Springer Texts in Business and Economics

More information about this series at http://www.springer.com/series/10099

Dmitry Ivanov • Alexander Tsipoulanidis •
Jörn Schönberger

Global Supply Chain and Operations Management

A Decision-Oriented Introduction to the Creation of Value

Dmitry Ivanov
Department of Business Administration
Berlin School of Economics and Law
Berlin, Germany

Alexander Tsipoulanidis
Department of Business Administration
Berlin School of Economics and Law
Berlin, Germany

Jörn Schönberger
Faculty of Transportation and Traffic Science
 "Friedrich List"
Technical University of Dresden
Dresden, Germany

ISSN 2192-4333 ISSN 2192-4341 (electronic)
Springer Texts in Business and Economics
ISBN 978-3-319-24215-6 ISBN 978-3-319-24217-0 (eBook)
DOI 10.1007/978-3-319-24217-0

Library of Congress Control Number: 2016940194

© Springer International Publishing Switzerland 2017
This work is subject to copyright. All rights are reserved by the Publisher, whether the whole or part of the material is concerned, specifically the rights of translation, reprinting, reuse of illustrations, recitation, broadcasting, reproduction on microfilms or in any other physical way, and transmission or information storage and retrieval, electronic adaptation, computer software, or by similar or dissimilar methodology now known or hereafter developed.
The use of general descriptive names, registered names, trademarks, service marks, etc. in this publication does not imply, even in the absence of a specific statement, that such names are exempt from the relevant protective laws and regulations and therefore free for general use.
The publisher, the authors and the editors are safe to assume that the advice and information in this book are believed to be true and accurate at the date of publication. Neither the publisher nor the authors or the editors give a warranty, express or implied, with respect to the material contained herein or for any errors or omissions that may have been made.

Printed on acid-free paper

This Springer imprint is published by Springer Nature
The registered company is Springer International Publishing AG Switzerland

Dmitry Ivanov
To my parents who inspired the dreams and without whom this book would have never been completed
To my wife who makes the dreams come true inspiring with love and smile and without whom this book would have been completed much earlier
To my children: get inspired and climb, reach the peak, enjoy, stay inspired

Alexander Tsipoulanidis
To my family:
Joanna, Marina, Irini, Ursula and Reimar - I love you all!

To my father:
Ioannis (1934–2002) - I miss you!

Jörn Schönberger
For my family:
Maybe this book explains what I'm doing in the Lecture hall...

Preface

About This Book

In everyday life, all of us take supply chain and operations management (SCOM) decisions. If you move to a new flat, location planning is first necessary. Second, you need a plan of how to design the overall process. This includes capacity planning, transportation planning, and human resource planning. You also need to replenish some items and do procurement planning. Finally, a detailed schedule for the day of the move is needed.

Similarly, building a new house involves many SCOM decisions. Again, it starts with location selection. If you decide to coordinate the overall process by yourself, it is necessary to coordinate the entire supply chain of different manufacturers and workmen. In turn, they need the detailed data of your plans and forecasted data to plan their own process and sourcing activities. In order to avoid traffic jams at the building site, detailed coordination at the vehicle routing level is needed.

SCOM belongs to the most exciting management areas. These functionalities are tangible and in high demand in all industries and services. This study book intends to provide both the introduction to and advanced knowledge in the SCOM field. Providing readers with a working knowledge of SCOM, this textbook can be used in core, special, and advanced classes. Therefore, the book is targeted at a broad range of students and professionals involved in SCOM.

Special focus is directed at bridging theory and practice. Since the managers use both quantitative and qualitative methods in making their decisions, the book follows these practical knowledge requirements. Decision-oriented and method-oriented perspectives determine the philosophy of the book. In addition, because of the extensive use of information technology and optimization techniques in SCOM, we pay particular attention to this aspect.

Next, a strong global focus with more than 80 up-to-date cases and practical examples from all over the world is a distinguishing feature of this study book. The

---

The original version of this book was revised. An erratum to the book can be found at (DOI: 10.1007/978-3-319-24217-0_15).

Interactive Case-Study Map: 80 cases on supply chain and operations management across the globe!

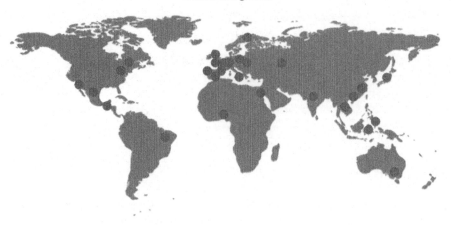

Fig. 1 Interactive case-study map in the e-supplement

case studies encompass different industries and services and consider examples of successful and failed SCOM practices in Europe, America, Asia, Africa, and Australia.

Finally, following the expectations of modern students and the positive teaching experiences in SCOM over the past 10 years, we divided this textbook into a hardback and an electronic part. In the hardback, basic theoretical concepts, case studies, applications, and numerical examples are explained. The e-supplement supports the hardback and provides students and teachers with additional case studies, video streams, numerical tasks, Excel files, slides, and solutions (see Fig. 1).

The e-supplement of this book can be accessed via the URL www.global-supply-chain-management.de without further registration. For course instructors, a special area is set up that contains further material. The e-supplement is updated with additional topics, exercises, and cases.

The book consists of 14 chapters divided into three parts:

Part I Introduction to Supply Chain and Operations Management
- Chapter 1 Basics of Supply Chain and Operations Management
- Chapter 2 Examples from Different Industries, Services and Continents
- Chapter 3 Processes, Systems and Models

Part II Designing Operations and Supply Network: Strategic Perspective
- Chapter 4 Supply Chain Strategy
- Chapter 5 Sourcing Strategy
- Chapter 6 Production Strategy
- Chapter 7 Facility Location

- Chapter 8 Transportation and Distribution Network Design
- Chapter 9 Factory Planning and Process Design
- Chapter 10 Layout Planning

Part III Matching Demand and Supply: Tactical and Operative Planning
- Chapter 11 Demand Forecasting
- Chapter 12 Production and Material Requirements Planning
- Chapter 13 Inventory Management
- Chapter 14 Scheduling and Routing

Each *chapter* contains the following elements:

- Introductory case study
- Learning objectives
- Theory with practical insights and case studies
- Tasks with solution examples
- Key points and outlook
- Additional tasks and case studies placed in e-supplement
- Further supplementary materials: online tutorial, Excel files, and videos.

Each chapter starts with an introductory case study. Subsequently, major decision areas and methods for decision support are handled. Finally, applications can be trained based on additional case studies and numerical tasks. The summary of key points and an outlook end each chapter.

Throughout the book, practical insights are highlighted.

In the e-supplement, different additional materials can be found, highlighted in each chapter.

The advantage of using the e-supplement is that it offers the possibility of updating the case studies and to add additional materials more dynamically than producing new editions of the textbook. Another advantage is to be able to keep the hardback copy part quite short and concise. Finally, modern students are quite different from students who studied 20 years ago. They cannot imagine the study process without online resources.

The authors gratefully acknowledge all those who have helped us in bringing this book to publication. First and foremost, we have greatly benefited from the wealth of literature published on the subjects of SCOM and related topics. We thank Dr Marina Ivanov for coauthoring the Chap. 4 "Supply Chain Strategy" and Chap. 6 "Production Strategy." We would like to thank all our colleagues from Berlin School of Economics and Law and University of Bremen. The book has benefited immensely from their valuable insights, comments, and suggestions.

We thank companies AnyLogic, Knorr-Bremse Berlin Systeme für Schienenfahrzeuge GmbH, OTLG, REWE, and SupplyOn for permissions to prepare new case studies and use company materials. We thank our student assistants Benjamin Bock, Alexander Reichardt, Katharina Schönhoff, and Laura Seyfarth, who helped us to prepare case studies, tasks, and figures. In addition, we thank our PhD and master students Alex Bolinelli, Christina ten Brink gt Berentelg, Vikas Bhandary, Jonas Dahl, Nora Fleischhut, Irina Fensky, Daniel Jácome Ferrao, Diego Martínez Gosálvez, Fernanda Jubé, Laura Kromminga, Chensuqiu Lin, Abdul Mutallab Mukhtar, Sufyan Nasir, Carlos Ortega, Janna Piorr, Beatrix Schubert, Aneesh Somanath, Henrik Thode, Evelyn Wendler, and Chiu Hua Yi for contributing to preparation of case studies. We cordially thank Ms. Pat Baxter for thorough proofreading of the manuscript.

Finally, we wish to thank Mrs. Barbara Bethke and Mr. Christian Rauscher from Springer and the entire Springer production team led by Mrs. Britta Kirchner for their assistance and guidance in successfully completing this book.

Last but not least—we cordially thank our families who supported us enormously during our work on the book.

April 2016

Dmitry Ivanov
Alexander Tsipoulanidis
Jörn Schönberger

Companion Web Site

This book is accompanied by a free Web site www.global-supply-chain-management. de. On this Web site you will find a lot of up-to-date complementary material such as video streams, case-studies, Excel spreadsheet templates, tasks and answers, figures from the book, and simulation games. This area will be extended continuously.

About the Authors

Dmitry Ivanov

Prof. Dr. habil. Dr. Dmitry Ivanov is professor for Supply Chain Management at Berlin School of Economics and Law (BSEL). He has been *teaching* for 15 years the classes in operations management, production and supply management, supply chain management, logistics, management information systems, and strategic management at undergraduate, master's, PhD, and executive MBA levels at different universities worldwide in English, German, and Russian. He gave guest lectures, presented scholarly papers, and was visiting professor at numerous universities including Baruch College - City University of New York, The Hong Kong Polytechnic University, Imperial College London, University of Vienna, University of Bremen, Technical University Dortmund, University of West Scotland, State University of St. Petersburg, High School of Economics Moscow, St. Petersburg Institute of Informatics and Automation, and Fraunhofer Institute of Material Flow and Logistics.

His *research* explores supply chain structure dynamics and control, with an emphasis on global supply chain design with disruption consideration, distribution planning, and dynamic (re)-scheduling. He is (co-)author of structure dynamics control method for supply chain management. He applies mathematical programming, simulation, and control theoretic methods. Based on the triangle "process–model–technology," he investigates the dynamics of complex networks in production, logistics, and supply chains. Most of his courses and research are placed at the interface of supply chain management, operations research, industrial engineering, and information technology.

His *academic* background includes industrial engineering, operations research, and applied control theory. He studied industrial engineering and production management in St. Petersburg and Chemnitz and graduated with distinction. He gained his PhD (Dr.rer.pol.), Doctor of Science, and Habilitation degrees in 2006 (TU Chemnitz), 2008 (FINEC St. Petersburg), and 2011 (TU Chemnitz), respectively. In 2005, he was awarded a German Chancellor Scholarship.

Prior to becoming an academic, he was mainly engaged in *industry and consulting*, especially for process optimization in manufacturing and logistics and ERP systems. His practical expertise includes numerous projects on application of operations research and process optimization methods for operations design, logistics, scheduling, and supply chain optimization. Prior to joining BSEL, he has been professor and acting chair of Operations Management at the University of Hamburg.

He is the (co)-author of more than 250 *publications*, including three textbooks and a monograph "Adaptive Supply Chain Management". Professor Ivanov's research has been published in various academic journals, including International Journal of Production Research, European Journal of Operational Research, Journal of Scheduling, Transportation Research, International Journal of Production Economics, Computers and Industrial Engineering, International Journal of Technology Management, International Journal of Systems Science, Annual Reviews in Control, etc. He has been guest editor of special issues in different journals, including International Journal of Production Research and International Journal of Integrated Supply Management. He is an associate editor of International Journal of Systems Science and Editorial Board member of several international and national journals, e.g., International Journal of Systems Science: Operations and Logistics and International Journal of Inventory Research. He is Vice-Chair of IFAC TC 5.2 "Manufacturing Modelling for Management and Control" and Co-Chair of the IFAC TC 5.2 Working group "Supply Network Engineering". He is member of numerous associations, including INFORMS, German Academic Association for Business Research (VHB) and German Operations Research Society (GOR).

He regularly presented his research results and has been co-chair and IPC member of many international conferences where he has organized numerous tracks and sessions (including INCOM, EURO, INFORMS, OR, MIM, MCPL, IFAC World Congress, PRO-VE, ICINCO, DMO).

Alexander Tsipoulanidis

Prof. Dr. Alexander Tsipoulanidis, MBA, is professor for Operations Management at the Berlin School of Economics and Law (BSEL), lecturing Supply Chain and Operations Management in various programs leading to a bachelor's, master's, or MBA degree. Alexander is mechanical engineer and industrial engineer with a focus on factory, layout, and material flow planning. At the Engineering Faculty of the University of Bristol (UK), he proceeded with his doctorate (PhD) in which he explored the significant influence of Lean Engineering and product development as a part of the Lean Enterprise. He holds an MBA in Strategic Management from Anglia Ruskin University Cambridge (UK), where Alexander concentrated on competitive strategies at times of global Hyper-Competition.

During a Federal Ministry of Education and Research (BMBF) project that was scientifically supported by the Institute for Machine Tools and Factory Management (IWF) of the TU Berlin and the Fraunhofer Institute for Material Flow and Logistics (IML) in Dortmund, Alexander contributed to the "Production 2000" project regarding assembly-controlled logistics and value-added network works (Entwicklung von montagegesteuerten, integrierten Logistik- und

Wertschöpfungsketten; Rahmenkonzept Produktion 2000 des Bundesministeriums für Bildung und Forschung) from a materials logistics perspective. As such, he developed practical solutions for process synchronization and performance improvements within a network of small series producers.

Alexander Tsipoulanidis has been working approximately 20 years for international enterprises (e.g., ABB, DaimlerChrysler, and Bombardier Transportation). There, he had different roles at various production sites but also had executive positions at the global headquarters. His responsibilities have been related to capacity management of a European production network, planning of new factories, or the redesign of shop-floor layouts. Globally, he was conducting "Lean Operations Assessments" of production facilities, developed site continuous improvement plans, and implemented the related supply chain strategies. Furthermore, he defined lean and manufacturing-oriented product development processes and was involved in a restructuring initiative aiming to make the respective enterprise lean, efficient, attractive, and profitable.

His current research focuses on the fundamentals of Lean Thinking in combination with the usage of the Internet of Things/Machine to Machine (M2M) technology in diverse value-added domains. Recently, he has analyzed the development of lean and sustainable supply chain strategies in strong connection with the abovementioned technologies. Thus, Alexander's primary research objective is to explore the generation of competitive advantage by utilizing the Internet of Things in order to sustain Supply Chain and Operational Excellence at times of digitalization.

Jörn Schönberger

Prof. Dr. habil. Jörn Schönberger is professor for business management at Technical University of Dresden. He positions the Chair of Business Management, especially Transport Services and Logistics, as part of the Friedrich-List-Faculty of Transportation and Traffic Science. Prior to his current position, he has been professor for Operations and Supply Chain Management at Berlin School of Economics and Law (BSEL) and senior researcher at the University of Bremen. For several years, he has been guest professor at the University of Rennes 1 for IT and logistics. In 2010, he was a temporary professor (sine spe) for Operations Research and Supply Chain Management at RWTH Aachen.

Jörn Schönberger was visiting professor at the University of Vienna and visiting researcher at Copenhagen Business School. In addition, he is/was involved in several academic programs on different study levels at the University of Bremen, Technical University of Berlin, RWTH Aachen, University of Vienna, University of Rennes 1, European Business School, FOM University of Applied Sciences, University of Applied Sciences Bremen, Hamburg Distance University of Applied Sciences, as well as University of Applied Sciences HIWL. Most of his courses address topics at the interface between engineering and business management.

His research interests comprise model-based optimization and control of complex logistics systems. Furthermore, he investigates the synchronization of information and material flows. Another research direction covers the dynamics of complex logistics system. Based on methodologies from Mathematics, Operations Research, Artificial Intelligence, and Information systems, he investigates applications from the fields of logistics, transportation, and traffic, manufacturing, and sports management.

Jörn Schönberger received a diploma in mathematics in 2000 and a PhD (2004) in Business Management from the University of Bremen. His doctoral thesis was awarded by the German Operations Research Society. He gained his Habilitation degree for Business Management also from the University of Bremen in 2010.

He is author of two monographs and two textbooks as well as editor of some books. He (co-)authored several journal papers and numerous other publications. Regularly, he presents his research results on international scientific meetings. His service to the scientific community comprises the organization of several conferences as well as his work as a regular reviewer for the Deutsche Forschungsgemeinschaft (German Research Foundation) and several scientific journals as well as conferences. Jörn Schönberger is member of several scientific communities like the German Academic Association for Business Research (VHB) and the German Operations Research Society (GOR).

Besides his academic career, he regularly works as a freelance consultant. He is/was involved in projects related to information management, information processing, database development and application, as well as process optimization.

Contents

1 Basics of Supply Chain and Operations Management 1
  1.1 Introductory Case Study: The Magic Supply Chain and the Best Operations Manager 2
  1.2 Basic Definitions and Decisions 3
    1.2.1 Transformation Process, Value Creation and Operations Function 3
    1.2.2 Supply Chain Management 5
    1.2.3 Decisions in Supply Chain and Operations Management 6
  1.3 Careers and Future Challenges in Supply Chain and Operations Management 9
  1.4 Key Points 13
  Bibliography 14

2 Examples from Different Industries, Services and Continents 15
  2.1 Examples of Operations and Supply Chains in Manufacturing 15
    2.1.1 Nike: Sourcing Strategy in the Integrated Supply Chain 15
    2.1.2 Dangote Cement: Establishing Sophisticated Supply Chain Management in Africa 17
    2.1.3 Toyota: Supply Chain Disruption Management 20
    2.1.4 Adidas "Speedfactory": 3D Printing and Industry 4.0 in Supply Chain and Operations Management ... 21
  2.2 Examples of Operations and Supply Chains in Services 22
    2.2.1 SCOM in Restaurants: Case Study Starbucks Corporation 22
    2.2.2 Operations Management at Airport Madrid/Barajas ... 23
    2.2.3 Time-Critical Supply Chains: Disaster Management and Humanitarian Logistics 25
    2.2.4 Operations Issues in Car Sharing 28
    2.2.5 REWE: Expanding the Logistics Network 29

	2.3	Examples of e-Operations and Supply Chains	30
		2.3.1 Fab.com	30
		2.3.2 Homeplus: The Store Comes to Your Home	34
	Bibliography		35
3	**Processes, Systems, and Models**		37
	3.1	Introductory Case-Study: AirSupply	37
		3.1.1 E-procurement	38
		3.1.2 Vendor-Managed Inventory	39
		3.1.3 Implementation	40
	3.2	Business Process Management	41
		3.2.1 Process Optimization and Re-engineering	41
		3.2.2 Business Process Modelling	43
	3.3	Management Information Systems	45
		3.3.1 Role of Information Technology in Supply Chain and Operations Management	45
		3.3.2 Types of Management Information Systems	45
		3.3.3 Management Information Systems and Organization	46
		3.3.4 ERP Systems	47
		3.3.5 APS Systems	48
		3.3.6 SCEM and RFID	50
		3.3.7 Business Analytics and E-Business	52
	3.4	Problem Solving Methods and Research Methodologies	54
		3.4.1 Problems, Systems, and Decision-Making	54
		3.4.2 Models and Modeling	58
		3.4.3 Model-Based Decision-Making	59
		3.4.4 Quantitative Models and Operations Research	61
		3.4.5 Integrated Decision-Making Support	62
		3.4.6 Research Methodologies	63
	3.5	Key Points	65
	Bibliography		66
4	**Operations and Supply Chain Strategy**		69
	4.1	Introductory Case-Study "Quick and Affordable": Zara, UNIQLO & Primark	69
	4.2	Operations and Supply Chain Strategies	73
		4.2.1 Value Added and Costs	73
		4.2.2 Operations Strategies	74
		4.2.3 Supply Chain Strategies and "Strategic Fit"	74
	4.3	Supply Chain Coordination	79
		4.3.1 Bullwhip Effect	79
		4.3.2 Vendor-Managed Inventory	82
		4.3.3 Collaborative Planning, Forecasting and Replenishment	85
		4.3.4 Supply Chain Contracting	86

	4.4	Supply Chain Resilience and Sustainability	87
		4.4.1 Supply Chain Sustainability: Examples of Coca-Cola and Mercadona	88
		4.4.2 Supply Chain Resilience and Ripple Effect	91
	4.5	Key Points	93
	Bibliography		94
5	**Sourcing Strategy**		97
	5.1	Introductory Case Study "New Logistics Concept (NLK: Das Neue Logistik Konzept) at Volkswagen"	97
	5.2	Sourcing Process and Principles	100
		5.2.1 Procurement, Purchasing and Sourcing	100
		5.2.2 Sourcing Process	101
		5.2.3 Make-or-Buy and Outsourcing	102
		5.2.4 Organization of Sourcing Processes	105
	5.3	Sourcing Strategies	106
		5.3.1 Single vs. Dual and Multiple Sourcing	106
		5.3.2 Local vs. Global Sourcing	107
		5.3.3 Just-in-Time	110
	5.4	Supplier Relationship Management	111
		5.4.1 Strategic Supplier Analysis	112
		5.4.2 Supplier Selection	114
		5.4.3 Supplier Integration and Development	116
	5.5	Key Points	117
	Bibliography		118
6	**Production Strategy**		121
	6.1	Introductory Case-Study DELL vs. Lenovo	121
	6.2	Postponement and Modularization	126
		6.2.1 Problem: Mass Production or Product Customization	126
		6.2.2 Principles: Postponement and Modularization	126
		6.2.3 Examples of Postponement Strategies	127
	6.3	Push-Pull Views and Order Penetration Point	130
	6.4	Selection of a Production Strategy	132
		6.4.1 Types of Production Strategies	132
		6.4.2 Method: Lost-Sales Analysis	137
	6.5	Key Points	139
	Bibliography		139
7	**Facility Location Planning and Network Design**		141
	7.1	Introductory Case Study Power Pong Sports, China	142
	7.2	Supply Chain Design Framework	144
	7.3	Global Supply Chain Design	146
		7.3.1 Warehouse Location Problem and Its Formalization	146
		7.3.2 A Spreadsheet Approach to the WLP	149

	7.3.3	Branch-&-Bound: How the Solver Add-In Works	155
	7.3.4	Capacitated WLP	160
7.4	Regional Facility Location		166
	7.4.1	Management Problem Description	167
	7.4.2	A Mathematical Model of the Decision Situation	167
	7.4.3	Solving the Mathematical Model: Centre-of-Gravity Approach	168
7.5	Factor-Ranking Analysis		175
	7.5.1	Case-Study OTLG Germany	175
	7.5.2	Factor-Rating Method	175
	7.5.3	Utility Value Analysis	180
7.6	Key Points		184
Bibliography			186

8 Distribution and Transportation Network Design 189
8.1 Introductory Case Study: Bavarian Wood 190
8.2 Generic Transport Network Structures 192
8.3 Realizing Economies of Scale in Transportation 194
8.3.1 Consolidation of Shipments 194
8.3.2 Postponement 196
8.3.3 Milk-Runs 197
8.3.4 Transshipment 202
8.4 Trade-Off-Based Transportation Network Design 206
8.5 Capacity Allocation in a Many-to-Many Network 209
8.5.1 The Transportation Problem 210
8.5.2 Decision Model 210
8.5.3 Finding the First Feasible Model Solution 212
8.5.4 Optimality Check 216
8.5.5 Solution Improvement 217
8.6 Distribution Network Design 221
8.6.1 Case Study: ALDI vs. Homeplus 221
8.6.2 Types of Distribution Networks 224
8.6.3 Case Study: Seven-Eleven Japan 225
8.6.4 Transportation Modes 228
8.7 Key Points 231
Bibliography 231

9 Factory Planning and Process Design 233
9.1 Introductory Case-Study "Factory Planning at Tesla" 233
9.2 Factory Planning 235
9.2.1 Role of Factory Planning in SCOM 235
9.2.2 Processes of Factory Planning 236
9.3 Capacity Planning 240
9.3.1 Little's Law 242
9.3.2 Bottleneck Analysis/Theory of Constraints 244

		9.3.3	Drum, Buffer, Rope	245
		9.3.4	Break-Even Analysis	246
		9.3.5	Decision Trees	248
		9.3.6	Queuing Theory	250
		9.3.7	Simulation: Case Study AnyLogic	254
	9.4	Process Flow Structures		256
		9.4.1	Job Shop	256
		9.4.2	Batch Shop	257
		9.4.3	Assembly Line	257
		9.4.4	Continuous Flow	262
		9.4.5	Product-Process Matrix	262
	9.5	Lean Production Systems		263
		9.5.1	Lean Thinking	263
		9.5.2	Lean Production Principles	265
		9.5.3	Lean Supply Chain	269
	9.6	Modern Trends: Industry 4.0		271
	9.7	Key Points and Discussion Questions		273
	Bibliography			275
10	**Layout Planning**			279
	10.1	Introductory Case-Study "OTLG Ludwigsfelde"		279
	10.2	Layout Planning in Manufacturing		280
		10.2.1	Fixed Position Layout	281
		10.2.2	Process Flow Layout	282
		10.2.3	Product Flow Layout	284
		10.2.4	Cell-Based Layout	288
	10.3	Layout Planning in Warehouses		290
		10.3.1	Incoming Area	290
		10.3.2	Storage Area	291
		10.3.3	Put-Away and Order Pick-Up	291
		10.3.4	Layout Concepts	292
	10.4	Methods of Layout Planning		293
		10.4.1	REL-Charts	293
		10.4.2	Quadratic Assignment Problem	295
		10.4.3	Simulation: Modeling Operations at Pharmaceutical Distribution Warehouses with AnyLogic	297
	10.5	Key Points		299
	Bibliography			300
11	**Demand Forecasting**			301
	11.1	Introductory Case Study		301
	11.2	Forecasting Process and Methods		304
		11.2.1	Forecasting Process and Time Horizons	304
		11.2.2	Forecasting Methods	305
		11.2.3	Forecasting Quality	307
	11.3	Statistical Methods		308

		11.3.1	Linear Regression	308
		11.3.2	Moving Average	310
		11.3.3	Simple Exponential Smoothing	312
		11.3.4	Double Exponential Smoothing	313
	11.4	Key Points and Outlook		314
	Bibliography			315
12	**Production and Material Requirements Planning**			**317**
	12.1	Introductory Case-Study SIBUR: Integrated Operations and Supply Chain Planning		318
	12.2	Planning Horizons/MRP-II		321
	12.3	Sales and Operations Planning		322
		12.3.1	Role of Sales and Operations Planning	322
		12.3.2	Options for Aggregate Planning	324
		12.3.3	Methods for Aggregate Planning	325
	12.4	Sales and Production Planning with Linear Programming		328
		12.4.1	Problem Description	328
		12.4.2	Method: Linear Programming	329
		12.4.3	Graphical Solution	331
	12.5	Master Production Schedule and Rolling Planning		333
		12.5.1	Master Production Schedule	333
		12.5.2	Rolling Planning	334
	12.6	Material Requirements Planning		335
		12.6.1	Bill-of-Materials	336
		12.6.2	MRP Calculation	338
	12.7	Key Points		342
	Bibliography			342
13	**Inventory Management**			**345**
	13.1	Introductory Case-Study: Amazon, Volkswagen and DELL		345
	13.2	Role, Functions and Types of Inventory		346
	13.3	Material Analysis		348
		13.3.1	ABC Analysis	348
		13.3.2	XYZ Analysis	351
	13.4	Deterministic Models		354
		13.4.1	EOQ Model	355
		13.4.2	EOQ Model with Discounts	358
		13.4.3	EPQ Model	360
		13.4.4	Re-order Point	361
	13.5	Stochastic Models		362
		13.5.1	Service Level and Safety Stock	362
		13.5.2	Single Period Systems ("Newsvendor Problem")	366
		13.5.3	Safety Stock and Transportation Strategy: Case DailyMaersk	368

13.6	Inventory Control Policies	370
	13.6.1 Fixed Parameters	371
	13.6.2 Dynamic View	375
13.7	Dynamic Lot-Sizing Models	375
	13.7.1 Least Unit Cost Heuristic	376
	13.7.2 Silver-Meal Heuristic	377
	13.7.3 Wagner-Whitin Model	379
13.8	Aggregating Inventory	381
13.9	ATP/CTP	383
13.10	Key Points and Outlook	385
	Bibliography	387

14 Routing and Scheduling 389

14.1	Introductory Case Study RED SEA BUS TRAVEL	390
14.2	Shortest Paths in a Network	391
	14.2.1 Outline of the Shortest Path Problem (SPP) in a Network	391
	14.2.2 Mathematical Graphs	393
	14.2.3 The SPP as Graph-Based Optimization Model	393
	14.2.4 Dijkstra's Algorithm for the Identification of a Shortest s-t-Path	394
14.3	Round Trip Planning/Travelling Salesman Problem	397
	14.3.1 Travelling Salesman Problem	398
	14.3.2 A Mixed-Integer Linear Program for TSP-Modelling	401
	14.3.3 Heuristic Search for High Quality Round Trips	402
14.4	Vehicle Routing	409
	14.4.1 Case Study ORION: Vehicle Routing at UPS	410
	14.4.2 Decision Situation Outline	411
	14.4.3 Current Approach for the Route Compilation	412
	14.4.4 Capacitated Vehicle Routing Problem	414
	14.4.5 The Sweep Algorithm	417
14.5	Machine Scheduling	421
	14.5.1 The Problem of Scheduling a Machine	421
	14.5.2 Priority Rule-Based Scheduling	424
	14.5.3 Scheduling Algorithm of Moore	426
	14.5.4 Scheduling Two Machines in a Flow Shop	427
	14.5.5 Further Challenges in Machine Scheduling	430
14.6	Key Points	430
	Bibliography	432

Erratum to: Global Supply Chain and Operations Management E1

Appendix Case-Study "Re-designing the Material Flow in a Global Manufacturing Network" 435

Index 441

Basics of Supply Chain and Operations Management

Learning Objectives for this Chapter

- What is transformation process and value creation?
- What is an operations and operations management?
- What is supply chain and supply chain management?
- Which decisions are in the scope of supply chain and operations management?
- Which objectives are used to measure performance of supply chain and operations management?
- Which qualifications should obtain a future supply chain and operations manager?
- Which career paths are possible for supply chain and operations managers?

Find additional case-studies, Excel spreadsheet templates, and video streams in the *E-Supplement* to this book on www.global-supply-chain-management.de!

1.1 Introductory Case Study: The Magic Supply Chain and the Best Operations Manager

Santa Claus is one of the best supply chain (SC) and operations managers in the world. He achieves incredible *performance*: he always delivers the right products, at the right place and at the right time. And this is despite highly *uncertain demand* and a very complex SC with more than two billion customers.

His *strategy* and *organization* is customer-centred and strives to provide maximal children satisfaction. The organization of the supply chain and operations management (SCOM) is structured as follows. The customer department is responsible for processing all the letters from children from all over the world. This *demand* data is then given to the supply department. The *supply* department is responsible for buying the desired items from suppliers worldwide. The core of the supply department is the global purchasing team which is responsible for *coordinating* all the *global* purchasing activities.

Since many of the children's wishes are country-specific, the regional *purchasing* departments (so-called lead buyers) are distributed worldwide and build optimal *SC design*. In some cases, the desired items are so specific that no supplier can be found. For such cases, Santa Claus has established some production facilities and located them globally to minimize total *transportation* costs and to ensure *on-time delivery* of all the gifts for Christmas.

The customer department regularly analyses children's' wishes. It was noticed that there are lots of similar items which are asked for each year. In order to reduce purchasing fixed costs and use *scale effects*, Santa Claus organized a network of *warehouses* worldwide. Standard items are purchased in large batches and stored. If the actual demand in the current year is lower than *forecasted demand*, this is not a problem—these items can be used again in the following year. Since there are millions of different items in each warehouse, Santa Claus created optimal *layouts* and *pick-up* processes in order to find the necessary items quickly and efficiently.

The SC and operations planning happens as follows. In January, Santa Claus and the customer department start to analyse the previous year's demand. During the first 6 months of the year, they create a projection of future demand. The basis for such a forecast is statistical analysis of the past and identification of future trends (e.g., new books, films, toys, etc.). After that, the supply department replenishes the items and distributes them to different warehouses. The production department *schedules* the *manufacturing* processes. From October, the first letters from children start to arrive. The busy period begins. From October to December, Santa Claus needs lots of assistants and enlarges the workforce.

The operations and SC execution is now responsible for bringing all the desired items to children. It comprises many activities: transportation, purchasing and manufacturing. Children are waiting impatiently to start the incoming goods inspection. No wrong pick-ups and bundles are admissible and no shortage is allowed. More and more, children's wishes are not about items but rather about some events which they want to happen (e.g., holidays, etc.). *Service operations* are also in the competence of Santa Claus. In addition, Santa Claus has established the most *sustainable* SC in the world based on *transportation* by sledges. Sometimes, the letters with very unusual wishes come in the very last moment but Santa Claus's SC is prepared for the unpredictable—lastly it is a magic SC.

1.2 Basic Definitions and Decisions

1.2.1 Transformation Process, Value Creation and Operations Function

One of the basic elements in management is the creation of *added value*. *Operations* is a function or system that transforms inputs (e.g., materials and labour) into outputs of greater value (e.g., products or services); in other words, the operations function is responsible to *match demand and supply* (see Fig. 1.1):

The transformation process is the traditional way to think about operations management in terms of *planning* activities. In practice, SC and operations managers spend at least a half of their working time to handle different uncertainties and risks. That is why *control* function becomes more and more important to establish feedbacks between the planned and real processes.

The *operations* function along with marketing and finance is a part of any organization (see Fig. 1.2).

Operations management is involved with managing the resources to produce and deliver products and services efficiently and effectively.

Operations management deals with the design and management of products, processes, and services, and comprises the stages of sourcing, production, distribution and after sales.

Fig. 1.1 Input-output view of operations function

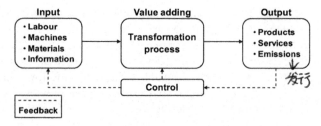

Fig. 1.2 Role of operations in organization

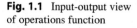

Fig. 1.3 Objective triangle of operations and supply chain performance

Measurement of operations and SC *performance* is typically related to the objective triangle "costs-time-quality" (see Fig. 1.3):

The importance of these objectives is *dynamic*, i.e., it changes in time since operations management has a long history. Over the last 60 years, a transition from the producers' market to the customers' markets has occurred. This transition began in the 1960s with an increasing role of marketing in the conditions of *mass production* of similar products to an anonymous market. This period is known as the *economy of scale*. After filling the markets with products, the quality problems came to the forefront. In the 1970s, total quality management (TQM) was established.

The increased quality caused the *individualization* of customers' requirements in the 1980s. This was the launching point for the establishment of the economy of the customer. This period is characterized by efforts for optimal inventory management and a reduction in production cycles.

In the 1980–1990s, handling a high product variety challenged operations management. Another trend was the so-called *speed effect*. The speed of reaction to market changes and cutting time-to-market became even more important. Consequently, the optimization of internal processes simultaneously with external links to suppliers was rooted in the concepts of lean production and just-in-time (JIT).

Throughout the 1990s, companies concentrated on development approaches to core competencies, outsourcing, innovations and collaboration. These trends were caused by globalization, advancements in IT and integration processes into the world economy. Particularly in the 1990s, the paradigm of supply chain management (SCM) was established that shapes developments in SCOM in the twenty-first century.

1.2 Basic Definitions and Decisions

In 2010–2015, such trends like risk management, SC resilience and flexibility, intelligent information technologies, e-operations, leanness and agility, the servitization of manufacturing, outsourcing and globalization, smart manufacturing and Industry 4.0 shaped the SCOM landscape in practice and research.

1.2.2 Supply Chain Management

A supply chain (SC) is a network of organizations and processes wherein a number of various enterprises (suppliers, manufacturers, distributors and retailers) collaborate (cooperate and coordinate) along the entire value chain to acquire raw materials, to convert these raw materials into specified final products, and to deliver these final products to customers (see Fig. 1.4).

Supply chain management (SCM) is a cross-department and cross-enterprise integration and coordination of material, information and financial flows to transform and use the SC resources in the most rational way along the entire value chain, from raw material suppliers to customers. SCM is one of the key components of any organization and is responsible for balancing demand and supply along the entire value-adding chain (see Fig. 1.5).

SCM integrates production and logistics processes. In practice, the production, logistics and SCM problems interact with each other and are tightly interlinked. Only two decades have passed since enterprise management and organizational structure have been considered from the functional perspective: marketing, research and development, procurement, warehousing, manufacturing, sales, and finance. The development of SCM was driven in the 1990s by three *main trends*: customer

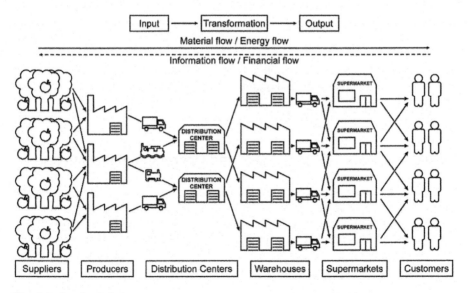

Fig. 1.4 Supply chain

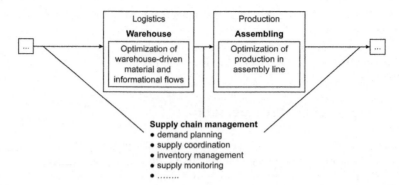

Fig. 1.5 Functions of logistics, production, and SCM in a value chain [from Ivanov and Sokolov (2010)]

orientation, markets globalization and establishing an information society. These trends caused changes in enterprise competitive strategies and required new adequate value chain management concepts.

The first use of the term "SCM" is commonly related to the article "SCM: Logistics Catches up with Strategy" by Oliver and Webber (1982). They set out to examine material flows from raw material suppliers through SC to end consumers within an integrated framework that has been named SCM. The origins of SCM can be seen in early works on postponement, system dynamics and the bullwhip effect (Forrester 1961), cooperation (Bowersox 1969), multi-echelon inventory management (Geoffrion and Graves 1974), JIT, and lean production.

SCM, as the term implies, is primarily directed to the inter-organizational level. Another successful application of SCM depends to a very large extent on the intra-organizational changes. Even the collaborative processes with an extended information systems application are managed by people who work in different departments: marketing, procurement, sales, production, etc. The interests of these departments are usually in conflict with each other. Hence, not only outbound synchronizations but also internal organizational synchronization are encompassed by SC organization.

1.2.3 Decisions in Supply Chain and Operations Management

The main management task is to make decisions. *Chocolate SC* can be used as an illustrative example to depict basic decisions in SC and operations management (SCOM). What happens between the cocoa pods harvest and placing chocolate on the shelves in a supermarket? A complex SC should be built between raw material suppliers and end customers (see Fig. 1.6). To produce chocolate, cocoa pods are first harvested from cocoa trees, e.g. in Côte D'ivoire. Cocoa pods are then moved by donkeys to a processing station where they are packed into special carrier bags to avoid damages during transportation by container ship.

1.2 Basic Definitions and Decisions

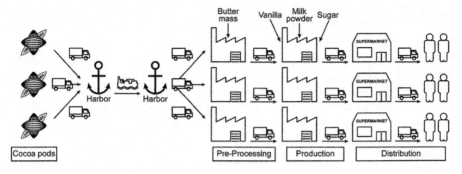

Fig. 1.6 Chocolate supply chain

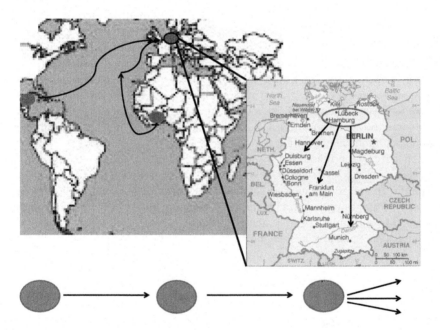

Fig. 1.7 Global view of the chocolate supply chain

At the harbor, the bags are packed into special containers and moved to a container ship that will bring them, e.g., to Hamburg (see Fig. 1.7).

Simultaneously, from harbors in Guatemala and Madagascar container ships with vanilla start. Along with sugar and milk powder, vanilla belongs to the components needed for chocolate production. Sugar and milk powder are typically sourced locally to avoid long transportation ways. Simultaneously, from harbors in Guatemala and Madagascar container ships with vanilla start.

Along with sugar and milk powder, vanilla belongs to the components needed for chocolate production. Sugar and milk powder are typically sourced locally to avoid long transportation ways. After unloading at Hamburg harbor, where up to 200,000 tons of cocoa pods are transshipped each year, the transportation is continued by trucks.

First, cocoa pods are delivered to preliminary processing plant to produce cocoa butter and cocoa mass which are then moved in trucks by road to chocolate manufacturers. After getting all the components, multi-stage manufacturing process can be started, the final result of which is chocolate. Chocolate is then packed and delivered in large batches at pallets to distribution centers from which small batches are finally delivered to supermarket.

It can be observed from the chocolate SC as well as from the introductory example of the Santa Claus's SC that the responsibilities of SCOM managers can be divided into sourcing, production, distribution, transportation and SCM (see Fig. 1.8).

The responsibilities of SCOM managers are really multi-faceted (see Fig. 1.9). The decision-making area in SCOM ranges from strategic to tactical and operative levels. *Strategic* issues include, for example, determination of the size and location of manufacturing plants or distribution centres, decisions on the structure of service networks, factory planning, and designing the SC. *Tactical* issues include such decisions as production or transportation planning as well as inventory planning. *Operative* issues involve with production scheduling and control, inventory control, quality control and inspection, vehicle routing, traffic and materials handling, and equipment maintenance policies.

This description holds true for many different organizations like global brand manufacturer such as Apple or Toyota, major retailers such as Tesco or Wal-Mart, nonprofit organizations such as International Red Cross, local petrol stations or hospitals. Purchasing, assembly, shipping, stocking and even communicating are just a few examples of the many different actions unfolding within these organizations, united by a single purpose: to create value for a customer.

Fig. 1.8 House of SCOM

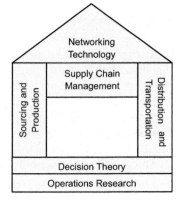

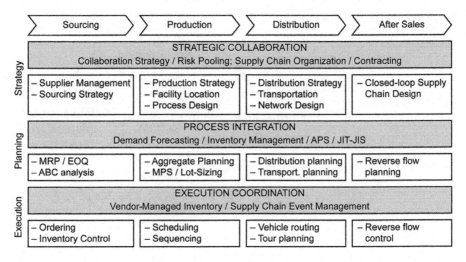

Fig. 1.9 Decision matrix in supply chain and operations management

1.3 Careers and Future Challenges in Supply Chain and Operations Management

SCOM is everywhere! SCOM specialists should obtain different qualifications since SCOM is multi-disciplinary in its nature (see Fig. 1.10). There are many *skills* and attributes which are important for SC and operations managers to succeed in the operations environment. Those are:

- systems and engineering knowledge
- leadership and strong communication skills
- general multidisciplinary business knowledge
- strong analytical problem solving abilities and quantitative skills
- negotiation and presentation skills

To become an SC or operations manager, it is important to be able to communicate well with people from all departments. There is a strong relationship between the SCOM function and other core and support functions of the organization, such as accounting and finance, product development, human resources, information systems and marketing functions. Another important skill is time management.

Some of the *job responsibilities* common to SCOM are as follows:

- coordinating business processes concerned with the production, pricing, sales and distribution of products and services
- managing workforce, preparing schedules and assigning specific duties;
- reviewing performance data to measure productivity and other performance indicators

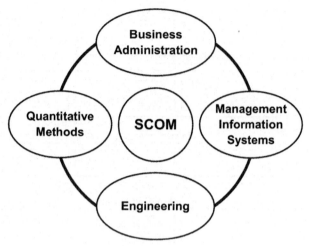

Fig. 1.10 Multi-disciplinary view of supply chain and operations management

- coordinating activities directly related to making products/providing services
- planning goods and services to be sold based on forecasts of customer demand;
- managing the movement of goods into and out of production facilities
- locating, selecting, and procuring merchandise for resale, representing management in purchase negotiations
- managing inventory and collaborating with suppliers
- planning warehouse and store layouts and designing production processes
- process selection: design and implement the transformation processes that best meet the needs of the customers and firms
- demand forecasting and capacity planning
- logistics: managing the movement of goods throughout the SC
- risk manager: pro-active SC design, risk monitoring, and real-time coordination in the case of disruptions

SC and operations managers have strategic responsibility but also control many of the everyday functions of a business or organization. They oversee and manage goods used at the facility such as sales merchandise, inventory or production materials. SC and operations managers also authorize and approve vendors and contract services at different locations worldwide. Starting positions for SCOM typically comprise operative responsibilities in procurement or sales departments and work as for example a consultant, customer service man-ager or a SC analyst. With 5–10 years of practical experience, such positions as purchasing manager, transportation manager, international logistics manager, warehouse operations manager or SC software manager can be achieved. With 10 or more years of experience, vice president for SCOM is a realistic position.

SCOM positions may include jobs in production planning, inventory control, materials control, work scheduling, quality control, and operations analysis. There

1.3 Careers and Future Challenges in Supply Chain and Operations Management

are a wide variety of career options in the field of SCOM. Some key opportunity areas are as follows:

- Operations manager
- Business analyst
- Production planner
- Operations analyst
- Materials manager
- Quality control specialist
- Project manager
- Purchasing manager
- Industrial production manager
- Facility coordinator
- Logistics manager
- Risk manager

Consider some of these and other possible *careers in SCOM* more detailed.

- *Plant managers* supervise and organize the daily operations of manufacturing plants. For this position, expertise in activities such as production planning, purchasing and inventory management is needed.
- *Quality managers* aim to ensure that the product or service an organization provides is fit for purpose, is consistent and meets both external and internal requirements. This includes legal compliance and customer expectations. A quality manager, sometimes called a quality assurance manager, coordinates the activities required to meet quality standards. Use of statistical tools is required to monitor all aspects of services, timeliness and workload management.
- *Process improvement consultants* take over activities which include designing and implementing such activities as lean production, six sigma and cycle time reduction plans in both service and manufacturing processes.
- *Analyst* is a key member of the operations team supporting data management, client reporting, trade processes, and problem resolution. They use analytical and quantitative methods to understand, predict and improve SC processes.
- *Production managers* are involved with the planning, coordination and control of manufacturing processes. They ensure that goods and services are produced at the right cost and level of quality.
- *Service manager* plans and directs customer service teams to meet the needs of customers and support company operations.
- *Sourcing managers* are involved with commercial and supplier aspects of product development and sourcing projects. They conduct supplier analysis, evaluate potential suppliers, and manage the overall supplier qualification process, develop and create sourcing plans, request for proposals and other sourcing documents, evaluate and recommend purchasing and sourcing decisions.

- *International logistics manager* works closely with manufacturing, marketing and purchasing to create efficient and effective global SC.
- *Transportation manager* is responsible for the execution, direction and coordination of transportation. They ensure timely and cost effective transportation of all incoming and outgoing shipments.
- *Warehouse manager* is responsible for managing inventory, avoiding stock-outs and ensuring material replenishment at minimal costs.
- *Risk manager* analyses possible risks, develops pro-active operations and SC design, monitors risks and coordinates activities for stabilization and recovery in the case of disruptions.

Since all organizations have an operations function there are many sectors which would need SCOM. Those sectors include but are not limited to:

- Manufacturing companies
- Retail establishments
- Logistics
- Hospitals
- Banks and insurance companies
- Restaurants
- Airlines and airports
- Entertainment parks
- Building and construction companies
- Public transportation companies
- Government agencies
- Research corporations.

SC and operations managers work in an exciting and dynamic environment. This environment is the result of a variety of challenging forces, from globalization of world trade to the transfer of ideas, products and money via the internet. Some of the *challenges* are as follows:

- globalization and collaboration with suppliers and customers worldwide
- issues of flexibility and resilience
- shorter product lifecycles and fast changing technology, materials and processes (e.g., additive manufacturing, internet of things, and Industry 4.0)
- sustainability and mass customization
- higher requirements on multidisciplinary knowledge and competencies.

> ▶ **Practical Insights** Excellence in Supply Chain and Operations Management becomes a competitive advantage for companies. This requires a new kind of leader to manage complexity, risks and diversity in global SCs and operations. This textbook provides you with the strategic, management and analytical skills you need to launch your

international career in global SCM, operations, and logistics. Three pillars build the textbook framework: practical orientation and creation of working knowledge, methodical focus, and personal development of students with the advancing of their communication, interaction and organizational skills with the help of case-studies and business simulation games.

A career in SCOM has many opportunities. The job itself is also diverse, due to the varied tasks completed by SC and operations managers. Another advantage is the high income expected, especially for experienced SC and operations managers. On the other hand, there may be long working hours and a stressful job. Operations and SC managers generally have to work in a changing environment so they have to be flexible. As can be seen in the real job offers, flexible managers with the willingness to travel a lot are always in demand.

Example *Jeff Williams is Apple's Senior Vice-President of Operations*
Jeff leads a team of people around the world responsible for end-to-end supply chain management and dedicated to ensuring that Apple products meet the highest standards of quality. Jeff joined Apple in 1998 as head of worldwide procurement and in 2004 he was named vice-president of operations. In 2007, Jeff played a significant role in Apple's entry into the mobile phone market with the launch of the iPhone, and he has led worldwide operations for iPod and iPhone since that time. Prior to Apple, Jeff worked for the IBM Corporation from 1985 to 1998 in operations and engineering roles. He holds a bachelor's degree in Mechanical Engineering from North Carolina State University and an MBA from Duke University.
Source: https://www.apple.com/pr/bios/jeff-williams.html

1.4 Key Points

Operations is a function or system that transforms inputs into outputs of greater value. *Operations management* is involved with managing the resources in order to produce and deliver products and services. It comprises the stages of sourcing, production, distribution and after sales. *A supply chain* is a network of organizations and processes along the entire value chain. SCM is a collaborative philosophy and a set of methods and tools to integrate and coordinate local logistics processes and their links with the production processes from the perspective of the entire value chain and its total performance.

SCOM is everywhere: in production, logistics, healthcare, airlines, entertainment parks, passenger transport, hotels, building and construction, etc. Key objectives of SCOM are costs, time, quality, and resilience. Career is SCOM is really multi-facet and requires multi-disciplinary knowledge that comprises the elements from business administration, optimization, engineering, and information systems. As examples of *logistics problem*s, warehouse management, transportation optimization, procurement quantity optimization, inventory management, cross-docking design, inter-modal terminals design, etc. can be named. Accordingly, production management deals with optimizations in assembly lines, production cells, etc. As examples of *SCM problems*, supply chain design, demand planning, and supply coordination can be named.

Bibliography

Bowersox DJ (1969) Physical distribution development, current status, and potential. J Marketing 33:63–70
Bowersox DJ, Closs DJ, Copper MB (2012) Supply chain logistics management, 4th edn. McGraw-Hill, Boston
Choi TM (ed) (2016) Service supply chain systems. CRC Press, London
Chopra S, Meindl P (2015) Supply chain management: strategy, planning and operation, 6th edn. Pearson, Harlow
Christopher M (2011) Logistics and supply chain management. Creating value-adding networks, 4th edn. FT Press, New Jersey
Clegg B, MacBryde J, Dey P (2013) Trends in modern operations management. Int J Oper Prod Manag 33(11/12)
Das A (2016) An introduction to operations management. CRC Press, Boca Raton, FL
Dolgui A, Proth J-M (2010) Supply chain engineering: useful methods and techniques. Springer, Berlin
Forrester JW (1961) Industrial dynamics. MIT Press, Cambridge
Foster ST, Sampso S, Wallin C, Webb S (2016) Managing supply chain and operations: an integrative approach. Pearson
Francis M, Fisher R, Thomas A, Rowland H (2014) The meaning of 'value' in purchasing, logistics and operations management. Int J Prod Res 52(22):6576–6589
Geoffrion AM, Graves GW (1974) Multicommodity distribution system design by benders decomposition. Manage Sci 29(5):822–844
Greasly A (2013) Operations management, 3rd edn. Wiley, New York
Heizer J, Render B (2013) Operations management: Sustainability and supply chain management, 11th edn. Pearson, Harlow
http://careersinsupplychain.org
http://www.apics.org
Ivanov D, Sokolov B (2010) Adaptive supply chain management. Springer, London
Oliver RK, Webber MD (1982) Supply chain management: logistics catches up with strategy. In: Christopher M (ed) Logistics: the strategic issues. Chapman & Hall, London
Simchi-Levi D, Kaminsky P, Simchi-Levi E (2007) Designing and managing the supply chain: concepts, strategies and case studies, 3rd edn. McGraw-Hill, Boston
Slack N, Brandon-Jones A, Johnston R (2013) Operations management, 7th edn. Pearson, Harlow
Stadtler H, Kilger C, Meyr H (2015) Supply chain management and advanced planning, 5th edn. Springer, Berlin

Examples from Different Industries, Services and Continents

Learning Objectives for This Chapter

- Examples of SCOM in manufacturing
- Examples of SCOM in services
- Examples of e-operations and supply chains

2.1 Examples of Operations and Supply Chains in Manufacturing

2.1.1 Nike: Sourcing Strategy in the Integrated Supply Chain

Since its establishment, Nike has evolved into a global enterprise providing trainers and sports garments to customers worldwide. Now the company has several brands, operating their business in 170 countries, employs 38,000 staff, and possess 100 sales and 65 administrative offices across the world. Nike owns 700 retail stores and works with 900 contracted factories, which manufacture a wide variety of products for Nike. Nike's revenue in 2012 was $24,128m, cost of sales was $13,567m, and inventory was $3350m.

A *sourcing strategy* is essential for Nike since the company's production and logistics strategy is based on *outsourcing* (see Fig. 2.1).

Nike is executing a long-term sourcing consolidation strategy and streamlining its SC operations. In 2007 Nike began assessing the contract manufacturing base and undertaking a multi-year strategy in order to:

Find additional case-studies, Excel spreadsheet templates, and video streams in the *E-Supplement* to this book on www.global-supply-chain-management.de!

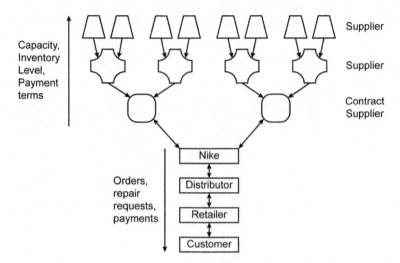

Fig. 2.1 Nike's supply chain

- streamline SC to focus on a number of contract manufacturing groups;
- build a strong and sustainable sourcing base for greater operational efficiencies and future growth;
- identify sub-contractors able to deliver best performance of products and innovation;
- align sub-contractors in terms of Nike's corporate responsibility principles.

Nike has been shifting from a risk-reduction focus—which devotes time and attention to the lowest factory performers—to a strategy that invests time and attention in strengthening relationships with the factories operating at the highest performance levels.

A new manufacturing index (MI) was implemented in 2012. It integrates scores from key performance areas into a single scoreboard rating that groups factories as Gold, Silver, Bronze, Yellow or Red. Contract factories that are able to consistently exceed Nike requirements in the equally weighted areas of quality, costs, delivery and sustainability performance management, and show consistent performance leadership in the industry, will achieve a Silver rating in the MI. Contract factories that go beyond industry and are demonstrating innovation and benchmark performance within the broader manufacturing landscape will achieve Gold. At a minimum, factories in Nike's SC will be expected to achieve and sustain a Bronze rating, indicating that factories can meet their baseline standards and can self-govern through integrated systems and a lean approach.

The MI creates one overall score for each contract factory, enabling a consistent and comprehensive conversation about Nike's business with that factory. Nike develops incentives and sanctions based on the MI ratings. For example, Silver- and Gold-rated factories will be able to self-audit and calibrate with Nike staff and will have access to a range of Nike's technical assistance, leadership and education resources, as well as possible innovation or community co-investment, and priority consideration for orders.

Nike initiated several schemes to make its SC more sustainable and environmentally friendly. Nike has set up Sustainable Manufacturing & Sourcing-Sustainable—a new organizational structure within the company that brought together labour compliance, health, safety and environment, lean manufacturing, human resources management, climate and energy, waste and water management.

In 2005, Nike disclosed its factory list. A SC map of Nike can be seen online at http://nikeinc.com/pages/manufacturing.

You can use this case-study in chapters (i.e., Chap. 5) for the following *discussions:*

- What advantages and disadvantages would you see in the outsourcing strategy?
- Select and calculate at least two performance indicators to evaluate the inventory management performance at Nike!
- What do you think of the MI at Nike from the position of a contract manufacture?

2.1.2 Dangote Cement: Establishing Sophisticated Supply Chain Management in Africa

The African economy has undergone fundamental changes over the last decade. However, in most African countries, particularly the lower income countries, infrastructure emerges as a major constraint on doing business. The distribution network of Africa comprises waterways, airways, railways, roads and pipelines.

The Dangote Group is one of the most diversified business conglomerates in Africa with a reputation for excellent business practices and product quality, with its operational headquarters in Lagos, Nigeria in West Africa. The group's activities encompass cement, sugar, food, and poly products manufacturing, sugar and salt refining, flour milling, and logistics port management.

The SC in Dangote Cement has the following structure (see Fig. 2.2):

Dangote Cement is a fully integrated cement company and has projects and operations in Nigeria and 14 other African countries. Dangote Cement's production capacity in Nigeria comprises three existing cement plants in Obajana, Ibese and Gboko. The combined production capacity is about 20 million tonnes per year. The Obajana Cement Plant (OCP) located in Kogi State is reputed to be one of the largest cement plants in the world.

The Dangote Group has experienced growth in the quality of its goods and services, focusing on cost leadership and efficiency of its human capital. The group's core business focus is to provide local products and services that meet the basic needs of the population. Through the construction and operation of large-scale manufacturing facilities in Nigeria and across Africa, the group is focused on building local manufacturing capacity to generate employment and provide high-quality goods.

The raw materials required to produce cement (calcium carbonate, silica, alumina and iron ore) are generally extracted from lime stock rock, chalk, clayey schist or clay. Dangote Cement owns or has licenses for the quarries/deposits which are located near their manufacturing plants. Dangote Cement presently has operations in six African countries: Cote D'Ivoire, Guinea, Ghana, Liberia, Sierra Leone and

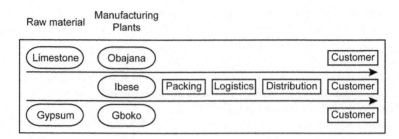

Fig. 2.2 Dangote cement's supply chain

Togo. Dangote Cement's expanded African operations will include factories in South Africa, Senegal, Cameroon, Gabon, Benin, Ethiopia, Tanzania, Zambia and the Republic of Congo. The company has deployed modern robotic laboratories in all its cement plants. These modern laboratories are operated by trained personnel and are provided with the latest technologies, practices and standards.

2.1.2.1 Supply Chain Management

Dangote Cement adopts a fully integrated SCM model. The SC is managed as a single entity thus ensuring information flows throughout the entire system. Dangote Cement runs an integrated make-to-order model which requires tracking of customer demand in real time and that is the reason why Dangote adopted CPFR (collaborative planning forecasting, and replenishment) in order to balance demand and supply with the help of distributors and retailers. All members of the SC are involved and freely share planning, demand, forecasting and inventory information among themselves. Collaboration is ensured in drawing up production, marketing and shipment plans. All processes from raw materials extraction, through the value-adding processes to distribution channels are interlinked within the organization.

2.1.2.2 Logistics Management

The biggest challenge for Dangote Cement, and for the industry, is to tackle logistics and distribution costs, as cement has to be moved to markets from production centres. Being one of the largest cement producers in Africa, the company uses the cost-efficient sea transportation to supply its Pan-African operations. Two dedicated export water terminals located in Calabar and Lagosare are used for freighting cement from Nigeria through international transportation to their markets.

Road transportation is the most widely used form of transportation utilized by Dangote Cement. It is the only option for landlocked nations and the most viable in most other African nations because of the poor rail infrastructure (the company is in active consultation with various governments for a possible revival of the railways to enable cheaper distribution costs).

Dangote Cement enjoys the benefit of its in-house transport fleet to ensure SC efficiency. The company has an own fleet of trucks as well as "Dantrans", which is a subsidiary of the Dangote Group and provides freight services with a fleet of over 3000 trucks under commercially competitive terms to members of the group to facilitate transport of raw materials from the sea ports to factories located inland, and for the distribution of finished goods. The fleet of trucks and haulage is monitored by trace and tracking (T&T) systems. Dangote Cement has its own depots and warehouses in several locations to serve various dealers, corporate and institutional buyers.

The fleet is deployed strategically across Nigeria to ensure the company's cement has access to every corner of the country. To mitigate any disruption, regional transport hubs are backed by fully fledged workshops to take preventive action and deliver maintenance. The company implements scientific logistic solutions to find means of effective distribution.

2.1.2.3 Distribution Management

Cement transportation and storage is capital intensive due to the high volume–weight relation of the product. Dangote Cement adopts a robust and pragmatic approach to ensure a smooth material flow throughout the distribution network. This is essential to meet customer demands at all times while minimizing SC costs.

Dangote Cement first began its operations in Nigeria as an importer and built six terminals in Lagos and Port Harcourt. Soon after, Nigeria's cement sector became self-sufficient, as a result of which two terminals that were built to import cement are now being used for export purpose. In addition, new terminals in other neighbouring countries have been built to expand the SC and distribute cement by road through the supply network and to the customer.

Dangote Cement has now invested in various strategic locations for depots across Nigeria to ensure quick supplies. Dangote Cement operates 67 owned warehouses and cement depots spread across various strategic locations in Nigeria to service the local market. They serve an ever growing list of authorized distributors who sell bagged cement to retailers and bulk users.

The company maintains close relations with all dealers offering attractive returns on cement sales as well as supporting dealers with prompt supplies through its dedicated haulage or through third-party transportation. Dangote Cement has recently launched a special drive to enroll new dealers and distributors with simplified online, direct enrolment processes to further strengthen its distribution network. A vendor-managed inventory (VMI) system is used to maintain adequate cement inventory at all times on behalf of Dangote Cement under the terms of a contractual agreement with the authorized distributors. Retailers in turn purchase cement in bulk from the authorized distributors and sell in retail quantities to low-level end users.

Dangote Cement recently extended its ability to deliver cement directly to customers with investment in additional trucks and a call centre to deal with customer orders. Such a distribution model helps the company increase its market share by providing more options for customers and with value-added services.

2.1.2.4 Sustainability Management

Cement manufacturing causes environmental impacts at all stages of the process. These include emissions of airborne pollution in the form of dust, gases, noise and vibration when operating machinery and during blasting in quarries; also damage to the countryside from quarrying. Equipment to reduce dust emissions during quarrying and the manufacturing of cement are widely used. Further equipment to trap and separate exhaust gases are coming into increased use. Environmental protection also includes the re-integration of quarries into the countryside after they have been closed down by returning them to nature or re-cultivating them. Some of the company's sustainability measures include: usage of filters for minimal dust emission; usage of fossil fuel in order to reduce emissions of greenhouse gases; usage of natural gas for power generation; dust-free manufacturing by covering raw material and process conveyers; usage of covered conveyer belts from lime stone mines to plant in order to minimize vehicles movement; usage of environmentally friendly polypropylene bags for packing; utilization of rain water to keep plant cool; and a water treatment plant in order to reuse water.

You can use this case-study in further chapters for the following discussions:

- What problems might Dangote Cement experience in future in its SC?
- Why can its own transportation fleet be seen as an advantage for Dangote Cement? Can you see any risks in its having its own transportation fleet?
- Describe Dangote Cement's production, logistics and distribution networks!
- How does Dangote Cement's main product influence its production, logistics and distribution strategies?
- What do you think about the introduction of direct shipments to customers?

2.1.3 Toyota: Supply Chain Disruption Management

A special focus of SCOM at Toyota is risk and disruption management. Many parts of the Toyota's SC are located in areas that are likely to be hit by an earthquake. As such, the risk that Toyota's SC would suffer from those disasters is rising, and the damage may severely impact production and other activities. Given this scenario, it is essential to assume that Toyota itself, with its restricted resources, would suffer and will have made preparations to affect early recovery. For these reasons, Toyota is reassessing its business continuity plan. The foremost premise of Toyota's business continuity plan is to work on preparedness before and recovery after disaster happens.

As a part of the *preparedness*, Toyota addressed the difficulty of "energy, information and transport network fragmentation" once disasters occur, and developed a hybrid car for the Miyagi Prefectural Police, installed with external power provision systems. Additional to providing good fuel efficiency and environmental performance through normal times, during disasters these cars can be driven on fuel or electricity, and even have a power supply function that allows electricity to be drawn from the car.

Toyota's help in *disaster recovery* areas is illustrated by its sending workers to its production sites within the disaster affected areas, where they can be engaged in numerous activities such as restoring facilities and distributing disaster relief supplies. Worker volunteers from the Toyota Corporation are continuing to help with restoration efforts for individuals within the areas hardest hit by the latest disaster. Toyota additionally provides material support: trucks with relief supplies from the Toyota Corporation gathered at two local production sites.

Learning from such experiences, Toyota has prepared a nationwide framework for sending relief supplies to disaster affected areas that utilizes the warehouses and logistics network throughout Japan. Additional to stocking emergency supplies at the 34 distributors nationwide, Toyota has also built a framework for sending such relief supplies to distributors on disaster affected sites. Toyota attends them in order to deliver quick and reliable support for disaster affected sites, taking into consideration such possible problems as motor fuel shortages.

The risk management committee at Toyota organizes meetings twice a year to identify the risks that may affect business activities and to take preventative actions against negative impacts of those risks. The committee members include global chief risk officer (CRC), regional CRS's, and all senior managers and chief officers. They work to manage and prevent the major risks in the regions and report on any immediate and serious disruptions.

2.1.4 Adidas "Speedfactory": 3D Printing and Industry 4.0 in Supply Chain and Operations Management

Lot-size "1", 3D printing, Industry 4.0—all these concepts have been extensively developed in the last years. In December 2015, Adidas Group presented new "Speedfactory" concept that is going to implement these concepts in practice.

In 1993, Adidas Group ceased the manufacturing in Germany and outsourced its production to Asia. Long product development time, long lead times and long transportation ways have been characteristic for the supply chains of Adidas Group in the last 20 years. This should be changed in next years with a radical supply chain re-design.

In Speedfactory, new intelligent robot technologies with the use of 3D printing are going to be implemented for production of sport shoes. This new project of Adidas is a part of Industry 4.0 initiative and it has been developed in collaboration with universities RWTH Aachen and TU Munich. High quality production of individual designs will be possible with the new factory that is being currently built in Ansbach, Bavaria. Further factories, e.g., in U.S. are planned. The Speedfactory concept allows reacting faster to demand and produce close to the customer. Long transportation ways, lead times, and complex supply chains can be omitted.

Speedfactory combines the designing and manufacturing of sport products in an automated, decentralized, and flexible manufacturing process. It becomes possible to produce where it is needed and when it is needed. Therefore, customer requirements can be met even more flexible. A positive impact on the environment can be observed in regard to transportation and adhesion reduction.

Discussion
- What are the drivers of supply chain re-design at Adidas group?
- Which impact might have 3D printing and Industry 4.0 on product development time, lead time, and transportation ways?
- What sustainability issues can be addressed in Speedfactory concept?

2.2 Examples of Operations and Supply Chains in Services

2.2.1 SCOM in Restaurants: Case Study Starbucks Corporation

The Starbucks Corporation, founded in 1971, is one of the world's largest coffee house chains, with more than 17,240 coffee shops in over 50 countries. Starbucks' product portfolio consists of food items, as well as such beverage products as coffee specialties, tea and other refreshing drinks. Starbucks Corporation also offers roasted beans and several merchandise products. However, Starbucks' main product is coffee. Therefore and because of the large and complex global supply SC, this case focuses on the coffee bean only. In particular the company's production and sourcing strategy and its transportation network are considered.

Starbucks uses like most restaurants the production strategy make-to-stock, which means production is performed in expectation of a customer order. Reasons for that are the scale effects resulting for example in lower transportation and manufacturing costs and higher flexibility compared to other production strategies. To decrease the lead time of coffee deliveries and to further decrease the transportation costs, Starbucks aims to manufacture in the region where the coffee is sold. To reach the aim of regionalization of coffee manufacturing, Starbucks owns five coffee roasting plants, four of them located in the United States and another in the Netherlands. Additional to its company-owned coffee roasting plants, Starbucks works with 24 contract manufacturers in the United States, Canada, Europe, Asia and Latin America.

Starbucks has spread its production across a wide territory; nevertheless transportation, logistics and distribution are still the biggest part of Starbucks' operating expenses. Therefore the existence of an efficient and effective single, global logistics system is essential for the company. Figure 2.3 shows the SC of the Starbucks Corporation.

The company has a multiple sourcing concept. The suppliers of the coffee beans are mainly located in Latin America, Asia and Africa. To ensure ethical sourcing of the high quality coffee beans, Starbucks uses Coffee and Farmer Equity (C.A.F.E)

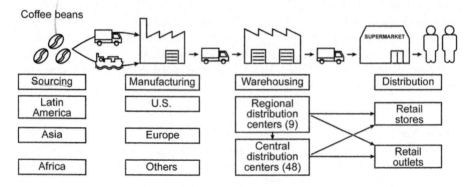

Fig. 2.3 Starbucks's SC

practices. C.A.F.E is a set of guidelines which evaluates the social, economic and environmental aspects of coffee production. This allows Starbucks to address the sustainability issues which have become very important in SCM.

Starbucks uses ships and trucks for transportation. The Starbucks Corporation normally delivers the unroasted beans in ocean containers to the United States and Europe. From the port of entry the goods get trucked to a storage site close to one of the coffee roasting plants. Once the beans are roasted and packaged the coffee is delivered to regional distribution centres by trucks. In total Starbucks runs nine regional distribution centres, five in the United States and two in Europe and an additional two in Asia. Each of the distribution centres covers 200,000 to 300,000 square feet. Other goods needed for running a coffee shop are also stored there. From there the products get delivered either directly to the store or to central distribution centres, which are smaller warehouses. In total the Starbucks Corporation has 48 central warehouses worldwide. From there the coffee beans and other products are frequently trucked to retail stores and retail outlets.

Discussion (Especially in Regard to Chap. 8)
1. What kind of production strategy does the Starbucks Corporation use and why?
2. What kind of sourcing strategy is Starbucks using, in terms of numbers of suppliers and geographical aspects?
3. Which mode of transportation does Starbucks use?
4. What kind of transportation network does Starbucks use—direct shipping or via distribution centres?

2.2.2 Operations Management at Airport Madrid/Barajas

Airport Madrid/Barajas is among the largest in Europe regarding the volume of passengers and aircraft operations. As all airports, Madrid/Barajas divides its process range in two different areas:

- Airside where activities related to aircraft operations happen, such as approach, taxiing and turnaround (fuelling, push-back, etc.);
- Landside the area next to terminal activities (parking, bus stations, etc.) The terminal is the most important component of the landside.

The airport's operational centre must coordinate not only airlines and air traffic control (ATC), but all other sub-actors involved in the whole process such as passengers, government and security, handling companies, luggage, technicians, etc. In the case of Madrid/Barajas all of those actors, sub-actors and stakeholders are controlled and coordinated through the airport management centre (AMC) under the real-time philosophy of modern airports.

The effectiveness of an airport is directly proportional to the number of start and landing operations performed per time period. But what happens if the arriving aircrafts do not get a taxiway clearance from the control tower, or there is no available gate to park at, or there are no available handling agents to load or unload the baggage? The AMC is therefore needed to coordinate every single operation that occurs at Madrid/Barajas airport, planning every movement and solving quickly any unexpected problems or conflicts.

A particular challenge of operations management at the airports is that operations processes are highly influenced by uncertain external factors. The most relevant one is the weather. Before the AMC was created, operations management was established to act under certain standards, and when standards varied (weather conditions, aircraft delays, apron, stands and gates not operative etc.), the system wasn't able to respond effectively.

In consequence, the airport managers agreed on the need to change the way in which all the actors were coordinated, commanded and controlled. This led to a change towards the AMC, with a real-time philosophy. The AMC is the centralized unit for an airport's operations created to manage all of its daily activities. Implementation became a big challenge and the most important step in terms of operations management ever carried out in Madrid/Barajas. The objectives of the AMC are as follows: to offer a general view of airport´s functioning at any time; to provide a unique point of contact for operators, agents and the airport's divisions; to support the integrated management of the systems; and to supervise the levels of service to optimize resources and re-duce the cost of operations.

The implementation of the AMC considered new subdivisions in terms of operations management, and made them all work together, well-coordinated and in the same physical space. The AMC became the unit where four different subdivisions of the airport's operations management (Aircraft Operations, Security, Passenger Services and Infrastructure) interact quickly and effectively under any kind of expected and unexpected situations with the help of information technologies like video-walls, infrared cameras, PDAs and communication devices.

The following case describes briefly how the AMC operates in the event of Snow Forecast, which usually happens in Madrid/Barajas at least twice every winter, and for which any airport should be prepared.

The plan of action is divided into six different phases:

Phase 1 Pre-activation
When an airport's METEO forecasts a 40 % or more probability of snow, it contacts the AMC, delivering an urgent message. The operations manager takes the lead and starts to coordinate all the means needed to prepare the airport for the upcoming situation. The manager on duty decides with the coordinator which plan to activate, and the way to proceed. This phase consists of localizing and informing stakeholders, technicians and drivers to warn them about the situation and the activation of the plan.

Phase 2 Positioning
In this phase the manager on duty will give the instructions to the coordinator of the AMC to allocate all the means requested in the 1st phase in their set-points at least 2 h before the snow is forecast.

Phase 3 Pre-acting

This phase will be activated 1 h prior to the snow forecast. The operations manager in coordination with the air traffic manager instructs the AMC coordinator to inform about and coordinate the so-called pre-acting phase. The technicians will start preparing the runways and spreading specific products over runways and the taxiways. These products will make the snow melt in contact with the surface. This will be carried out within 30 min; half an hour before it starts to snow.

Phase 4 Evaluation

The AMC in coordination with ATC (tower) starts coordinating the collection of information about the state of the airfield through the technicians, pilots and airfield operators. If the coefficient of friction of the runway is low, the service executive will give the instructions to activate the 5th phase.

Phase 5 Clearing Runways and Taxiways

If the manager on duty decides to act due to the low coefficient of friction, he will be in constant contact with ATC. The procedure will be as usual.

Phase 6 Cancelling

The manager on duty, together with the AMC coordinators, will evaluate the circumstances and proceed to the cancellation. The information will be disseminated to the rest of the agents involved.

Future development of the AMC is the collaborative decision making system which is the operations system that allows the stakeholders to enter and receive the real-time information that each one of them needs to operate more efficiently. The actors involved are ATC, aircraft operators, handling companies, airport operations and control flow management unit (CFMU). ATC gets information from the CFMU. Once ATC knows when exactly the aircraft will be landing, they will communicate to handling companies and airport operations, to be able to manage more efficiently the services provided to the aircraft.

Discussion Questions
- Which activities comprise airport operations management?
- What are the challenges of the airport operations management?
- Which role does information coordination play in airport operations management?

2.2.3 Time-Critical Supply Chains: Disaster Management and Humanitarian Logistics

Commonly, logistics is associated with the business field. However, in recent years particular efforts were directed at investigating severe *SC disruptions*, which can be caused, for example, by natural disasters, political conflicts, terrorism, maritime piracy, economic crises, destruction of information systems, or transport infrastructure failures. In this setting, humanitarian logistics becomes more and more

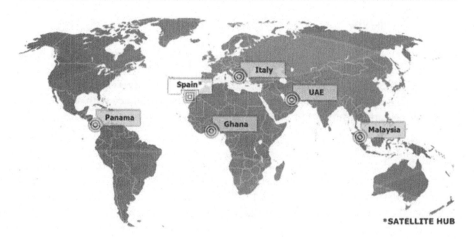

Fig. 2.4 Global supply emergency network for humanitarian logistics (source: World Food Program)

important. We can categorize natural disasters and man-made disasters such as wars and terrorist attacks.

Disaster/humanitarian logistics is a relatively new field which has just recently received more attention. This is due to increasing political conflicts along with the accelerating strength of natural disasters. The main challenge of humanitarian logistics is the coordination of activities in a destroyed environment. This can become extremely complex since almost all parameters are unknown up to the point of the disaster and even after the event. Not knowing the type or amount of goods, or the actual shipment location makes humanitarian logistics a particularly challenging field.

Each year more than 500 catastrophes of different kinds occur worldwide. The UN Humanitarian Response Depots (UNHRD), which is a UN organization under the head of the World Food Program, reacts quickly when disasters occur. Usually, the most necessary supplies are food and water. The organization has developed a concept whereby emergency supplies are stored in five hubs worldwide: in Ghana, UAE, Malaysia, Panama and Italy (see Fig. 2.4). The hubs also contain medical kits, shelter items and IT equipment. Through this network the UNHRD is able to start supplying goods to every country in the world within 1–2 days.

The effectiveness of the emergency aid response relies on logistics speed and efficiency, and for this reason increases the awareness of the crucial role of logistics in humanitarian relief operations. Time is the most important factor as it influences how many lives can be saved. Therefore, it is necessary that the mechanism is ready to work at any time. The disaster management cycle has four stages (Altay and Green 2006):

- *Mitigation* is a role played by the government, where the host government has the responsibility to put in place protocols and take action to reduce the probability of disasters.

- *Preparedness* refers to the various operations that occur before a disaster strikes. Here the physical network is design, and information and communication technology (ICT) systems are developed together with the bases of collaborators.
- *Response* is the various operations that are instantly implemented after a disaster occurs. First, all collaborators get involved; second, they try to restore in the shortest time possible the basic services and delivery of goods to the highest possible number of beneficiaries. Collaboration and coordination among the players are crucial.
- *Reconstruction* is the operations in the aftermath of a disaster. It involves rehabilitation and the aim is to address the problem from a long-term perspective, since the after-effects of the disaster can continue for a long period of time.

When a disaster does occur, the local government needs to request the World Food Program's help. First, food supplies are sent out immediately. Following that, employees are sent to disaster areas to access information about demands for goods. They also evaluate the best means of transporting the goods to the affected area. Next, the emergency operation is planned and budgeted. To receive financial aid the World Food Program will request funds from countries worldwide. Most funds are then received out of government expenditure. A team of logistics experts works on how to transport all the required goods to the area where the disaster occurred using all possible transportation means. Particular importance is assigned to reorganizing the ICT as it will help further operations through improved information flow. The World Food Program has an IT team which is specially trained to be able to set up the infrastructure within a day.

In November 2013 one of the strongest typhoons recorded, "Haiyan", hit the Philippines. It killed thousands and destroyed such infrastructure as roads, ports and hospitals. Many logistic problems were encountered right at the beginning:

- Most of the roads, airport and harbours were destroyed.
- Weather conditions after the typhoon were still bad (rain, strong winds, etc.)
- No electricity was available, due to lack of fuel for generators, which also led to mobilization problems.
- Acute shortages of food and water and lack of medical supplies or proper hospital facilities were observed.

The World Food Program was working closely with local government to provide as much help as possible. As soon as the typhoon hit, the organization supplied "high energy biscuits" and rice. Moreover, logistics and telecommunication support also were provided by the World Food Program. The goods financed by international donations were distributed via hubs in Cebu, Tacloban, Roxas, Ormoc and Guiuan on the Philippines.

But not only non-profit organizations take responsibility for humanitarian aid. DHL, which is a German logistics company, also engaged in activities on the Philippines in 2013. In cooperation with the UN the company built up a global network of disaster response teams (DRT). These teams consisted of volunteers employed at DHL and they are particularly trained for disaster situations. They are divided into three areas worldwide so as to be able to access all regions quickly. In the case of typhoon "Haiyan" the team supported the accessibility of the airport and increased throughput times so that goods could reach the victims faster. The DRT's greatest strength is their knowledge about logistics and how to solve crisis situations. Since building up in 2005, the teams have been successfully able to support victims of disasters more than 20 times.

For the future, the UN seeks to improve prevention. Naturally, it is impossible to reduce all risks to a minimum level but improving prevention measures is still an option. A 10-year plan called the Hyogo Framework for Action (HFA) is designed to reduce risks from natural disasters.

Questions
- What is the difference between business and humanitarian logistics?
- Which four stages are included in the disaster management cycle?
- Where can you see limitations of humanitarian logistics?
- What organizations belong to the stakeholders in humanitarian logistics?

2.2.4 Operations Issues in Car Sharing

The business model of car sharing appears to be relatively new. However, its origins can be found in Zurich, Switzerland, in 1948. Similar to car sharing today, in a "Sefage" (Selbstfahrergemeinschaft) people could use one car together without having to buy one of their own. Recently, changing preferences in passenger transport, particularly in bigger cities, have boosted the demand for car sharing. According to estimations of Navigant Research, global car-sharing revenue will grow to $6.2 billion in 2020, up from $1 billion in 2013 (Clark 2014). The advantages of car sharing are numerous, but high flexibility at low cost compared to possessing a car is probably the main reason why people increasingly choose car sharing. Business customers also benefit since they can use car sharing as an add-on for the company car fleet. Additionally, travel costs for employees can be reduced by using car sharing instead of taxis. But there is even more to car sharing. It decreases the total amount of cars in the city, which means less traffic volume and more parking spaces. Pollution is also decreased, especially since more and more car sharing providers offer hybrid or completely electric driven vehicles.

There are *two types of car sharing*: station-bound and free-floating. Station bound is the older version where the car is received and returned at the rental station. Most of the time now it is possible to return the car to a different station if it belongs to the rental company. Free-floating is non station-bound meaning the car can be rented and left anywhere within a particular area. Charges are paid based on a minute and/or kilometre based bill. This option of car sharing is more appropriate for short distances otherwise it can become rather expensive.

Car sharing providers are facing challenges in operations management concerning demand, capacity, location and cost planning. Usually, car sharing is

2.2 Examples of Operations and Supply Chains in Services

an additional business field for rental service providers or car manufacturers. For example, DriveNow is a subsidiary owned by BMW and SIXT. Car2Go was founded by Daimler and Europcar. These companies already have expert knowledge in demand forecasting and capacity planning, which makes it easier to evaluate the number of cars needed at different locations. The challenge faced in this field is meeting demand at peak-times and in different areas of the city.

For particular occasions such as a big football game it may happen that many vehicles are used to drive to one particular location. Accordingly, there may be a misallocation of cars within an area. It is easy for car sharing providers to track these actions via GPS. To solve the problem, employees can be hired to spread the vehicles throughout the city. This option can be quite expensive, as employees need to be transported to the cars themselves too. A cheaper option is to offer benefits for customers such as free miles, bonus points or other discounts.

Cost planning can also constitute an issue for operations management. Most car sharing companies attempt to attract customers by offering free parking everywhere. Once a parking ticket is received the rental company pays the fee. Whereas charges for parking without a ticket used to be rather cheap, authorities have reacted by increasing the prices. Charging fees constitutes a variable cost that may be difficult to forecast.

Questions
- Which challenges of operations management are met by car sharing companies?
- What role does information technology play in car sharing?
- What do you think of sustainability issues regarding the car sharing concept?
- Compare station-bound and free-floating from an operations management perspective regarding the costs, time, quality, and management complexity.

2.2.5 REWE: Expanding the Logistics Network

With a turnover of more than 49.7 billion euros, more than 8000 supermarkets, a fleet of almost 2000 trucks which do 965,000 trips annually, covering a distance of 162 million kilometres and both collecting goods from suppliers as well as secondary delivering them to stores, and with 327,600 employees (2013), the REWE Group is one of the leading travel and tourism companies in Europe.

In 2008, an extensive logistics modernization began in the company. The objectives included an increase in warehouse productivity by 15 % per m^2, higher demand forecast accuracy, inventory reduction, and higher product availability rates as well as transportation cost reduction and sustainability.

At present, the company operates about 30 distribution centres (DC) in Germany. In 2011, a new DC in Oranienburg near Berlin was built for 60 million euros with an area of 52,500 m^2. The criteria for location selection were to shorten transportation routes and maximize efficiency across the network. About 325 employees in Oranienburg ensure the replenishment of REWE supermarkets with more than 12,000 SKU (stock keeping units). One hundred trucks deliver products to 330 supermarkets from Sassnitz und Jüterbog daily.

You can use this case-study in Chaps. 7 and 8 and analyse such questions like:

- What are the objectives of the logistics redesign at REWE? What trade-offs can you see?
- Which types of distribution networks do you know? Which type is implemented at REWE?
- What could be the reasons for looking for a new warehouse location near Berlin? Which selection criteria were important for the company?
- Which methods and/or models would you recommend to apply to facility location planning?
- Describe, based on the example of this case study, the basic steps in facility selection decisions!

2.3 Examples of e-Operations and Supply Chains

2.3.1 Fab.com

In this case study a business-to-consumer (B2C) e-commerce application of operations management is considered. As an example we look at Fab.com, one of the fastest growing B2C start-ups, and see why and how the company decided to transit from a flash sale to an inventory-based model.

We can learn in this case study:

1. how to determine the optimal location for a warehouse;
2. how to understand the trade-off "service level vs. costs";
3. how to determine a distribution strategy and what are the trade-offs between the number of warehouses and logistics costs;
4. which costs should be included in the facility location analysis;
5. how to improve and measure inventory management performance;
6. which information technologies exist to support SCOM decisions;
7. how to develop strategic collaboration with suppliers.

General Description

Fab.com started as a design-oriented e-commerce website selling fine design at affordable prices. Fab.com launched in June 2011, and has grown to serve two million registered users in less than 7 months; by December 2012, it has grown to serve over 10 million members and became one of the fastest growing e-commerce start-ups in the US, and even globally. The core of its business is the concept that was realized by a small design team and improved daily through careful analysis of user data. The vision is to create a one-stop online store for well-designed goods. But as Fab grew exponentially, it was facing serious on-time delivery and customer service issues.

Fab started and operated with its novel concept and marketing strategy, achieving customer-centric guidelines, and taking full advantage of the internet. A well-designed website, a user-friendly portal platform, a powerful backstage data processing system, accurate and efficient handling of daily customers resulted in rapid growth of registered members and revenue.

Mobile Commerce (M-Commerce) is a major focus for Fab. Customers with smartphones purchase products twice as often as those who visit the website, and tablet visitors purchase four times as often as web visitors. One-third of Fab's visitors are from these mobile devices and the company expects this number to rise to as much as 50 % in a year.

Social networking is also important for Fab. CEO Jason Goldberg himself is keeping a blog to announce or showcase anything about Fab; he is also quite active in interacting directly with customers' comments or feedback. Moreover, of the company's two million members, more than half came from sharing with friends. Fab was a partner in Facebook's Open Graph expansion, so that when people purchase on Fab, their purchases appear on their friends' Facebook feeds.

Problems with Which Fab Struggled

Due to an initial strategy to eliminate inventory risk, Fab decided not to buy any products until customers purchased an item online. To meet members' curious minds, Fab's ten buyers scour the world for products that fit Fab's unique aesthetic. This caused a situation where Fab could promise only a long delivery time of 16 days. The serious problem was that the customer service team was becoming overloaded with complaints. Customers wanted high-quality products delivered fast, since getting unique products delivered to them fast is far more important to them than just getting unique products.

Fab itself has found from their data history that a unique product delivered swiftly increases Fab's customer satisfaction, with the likelihood of repeats, and the propensity to promote Fab to one's friends fourfold over a similar product that takes longer to ship. Customers also requested better product descriptions and better product imagery.

Furthermore, Fab had been relying on so-called flash sales, where a limited amount of merchandise is sold in a short period of time. This requires shoppers to buy goods within a certain length of time. Such a concept was hard to operate on a large scale: running a flash-sales web-site is more time-consuming and requires long extra hours of work to ensure efficiency and good customer service at the same time. As the business grew, Fab realized they had the following issues:

1. Long delivery times caused low customer service satisfaction.
2. There as a shortage of favourable goods.
3. Labour costs were high.
4. As a small scale company, it had its limits and limitations.

Solutions

Earlier in 2013, the company shifted from a flash-sale site to an "online lifestyle shop" operated by a new inventory-based system with the following features.

Inventory-Based Management

Fab started to lease a warehouse, built its own SC, and purchased inventory. Now, products come into Fab's New Jersey warehouse and remain there until the sale ends, usually between three and 30 days. If a customer orders an item which is in stock, (around 75 % of what Fab sells) it starts shipping within 2 h. That's a huge change from the 16 days it typically took Fab to ship before. So far, by 2013, Fab has expanded its footprint of warehouses to more than 500,000 ft^2 across three locations, two in New Jersey and one in Eindhoven, the Netherlands.

Established Supplier Base

Fab relies on and supports original designers and makers, working with more than 20,000 product designers. Fab has its own supplier evaluation criteria list in accordance with its business concept. Fab collaborates with the designers directly by providing the platform where they can showcase and sell their goods. Alternatively, the collaboration is based on licensing new designs and manufacturing products on the designers' behalf or as authorized derivations and reproductions of their work. Thus, on one hand, it helps designers globally scale up their businesses; on the other hand, it secures Fab's supplier base.

Advance Information Technology

As Fab started focusing on an inventory-based business model, they designed processes and invested significantly in technology and engineering staff to help the company scale efficiently and reduce operating costs. Managing a global business forces a company to strengthen its SC. Fab elaborated on sourcing and planning as it consolidated merchandising, marketing and operations into a single unit in New York. Fab transited its business model from flash sales to a more scalable, inventory planning model in order to secure a greater consumer base and profitability. Fab is developing its in-house engineering talent and investing in technical systems that will power their growth and scale, with a business that can be managed with innovative technology and fewer people.

Fab also design systems to help the website to effectively and efficiently respond to customer issues, whether it is offering easy returns and quickly getting a replacement product shipped, or automatically crediting customers when prices drop. Fab now counts more than 110 employees in the product development and engineering organization.

Fab's key technology investments include:

- an inventory management system that provides visibility and control across all the facilities;
- a promotions framework that bubbles up the most compelling offers;
- innovative tools to help customers discover and find what's new;
- a personalization engine that provides personalized product recommendations and thus a more relevant shopping experience;
- a new and improved mobile shopping experience that enhances its leadership position in m-commerce.

2.3 Examples of e-Operations and Supply Chains

Improvement in Logistics

As logistics is thought to be a base requirement for any retailer, Amazon is heading towards same-day service; on 2013s "Cyber Monday", they even used drones to ensure 30-min deliveries; and eBay has a 1-h pickup from local retailers. Fab also focuses on building processes that optimize their transportation costs, as well as designing innovative inventory controls to efficiently move products between facilities. Fab has chosen warehouse locations that minimize shipping costs and reduce shipping times and have outfitted those facilities with their own technical systems. The result is that delivery times have dropped from 16 days to 3 days on average.

The logistics system development comprises the following features:

1. Previously, Fab outsourced their logistics in order to fundamentally improve on-time delivery. Now Fab aims to stop using third-party logistics firms to handle delivery planning. Instead, the company will bring all logistics operations in house and use an uninterruptable power supply (UPS) to transport products to customers.
2. Fab promises free shipping with a minimum order value (in the US, this is $49). But they also adopt an alternative shipping policy: free shipping on orders taking more than 5 working days; expedited shipping orders (an extra shipping cost) would be promised to be shipped within 1–3 working days. Thus, Fab is able to split the order flow and ensure the stability of their delivery timetable without affecting customer satisfaction level.

Summary

From Fab.com's case study, we can learn that e-commerce is a crucial opportunity for business success. As from the SCOM point of view, in order to fulfil the goal of being a global company and to remain profitable, the objectives of satisfying customers with fast delivery and the right products, and achieving lowest costs and highest margins, should be achieved. Continuous improvement of cost structures is critical in order to continue providing customers with exceptional service and benefits, which will result in the greatest possible long-term stakeholder value. Fab seems to focus on developing successful supply-chain management with efficient and effective inventory management, establishing supplier relationship management, investing in new facilities for stocking items and information technology, and improving logistics, to ensure a high level of customer satisfaction at minimal costs.

Discussion Questions for Future Chapters
- Analyse the advantages and disadvantages of flash-sale strategy! How can we improve this based on the inventory systems?
- Analyse trade-offs between delivery time and costs (include transportation, inventory and facility costs)!
- Where can you see how information technology has impacted on operations and SC management?
- Which methods of facility location could be applied at Fab.com?

- What can you say about Fab's decision on back-sourcing of logistics operations?
- If you had to analyse Fab's performance in comparison with other companies in the branch (such as Amazon), how would you proceed?

2.3.2 Homeplus: The Store Comes to Your Home

Tesco is known by the name Homeplus in South Korea and adapts its business model to better meet the needs and preferences of its local customers. In this regard, the following three aspects are particularly relevant:

- long working hours and little spare time
- high technology acceptance
- high store rent in major cities.

The concept is based on establishing a virtual store using m-commerce technology in which shoppers can browse through pictures of available products at a public place, in this case a subway station. The products can be selected by scanning the QR-code with a smartphone which uses a mobile application to directly order the selected products. The ordered products are then sent to the customer's home within the same day. Deliveries are arranged to arrive in minutes or hours, rather than days, so the groceries will be in the shopper's kitchen that night and there is no need to wait in to collect them.

The virtual store fits perfectly the expectations of the local customers; their sales increased 130 % in 3 months, and their number of registered users went up by 76 %. The virtual m-commerce store might be more suitable for the Korean market than most other markets. Yet the benefits such as shorter shopping times, convenient order and payment services and home delivery may also become more and more appreciated around the world, just as more and more countries will reach similar smartphone acceptance rates to South Korea. From an SCM perspective, additional benefits can be achieved.

Most notably, physical stores can be eliminated leading to a more cost-efficient SC with direct shipping as a distribution strategy. The entire purchasing process can be automated without any human intervention from the retailer's side. With fewer centralized distribution centres higher customer service (product availability) rates as well as reduced safety stock can be achieved. However, delivery costs for very small quantities could become a serious issue, depending on the customers' order behaviour and stores' delivery pricing policy.

You can use this case-study in further chapters for the following discussions:

- Consider trade-offs between inventory costs, number of warehouses, and transportation costs. Explain the efficiency issues in this case study based on these trade-offs.
- Which distribution strategy is used by Homeplus in South Korea?
- Is it possible to implement a virtual store in your country? What challenges might be encountered?

Bibliography

Bowersox DJ, Closs DJ, Copper MB (2012) Supply chain logistics management, 4th edn. McGraw-Hill, Boston
Chopra S, Meindl P (2012) Supply chain management. Strategy, planning and operation, 5th edn. Pearson, Harlow
Gleissner H, Moeller K (2011) Case studies in logistics. Gabler, Wiesbaden
Greasly A (2013) Operations management, 3rd edn. Wiley, New York
Heizer J, Render B (2013) Operations management: sustainability and supply chain management, 11th edn. Pearson, Harlow
Slack N, Brandon-Jones A, Johnston R (2013) Operations management, 7th edn. Pearson, Harlow

References for Sect. 2.1.1

www.nike.com

References for Sect. 2.1.2

http://dangote-group.com/
http://dangcem.com/

References for Sect. 2.1.3

http://www.toyota-global.com
Marsh P, Brown K, Anderlini J, Johnston T, Waldmeir P, Jung-a S, Rickards J, Weitzman H, Ward A (2011) Japan crisis impact on the SC: Global industries consider their options. Financial Times Europe, 17 March, p 16

References for Sect. 2.1.4

Adidas Group (2016) http://www.adidas-group.com/de/medien/newsarchiv/pressemitteilungen/2015/adidas-errichtet-erste-speedfactory-deutschland/. Accessed 27 May 2016
Zühlke K (2015) Industrie 4.0 in der Praxis: adidas errichtet erste Speedfactory in Deutschland. http://www.elektroniknet.de/elektronikfertigung/strategien-trends/artikel/126153/. Accessed 27 May 2016

References for Sect. 2.2.1

Cooke JA (2012) From bean to cup: how starbucks transformed its supply chain. *Supply Chain Quarterly*, 4
Starbuck Corporation 2014 [Online] www.starbucks.com, Accessed 01.09.2014

References for Sect. 2.2.2

Oleaga MA (2013) The AMC – New concept of Airport Management // El CGA – Nuevo concepto de gestión operativa

Pascual VMS (2012) The effect of the meteorological conditions to airports operations, Itavia

References for Sect. 2.2.3

Altay N, Green WG (2006) OR/MS research in disaster operations management. Eur J Oper Res 175:475–93

DHL GmbH (2013) *Disaster Response Teams leisten Katastrophenhilfe.* http://www.dpdhl.com/de/verantwortung/katastrophenmanagement/katastrophenhilfe_drt.html, accessed 21 Mar 2014

Ivanov D, Sokolov B, Dolgui A (2014) The Ripple effect in supply chains: trade-off 'efficiency-flexibility-resilience' in disruption management. Int J Prod Res 52(7):2154–72

Spens K, Kovács G (2009) Identifying challenges in humanitarian logistics. Int J Phys Distr Log Manag 39:506–28

Van Wassenhove L (2006) Humanitarian aid logistics: supply chain management in high gear. J Oper Res Soc 57:475–89

World Food Programme (2014) *Responding to emergencies.* http://www.wfp.org/emergencies, accessed 20 Mar 2014

References for Sect. 2.2.4

Clark J (2014) What's next for car sharing? Europe Autonews. http://europe.autonews.com/article/20140207/ANE/140209903/whats-next-for-car-sharing, accessed 21 Apr 2014

https://www.car2go.com

https://drive-now.com/

References for Sect. 2.2.5

http://www.rewe-group.com

http://supplychainanalysis.igd.com

References for Sect. 2.3

Strother J (2011) BBC news – shopping by phone at South Korea's virtual grocery

The Telegraph (2011) Tesco builds virtual shops for Korean commuters

Processes, Systems, and Models 3

Learning Objectives for This Chapter

- Interrelations between business processes, quantitative models, and information systems
- Role of business process management in operations and supply chains
- Effects of management information systems in SCOM
- Management information technologies, e.g., ERP, APS, WMS, RFID
- Planning, problem, and decision
- Role of models and modelling in decision-making
- Quantitative methods of decision-making

3.1 Introductory Case-Study: AirSupply

Each time an aircraft is made, it is the result of assembling a multitude of parts representing a very large volume of orders. And what's true for the aircraft assembly line is true for the whole aerospace industry where not only aircraft but also helicopters and satellites are built. Parts for manufacturing are coming from multiple suppliers from all over the world. Most of them are quite complex and need to fulfill highest quality standards. Each time delay can cause very high costs. It is essential that all suppliers involved in the manufacture of an aircraft have a real-time visibility of the progress of demand and inventory to adapt to fluctuations and changes of customer requirements. If so, it is essential for customers and suppliers to have a common tool that will enable them to better collaborate and to gain visibility over demand as well as inventory (see Fig. 3.1).

Find additional case-studies, Excel spreadsheet templates, and video streams in the *E-Supplement* to this book on www.global-supply-chain-management.de!

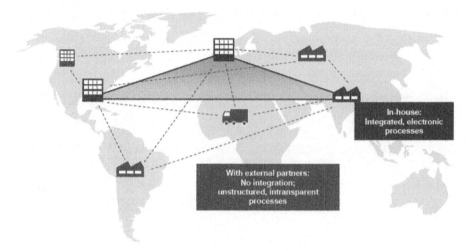

Fig. 3.1 Internal and external process integration in the supply chain

Such a tool can be seen in the example of SupplyOn's AirSupply solution that was developed in collaboration with Airbus/EADS and other major manufacturers and suppliers in the European aerospace industry. If AirSupply is mainly characterized by the networking of the whole Aerospace & Defense supply line, its main innovation lies in the fact that it will provide all users with one single tool. In other terms, the same view on demand and inventory data. The solution combines major new technologies such as cloud computing, software as a service (SaaS) and e-procurement. It was developed in cooperation with SupplyOn which had many years of experience with web-based SCM solutions in the automotive industry.

AirSupply offers services for a number of SC processes, covering the entire product cycle. The following main functions are provided (see Fig. 3.2):

- Forecast collaboration
- E-Procurement
- Vender managed inventory (VMI)

Consider some of these processes in detail.

3.1.1 E-procurement

AirSupply is a solution for an integrated SC where e-procurement plays a crucial role. Other than traditional procurement using enterprise resource planning (ERP) and simple EDI (electronic data interchange) communication, the e-procurement

3.1 Introductory Case-Study: AirSupply

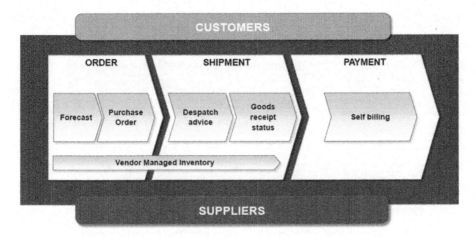

Fig. 3.2 Processes in supply chain management

solution provides real-time visibility of demand fluctuations and closer networking between suppliers and customers all having the same view on demand.

Many of the other characteristics of the aerospace industry, such as complex parts and high-quality standards make SC visibility and collaboration crucial competitive factors. Each airplane is produced according to individual customer requirements and several millions of parts are required at the right time while inventories are minimized and delays are costly. Especially for suppliers using expensive parts from other suppliers, the financial risk can be high, but can be mitigated through the e-procurement solution.

The following description of the purchase order process gives an example of how AirSupply facilitates SC processes. After the customer creates the purchase order (PO) in their ERP, three different scenarios can be supported by AirSupply:

- The supplier accepts the PO without changes.
- The supplier accepts the PO with changes. The customer either accepts or makes a new proposal.
- The supplier accepts the PO without changes, but the customer requests a modification. The supplier can accept and dispatch the goods or otherwise, the customer makes a new proposal.

AirSupply automatically synchronises the PO information from the cloud to the ERP system.

3.1.2 Vendor-Managed Inventory

The VMI process in particular shows a very strong need for integrated SC information systems (see Fig. 3.3).

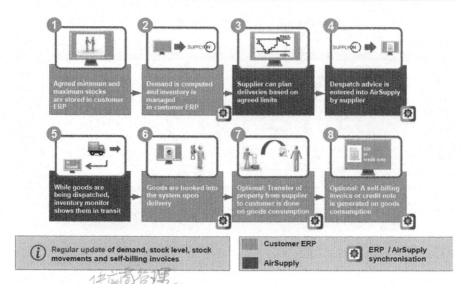

Fig. 3.3 Vendor-managed inventory process

In VMI, the supplier (or vendor) is responsible for managing the supply and usually agrees with the customer on a minimum and a maximum inventory level. This requires that the suppliers have timely and accurate information on the customer's inventory levels at any time. AirSupply strongly supports this SCM strategy by automatically advising suppliers when customers' inventory levels are critically low. Also, suppliers can simulate deliveries to make adjustments prior to actually dispatching goods.

Closer collaboration has helped reduce safety stock and improve the service level with the use of VMI. Also manual work is cut down as supplier data doesn't need to be entered and disputes linked to reception, inspection and billing can be reduced.

3.1.3 Implementation

AirSupply is based on a Hybrid Cloud with SaaS (software as a service) solution that allows managing established internal processes. More than 1000 suppliers were integrated into AirSupply by the end of 2012, and the solution connects all major firms of the European aerospace industry and has become its dominating platform. The common cloud platform enables standardized and integrated procurement processes while at the same time offering customized services to each individual company. Since cloud computing helps companies keep their hardware and software investments more flexible and overall lower, AirSupply offers a huge savings potential. Furthermore, cloud computing providers can guarantee a high level of data security and service reliability that a single company's IT, especially of a smaller company, could hardly do. At first glance, cloud services are particularly attractive for small and medium-sized enterprises (SMEs) that want to access massive computing power and specialized software with low fixed costs. For larger companies, the importance of having control over their IT infrastructure to secure and protect crucial internal processes could rather outweigh the benefits of cloud computing. However, the hybrid cloud solution can achieve the best combination of internal and external, fixed and variable IT systems for any company.

Discussion
1. What benefits of cloud computing for SC integration can you identify?
2. What benefits and drawbacks of e-procurement can you identify?
3. What do you think on how does the AirSupply platform encourage its users to increase collaboration and develop mutual trust to share information along the SC?
4. What could prevent industry members from joining AirSupply?

3.2 Business Process Management

3.2.1 Process Optimization and Re-engineering

A process is a content and logic sequence of functions or steps that are needed to create an object in a specified state. A *business process* is a network of activities for accomplishing a business function. Processes have input and output parameters and may be tied to functional area or be cross-functional. Today companies are organized on the process basis. As said by W. Edwards Deming (Professor at Columbia University; 1900–1993), "if you can't describe what are you doing as a process, you don't know what are you doing."

Examples of processes include the following areas:

- Manufacturing and production, e.g., assembling the product
- Sourcing, e.g., selecting suppliers
- Human resources, e.g., hiring employees

Consider as an example process "Order fulfilment" (Fig. 3.4):

It can be observed that fulfilling a customer order involves a complex set of steps that requires the close coordination of the sales, accounting, and manufacturing functions. The basic concept for managing processes in an organization is called *business process management (BPM)*. BPM contains a variety of tools, methodologies to analyze, design, and optimize processes. BPM comprises the following steps (Hammer and Champy 1993).

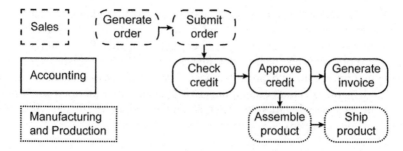

Fig. 3.4 Business process "Order fulfillment" [based on Laudon and Laudon (2013)]

- Identify processes for change
- Analyze existing processes
- Design the new process
- Implement the new process
- Continuous measurement

Processes can be optimized subject to finding their best state with regard to

- costs,
- capacity,
- time,
- quality,
- service level,
- reliability,
- flexibility, and
- sustainability.

The process analysis results may be characterized by *effectiveness* (the achievement of process goals) and *efficiency* (performing the process with minimum costs). Processes that are both effective and efficient are named optimal. Optimal processes are characterized by effectiveness, efficiency, controllability, stability, flexibility, analysability, observability, reliability, documentability and permanent improvement capabilities.

Most of the SCOM problems are involved with multiple objectives. The interrelation of objectives is named "trade-off" which means that a manager should find a compromise. For example, it is very difficult to achieve both low inventory and high customer service level, or both high capacity utilization and short lead-time.

> ▶ **Practical Insights** *Sustainability* becomes more and more important in process optimization in production, logistics, and services. Consider two apples in a German supermarket: an apple from South Africa and an apple from Germany. Which apple is more sustainable? Different costs such as transportation and warehouse costs should be considered in the analysis. In autumn, the German apple would be more sustainable. But in spring, the apple from

South Africa is more sustainable despite of transportation emissions because of high warehousing costs and corresponding energy consumption and emissions in Germany.

Process optimization in organizations is known under the name *business process re-engineering (BPR)*. BPR is an organization-wide philosophy of continuous process improvement. It comprises different views of process management such as operational, organizational, ethical, etc.

> ▶ **Practical Insights** Options for process improvement lie frequently in coordination area. For example, in the automotive industry, the supply cycle between a customer order and car delivery is approximately 60 days. The car assembly itself takes into account only 2 days. This means that the value-adding processes comprise less than 5 % of total supply cycle. 95 % are planning and coordination activities. Here a huge optimization potential can be found.

In SCs, the following options can be considered for *process improvement*:

- SC design and configuration (i.e., new market acquisition, too long time-to-market, non-resilient SC design);
- SC planning (weak flow capacities and too long a supply cycle);
- SC operations (false priorities of customers' orders, imbalance of capacities and order volumes, too frequent disruptions and high costs for their recovery);
- SC performance evaluation (performance of different departments such as logistics, transport and production is evaluated local for each department without any general links from the SCM perspectives); and
- SC execution (different levels of managers' qualifications, false or incomplete process documentation, weak consistency in process performance evaluation).

3.2.2 Business Process Modelling

In order to perform process optimization, as-is processes should be described-*Process models* describe the SCOM activities from an information processing perspective. Process modelling can be referred to as descriptive modelling and serves as an interface for information systems development.

For *business process modelling*, a number of techniques and tools can be used. The most popular of these are as follows:

- SCOR (Supply Chain Operations Reference),
- ARIS (Architecture of Information Systems),
- UML (Unified Modelling Language) and
- IDEF (Integration Definition for Function Modelling).

These approaches can also be used to model the *workflow* of decision–making processes. The process modelling serves for (1) describing processes and structures and (2) for clear illustrating those entities. For these purposes, different solutions have been developed, e.g., activity diagrams in UML and event-process chains (EPC) in ARIS.

The business process models have typically the following elements:

- Activities—Transform resources and information of one type into another type
- Decisions—A question that can be answered Yes or No
- Roles—Sets of procedures
- Resources—People, or facilities, or computer programs assigned to roles
- Repository—Collection of business records

One of the well-known models to describe the SC processes and measure their performance is SCOR (Supply Chain Operations Reference Model) (see Fig. 3.5).

SCOR model structure is not difficult to understand. Just imagine, you are about to organize a party. What decisions are involved with? First, we need to plan. Then we need to source food and drinks. Next step is to make the party. Finally, your guests need to be delivered to their homes. The same principles are used in SCOR model structure. It contains description of planning, sourcing, making, delivering, and return processes in the SC at different levels of abstraction.

The main value of SCOR from the business process modelling point of view is the standardized business process models that are interlinked at three levels. Besides, a coherent system of performance indicators is correlated with the process models. Finally, the data origins to calculate the performance indicators are explicitly provided. A *SCOR* project typically contains the following stages:

- Business process modelling
- Benchmarking analysis
- Business process re-engineering
- Process reference model

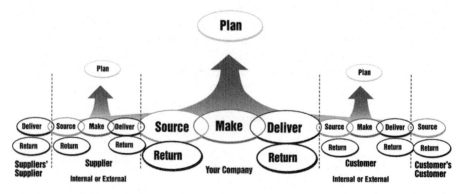

Fig. 3.5 SCOR model (source: www.supply-chain.org)

3.3 Management Information Systems

3.3.1 Role of Information Technology in Supply Chain and Operations Management

SCOM managers say: Where information is missing, material is also missing. A universal property of the management processes, irrespective of the problem domain, is that it has a notably *informational nature*, i.e. is connected, first of all, with the collection, processing, analysis and usage of data, information, and knowledge.

Management Information Systems (MIS) collect, process, store, and distribute information in order to support decision making, coordination, and control. MIS use data, i.e. are streams of raw facts. Information is data shaped into meaningful form. For companies, MIS is an instrument for *creating value*. Investments in right information technology (IT) can result in superior returns regarding productivity increases, revenue increases, and superior long-term strategic positioning. On one hand, MIS automate steps that were done manually previously. On other hand, MIS enable entirely new processes by changing flow of information, replace sequential steps with parallel steps, eliminating delays in decision making, and support new business models.

3.3.2 Types of Management Information Systems

The extensive development of IT for SCOM began in 1980s. In 1970s, first functions like accounting were automated. In 1980s, material requirements planning (MRP), sales and operations planning (S&OP), and MES (manufacturing execution systems) have been developed. At the same time, additional functions like product design and quality control have been captured under the umbrella of CIM (computer integrated manufacturing).

Along with great advantages and help for managers, these systems were so called island solutions, without integration with each other. Since these systems have used the same data to a great extent, in 1990s, integrated enterprise planning systems (ERP) have been developed.

In the twenty-first century, SCM caused the development of APS (advanced planning and scheduling) systems and different IT for SC collaboration. At present, mobile technologies, internet of things, smart manufacturing and Industry 4.0, Radio Frequency IDentification, e-business, and cloud computing belong to the trends of IT development for SCOM.

The variety of the existing IT can be distinguished in the following groups.

Planning at the Enterprise Level
- ERP (Enterprise Resource Planning)
- MES (Manufacturing Execution Systems)
- WMS (Warehouse Management Systems)

Planning and Control for SC Coordination
- APS (Advanced Planning Systems)
- TMS (Transportation Management Systems)
- SCEM (SC Event Management)

Real-Time Control
- RFID (Radio Frequency Identification)
- T&T (Trace and Tracking)
- ASN (Automated Shipping Notification)

Business Intelligence
- OLAP (On Line Analytical Processing)
- DSS (Decision Support Systems)
- Data miming and Big Data
- Cloud computing

SC Communication and Data Interchange
- EDI (Electronic Data Interchange)
- E-Commerce
- XML (Extensible Markup Language)
- Mobile technologies, Android

We will consider some of them further in this chapter.

3.3.3 Management Information Systems and Organization

IT provide a new level of coordination capabilities in SCs and enable a breakthrough in SC responsiveness and flexibility. Modern IT can potentially enable almost any integration and coordination concept. More important problems for efficient coordination lie in the organization sphere, collaboration culture and trust.

First, the issues of *investments in IT* infrastructure should be highlighted. It is to decide on the amount to spend on IT. IT can be bought, but also rented or used via cloud computing. IT can also be available via outsourcing. Whatever option is selected, *total cost of ownership (TCO)* model for costs analysis should be used. It analyzes direct and indirect costs. Note that hardware and software costs account for only about 20 % of TCO. Other costs include installation, training, support, maintenance, infrastructure, downtime, space, and energy. TCO can be reduced by the use of cloud services, greater centralization and standardization.

Second, *IT project management* is a critical issue. As in any project management, activities in an IT project include planning work, assessing risk, estimating resources required, organizing the work, assigning tasks, controlling project execution, reporting progress, and analyzing results. Five major variables for planning an IT project are as follows: scope, time, cost, quality, and risk.

3.3 Management Information Systems

In spite of sophisticated project management, empirical data shows that 30–40 % of IT projects exceed schedule and/or budget or fail to perform as specified. Frequently, the reasons are as follows: fail to capture essential business requirements, fail to provide organizational benefits, complicated, poorly organized user interface, and inaccurate or inconsistent data.

A road map in an IT project should be elaborated at all the management levels at include the following parts:

- Purpose of the plan
- Strategic business plan rationale
- Current systems/situation
- New developments
- Management strategy
- Implementation plan
- Budget

Third, the issue of *global organizations* becomes a critical challenge for many IT infrastructures, especially in global SCs. Unfortunately, many companies fail in building right IT for their global SCs. Consider as an example a typical scenario of disorganization on a global scale. A multinational consumer-goods company based in United States and operating in Europe would like to expand into Asia. World headquarters and strategic management are located in United States. The only centrally coordinated information system is financial controls and reporting. The company is divided into separate regional, national production and marketing centers. Foreign divisions have separate IT systems, E-business systems of different divisions and centers are incompatible. In addition, each production facility uses different ERP system, different hardware, and so on.

Recommendations on the right organization of IT in global companies include the following issues. First, it can be advised to share only core systems which support functionality critical to the company. Systems that share some key elements can be partially coordinate. It is not advisable to be totally common across national boundaries. Local variation is desirable since IT need to suit local requirements.

3.3.4 ERP Systems

Enterprise resource planning (ERP) systems comprise integrated software modules and a common central database. ERP modules include but are not limited to:

- Production Management
- Inventory Management
- Sales
- Human resources
- Marketing
- SCM

Modules can be seen as a number USB sticks which can be purchased all together or isolated. ERP working principle is based on collecting data from different departments of a firm for use in nearly all of firm's internal business activities. The advantage is that information entered in one process is immediately available for other processes. ERP uses

- master data (they do not change frequently, e.g., bill-of-materials) and
- process data (they change operative, e.g., current inventory level)

Advantages of ERP are as follows:

- Provides integration of the SC, production, finance, and marketing
- Creates a commonality of databases
- Can incorporate improved best processes
- Increases communication and collaboration between business units and sites
- Has an off-the-shelf software database
- May provide a strategic advantage and increase company assets

To the *limitations* of ERP belong:

- Can be very expensive to purchase and even more so to customize
- Implementation may require major changes in the company and its processes
- Can be so complex that many companies cannot adjust to it
- Involves an ongoing, possibly never completed, process for implementation
- Expertise is limited with ongoing staffing problems

> ▶ **Practical Insights** An integrated ERP system is costly. Its implementation will change organisation processes and structure. The project will take into account many years. At the same time, there are many companies with "self made" software for production planning, accounting, etc. The question is: should we buy new ERP or develop and integrate self-made solutions? There is no unique answer to this question. There are companies which develop their own solutions. In other cases, new ERP projects were successful. The key success factors here depend much on the correspondence of the existing IT to the current and future needs of the company. It is also important how qualified and organized is the IT department at the firm.

3.3.5 APS Systems

At the beginning of the twenty-first century, SCM topics become more and more important. Some important modules like "SC design" and "Distribution planning" were missing in ERP. In addition, ERP provided very limited support for

3.3 Management Information Systems

mathematical optimization in scheduling. ERP had also some other restrictions like planning against unlimited capacities. That is why new generation of APS systems has been developed (Stadtler et al. 2015) (see Fig. 3.6).

An APS extract data from ERP and uses them for optimization. Consider an example for scheduling in APS (see Fig. 3.7):

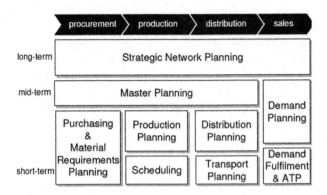

Fig. 3.6 Structure of APS system (Stadtler et al. 2015)

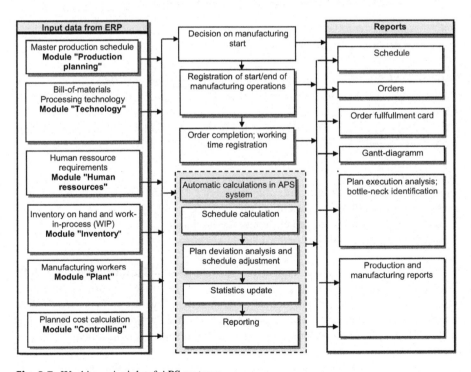

Fig. 3.7 Working principle of APS systems

APS system:

- extracts some input data from different ERP modules,
- performs automatic calculation on the basis of scientific optimization methodology, and
- generates reports.

APS modules are mainly dedicated to deterministic planning. However, there are uncertainties on both the inbound (unreliable suppliers, machine breakdowns) and the outbound (unknown customer demand) side. In order to hedge against uncertainty, buffers have to be installed—either in the form of safety stocks or safety times.

APS practical application is not an easy task. First, there is a discrepancy between the expectations of companies and the capabilities of the software. Second, optimization models can often not be solved within reasonable time limits, especially if interactive planning is desired. Third, the willingness to share information, e.g. about costs or capacities, is often rather limited, problems in using generic model formulations, which are often not sufficiently tailored to the needs of the specific application environment. APS appear to be most successful for intra-company SCs with centralized logistics control (Günther 2005).

3.3.6 SCEM and RFID

ERP and APS systems support planning activities. For *real-time control*, other systems are used. We consider two IT for the *control* stage: SCEM and RFID. Supply Chain Event Management (SCEM) aims at a timely identification of deviations or in SCs. A basis for the *alerting* and disruption recovery is a tolerance area of execution parameters' admissible deviations. SCEM is composed of five main functions:

- monitoring of processes
- notification about an impermissible parameter deviation
- simulating possible adjustment actions
- selecting a control action to eliminate the deviation
- measuring on the basis of performance indicators.

SCEM is based on three *main drivers*. First, the tracking and tracing (T&T) systems, RFID, and mobile devices are used to provide current in-formation about a process execution. Second, the method of management by exception is used to filter information and to compare actual parameter values with planned ones. Third, the method of event-oriented planning is used to reveal sensitive adjustment actions in the case of negative events.

One of the basic technologies to facilitate the feedbacks in the SC execution is RFID. In recent years, the applications and research literature on RFID have grown exponentially. RFID is an automatic identification technology composed of RFID

3.3 Management Information Systems

Table 3.1 Advantages and limitations of RFID for SCOM

Advantages	Limitations
Up-to-date data	Costs
Contact-free	Technical issues
"Bulk"-reading	Privacy issues
Protection/security	Heat resistance

tags and specialized RFID readers. *Tags* are also called RFID transponders (abbreviation of transmitters-responders). Tags are attached to or incorporated in any kind of object (product, tool, animal, goods, human being, etc.) for the purpose of identification and tracking using radio waves. RFID *readers* read the information on tags and transfer it to a processing device. RFID technology when applied to SCOM can provide several crucial advantages but has also some limitations (see Table 3.1).

The common target of RFID is to reduce costs created by manual operating, accelerate data receipt and transmission, and increase the preciseness and quality of data. RFID technology allows *tracking products throughout the SC* from supplier delivery to warehouses and points of sale. This contributes to the reduction of uncertainty of fluctuations in processes, improvement of the readability of the quantity and quality of items produced, improvement of safety (in particular, reduction of counterfeiting) and reduction of waste and theft. Some figures are listed below:

- The reduction of error when picking a product in inventory is at 5 %.
- Thefts at retailers are reduced by 11–18 %.
- Shrinkage at retailers decreases and becomes 0.78 % instead of 1.69 %.
- Thefts on shelves decrease by 9–14 % while the reduction ranges between 40 and 59 % in stores.
- Stock availability increases by 5–10 %.

RFID is also believed to provide crucial benefits in ensuring SC stability/continuity by means of improved information sharing and SC monitoring support through a faster exception management. SCs can potentially become more flexible, responsive, agile and secure by applying RFID.

Reduction of labor cost due to RFID is evaluated at 30 % in distribution, 17 % or 7.5 %, depending on the study, for retail stores. Other estimations claim that saving in receipt of products in inventory facilities is 7.5 % or 5–40 %, depending on the study. Other figures are 9 % in manufacturing, 90 % or 100 % in physical inventory counting, 0.9–3.4 % in stores.

At the same time, the existing studies underline that RFID does neither explain nor solve the fluctuations of customer demand, transportation times, and inventory levels. It identifies and processes the data in the volume according to the tags, readers and middleware functionalities, and at the places where they are installed. RFID also does not propose any control actions that should be taken to adapt a SC in the case of changes or disruptions at the execution stage.

3.3.7 Business Analytics and E-Business

During the last decade, new IT for SCOM has been developed. Details of managerial and technical implementation on these technologies differ, but most of them share attributes of intelligence. Since SCOM depends on the use of IT, in the coming years these new tools will change the landscape of managerial concepts and decision support systems for SCOM. Associating (and even embedding) IT and intelligence into SC planning and organisational structures has been discussed for over 10 years now. However, questions remain about the benefits and obstacles in allowing orders, deliveries and products to be able to plan and control their own progress through a SC. With the new IT, data management becomes a competitive advantage for companies. To the trends in IT development for SCOM belong:

- Business Intelligence (BI) and data mining
- Cloud computing and SaaS (software as a service)
- E-Business, net marketplaces (e-hubs) and virtual enterprises
- IoS—Internet of Services/Internet of Things and Industry 4.0

BI comprises data and software tools for organizing and analyzing data. It is used to help managers and users make improved decisions. Presently, so called Big Data issues becomes more and more important. Data mining belongs to the group of business analytics that comprises tools and techniques for analyzing data.

With the help of *cloud computing*, hardware/software can be used as a service without buying IT. It allows companies to minimize IT investments. The drawbacks are the concerns of security and reliability.

E-business consists of the use of digital technology and Internet to drive major business processes.

> ▶ **Practical Insights** In many e-commerce service SCs, especially in start-ups, the managers focus rather on the link warehouse-customer and frequently undervalue the link supplier-warehouse. In manufacturing SCs the focus is rather on the link supplier-production and the customer may play underordinated role in SCOM decisions. It is therefore important to consider integrated SC from suppliers to customers for both service and manufacturing SCs.

E-commerce is a subset of e-business and consists of buying and selling goods and services through Internet. Presently, M-Commerce solutions are being developed to include mobile IT into SCOM. In order to implement E-business, *Electronic data interchange (EDI)* technology is used. EDI ensures computer-to-computer exchange of standard transactions such as invoices, purchase orders. Major industries have EDI standards that define structure and information fields of electronic documents. More companies are increasingly moving toward private networks that allow them to link to a wider variety of firms than EDI allows and share a wider range of information in a single system.

▶ **Practical Insights** Consider an example. Harley Davidson was facing problems with their suppliers, as the relationships were sub-par and unsophisticated. Engineers focused on the supplier's technical innovation and failed to consider whether the supplier could produce the necessary volume, deliver on schedule, or meet cost targets. As a result, supplier components came in late and production was often put at risk. To resolve this problem, the company developed an internet-based SCM strategy where a web portal was created enabling Harley Davidson and its suppliers to conduct transactions, from placing purchase orders to invoicing, on the internet. Nearly 300 of Harley's 695 parts suppliers logged into applications through the supplier portal. Suppliers can view production forecasts, account status, and are able to submit shipment notices and receive inventory-replenishment alerts. The portal has allowed Harley to achieve lower costs, consistent quality, and improved delivery performance.

Net marketplaces (e-hubs) are single markets for many buyers and sellers. They can be industry-owned or owned by independent intermediary. E-hubs generate revenue from transaction fees and other services. The market principle use prices established through negotiation, auction, or fixed prices.

In many industries, hierarchical SCs with pre-determined suppliers' structures and long-term product programs evolve into *virtual enterprises and collaborative networks*. Their special feature lies in a customer-oriented networking of core competences and flexible configurable SCs, conditioned by an enlargement of alternatives to search for suitable partners for a cooperation enabled by Internet technologies.

The main objective of a *virtual enterprise* is to allow a number of organizations to develop a common working environment or virtual breeding environment with the goal of maximizing flexibility and adaptability to environmental changes and developing a pool of competencies and resources. SCs in virtual enterprise are based on a customer-oriented networking of core competences through a partner selection from a pool of available suppliers in a virtual environment according to customer requirements. Virtual enterprises focus on speed and flexibility. A virtual enterprise is enabled by building a united information space with extensive usage of Web services.

Virtual enterprise structures are highly dynamic and their life cycles can be very short. Remarkable are alternatives for SC configuration. It is a great advantage to react quickly to customers' requirements. A virtual enterprise also builds a structural-functional reserve for the running of a SC. Unfortunately, virtual enterprises are mostly considered from the information perspective without dealing properly with managerial and organizational aspects. Our practical experiences show that there are only a few (if any) organizations that have managed to apply the main idea of a virtual enterprise—collaborate for a short time and then disperse, perhaps to form new networks with other enterprises. There are two main obstacles: trust and technical project documentation.

The development of the *Internet of Things* in a manufacturing context has been called *Industry 4.0* with reference to the three prior industrial revolutions that are the steam machine; assembly line manufacturing, and computer integrated manufacturing (CIM). Even in our everyday life, WLAN-based communication of different devices such as refrigerators and kitchen stoves with the smartphones is possible. In Industry 4.0 manufacturing, both machines and materials are equipped with interconnected sensors in *cyber-physical systems* and take an active role the process and optimise it. The products and the machines communicate to each other by themselves. Materials will be able to communicate their purpose to the machines making product lifecycles faster and more flexible. Important component of Industry 4.0 is *additive manufacturing* technology, especially 3D printing.

> ▶ **Practical Insights** Business Analytics and Industry 4.0 are expected to be path-breaking concepts for SCOM in near future. All management activities are about data and information. By now, the state-of-the-art IT allow storing and transmitting a huge amount of data. The managers need to analyze all this data, to extract the necessary data, and transfer this data into information. In future, the managers will get the information needed at the right place, at the right time, and at the right quality. The preliminary actions for sorting and combining data will be done automatically by Business Analytics and Industry 4.0.

3.4 Problem Solving Methods and Research Methodologies

A baker bakes bread. A bus driver drives the bus. What do managers do? They take decisions. Decisions are taken to solve problems. Decisions can be taken regarding planning and control of operations and SCs. In this paragraph we learn basic problem solving methods in SCOM.

3.4.1 Problems, Systems, and Decision-Making

For a *problem* to exist there must be an individual (or a group of individuals), referred to as the problem owner (decision maker) that:

- is dissatisfied with the current state of affairs within a real-life context, or has some unsatisfied present or future needs, i.e. has some goals to be achieved or targets to be met;
- is capable of judging when these goals, objectives, or targets have been met to a satisfactory degree; and
- has control over some aspects of the problem situation that affect the extent to which goals, objectives, or targets can be achieved (Daellenbach and McNickle 2005).

Rather than to assume that we have a well-structured problem with clearly defined objectives and alternative courses of action, it is better to:

- represent the problem situation where the issues are still vague, fuzzy
- gain a more comprehensive understanding of the various issues involved in decision-making
- formulate a right problem that ensures an appropriate level of detail to provide insights into the problem solution
- perform decision-making within the context of systems.

Most of the problems exist in the system context. A *System* is a set of interrelated entities, comprising a whole unity where each component interacts with or is related to at least one other component and they all serve a common objective. *Environment* is the aggregate of elements that do not belong to the system but influence it.

One of the basic system characteristics is its structure. *Structure* is the characteristic of steady links and interaction modes of system's elements; structure determines the system's integrity, basics and building of organization and functioning; structure is a framework of a system. Since in practice, many SC structures can be disrupted (e.g., Toyota' SC was badly affected by the tsunami in March 2011), we can talk about SC *structure dynamics* (Ivanov et al. 2010).

Dynamics is a system's change and evolution in the form of changes in object and process states in space and time as driven by perturbation and control influences of both planned nature to transit from a current state to a desired one and adaptation nature to adapt a system to a changed execution environment.

Decision is a selection of an activity (or a set of activities) to handle from several alternatives. Decisions are subject to constraints which limit decision choices and objectives making some decisions preferred to others. A selection of a managerial decision leads the system goal-oriented to the output performance. The decisions shape the system behaviour with regard to a certain goal (or multiple goals). Objectives and criteria play the most important role in taking decisions.

> ▶ **Practical Insights** Each management decision has two components. The first one is an *analytical component* and the second one is the *behavioral* component. The analytical part of the decisions is supported by the *quantitative analysis* business analytics methods. The behavioral part of the decisions is based on the intuition and leadership qualities of the decision-maker as well as on the external environment *behavior prediction and reaction* in regard to the decisions of suppliers, retailers, and customers.

Performance is a complex characteristic of the goal results of the system's functioning; potential and real performance, taking into account the conformity of the achieved results with the goals set by management at the planning stage.

Performance is measured with certain metrics or indicators (e.g., customer service level, on-time delivery, costs, etc.)

Basic problems in decision-making are as follows:

- optimality
- multiple objectives
- risk and uncertainty, and
- complexity.

3.4.1.1 Optimal Decisions and Multiple Objectives

Optimal decision is the best one. Optimal decisions are very "fragile" and presume certain problem dimensionality, fullness and certainty of the model. Besides, the optimal solutions are usually very sensitive to deviations. Moreover, the decision making is actually tightly interconnected with dynamics and should be considered as an adaptive tuning process and not as a "one-way" optimization.

> ▶ **Practical Insights** Consider an example. A typical optimization problem is determination of optimal order quantity for some purchased items. This optimization is based on the reduction of ordering and inventory holding costs. If so, the calculated order quantity is optimal only for purchasing department. At the same time, this problem is tightly interconnected with transportation planning and customer service level improvement. So the real problem situation which exists is integrated inventory optimization.

The problems of applying optimization-based decision-making are interrelated with complexity, uncertainty and multiple objectives. A particular feature of optimal decisions is *multi-objective* decision making by managers with their own preferences that, in their turn, are always changing. Hence, it becomes impossible to build any general selection function for multi-criteria decision making. Finding optimal solutions is possible but it can be very time-consuming. However, these optimal solutions can be used for benchmarking to estimate the quality of solutions obtained by heuristics or simulation models (see further in this chapter).

Multiple objectives are conflicting in the sense of competing for common resources to achieve variously different performance objectives (financial, functional, environmental, etc.). A multi-criteria decision making (MCDM) strategy employs *trade-off* analysis techniques to identify compromise designs for which the competing criteria are mutually satisfied in a Pareto-optimal sense. One example of the up-to-date techniques for MCDM is TOPSIS. For more detailed information on decision-making theory, we refer to the study books on operations research, decision theory, and quantitative analysis in management, e.g., Taha (2009), Render et al. (2012), Dolgui and Proth (2010), Yalaoui et al. (2012).

3.4.1.2 Risk and Uncertainty

Uncertainty is one of the most critical issues in taking decisions. *Uncertainty* is a system property characterizing the incompleteness of our knowledge about the system and the conditions of its development. Uncertainty is a polysemic term (poly—many, sema—a sign). Historically, the first terms related to uncertainty were accident, probability and possibility, which we relate to Aristotle. Up to the twentieth century, the mathematical basics of uncertainty factor description were founded on probability–frequency interpretation and are related to Pascal, Ferma, Bernoulli and Laplace. Modern probability theory is based on the research of Kolmogorov, who introduced an axiomatic definition of probability as a measure related to a system of axioms of a so-called probability space.

Uncertainty initiates risk. *Risk management* is a methodological approach to the management of outcome uncertainty. The concept of risk is subject to various definitions. Knight (1921) classified under 'risk' the 'measurable' uncertainty. From the financial perspective of Markowitz (1952), risk is the variance of return. From the project management perspective, risk is a measure of the probability and consequence of not achieving a defined project goal. According to March and Shapira (1987), risk is a product of the probability of occurrence of a negative event and the resulting amount of damage.

Generally, in decision theory, risk is a measure of the set of possible (negative) outcomes from a single rational decision and their probabilistic values. A particular feature of risk management in SCs (unlike in technical systems) is that people do not strive for a *100 % guarantee* of the result: they consciously tend to take risks. We point out the problem of contradiction between *objective risk* (determined by experts, applying quantitative scientific means) and *perceived risk* (perception of managers).

There are three types of uncertainty affecting SCOM (Klibi et al. 2010):

- random uncertainty (i.e., problem in coordination demand and supply)
- hazard uncertainty (unusual events with high impact)
- deep uncertainty (severe disruptions) no information (game theory and utility functions);

According to the certainty of data the following cases can be classified:

- no information (treated in game theory and utility functions);
- vague information (treated in fuzzy theory);
- random and stochastic information (treated in probability theory);
- determined information (treated in analytical models)

The uncertainty factors are usually divided into two groups:

- stochastic factors and
- non-stochastic factors.

The first group can be described via probability models. For the formal description of non-stochastic uncertainty, fuzzy description with known membership functions, subjective probabilities for the uncertainty factors, interval description, and combined description of the uncertainty factors are used.

3.4.2 Models and Modeling

The concept of a model is widely applicable in natural human languages and is a general scientific term. It is characterized by polysemy, that is, widely expressed and reflecting different meanings of this concept depending on the applications and contexts. At present, there are several hundred definitions of the concept of a model and modelling. In summing up different definitions, the following views of models and modelling can be presented.

A *model* is:

- a system whose investigation is a tool for obtaining information about another system;
- a method of knowledge existence; and
- a multiple system map of the original object that, together with absolutely true content, contains conditionally true and false content, which reveals itself in the process of its creation and practical use.

Modelling is one of the stages of cognitive activity of a subject, involving the development (choice) of a model, conducting investigations with its help, obtaining and analysing the results, the production of recommendations, and the estimation of the quality of the model itself as applied to the solved problem and taking into account specific conditions (Fig. 3.8).

Because of the *finiteness* of the designed (applied) model (a limited number of elements and relations that describe objects belonging to infinitely diverse reality) and the *limited* resources (temporal, financial and material) supplied for modelling, the model always reflects the original object in a simplified and approximate way.

However, the human experience testifies that these specific features of a model are admissible and do not oppose the solution of problems that are faced by subjects.

Fig. 3.8 Modelling stakeholders

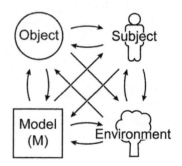

3.4.3 Model-Based Decision-Making

In each decision, managers use both quantitative and qualitative models. Quantitative analysis is a scientific approach to managerial decision making in which raw data are processed and manipulated to produce meaningful information. Consider an example.

Case Study "Re-designing the Material Flow in a Global Manufacturing Network"
Problem description
Consider an enterprise that produces systems for energy transmission and has two locations: factory A is located in Europe and factory B is located in China. Both factories have deep manufacturing penetration; in other words they are able to produce almost all the components and modules needed for the final product assembly. Both factories can assemble the same final products from the same components, known as shared components. The final assembly always takes place in the country where the customer builds its energy system. It should be analysed to see whether the production of the shared components can be distributed within the network so that total network costs are minimized.
Model development
Each manager applies to each decision both quantitative and qualitative methods. From the mathematical point of view, the problem can be represented as a number of origin points with some capacities and destination points with some demand. The production volumes should be delivered to the customers in such a way that total costs are minimized. This is a well-known problem in operations research, namely the transportation problem. At the same time, the problem also comprises costs and risks which cannot be quantified within an optimization model, and therefore additional qualitative analysis will be needed.
Input Data
At the first stage, four options for process design have been formulated:

1. Local manufacturing at A and B
2. Manufacturing at A for A and B
3. Manufacturing at B for A and B
4. Mixed manufacturing at A and B for A and B

For the development of the mathematical model, the following data is needed:

- origin points
- destination points
- production capacity at the origin points A_i
- demand at the destination points B_j
- costs for production and transportation of a product unit from A_i to B_j

Solution development
The particular feature of the problem considered is that origin and destination points are actually identical. The model has then the standard format of the

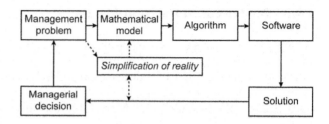

Fig. 3.9 Model-based decision-making process

transportation problem and can be solved with the help of Excel Solver. Final decisions should be taken based on the analysis of both quantitative optimization results and managerial qualitative analysis.

Results implementation

From the cost efficiency point of view, option 2 could be selected. However, some crucial risks exist. First, single sourcing strategy is very risky since production and delivery shortages can occur. Second, if manufacturing in Germany should be relaunched, implementation costs would be very high.

The model-based decision-making process is shown in Fig. 3.9.

We can observe that a *real management problem* is the initial point of the decision-making process. An example can be facility location problem where we are given demand in some markets, possible locations and capacities of new facilities, fixed costs for having a facility in the SC, and transportation costs from each location to each market. We are seeking for the decision where to locate the facilities and which quantities should be shipped from the facilities to the markets.

Next step is to transform the real problem into the *mathematical model*. For this transformation, we need to reduce the *complexity* of reality. This inevitably results into simplification of reality. For example, we would assume deterministic capacity in our facility location model instead of considering fluctuations in demand.

We do this simplification in order to represent the management problem in the mathematical model in such a way so that this model can be solved with the helped of existing *algorithms* in a reasonable time. In our example, we formulate facility location problem as a mixed-integer linear programming model that can be solved with the help of simplex and branch&bound algorithms.

For implementation, *software* is needed. Small instances can be solved with the help of Excel solver, but for real data, professional solver such as CPLEX, Lindo, AMPL, Matlab, GAMS, Gurobi, and XPRESS exist. Software will calculate the *solution*. In our example, it would be the solution comprising the suggestions on where to open the facility locations and which product quantities should be shipped from each opened location to each of the markets so that total production and logistics costs is minimal.

Software calculated this solution. The most important question now is as follows: is this solution automatically our *decision*? NO! This is a solution to the mathematical problem. Now it is the stage where management expertise is needed to transfer this mathematical solution into the managerial decisions. First of all, simplifications of reality should be reviewed. Second, so called *soft facts* such as

3.4 Problem Solving Methods and Research Methodologies

risks, flexibility, etc. should be included in the analysis. That is why we prefer talking about *decision-support quantitative methods*.

3.4.4 Quantitative Models and Operations Research

Quantitative models for SCOM can be divided into three primary approaches. These are optimization, simulation and heuristics. Hybrid models (e.g., optimization-based simulation models) also exist. *Optimization* is an analysis method that determines the best possible option of solving a particular operations or SC problem. Optimization has been a very visible and influential topic in the field of SCOM. The drawback of using optimization is difficulty in developing a model that is sufficient detailed and accurate in representing complexity and uncertainty of SCM, while keeping the model simple enough to be solved.

Simulation is imitating the behaviour of one system with another. By making changes to the simulated SC, one expects to gain understanding of the dynamics of the physical SC. Simulation is an ideal tool for further analysing the performance of a proposed design derived from an optimization model (Sterman 2000, Ivanov 2016).

Heuristics are intelligent rules that often lead to good, but not necessarily the best, solutions. Heuristic approaches typically are easier to implement and require fewer data. However, the quality of the solution is usually unknown. An option to estimate the quality of heuristic algorithms may be the usage of optimization as a tool for "ideal" solutions to problems.

Operations Research (OR) is the application of advanced analytical methods to help make better decisions (INFORMS definition). OR deals with problems that may be described with mathematical models to find optimal or good solutions. An overview of OR-based methods is presented in Fig. 3.10. Basic OR methods and their application to SCOM include but are not limited to:

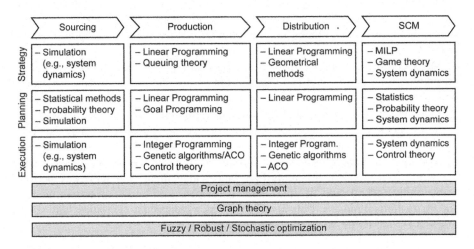

Fig. 3.10 OR methods for SCOM

- Linear programming (production planning; revenue management)
- Integer programming/Combinatorial Optimization (scheduling, routing)
- Mixed integer linear programming (MILP) (SC design)
- Dynamic programming/Graph Theory (dynamic lot-sizing/SC contracting)
- Network theory (project management)
- Queuing theory (waiting lines: call centers, hotline services, process design, entertainment parks, services)
- Simulation (SC design, bullwhip-effect, etc.)
- Heuristics (genetic algorithms, ant colony optimization (ACO), application to scheduling and routing problems)
- Fuzzy/Robust/Stochastic optimization (data uncertainty)

The application of many of these methods to different SCOM problems will be considered in further chapters of this book.

3.4.5 Integrated Decision-Making Support

Having read previous materials of this book, you have already got an overview on:

- Decision-makers in SCOM
- Business processes in SCOM
- Methods of decisions-making support in SCOM
- IT in SCOM

Before starting to consider processes and decision-support methods in details, let us summarize our knowledge to the triangle "*Process→Model→IT*". Process modelling and re-engineering are basic preliminaries for successful application of quantitative models and IT. All these three components are tightly interrelated with each other. The main blocks required for successful SCOM are presented in Fig. 3.11.

Many companies make a mistake while starting optimization directly with IT introduction. First, it should be clearly stated which data are necessary for which optimization models. Second, these data should be brought into correspondence with the business processes and organizational structure.

In the block "Enterprise Supply Chain", typical functionality of ERP and APS systems can be used. In the block "Integrated SC", special EDI-driven software for SC coordination and collaboration are required. Finally, the block "Services and analytics" is responsible for reporting, data management, and KPI (key performance indicator) control. All these models are based on business process models and mathematical models. Data management also comprises integration with some external IT like RFID, payment security systems, etc.

3.4 Problem Solving Methods and Research Methodologies

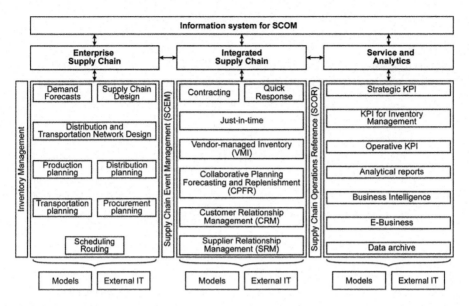

Fig. 3.11 Information system for SCOM

In Table 3.2, we summarize quantitative methods used in selected modules of the SCOM information system.

In the next chapters of this book, we will learn many of these problems, models and methods in detail.

3.4.6 Research Methodologies

Quantitative methods, modeling and optimization is one popular direction of conducting research in SCOM. Other research methodologies are qualitative-oriented and include case-study research, action research, surveys and interview-based research (Kotzab et al. 2005; Yin 2014).

Case-study research is based on deductive analysis of existing practical examples described in literature. Single case, some isolated cases, or even embedded cases can be analysed to develop some general recommendations for a problem.

Action research presumes active participation of the investigator in the problem solving. It can be, e.g., a traineeship in a company where students are involved into a project. Unlike in case-study research, results of the project are typically unknown at the beginning. In ongoing project, comparison of "as-is" and "to-be" states can be complicated. Benchmarking analysis can be successfully used here.

Surveys and interview-based research presumes data collection from different sources, e.g., interview of some experts in a particular area. The questionnaires are designed and evaluated with the help of statistical methods. Frequently, structural equation method is used.

Table 3.2 Data, decisions, and methods in SCOM [based on Ivanov (2010)]

Input data	Performance indicators	Examples of solution methods	Result (output)
Demand forecasting			
Statistical sales data	Forecast error minimization	Exponential smoothing; Regression analysis	Demand forecast
Supply chain design			
Location data Demand forecasts; Capacity data; Transportation (time, costs, etc.)	Cost minimization	Center-of-Gravity Warehouse Location Problem (WLP) CPLM (Capacitated Plant Location Model) Location-Allocation Model	How many production and distribution centers are needed, where, and of what capacity?
Distribution-transportation network design			
Customers and Suppliers Supply Chain Design Demand forecasts; Transportation (time, costs, etc.)	Cost minimization; Service level maximization	Transportation problem and its multi-stage modifications	Which products and of what quantity should be shipped to which destinations?
Inventory management			
Demand; Lead-time Holding, ordering, and warehousing costs Service level; Capacity data	Cost minimization; Service level maximization	Cycle inventory optimization (EOQ/EPQ); Safety inventory optimization; Multi-echelon inventory management; ATP/CTP	When and how much to order? What is optimal service level? Where to place inventory in the SC?
Sales and operations planning			
Demand Costs Inventory Capacity	Cost minimization Revenue maximization	Mathematical programming	Aggregate plan for 1–18 months
Distribution and transportation planning			
Sales and Operations plan Costs Inventory Transportation Capacity	Cost minimization	Mathematical programming, Heuristics	Aggregate plan for 1–18 months

(continued)

Table 3.2 (continued)

Input data	Performance indicators	Examples of solution methods	Result (output)
Scheduling and routing			
Master production schedule; Machine capacity; Due dates; Costs	Minimize completion time Maximize utilization of facilities Minimize work-in-process (WIP) inventory Minimize flow time	Combinatorial optimization, Heuristics	Schedules and delivery routes

3.5 Key Points

Organizations are structured by processes. Any organization or business strategy is influenced by technology. A business process is a network of activities for accomplishing a business function. The basic concept for managing processes in an organization is called business process management and contains a variety of tools, methodologies to analyze, design, and optimize processes. The analysis of process results may be characterized by effectiveness (the achievement of process goals) and efficiency (performing the process with mini-mum costs). Process models describe the SCOM activities from an information processing perspective.

At the enterprise level, such MIS like ERP, WMS and TPS systems are used. At the SC level, APS and SCEM systems can be applied. During the last decade, new IT for operations and SC integration have been developed. Examples include data mining, cloud computing, physical internet, pattern recognition, knowledge discovery, early warning systems, to name but a few. To the trends in IT development for SCOM belong Business Intelligence and data mining, cloud computing and SaaS, E-Business, and Industry 4.0.

In each decision, managers use both quantitative and qualitative models. Quantitative methods are based on Operations Research techniques. Qualitative research methodologies include case-study, action, and survey research.

Acknowledgement The introductory case-study is based on the materials of SupplyOn and is written with permission of SupplyOn. We thank Ms. Cornelia Staib, Mr. Arvid Holzwarth (MBA) and Mr. Jonas Dahl for their help in preparing this case-study.

Bibliography

Borshev A (2013) The big book of simulation modeling. AnyLogic North America, Chicago, IL
Bramer M (2013) Principles of data mining, 2nd edn. Springer, London
Camarinha-Matos LM, Afsarmanesh H (2007) A comprehensive modeling framework for collaborative networked organizations. J Intell Manuf 18(5):529–542
Chandra C, Grabis J (2007) Supply chain configuration. Springer, New York
Chatfield DC, Harrison TP, Hayya JC (2009) SCML: an information framework to support supply chain modeling. Eur J Oper Res 196(2):651–660
Daellenbach HG, McNickle DC (2005) Management science. Decision making through systems thinking. Palgrave Macmillan, Basingstoke
Dolgui A, Proth J-M (2010) Supply chain engineering: useful methods and techniques. Springer, Berlin
Gunasekaran A, Ngai EWT (2004) Information systems in supply chain integration and management. Eur J Oper Res 159(2):269–295
Günther H-O (2005) Supply chain management and advanced planning systems: a tutorial. In: Günther H-O, Mattfeld DC, Suhl L (eds) Supply chain management und logistik. Physica-Verlag, Heidelberg, pp 3–40
Hammer M, Champy J (1993) Reengineering the corporation: a manifesto for business revolution. Harper Collins, New York
Heizer J, Render B (2013) Operations management: sustainability and supply chain management, 11th edn. Pearson, Harlow
Ijioui R, Emmerich H, Ceyp M (2007) Supply chain event management: konzepte, prozesse, erfolgsfaktoren und praxisbeispiele. Physica-Verlag, Heidelberg
Ivanov D (2010) A framework for aligning (re)planning decisions on supply chains strategy, design, tactics, and operations. Int J Prod Res 48(13):3999–4017
Ivanov D (2016) Operations and supply chain simulation with AnyLogic 7.2. Available at www.anylogic.com/books
Ivanov D, Dolgui A (2013) Editorial to 'Intelligent information and product technologies for supply chain integration'. Int J Integr Supply Manage 8(1/2/3):1–5
Ivanov D, Sokolov B, Kaeschel J (2010) A multi-structural framework for adaptive supply chain planning and operations control with structure dynamics considerations. Eur J Oper Res 200(2):409–420
Klibi W, Martel A, Guitouni A (2010) The design of robust value-creating supply chain networks: a critical review. Eur J Oper Res 203(2):283–293
Knight F (1921) Risk, uncertainty, and profit. Hart, Schaffner, and Marx Prize Essays 31. Houghton Mifflin, Boston and New York
Kohli R, Grover V (2008) Business value of IT: an essay on expanding research directions to keep up with the times. J Assoc Inform Syst 9(1):23–39
Kotzab H, Seuring S, Müller M, Reiner G (eds) (2005) Research methodologies in supply chain management. Physica-Verlag, Heidelberg
Kroenke DM (2013) MIS essentials, 3rd edn. Pearson, Harlow
Laudon KC, Laudon JP (2013) Management information systems, 13th edn. Pearson, Harlow
March JG, Shapira Z (1987) Managerial perspectives on risk and risk taking. Manag Sci 33:1404–1418
Markowitz H (1952) Portfolio selection. J Finance VII(1):77–91
Motiwalla L, Thompson J (2012) Enterprise systems for management, 2nd edn. Pearson, Harlow
Render B, Stair RM, Hanna ME (2012) Quantitative analysis for management, 10th edn. Pearson, Harlow
Schönberger J (2011) Model-based control of logistics processes in volatile environments: decision support for operations planning in supply consortia. Springer, New York

Stadtler H, Kilger C, Meyr H (2015) Supply chain management and advanced planning, 5th edn. Springer, Berlin
Sterman J (2000) Business dynamics: systems thinking and modeling for a complex world. McGraw-Hill, London
Taha HA (2009) Operations research: an introduction, 9th edn. Pearson, Harlow
Yalaoui A, Chehade H, Yalaoui F, Amodeo L (2012) Optimization of logistics. Wiley, New York
Yin RK (2014) Case study research: design and methods (Applied social research methods), 7th edn. Sage Publications, London

Operations and Supply Chain Strategy

Learning Objectives for This Chapter

- Operations strategies and "strategic fit"
- Efficient and effective supply chain strategies
- Bullwhip-effect
- Vendor-managed Inventory (VMI)
- Collaborative Planning, Forecasting, and Replenishment (CPFR)
- Supply chain resilience and sustainability
- Ripple effect

4.1 Introductory Case-Study "Quick and Affordable": Zara, UNIQLO & Primark

Zara's Three Success Factors: Speed, Speed, and Speed

Zara is a global fashion retailer selling its goods around the world. The retailer's international footprint proves that national borders are no hindrance to a shared fashion culture. Founded in 1975, the Spanish retailer Zara presently has over 2100 stores strategically located in leading cities across 88 countries (https://www.inditex.com/brands/zara), launches more than 10,000 new designs each year, and is recognized as one of the world's principal fashion retailers. It belongs to the INDITEX Group, which also holds common brand names like Pull&Bear, Bershka and Stradivarius. In 2012 net sales of INDITEX were equal to 15,946 million euros, making it the fifth largest and fastest growing fashion retailer worldwide.

Find additional case-studies, Excel spreadsheet templates, and video streams in the *E-Supplement* to this book on www.global-supply-chain-management.de!

Zara is commonly known for its always up-to-the minute styles and products. The main key to their corporate strategy is their SC strategy. The following statement by INDITEX gives a first hint towards this exclusive strategy: "Our approach to fashion—creativity, quality design and rapid turnaround to adjust to changing market demands—has allowed us to expand internationally at a fast pace and has generated an excellent public response to our retailers' collections" (Inditex 2014).

While many retailers design and produce around 80 % of their season's inventory, Zara keeps back 50 % to be produced in the middle of the season. This way they can react if hot trends of the current season are for example skinny instead of boot-cut jeans. A full team of fashion experts keeps an eye on upcoming trends in each country on university campuses, night clubs and fashion shows. All research and design activities are steered from Zara's headquarters in La Coruña in Spain. For production Zara has its own high tech factories and a number of subcontractors. However, Zara keeps outsourcing to a minimum level and produces mainly in developed countries to provide better quality control. To keep responsiveness at the highest level many garments are kept in a generic unprinted stage. This approach is called postponement strategy, as products can be modified from generic to finish according to customer demand.

Procurement offices in the UK, China and the Netherlands deal with all purchasing activities. In manufacturing Zara links the two sites of SC strategies. On one site they import 40 % of their products as finished goods from low-cost countries. This strategy is used for "basics" products that are unchanged by fashion trends such as white and black T-shirts. All other materials are bought from Mauritius, New Zealand, Australia, Morocco, China, India, Turkey, Korea, Italy and Germany. Zara tries to source local instead of global, thus reducing transportation costs.

Short lead times are another key factor for Zara. Where other fashion companies supply every three months, Zara replenishes its stores twice a week. The company provides the necessary fundamentals for subcontractors to accomplish their agreed delivery times.

To implement its SC strategy ZARA redesigned inventory management correspondingly. Previously, goods were shipped from two central warehouses to each of the stores, based on requests from individual store managers. These local decisions, when assessed on a global scale, inevitably led to inefficient warehouse, shipping and logistics operations. Production overruns, inefficient SCs, and an ever-changing marketplace (to say the least) caused Zara to tackle this problem.

A variety of SCOM models was used in redesigning and implementing an entirely new inventory management system. The new centralized decision-making system replaced all store-level inventory decisions, thus providing results that were more globally optimal. Since implementation, having the right products in the right places at the right time for customers has increased sales from 3 to 4 %.

Inventory at Zara is kept a smidge under the estimated sales levels. For example, if demand increases immensely for clutch purses, they can assign emergency orders. Hence, the company is commonly able to deal with sudden demand changes. However, when the opposite was the case, Zara's management evaluated potentially lost customers as less costly than slow moving or last season's products. Speed is Zara's key strategy. All products are to leave the warehouse after a maximum of 3 days. At the end of each season Zara reduces its products up to 30 % to sell remaining stocks.

All items arrive at the stores ironed, on hangers and with price tags, saving valuable time for staff. Zara's pricing is based not on the classical cost plus margin principle, but on setting prices according to comparable items in the local market. This way it is possible that the same product has a different price in each European country. To make price tagging easier Zara previously attached a tag on its goods showing all prices. In this way goods could easily be shifted from one country to another with reduced complexity. Nowadays, bar codes are used to tag the products, and these can be read via a scanner, showing the local price in the local store. This also enables Zara to keep up-to-date information when and where goods are sold. All information is analysed at headquarters so that particular strategies can be adapted if necessary.

Marketing is minimized, as Zara sees all promotion activities as distracting for the customer. The company has managed to present itself as a fashion retailer with ever-changing and up-to-date styles with good quality at affordable price levels. Customers value exactly these assets—making all additional marketing efforts unnecessary.

UNIQLO: Basic, Casual Wear at Top Quality

UNIQLO does the exact opposite of Zara but is no less successful. UNIQLO is one of the largest and fastest growing Japanese companies and ranks third among fashion retailers worldwide following Gap and Marks & Spencer. The mother company, FAST RETAILING CO. LTD, which also owns brand names GU and Theory, was founded in 1963 in Japan, where it still has its head office in Yamaguchi-City. High-quality and affordable products are valued more highly than chasing the newest trend.

Products are rather casual and basic, making them occasion- and age-less but still stylish, using various colours and cuts. This way UNIQLO meets customer demand independently from clothes being presented on the catwalk at the moment.

UNIQLO has multiple production and purchasing offices in Asia which look after more than 100 suppliers each week. In this way the company is able to maintain good quality control over their outsourced partners. If issues concerning quality arise they are instantly taken to the production units where means for improvements are found. Currently, UNIQLO is seeking to expand their purchasing and production facilities to meet demand in the United Kingdom and the United States.

UNIQLO controls its inventory carefully trying to maintain optimum inventory levels each week. At the end of each season products are sold for 20–30 % less than the initial price to get rid of inventory.

Additionally, the fashion retailer has found a new place for selling clothes: railway stations. The concept works fabulously for UNIQLO. Shinjuku Station is Tokyo's biggest rail station where the UNIQLO store meanwhile ranks 6 from all

770 UNIQLO stores. Popularity has also risen among so-called one-day packs with basics like socks and underwear.

UNIQLO follows the SPA model (specialty store retailer of private label apparel) which is a specialized model of fashion retailer tracking all business activities from point of origin up to point of sale. This approach enables UNIQLO to improve constantly but also quickly its business processes giving the company an advantage over its competitors. Through long-term relationships to the suppliers UNIQLO is always seeking ways of better improving the SC. This also affects selling prices. By optimizing its SC, the company has been able to lower prices up to one third compared to its competitors.

UNIQLO promotes its products on posters, flyers or TV, also hinting which items will be put out for sale the following week.

Primark: It's All About Money
A lot for a little is what customers value when visiting Primark stores, while leaving with huge bags full of new fashionable clothes which cost not even half of what competitors offer. Primark belongs to Associated British Foods, a company selling food and clothes. Since the first store opened in Dublin, Primark has quickly expanded and today counts more than 250 stores all over Europe. In the future, the company plans to open more stores in even more countries.

The product is based on simple designs with fashionable prints. To save costs Primark focuses on selling only the most popular sizes.

Primark's customers demand catwalk fashion items at supermarket price levels. That's why it is all about money for Primark. Primark's products are sourced from more than 600 suppliers, mainly from low-cost countries. Buying and selling in high volumes and using economies of scale also allow Primark to cut down selling prices for the customer. The company uses off-season times to produce in advance and uses cheaper production periods. Primark uses a typical efficient make-to-stock strategy where the focus is to—guess what?—cut costs.

Additionally, Primark puts little mark-up on their products and avoids marketing efforts, as it trusts to mouth-to-mouth advertising. Hence, prices are comparatively low.

In the past, criticism has risen towards sustainability issues regarding low-cost retailers, as many workers in low-cost countries have to suffer poor working conditions. This has also caught the attention of some customers, which is why retailers such as Primark try to counter a negative ethical image.

Discussion Questions
1. What is the danger of mixing elements ("hybrid strategy") from both agile and lean SC strategies?
2. Contrast and compare Zara, UNIQLO and Primark concerning their primary goal, product design, manufacturing, inventory, supplier, lead time and pricing strategy.
3. What aspects may be critical about each SC strategy?
4. What do you think of UNIQLO's decision to open new facilities in UK and US?

5. Which roles does information technology play for SC coordination?
6. How do the SC strategies of Zara, UNIQLO and Primark support their competitive strategies to achieve "strategic fit"?
7. Are you concerned about sustainability issues in apparel SCs?

4.2 Operations and Supply Chain Strategies

4.2.1 Value Added and Costs

Value added and costs are two basic dominants in SCOM. Value creation can be achieved in different ways, e.g., through innovation, unique service or quality. Any process has value-added steps but also needs resources which increase the costs. Obviously, good processes have to be designed with a high degree of value-adding time and short periods of non-value added time. This would increase both *effectiveness and efficiency*.

However, in practice we can observe quite opposite situations. In many cases, value-added steps hardly comprise more than 20 %, more realistically estimations are about 5–7 % (Vrijhoef and Koskela 2000; Christopher 2011). This relation between value-added time and costs can be depicted as shown in Fig. 4.1.

It can be observed on the example of car manufacturing that value-added time is much shorter as compared with the increase in costs. The general recommendation is therefore to condense the cost creation steps to reduce the lead-time and increase the service level. A nice example is a doctor who has to remove a tick. The act itself needs 10 s but the patient will spend at least 10 min in the room since 9 min and 50 s will be required to fill in numerous forms and medical insurance documents. In this case, the value-added time is 1.7 %.

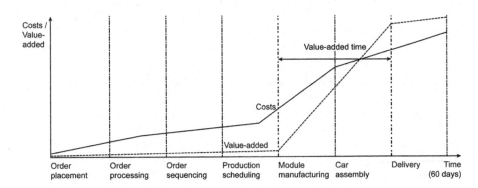

Fig. 4.1 Value-added and costs

4.2.2 Operations Strategies

Since different ways exist to create value and reduce costs, different operations strategies can be classified as follows:

- Innovation strategy
- Efficiency strategy
- Quality strategy
- Service strategy

The main driver in *innovation strategy* is great product or service innovation. Creating value through unique product or service properties may significantly increase company margins while maintaining cost efficiencies. An example is Apple, with the transition from iPhone3 to iPhone4. While the manufacturing costs were only slightly increased, the price was almost doubled. SCM in the innovation strategy should enable smooth and fast new product introduction and sales increase.

In *efficiency strategy*, price is the main competitive advantage. IKEA is well known for its highly efficient logistics and manufacturing. All the steps in the value chain support the efficiency strategy. Starting with consideration of manufacturing and logistics already at the product design stage, the operations at IKEA follow this philosophy in all other areas such as production, sourcing and shipments (Heizer and Render 2013).

Quality strategy ensures competitive advantage based on superior product properties. "Made in Germany" has been associated with high quality standards for many years. For such products, costs may be higher since in all the operational areas decisions are taken in favour of quality. Quality control mechanisms are crucial for ensuring high quality in the SCs.

Service or *responsiveness strategy* means high priority of customer preferences in operations decisions. Zara is known for its highly responsive operations and SCs. This becomes possible through sophisticated facility location planning and production in small batches. Both creates additional costs but they are overcome by higher value-added (Chopra and Meindl 2012).

4.2.3 Supply Chain Strategies and "Strategic Fit"

A SC strategy should correspond to competitive and operations strategy. Matching enterprise competitive strategy and SC strategy is named "strategic fit" (Chopra and Meindl 2015). *Strategic fit* presumes alignment of objectives in different departments with the overall SC objectives. For example, typical decisions in marketing relate to product mix and pricing. This should be brought into correspondence with logistics decisions such as transportation, packaging, and transshipment.

SC strategies and SC contributions to competitive and operations strategies are shown in Table 4.1. A SC strategy does not commonly target only one aspect. Just decreasing prices to the lowest level may be an option. At the same time, a SC

4.2 Operations and Supply Chain Strategies

Table 4.1 SCM strategies [based on Cohen and Roussel (2013)]

Strategy	Advantages	Competitive basis	SCM contribution
Innovation	Unique brand or technology	Innovative and high demanded products	Quick introduction of new products and innovation
Costs	Cost-efficient organization	Low prices in product segment	Efficient, lean SC organization
Service/Response	Flexibility	Customer-orientation	Agile SC is developed from customer point of view
Quality	High-quality products	Unique product properties	Quality control along the SC

Table 4.2 Efficient and responsive SC strategies [based on Fisher (1997)]

Criterion	Efficient supply chains	Responsive supply chains
Primary goal	Supply demand at the lowest cost	Respond quickly to demand
Product design strategy	Maximize performance at minimum product cost	Create modularity to allow postponement of product differentiation
Pricing strategy	Lower margins because price is a prime customer driver	Higher margins because price is not a prime customer driver
Manufacturing strategy	Lower costs through high utilization	Maintain capacity flexibility to buffer against demand/supply uncertainty
Inventory strategy	Minimize inventory to lower cost	Maintain buffer inventory to deal with demand/supply uncertainty
Lead time strategy	Reduce, but not at the expense of costs	Reduce aggressively, even if the costs are significant
Supplier strategy	Select based on cost and quality	Select based on speed, flexibility, reliability and quality

strategy needs to be matched to company and customer requirements. Consider in detail efficient and responsive SC strategies (see Table 4.2). Characteristics of agile SCs are fast response to customer demand, low inventory and flexible suppliers. Also, lead times are reduced to enable swift reaction to demand fluctuations. Margins are comparatively high to suitably fulfill the company's financial needs. Responsive SCs are best fit where market requirements are unpredictable and changeable.

When looking at lean SCs, almost the opposite is the case. The market situation is stable in demand and price. The variety of products is also comparatively low. Efficient SCs concentrate mainly on lowering cost via high capacity utilization, minimizing inventory, and contracting suppliers from low cost countries. Accordingly margins are kept at a low level. Lean SC strategies also try to reduce lead time but not at the expense of higher costs.

While choosing a strategy, it is sometimes advisable to go for a mixed approach. A poor strategy might endanger the company, perhaps by its not positioning itself prominently enough in the market, with the additional risk of encountering other negative aspects. Some situations require a clear position in the lean or agile SC. However, many companies have a wide product range. For some products market conditions may be stable; for others, however, they may be volatile and unpredictable. For these companies a hybrid strategy applying elements of responsiveness and efficiency for their particular products is advisable.

As a part of SC strategy, the definition of pre-assembled components, modules or systems is paramount. These modules or systems should be pre-tested and should be ready to install shipped directly from the supplier to the point of usage on the shop floor of the producer. Furthermore the early cooperation between the supplier of the modules and its customer will also help to increase the usage of standard parts in higher volumes, which will also result in reduced costs due to the economies of scale.

Case-Study Agile Supply Chain in the Latin American Food Industry

Production companies for consumer goods, distributors and retailers suffer nowadays from high pressure from competitors. The challenge for SCOM is to respond fast to market changes and customer demand, while at the same time reducing costs. This case study reviews the main initiatives and the results of a SC optimization project which took place in one of the world's leading nutrition companies for babies and children in Latin America. The underlying company merchandises more than 70 products in over 50 countries. The objective of the SC optimization was to increase the SC agility by synchronizing all the processes involved in order to reduce the overall lead time. Every process was redesigned to deliver only what was needed by the next process, and only when the next process needed it.

Agile SC can be defined as a "network of different companies, possessing complementary skills and integrated with streamlined material, information and financial flow, focusing on flexibility and performance" (Costantino et al. 2012); that was also the focus of the initiatives that were implemented on this case study.

The project was implemented in the Latin American division which has its headquarters, production site and distribution centres in Mexico and its distributors in eight countries in Latin America. The project was divided into four phases (see Fig. 4.2).

The first phase describes the *Analysis*, where the company's current situation of its chain was analysed and defined. The second phase, the *New System Design*, had as its objective the strategic development of new processes to enable SC agility. The third phase, the *Pilot Implementation*, applied the new processes on a representative product family. The last phase, the *Roll Out*, embraces the total implementation of all products and markets.

Within the analysis phase, the total lead time (the time from supplier until sale to final customer) was mapped. It indicated 188 days for Mexico and 295 days to export to Latin America (which is the average for all countries). The fairly long lead time was mainly caused through high inventory levels and large production batch sizes. At the same time, fill rates at the retail stores indicated less than 90 %, and shelf life varied from 0 (out of stock) to 139 days, mainly caused by poor forecast accuracy and replenishment strategies. Hence, the main obstacles faced at the beginning of the project were high inventory levels, long response and lead times,

4.2 Operations and Supply Chain Strategies

Fig. 4.2 Phases in the supply chain optimization project

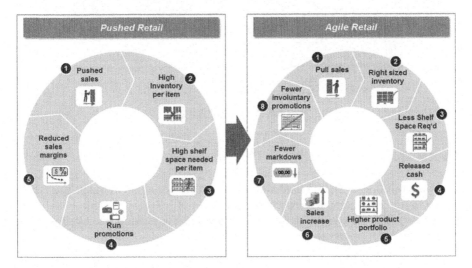

Fig. 4.3 Transition from push to agile SC

all of them mainly caused through large batch sizes produced at production facilities. The overall number of products was pushed downstream through the distribution channels without alignment with real demand. The distributors, holding high inventory levels, were also used to push the products to their respective markets. Further downstream, the retailers offered discounts and ran promotions in order to move the inventories pushed on from the distribution channel, generating pressure on sales margins. The pressure on margins is subsequently passed on upstream, since volume discounts usually result in lower margins for distributors and manufacturers (see Fig. 4.3).

After a detailed analysis of the information and material flow, the future vision and implementation plan were detailed at the second phase of the project: New System Design Phase. The design for installing new processes included synchronization tools for all processes for all points of the SC, in order to align production, consumption and material movements (see Fig. 4.4).

The current information systems also needed to be redesigned in order to be able to deal with the new process structures. A very important point was the definition of scheduling methodologies and the definition of production and transportation lot sizes.

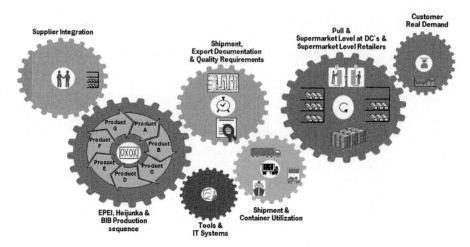

Fig. 4.4 Agile supply chain. EPEI: Every Part Every Interval, BIB: Batch-In-Batch

At the roll-out phase, the implemented processes needed to be stabilized for all products, markets, suppliers and customers. In the result, it became possible to decrease the lead time by 80 % from supplier to local consumers and by 55 % from supplier to export markets.

During the pilot implementation, a production plan with a higher "production frequency" and smaller lot sizes was implemented for one production family. Synchronization processes and systems were introduced for the main suppliers and customers. For this product family, 72 % of inventory reduction has been achieved.

Introducing an "agile SC" concept allowed a reduction in inventory shortages, to decrease lead time, while at the same time reducing inventory levels throughout the entire SC. In the underlying project case, this was achieved by using transparent point-of-sale (POS) data as input, which reflects real customer demand. Consequently, customers find a fresher product, when they need it and where they want it, thus increasing sales, turnover and revenue all along the SC. The real end-customer demand combined with higher production frequencies allows adjusting correct size inventory levels for all points in the SC, be it local or global. Adequate inventory levels and higher production frequency not only reduce lead times but also allow for a faster response to consumer demand. Hence, replenishments are managed on lower volumes but with higher frequency.

Implementing agile systems brought various advantages to the SC. Since production is in response to real demand, the company is less likely to build up unnecessary inventories thus freeing up cash, and reducing working capital as well as costs for expensive warehouses, distribution centres and obsolete products. Sales on the retailers' side also increase as service levels were improved and fresher products were replenished more frequently to fill the shelves to an adequate inventory level.

4.3 Supply Chain Coordination

4.3.1 Bullwhip Effect

The *bullwhip effect* is not a new phenomenon in the industrial world (Forrester 1961). The effect can be explained as magnification of variability in orders in the SC. In other words, irregular orders in the downstream part of the SC become more distinct upstream in the SC. This variance can interrupt the smoothness of the SC processes as each link in the SC will over- or under-estimate product demand, resulting in exaggerated fluctuations (see Fig. 4.5).

Many retailers each with little variability in their orders can lead to greater variability for a smaller number of wholesalers, and can lead to even greater variability for a single manufacturer. Main reasons for the bullwhip effect can be divided into behavioural and operational areas (Lee et al. 1997; Sterman 2000):

Behavioural Causes
- misuse of base-stock policies
- misperceptions of feedback and time delays
- panic ordering reactions after unmet demand
- perceived risk of other players' bounded rationality.

Operational Causes
- dependent demand processing (demand is non-transparent and causes distortions in information in the SC)
- lead time variability

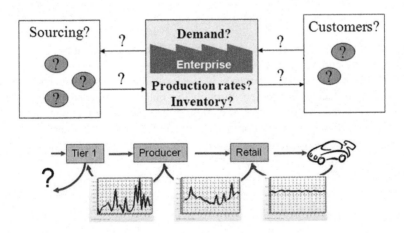

Fig. 4.5 Bullwhip-effect in the SC

Table 4.3 Elimination of bullwhip-effect

Reason for bullwhip effect	Countermeasures
Demand non-transparency	Information coordination
Neglecting to order in an attempt to reduce inventory	Automated ordering and monitoring of inventory in order to avoid overstock or shortage
Order batching	Coordinated and accurate lot size definition
Promotions	Use of everyday low prices (EDLP) instead of promotions
Shortage gaming	Validation of customer demand through historical data of customer ordering
Product returns	Policies to control returns or canceled orders.

- lot-sizing/order synchronization
- quantity discount
- trade promotion and forward buying
- anticipation of shortages.

Negative consequences, higher safety stocks, inefficient production (surplus or shortage), and low or peek utilization of distribution channels can be recognized. As countermeasures for bullwhip effect, the following can be identified (Table 4.3).

Consider how demand non-transparency leads to the bullwhip-effect.

> ▶ **Practical Insights** In order to reduce bullwhip-effect it can be recommended to avoid panic ordering reactions in case of unexpected demand fluctuations. It is advisable to take into account time lags between orders and deliveries throughout the supply chain. It is always to understand: where is the demand, where is inventory, and where is the costs.

Task 4.1. Bullwhip Effect: Focus on Demand Non-transparency

A fast-moving consumer goods (FMCG) company is facing slight demand variation which is leading to huge variation in stocks on the supplier side. The company delivers its product to consumers through the manufacturer and three suppliers. Because of the relatively low cost of changing the production rate compared to the cost of carrying inventory, the company has decided to change its production rate in order to reduce the capital commitment in the form of finished product. The task shows the effect on the manufacturer of a 10 % decrease in demand from customers.

4.3 Supply Chain Coordination

Table 4.4 Demand data

	Demand old	Order old	Safety stock old
Customer	1200	1200	300
Manufacturer	1200	1200	300
Supplier #1	1200	1200	300
Supplier #2	1200	1200	300
Supplier #3	1200	1200	300

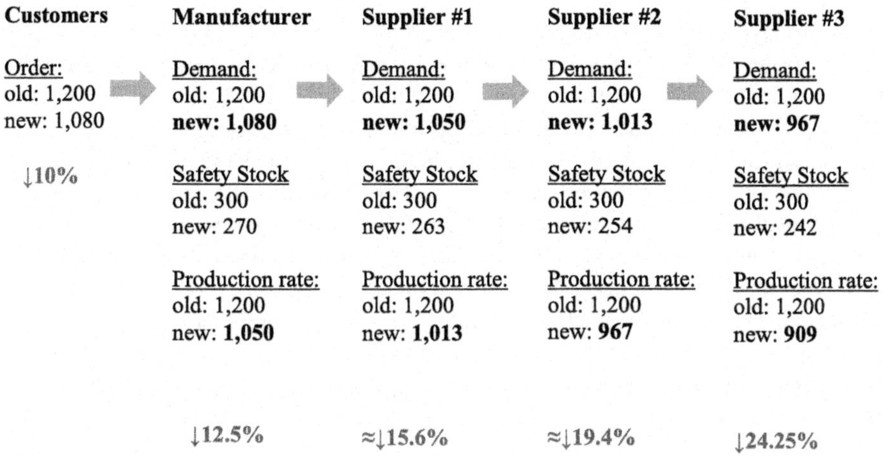

Customers

Order:
old: 1,200
new: 1,080

↓10%

Manufacturer

Demand:
old: 1,200
new: **1,080**

Safety Stock
old: 300
new: 270

Production rate:
old: 1,200
new: **1,050**

↓12.5%

Supplier #1

Demand:
old: 1,200
new: **1,050**

Safety Stock
old: 300
new: 263

Production rate:
old: 1,200
new: **1,013**

≈↓15.6%

Supplier #2

Demand:
old: 1,200
new: **1,013**

Safety Stock
old: 300
new: 254

Production rate:
old: 1,200
new: **967**

≈↓19.4%

Supplier #3

Demand:
old: 1,200
new: 967

Safety Stock
old: 300
new: 242

Production rate:
old: 1,200
new: **909**

↓24.25%

Fig. 4.6 Implications of the demand fluctuations on production rates

For any supplier the following formula is used to calculate the production rates:

$$\text{New order/production rate} = \text{Demand new} - \text{Safety stock old} + \text{Safety stock new} \quad (4.1)$$

Initial data for analysis is presented in Table 4.4.

Now demand decreases by 10 %. Safety stock is 25 % of demand and is therefore able to cover demand of 1 week. New demand correlates with the new production rate of the predecessor SC member (see Fig. 4.6).

Each player in the SC assumes that demand forecast (or orders) for the next period is the same as in the current period. Following this assumption each supplier will be the same as in the current period. Following this assumption each supplier will be planning their production rate to cover the demand/order for the next period, which will be equal to the demand/order for the current period (e.g., new demand of supplier #3 orients itself by new production rate of supplier #2). The problem will be that only the manufacturer can see the changes in demand on the customer side. Other players in the SC cannot see the changes in demand because of non-transparency. For that reason the players will change their production rate and safety stocks because the predecessor changed his order without pre-informing other SC partners.

We can observe that a lack of demand transparency affects the shortage. For example, Supplier #3 will not produce the right amount of pieces for customers' orders to satisfy their demand.

It can be concluded that changes on the customer side increase order quantity through the SC if demand is non-transparent. In general, communication, validation of demand, information sharing, and computer aided ordering and better pricing strategy can help reduce the bull-whip effect in this situation.

4.3.2 Vendor-Managed Inventory

Inventory typically exist to manage uncertainty of supply and demand (safety stock) and to take advantages of economy of scale (cycle inventory). At the same time, modern markets require more flexibility from SCs. Customer orders and demand change frequently. In building up high inventory, companies can increase their flexibility on one hand. On the other hand, if demand changes, these inventory mountains will lead to losses. Consider a short example. HP and Canon worked jointly on the Laserjet printer production. Canon produced engines for different types of printers. However, HP was able to indicate changes in demand only 3 months in advance. Canon needed 6 months to change its production plans. As demand for Laserjet III drastically decreased, a huge number of engines for this printer type was in inventory and had to be written off (the Laserjet-mountain).

In order to face this challenge, SC coordination strategies extensively use Internet and new IT. The ideas of these concepts are as follows (Heizer and Render 2013):

- Coordination instead of uncertainty
- "Replace inventory with information"
- Integrated SC
- Transparency of demand and inventory

At the plant level, inventory is an insurance against the unknowns; in the SC these "unknowns" became "known" through collaboration. Inventories in SCM are leverages of SC reliability and flexibility rather than buffers against a blind uncertainty.

One of the strategies for SC coordination is vendor-managed inventory (VMI). With VMI, the vendor controls inventory at the buyer side. The Buyer provides information on inventory and sales (see Fig. 4.7).

VMI is a special concept of restocking and replenishing the inventory that originated in retail business, the line of business where stock availability is a significant if not a crucial factor of company´s success. With VMI, the vendor takes responsibility for inventory management at the buyer side. The buyer provides certain information to a supplier, the supplier takes full responsibility for maintaining an agreed inventory level of the material, usually at the buyer's consumption location (usually a store). A third party logistics provider (3PL) can be involved to control the required level of inventory by adjusting the demand and supply gaps.

The main difference of this concept is that the real-time inventory information is made available to the supplier (manufacturer of a wholesaler) and a customer (distributor or retailer) relinquishes the control of inventory to him. Vendor reviews

4.3 Supply Chain Coordination

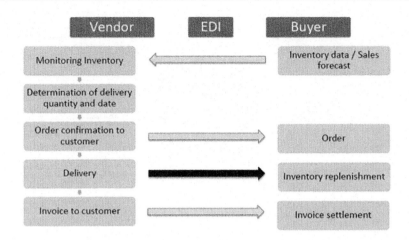

Fig. 4.7 Vendor-managed inventory strategy

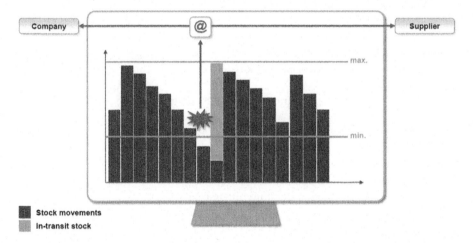

Fig. 4.8 Alerting concept in VMI (based on SupplyOn, used with permission)

every item that a customer carries and is responsible for the inventory plan. Efficiency increase of process activities is based on Electronic Data Interchange (EDI) and collaborative SC organization (see Fig. 4.8).

The supplier receives an insight into stock level and demand forecast and ensures that the stock is within agreed limits. Consider an example of the VMI process in SupplyOn (Fig. 4.9).

The following steps are included into the VMI process in SupplyOn (Fig. 4.9):

- agree on minimum and maximum stock limits
- demand and inventory is transmitted from the internal ERP system to SupplyOn

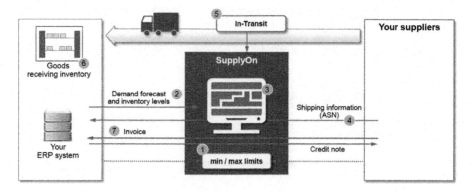

Fig. 4.9 VMI in SupplyOn (based on SupplyOn, used with permission)

- demand and inventory is shown in the Inventory Monitor, thus the supplier can plan deliveries based on the agreed limits
- ASN (Advanced Shipment Notification) is entered by the supplier and transmitted to the internal ERP system
- while the goods are being dispatched, the Inventor Monitor shows them as in-transit quantities
- goods are booked into the system upon delivery and become visible in the Stock Monitor
- invoice or credit note is generated as soon as the goods have been booked

Advantages of VMI are as follows:

For Vendor
- Early recognition of fluctuation in demand
- Optimization of production planning; increased volume
- Forces disciplines: measurements and communication
- Better planning and resource use via visibility
- Improved market analysis and elimination of non-value-added activities
- Closer customer ties and preferred status

For Buyer
- Increase of inventory availability
- Reduction of procurement activities
- Fewer stock-out with higher inventory turnover
- Optimal product mix
- Lower operating, purchasing and administrative costs
- SC relationship strategic strength
- Greater customer satisfaction and increased sales

For Overall SC
- Optimization of inventory management and cost reduction
- Decrease of fixed capital (stocks)

- Improvement of financial planning
- Supports long-term collaboration

For End-User
- Increased service level and reduced stock outs

However, it is proven that a sustainable VMI requires trust from both parties and willingness to invest (e.g. switching costs, EDI, etc.) Closer relationship implies more interdependency and cooperation. So, a customer needs to be ready to communicate promotions and other marketing campaigns with the supplier so that additional items can be available on time. Among other limitations of VMI are unforeseeable risks as employee strikes in case of stock outs and customer loss risk.

Limitations of VMI can be stated as follows:

- Trust in the SC should be high
- High costs of implementation and investments in IT; dependence on EDI
- Customer loss risk
- Non-foreseeable risks: employee strikes
- VMI mostly benefits end user and seller while vendor does most of the work
- Additional processing activities for vendor (costs)
- Supplier dependent buyer

VMI concept has been proved to be efficient for the following cases:

- Items with high a consumption amount
- Items with a high consumption value (compare with ABC analysis)
- Traditional procurement activities should be changed.

Lastly, VMI is suggested for the lines of business with multiple outlets and with a potential of a long-term partnerships between a vendor and a customer. Simply put, a major retail store chain is more likely to benefit from the VMI and recover the capital invested in switching to VMI than a small family-owned convenient store. VMI is recommended specifically for industries like retail, pharmaceutical, automotive, high-tech and other where the inventory expectation is a significant factor for a company to have a competitive advantage.

4.3.3 Collaborative Planning, Forecasting and Replenishment

Collaborative Planning, Forecasting and Replenishment (CPFR) aims at integration and coordinating actors and processes in the SC regarding the planning and fulfillment of customer demand, production and inventory (see Fig. 4.10). CPFR states cooperative management of demand and supply through joint visibility and replenishment of products in the SC. CPFR is based on information exchange

Fig. 4.10 CPFR strategy

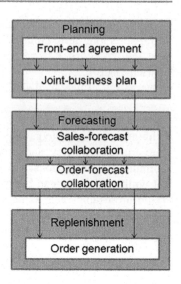

between suppliers and retailers that helps in planning and satisfying customer demands through a joint system of shared information. CPFR includes three basic stages:

In the planning phase, definition of collaboration areas, responsibilities and description of collaboration mission, objectives and framework takes place. Trading partners share the business plans and organizational information. Category information such as definition roles, strategies and tactics are needed to be explored. Seasonal events and frameworks for all events should be shared at this stage.

In the forecasting phase sales and order forecasts are needed to be performed and shared. Moreover exceptions for these forecasts should be classified. Events, promotion plans for products, new product information, individual forecast, forecast constraints related to the sales should be shared.

In the replenishment area, lead time, logistics data, location changes, current inventory levels, inventory in transit, and POS (point-of-sale) data should be shared. In the last phase, committed order from order forecasts should be generated.

4.3.4 Supply Chain Contracting

A supply contract specifies parameters governing the buyer-supplier relationship (Chopra and Meindl 2010). *Contracts* have significant impact on the behavior and performance of all stages in an SC. Two groups of contracts can be distinguished:

- Contracts for product availability and SC profit and
- Contracts to coordinate SC costs

In the first group, the supplier designs a contract that encourages the buyer to purchase more items and increase the level of product availability. In other words, the supplier shares a part of the buyer's demand uncertainty. In this group, the following contracts are included:

- Buyback or returns contracts (a salvage price is used at which a retailer can return unsold inventory to a certain amount)
- Revenue-sharing contracts (a share of the retailer's revenue is paid to the supplier)
- Quantity flexibility contracts (the manufacturer allows the retailer to change the quantity ordered after observing demand).

Contracts to coordinate SC costs are based on quantity discount contracts. A *quantity discount contract* decreases overall costs but leads by tendency to higher lot sizes. This in turn facilitates higher levels of inventory in the SC. It is typically reasonable for commodity products for which the supplier has high fixed costs per lot.

4.4 Supply Chain Resilience and Sustainability

SCs influence the environment and are influenced by it. In the light of ecological problems, natural disasters, and society development challenges, the necessity for new viewpoints on SCM has become even more obvious. The former paradigm of overall and unlimited customer satisfaction has naturally failed because of the limited resources for this satisfaction.

In these settings, the duality of the main goals of SCM—maximizing the service level and minimizing costs—will be enhanced by the third component—maintaining SC *resilience* and *sustainability*. This triangle goal framework will build the *new SCM paradigm* that can be formulated as the maintenance of resilience and the harmonization of value chains with possibly full customer satisfaction and cost-efficient resource consumption for ensuring the performance of production-ecological systems at the infinite time horizon (see Fig. 4.11).

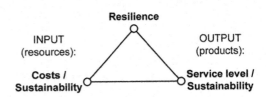

Fig. 4.11 Supply chain management resilience and sustainability

4.4.1 Supply Chain Sustainability: Examples of Coca-Cola and Mercadona

SC sustainability is based on triple-bottom-line "economy-ecology-society". Joint consideration of all these elements is crucial for SCM in long-term perspective. In SCM such concepts like "Closed-Loop Supply Chain" and "Reverse Logistics" have been developed. They are based on the idea that SC does not end at the point of sale but can be seen as a cycle including the after-sale area. We exemplify SC sustainability issues based on two case-studies of Coca-Cola and Mercadona.

Case Study Coca-Cola

The Coca-Cola system created a value chain based on strong partnerships with suppliers, distributors and retailers. The Coca-Cola Company itself only manufactures the bases of the beverages such as syrups and concentrates. It then distributes and sells these to their bottling partners (over 250 worldwide), located in every country where the products of Coca-Cola are sold (see Fig. 4.12).

The bottling partners manufacture packages and distribute the drinks as branded beverages to the points of sales (POS). The bottling partners also organize collaboration with suppliers. For example, Coca-Cola Beverages Vienna has had a long-term collaboration with SIG, a leading supplier of liquid packaging materials. Coca-Cola and SIG have recognized and embraced CPFR (collaborative planning, forecasting and replenishment). SIG has electronic access to inventory levels and sales forecasts at Coca-Cola with no time delay (previously up to 15 days late). Coca-Cola receives exact delivery quantities and times. This has enabled Coca-Cola to reduce inventory levels of packaging material by 50 %. This drastically reduces the processing time for orders and increases customer lock-in.

The bottling partners stay in close contact with grocery stores, supermarkets, convenience stores, cinemas and all other customers providing drinks from Coca-Cola. After selling the beverages to customers, consumers are able to buy all Coca-Cola products from the different POS. Because every empty Coca-Cola bottle is recyclable it is up to consumers to take responsibility for recycling.

The whole value chain is based on the fact that the company and its suppliers don't go through a process from manufacturing to distributing the products to the consumer, but consider a closed loop from manufacturing to using, and recovering material again for manufacturing. On the one hand this minimizes productions costs and on the other hand helps protect the environment. Coca-Cola contributed for instance US$2b to the planting of 25,000 acres of orange groves, thereby creating approximately 4100 jobs.

Because water is essential to the health of communities and communities are built out of the people who are buying drinks from Coca-Cola, the company needs to find a way to replenish their water. To provide access to clean water and therefore create sustainable water provision for communities and of course also for the production of the beverages, Coca-Cola contributed US$18.4m in 2012 to support 58 water initiatives worldwide. Besides that, up until 2020 Coca-Cola plans to

4.4 Supply Chain Resilience and Sustainability

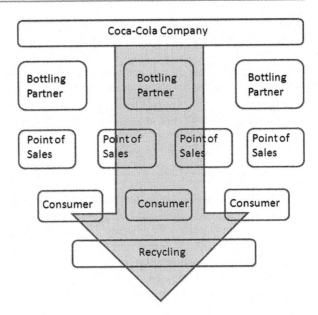

Fig. 4.12 Coca-Cola supply chain

manage water-neutral beverages, and has already reduced the water use for 1 l of product, reduced from 2.36 l in 2009 to 2.12 l in 2012.

In addition, supporting different projects on recycling and recovering used material and the development of new technologies plays a crucial role in making the packaging process more sustainable. In 2009 the Coca-Cola system developed Plant Bottle packaging, a polyethylene terephthalate (PET) plastic bottle made partially from plants and is completely recyclable.

Regarding new technologies and the upcoming ecological dimension, Coca-Cola also introduced many projects concerning climate change. Coca-Cola powers their trucks with a mix of efficient alternative fuels, for instance biodiesel or natural gas. In North America more than 750 trucks distributing products from Coca-Cola use about 30 % less fuel than they would with conventional diesel.

Case-Study Mercadona

The *objective* of this case study is to analyse how a company can efficiently implement a sustainable SC without having a negative impact on its turnover. Coordination of the value chain from positions of intermodal logistics and a closed-loop SC makes it possible to decrease costs, improve on-time delivery and company image, and achieve higher customer satisfaction. All these factors result in positive effects on turnover.

Mercadona is a family business founded in Valencia and is the largest Spanish supermarket chain in terms of a turnover of €19,077m in 2012. In 1981, the company had only eight shops in Valencia. Up to today this has risen to a considerable count of 1411 stores and 74,000 employees.

Mercadona is called the "Toyota of retail" because of its continuous improvement of *lean processes*. To name just a few of these, the company: packs fruit loose instead of selling it in containers to save packaging material; sells only a limited number of goods, so it can reduce cost due to the decreased variability; has redesigned packaging to optimize transportation. Mercadona says profit is not the primary goal, but rather investing in long-term development, for example of their employees. Being lean and always being one step ahead of their competitors is a part of Mercadona's strategy. The whole SC supports this *strategy* of leanness and innovation to remain both efficient and effective in modern volatile markets. The target of recent years was to find a way to generally become more *sustainable*. The Mercadona Board of Management looked particularly at its SC.

Mercadona initially organized *transportation* of its products by trucks and collaborated with the logistics company Acotral, which increasingly suffered delays due to road traffic. Since many goods are going from the supplier in Sevilla in the south of Spain to Valencia in the east, usage of rail services for the largest part of the distance was discussed as an option.

Renfe, a former state-owned train company, was suffering immensely from market liberalization. To secure their financial position they were seeking a new strategy. Offering transporting solutions to supermarket chains became an attractive option.

Hence, Mercadona, Arcotral and Renfe arrived at a collaborative agreement to involve rail as a transportation mode. The new *intermodal logistics* process was designed as follows. From the supplier in Seville the products were transported by truck to the rail terminal in Seville. Here the goods were *transhipped*, with Renfe taking the goods on two trains twice a week to Valencia. Of course this concept only worked for non-fresh goods such as sugar and non-food goods such as batteries. From the Valencia rail terminal Arcotral picked up the goods and brought them to Mercadona's distribution centre to supply the regional supermarkets.

The crucial element of the redesigned SC was the *coordination* between the companies. Renfe had to customize its services to be able to transport such a large amount of goods to Mercadona. Moreover, collaborative agreements can be successful only if based on trust and a *win-win* situation for all. As previously stated, Renfe customized their services. Further changes on their side included a *communication* tool which enabled *tracking* of the product at each stage of the transportation process. Mercadona then incorporated this communication tool into its own system which made it possible to have *visibility* throughout the whole SC. By offering this transportation solution Renfe had developed a new business concept. With such key customers as Mercadona they resolved their own financial situation and secured market position. In its turn, Mercadona became less vulnerable to road traffic, hence deliveries were rarely delayed. This also saved costs of maintaining safety stocks. While using rail, there were fewer noise emissions, traffic jams and accidents occurring, with a total of 12,000 tons less CO_2 emissions each year. Mercadona demonstrated a best-practice example of how a company can, when implementing it correctly, increase sustainability and additionally receive positive effects on their business processes and turnover.

Discussion Questions
1. The case study shows positive real-life examples which can be applied to other business. Even though Mercadona is a first-class example of implementing sustainability in SCM, where can you see possible limitations of this concept?
2. Consider a new SC redesigned within the collaborative agreement by Mercadona, Renfe and Arcotral. At which point could a reverse flow/closed-loop SC be implemented?
3. As stated in the case study, collaborative agreements only work on "trust and a win-win situation for all". What challenges can you see which could become critical for the SC?

4.4.2 Supply Chain Resilience and Ripple Effect

The risks in the SC can be classified into demand, supply, process, and structure areas (see Fig. 4.13). Risks of demand and supply uncertainty are related to the random uncertainty and business-as-usual situation. Such risks are also known as *recurrent* or *operational risks*. SC managers achieved significant improvements at managing global SCs and mitigating recurrent SC risks through improved planning and execution (Chopra and Sodhi 2014). In 2010–2014, SC disruptions occurred in greater frequency and intensity, and thus with greater consequences. Such *disruptive risks* represent now a new challenge for SC managers (Simchi-Levi et al. 2015). Let us concentrate on the disruption side.

First, globalization and outsourcing trends make SC more complex and less observable and controllable. According to complexity theory, such systems become more sensitive to disruptions. Special focus in this area is directed to disruptions in transportation channels. Second, the efficiency paradigms of lean processes, single sourcing, etc. have failed in disruption situations. As a consequence, SC became more vulnerable even to minor perturbations. Any disruption in a global SC, especially in its supply base, does immediately affect the entire SC. Third, with the increased specialization and geographical concentration of manufacturing, disruptions in one or several nodes affect almost all the nodes and links in the SC. Fourth, IT became the crucial element of global SCs, since disruptions in IT may have significant impacts on disruptions in material flows.

Fig. 4.13 Supply chain risks (Ivanov et al. 2014)

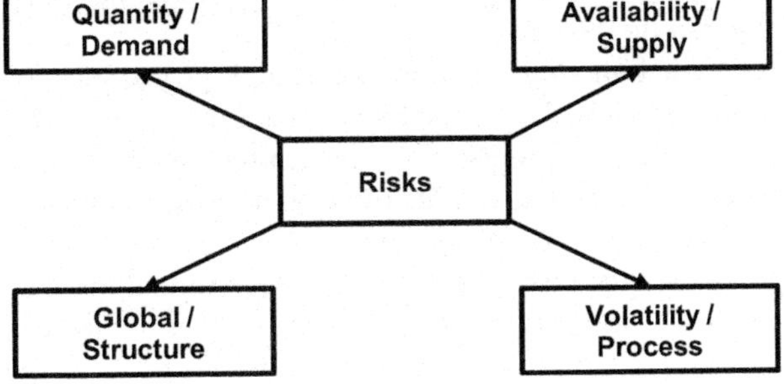

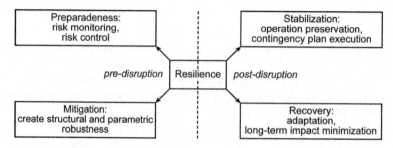

Fig. 4.14 Supply chain resilience (Ivanov et al. 2014)

Under resilience, we understand the ability to maintain, execute and recover (adapt) the planned execution along with achievement of the planned (or adapted, but yet still acceptable) performance. Building the resilient SC is based on mitigating risks, preparedness to disruptions; stabilization and recovery (see Fig. 4.14).

Basic areas of resilience include system, process and product resilience. To the basic elements to increase the SC resilience belong the following (Pettit et al. 2013; Chopra and Sodhi 2014):

- Back-up suppliers
- Excessive inventory
- Excessive capacity
- Information coordination and data transparency
- Process flexibility
- Product flexibility

Coordination and sourcing strategies in SC are also typical in practice. Many companies also invest in structural redundancy (e.g., Toyota extends its SC subject to multiple-sourcing and building new facilities on the supply side). All these four elements of resilience can be seen as strategies for mitigating at the *pre-disruption* stage and reacting at the *post-disruption* stage in the resilience framework.

For practical implementation, it is important to understand that risk and resilience analysis means little unless they are brought into correspondence with their impact on cost efficiency. The trade-off "efficiency-flexibility-resilience" becomes more and more important in SCOM and has been recently considered as *ripple-effect* in the SCs (Ivanov et al. 2014).

While bullwhip effect describes high-probability-low-impact risks, ripple effect focuses on low-frequency-high-impact disruptions. Ripple effect in the SC results from disruption propagation of an initial disruption towards other SC stages in the supply, production, and distribution networks (Fig. 4.15).

Ripple effect is not an infrequent occurrence. In many examples, SC disruptions go beyond the disrupted stage; i.e., the original disruption causes disruption propagation in the SC, at times still higher consequences are caused. Ripple effect is a

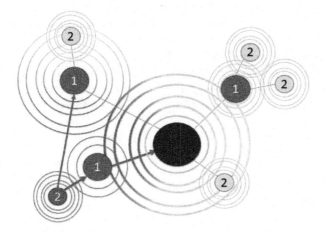

Fig. 4.15 Disruption propagation in the supply chain

phenomenon of disruption propagations in the SC and their impact on output SC performance (e.g., sales, on-time delivery, and total profit). Ripple effect may have more serious consequences than just short-term performance decrease. It can result in market share losses (e.g., Toyota lost its market leader position after tsunami in 2011 and needed to redesign SC coordination mechanism or company value decrease. Hendricks and Singhal (2005) quantified the negative effects of SC disruption through empirical analysis and found 33–40 % lower stock returns relative to their benchmarks over a 3-year time period that started 1 year before and ended 2 years after a disruption, large negative effects on profitability, a 107 % drop in operating income, 7 % lower sales growth and an 11 % growth in costs, 2 years at a lower performance level after a disruption.

Ripple effect is also known as *"domino effect"* or *"snowball effect"*. The reasons for ripple effect are not difficult to find. With increasing SC complexity and consequent pressure on speed and efficiency, ever large number of industries comes to be distributed worldwide and concentrated in jowl industrial districts. In addition, globalized SCs depend heavily on permanent transportation infrastructure availability. Mitigation and recovery strategies for ripple effect are considered in the SC resilience framework (Fig. 4.14).

4.5 Key Points

A SC strategy is one of the most important strategies in the enterprise. It should correspond to competitive and operations strategy. Such an alignment is named "strategic fit". SC strategies can be based on costs, agility, innovation, or quality. Frequently, hybrid strategies are very successful.

One of the crucial issues in SCM is SC coordination. Failed coordination in the SC can lead to bullwhip effect. It can be prevented with the help of information coordination, sharing data about sales, demand forecasts, and inventory. VMI and CPFR are examples of coordination strategies. Sophisticated SC contracting can also help in ensuring better SC coordination.

Finally, sustainability and resilience become more and more important in SCM. Bottom-line "economy-ecology-society" has direct impact on future development of SCM. Resilient SCs are expected to continue their execution even if severe disruptions are encountered and parts of the SC are destroyed.

Acknowledgements We thank Mr. Alex Bolinelli for preparation of the case study "Agile Supply Chain in the Latin American Food Industry".

Bibliography

Burke GJ, Carrillo JE, Vakharia AJ (2007) Single versus multiple supplier sourcing strategies. Eur J Oper Res 182(1):95–112
Chopra S, Meindl P (2012) Supply chain management. Strategy, planning and operation, 5th edn. Pearson, Harlow
Chopra S, Sodhi MS (2014) Reducing the risk of supply chain disruptions. MIT Sloan Manag Rev 55(3):73–80
Christopher M (2000) The agile supply chain: competing in volatile markets. Ind Market Manag 29(1):37–44
Christopher M (2011) Logistics and supply chain management. Creating value-adding networks, 4th edn. FT Press, New Jersey
Cohen S, Roussel J (2013) Strategic supply chain management: the five core disciplines for top performance, 2nd edn. McGraw-Hill, Boston
Costantino N, Dotoli M, Falagario M, Fanti MP, Mangini AM (2012) A model for supply chain management of agile manufacturing supply chains. Int J Prod Econ 135(1):451–457
Ernst R, Kamrad B (2000) Evaluation of supply chain structures through modularization and postponement. Eur J Oper Res 124(3):495–510
Fahimnia B, Tang CS, Davarzani H, Sarkis J (2015) Quantitative models for managing supply chain risks: a review. Eur J Oper Res 247(1):1–15
Fisher M (1997) What is the right supply chain for your product? Harv Bus Rev 1997:105–116
Forrester JW (1961) Industrial dynamics. MIT Press, Cambridge
Guide VDR, Wassenhove LNV (2009) The evolution of closed-loop supply chain research. Oper Res 57(1):10–18
Gunasekaran A, Laib K-H, Cheng TCE (2008a) Responsive supply chain: a competitive strategy in a networked economy. Omega 36(4):549–564
Haasis H-D, Kreowski H-J, Scholz-Reiter B (eds) (2008) Dynamics in logistics. Springer, Berlin
Hendricks KB, Singhal VR (2005) Association between supply chain glitches and operating performance. Manage Sci 51(5):695–711
Heizer J, Render B (2013) Operations management: sustainability and supply chain management, 11th edn. Pearson, Harlow
Ho W, Zheng T, Yildiz H, Talluri S (2015) Supply chain risk management: a literature review. Int J Prod Res 53(16):5031–5069
Ivanov D, Sokolov B, Dolgui A (2014) The ripple effect in supply chains: trade-off 'efficiency-flexibility-resilience' in disruption management. Int J Prod Res 52(7):2154–2172
Ivanov D, Sokolov B, Pavlov A (2014) Optimal distribution (re)planning in a centralized multi-stage network under conditions of ripple effect and structure dynamics. Eur J Oper Res 237(2):758–770
Ivanov D, Sokolov B (2010) Adaptive supply chain management. Springer, London

Knemeyer AM, Zinn W, Eroglu C (2009) Proactive planning for catastrophic events in supply chains. J Oper Manage 27(2):141–153

Kleindorfer PR, Singhal K, van Wassenhove LN (2005) Sustainable operations management. Prod Oper Manage 14(4):482–492

Lee HL, Padmanabhan V, Whang S (1997) Information distortion in a supply chain: the bullwhip effect. Manage Sci 43(4):546–558

Liberatore F, Scaparra MP, Daskin MS (2012) Hedging against disruptions with ripple effects in location analysis. Omega 40(2012):21–30

Lim MK, Bassamboo A, Chopra S, Daskin MS (2013) Facility location decisions with random disruptions and imperfect estimation. Manuf Serv Oper Manage 15(2):239–249

Losada C, Scaparra MP, O'Hanley JR (2012) Optimizing system resilience: a facility protection model with recovery time. Eur J Oper Res 217:519–530

Meisel F, Bierwirth C (2014) The design of make-to-order supply networks under uncertainties using simulation and optimization. Int J Prod Res 52(22):6590–6607

Pettit TL, Croxton KL, Fiksel J (2013) Ensuring supply chain resilience: development and implementation of an assessment tool. J Bus Logist 34(1):46–76

Sawik T (2016) On the risk-averse optimization of service level in a supply chain under disruption risks. Int J Prod Res 54(1):98–113

Schmitt AJ, Sun SA, Snyder LV, Shen ZJM (2015) Centralization versus decentralization: risk pooling, risk diversification, and supply chain disruptions. Omega 52:201–212

Schmitt AJ, Singh M (2012) A quantitative analysis of disruption risk in a multi-echelon supply chain. Int J Prod Econ 139(1):23–32

Simchi-Levi D, Schmidt W, Wei Y (2014) From superstorms to factory fires: managing unpredictable supply chain disruptions. Harvard Business Review, February

Snyder LV, Zümbül A, Peng P, Ying R, Schmitt AJ, Sinsoysal B (2016) OR/MS models for supply chain disruptions: a review. IIE Trans 48(2):89–109

Sokolov B, Ivanov D, Dolgui A, Pavlov A (2016) Structural analysis of the ripple effect in the supply chain. Int J Prod Res 54(1):152–169

Sterman JD (2000) Business dynamics: systems thinking and modeling for complex world. McGraw-Hill, Boston

Vrijhoef R, Koskela L (2000) The four roles of supply chain management in construction. Eur J Purch Supply Manage 6(3-4):169–178

Wilson MC (2007) The impact of transportation disruptions on supply chain performance. Transp Res E Logist Transp Rev 43:295–320

References for Sect. 4.1

Chopra S, Meindl P (2015) Supply chain management: strategy, planning, and operations, 6th edn. Pearson, London

Christopher M (2000b) The agile supply chain. Ind Mark Manag 29:37–44

Fast Retailing (2013) UNIQLO Business Strategy. http://www.fastretailing.com/eng/group/strategy/tactics.html, accessed 2 Mar 2014

Ferdows K (2003) New world manufacturing order. Ind Eng 35(2):29–31

Gunasekaran A, Lai K, Cheng TCE (2008b) Responsive supply chain: a competitive strategy in a networked economy. Omega 36:549–564

Heizer J, Render B (2011) Operations management, 10th edn. Pearson, London

Inditex (2014) Who we are. http://www.inditex.com/en/who_we_are/our_group, accessed 20 Feb 2014

Makioka H, Biragnet JP, Booker M (2009) Learning from the recession, the Japanese way. Business Week Online 16:18

Primark (2014) Über uns. http://www.primark.de/uber_uns/, accessed 3 Mar 2014

Slack N, Brandon-Jones A, Johnston R (2011) Operations management, 1st edn. Pearson Education, London

References for Sect. 4.4.1

Coca-Cola (2012) Global reporting initiative report 2012/2013
Senger E (2003) Supply chain prototyp mit coca-cola beverages. Universität St Gallen, St Gallen
Grüttner A (2010) Revolution im Einzelhandel – wenn der Kunde zum "Boss" wird. Handelsblatt, December 2010, www.handelsblatt.com
The Economist (2011) Spanish aisles. *The Economist*, June. http://www.economist.com
Mercadona (2013) https://www.mercadona.es
Renfe (2013) http://www.renfe.com
European Logistics Association (2010) http://www.elabestlog.org

References for Sect. 4.4.2

Simchi-Levi D, Schmidt W, Wei Y, Zhang PY, Combs K, Ge Y, Gusikhin O, Sanders M, Zhang D (2015) Identifying risks and mitigating disruptions in the automotive supply chain. Interfaces 45(5):375–390

Sourcing Strategy 5

Learning Objectives for This Chapter

- Role of purchasing, procurement, and sourcing in SCOM
- Basic elements of sourcing process
- Make-or buy vs. outsourcing
- Organization issues in sourcing
- Sourcing strategies according to number of suppliers, geographical supplier distribution, and sourcing principles
- Methods of spend analysis and supplier selection
- Elements of supplier relationship management (SRM)

5.1 Introductory Case Study "New Logistics Concept (NLK: Das Neue Logistik Konzept) at Volkswagen"

In 2011 new goals for 2018 for the Volkswagen Group have been announced: 20 % cost reduction; 50 % fewer complaints about defects in new vehicles; 30 great innovations; higher employee satisfaction; perfectly trained workers; only 8 weeks between start and full operation of serial production—and all of this with 25 % less environmental damage. These seven commandments need to be carried on an aluminum card by each VW production manager.

The new Volkswagen production system (VPS) and the new logistics concept (NLK) at Volkswagen (VW)

Despite many achievements, the Volkswagen Group is also facing many challenges concerning productivity, which is mainly influenced by production

---

Find additional case-studies, Excel spreadsheet templates, and video streams in the *E-Supplement* to this book on www.global-supply-chain-management.de!

and logistics. While the biggest competitor, Toyota, produces on average 30 vehicles per employee each year, at VW this number is only 17.

Other challenges are: different production processes at globally distributed VW locations; demand variations and missing flexibility in production and logistics; larger stocks as a consequence of separated production and logistics planning; and the continuous development of new technologies (e.g., hybrid and electrical vehicles).

Looking at Toyota, its success is traced back to lean production. Just-in-time (JIT) (no on-stock production and logistics), Kaizen (continuous improvement) and Jidoka (avoiding errors through intelligent automation) are the three pillars of lean production. The new Volkswagen production systems (VPS) and the new logistics concept (NLK) should improve production and logistics performance.

Through the new VPS-System, costs per vehicle should decrease by about €1500. This should be achieved through:

- introduction of flexible assembly lines, producing various models (e.g. the new VW plant in China can produce two different Golf models as well as two different Audi models on the same assembly line);
- standardization of production processes (e.g. one painting procedure for all 90 plants instead of 90 different ones as it is now the case);
- reduction in number of variations (e.g. only 28 variations of air-conditioning instead of 102 as it is now the case).

The VW Group follows an ambitious strategy with VPS and is facing big challenges. In the future more models of different brands need to be produced in one factory to be able to react more flexibly. VW is, as of now in its factories in emerging markets, building models of Skoda, Audi and Volkswagen in one factory. This has never happened in the past. The logistics concepts of the last 20 years no longer fit here.

NLK is used on a broad basis at AUDI and in the overall Volkswagen Group. The aim is the optimization of the supply process between suppliers and the Volkswagen Group. Through exact matching of supply schedules with shorter lead-times, improvement in the flow of goods will be achieved. Advantages for shipment handling on the supplier side will result in: shorter lead-times; better planning of production through "frozen periods"; and a reduction in production materials.

In the past VW has used inventory to supply production. To be able to react to any demand from production, materials had to have been stored. But if material just sits without moving, no value is added in the case of VW. It is a waste which is to be sustainably eliminated through the new system.

The idea is to make the processes leaner and thus reduce lead times. The production and logistics processes need to be synchronized. If production has a cycle time of 1 min, meaning that every minute one vehicle leaves the assembly line, then VW will also apply this cycle time to logistics, from the line back to the supplier. That is new. One can imagine it working like this: there would be cycled

5.1 Introductory Case Study "New Logistics Concept...

traffic in the direction of the line to the material input. If there are 20 parts in a bin, the bin needs to be interchanged after exactly 20 cycles; VW needs to apply the same cycle time back to suppliers.

In the development of the concept and its implementation all parties are intensively involved and make a substantial contribution. Collaboration with the factories' logisticians is very important. Mr. Stein, head of the NLK project said (Automobil-Produktion (2014)): "We are optimizing ourselves from inside to outside. We have a number of internal and external customer relationships within our processes, so the assembly line worker is a customer of the supplier. The optimized interaction within production was the starting point for consideration. We are speaking of a triangle; that means the assembly worker has a spot at the vehicle he is working on and a bin from which he gets the needed materials. Now the material availability is organized in a way where he literally does not have any walking routes and therefore the focus is on value-adding activities. Formerly, the materials were stored in multiple bins; today we are sequencing the material before sending it to the assembly line. This sorting is already happening, if possible, on the supplier side." Such a concept is called "supermarket". The materials are apportioned and prepared for each sequence in the line.

Next, the IT systems are indeed also one of the success factors of the project. As the Volkswagen Group has focused on reducing lead time, it is necessary to adjust EDI (electronic data interchange) flow by planning exact pick-up and delivery times. This way, during a pick-up of the goods the freight forwarder does not need to stop at only one supplier but can make multiple stops along a fixed route (so-called milk runs). This process needs to be visible in the new EDI flow. New to the NLK process is the use of the order message system, EDIFACT GLOBAL DELJIT, which documents precisely the order process for the goods.

It looks like this. The *retrieval module* processes the preview received for production planning. It is used for a rough classification of the scheduled pick-ups. More detailed orders/fine planning are processed through dispatch calls. In the *JIT module*, the dispatch calls received are shown. An overview of all orders can be seen and additionally printed out. The *JIT monitor* shows the orders, supervises all of the orders and tells the supplier when the next delivery is needed. On the JIT monitor information is split up in DELJIT by date and customer. The current delivery statuses are shown on the monitor and in addition provide information about all materials delivered. Each delivery is announced through an EDI *delivery note*. The transfer of delivery notes should be made during the dispatch of transport by the supplier. The goods that are to be delivered are also to be marked with a goods label. The former VDA4902 barcode label is replaced by the new *global transport label (GTL)*. There also exist optional modules for direct connection to the ERP systems. Radio-frequency identification (RFID) is also employed in material logistics. Readability of active and passive transponders is meanwhile excellent. However, it will be some time before there is broad implementation. The tags with which the bins have to be equipped are at the moment still too expensive.

The concept will be implemented step by step at all worldwide locations. Naturally, not everything can be achieved at once. The time frame is greatly influenced by product start in the factories. With a new product, new processes will also be used. Therefore complete implementation will stretch over the coming years. During this type of planning there is a programme that is constantly changing, unlike a project which is completed after a few years. VW has started to optimize their in-house area, and now they are starting to step outside, into supply and transporting networking. Close collaboration with suppliers and service providers will change the processes in- and outbound step by step.

Questions
- Describe the new development of production and logistics concepts at VW as follows: problem description → target → solution/changes → implementation → results.
- Which sourcing strategy is the VW group following?
- What is lean management?
- What do you understand by the term "cycle time"?
- Why is the synchronization of logistics and production processes important?
- Which information technologies are being used at VW in the new project?

5.2 Sourcing Process and Principles

5.2.1 Procurement, Purchasing and Sourcing

This section deals with the definition of procurement, purchasing, and sourcing which can be differentiated as follows (see Fig. 5.1).

According to Lysons and Farrington (2012), *purchasing* is "the process of procuring the proper requirement, at the time needed, for the lowest possible costs from a reliable source". Purchasing deals mostly with commercial activities and is related to transactional, ordering processes.

Procurement covers a broader scope than purchasing and covers both acquisitions from third parties and from in-house providers. It also involves options appraisal and the critical "make or buy" decision.

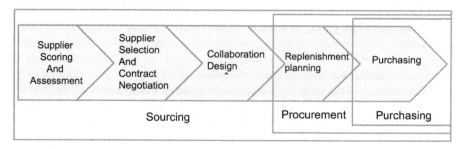

Fig. 5.1 Purchasing, procurement, and sourcing [adopted with changes from Mangan et al. (2008)]

Sourcing needs to be understood to be the entire "set of business processes required to purchase goods and services" (Chopra and Meindl 2012). The correlated activities range e.g., from the selection of suppliers, to drawing up contracts, product design and collaboration, to evaluation of supplier performance. Broadly speaking, sourcing is the process of establishing and managing the supplier relationships in the SC. In the narrow sense, sourcing is related to the activities and processes to provide the enterprise with materials, services, capital equipment, means of production, tools and supplies for work, etc. from external suppliers or partners. In practice, sourcing integrates the strategic and operative decision-making levels and coordinates supply strategy, procurement and purchasing activities. It is a fundamental element of SCOM as it is the linking process providing the organization with the inputs required for the creation of their products or services.

Sourcing is a very important activity in the SC. The purchased parts and materials can account for over 60 % of the cost of finished goods; for retail companies within the SC this can be as high as 90 %. The quality of purchased material, costs of goods bought, delivery of goods or services on time, supplier management, and supplier relationships are some of the factors that have a significant impact on SC performance and place particular demands on procurement managers. As sourcing is a very important and at the same time a very broad subject, this chapter focuses on the principles, processes and organizational aspects around the sourcing strategy in SCOM and its related activities.

5.2.2 Sourcing Process

In general, the *sourcing process* connects the supply side with the demand side, so that the so-called sourcing objects will be made available to the requestor. This is illustrated in a simplified way in Fig. 5.2, which depicts the high-level linkage between the requesting and the supplying side. In order to better understand the details behind these processes, it is important to develop a clear understanding about the content and objectives of the sourcing activities, which include the following elements:

- *Determination of material requirements:*
  i.e., the type, composition, configuration, quality, volume, location and timing for the delivery of the sourcing objects;
- *Order management:*
  i.e., determination of order volumes, frequencies, times and specification of logistical conditions. Also the supervision of accurate deliveries, goods reception, invoice control and approval can belong to the generic sourcing process;
- *Supplier base research, observation and analysis:*
  i.e., analysis and evaluation of the supplier base, assessment of potential new partnerships and elaboration of (strategic sourcing) recommendations, preparation of negotiations, contracts, etc.

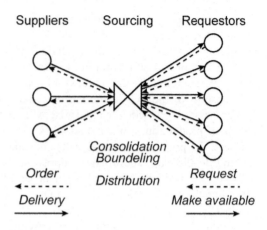

Fig. 5.2 Generic sourcing process [based on Kummer et al. (2013)]

- *Make or buy decisions:*
  Identification of internal/external value adding scope depending on the core competencies, but also comparison of capacities, lead times, costs, etc.
- *Supplier management:*
  i.e., auditing suppliers, running performance management assessments e.g., regarding on-time deliveries, quality, reliability, flexibility, etc. This is also related to supplier development or can initiate a substitution of suppliers.

It must be understood that sourcing objects can be product and non-product related. For example, in a restaurant, there are SCs both for food (i.e., product related sourcing) and for kitchenware (i.e., non-product related sourcing). Table 5.1 shows a selection of related examples, but of course the table could be extended by additional items.

Examples in Table 5.1 also indicate that a company is dealing with a large number of different suppliers on a daily basis and firms are also in regular contact with potential new suppliers. To make this a little bit more specific, we show an example of companies from the heavy investment goods industry (like turbines, planes, trains, etc.), in which approximately 35,000 suppliers are documented in the SRM System.

It is important to mention, that not all of these suppliers are of equal importance. The company will deal with some suppliers on a very regular basis and with some others more occasionally. Out of these 35,000 suppliers, for example, perhaps 500–600 form the core supplier base.

5.2.3 Make-or-Buy and Outsourcing

"*Make or buy*" is a strategic decision that determines if the sourcing objects are internally made or externally sourced. Such strategic decisions might also be related to the question of core competencies. Companies might even have their

5.2 Sourcing Process and Principles

Table 5.1 Examples of sourcing objects

Examples for product related sourcing objects	Examples for non product related sourcing objects
Raw material (e.g. metal plates, wood, stones, …)	Capital intensive equipment (e.g. cranes, milling machines, warehouse shelves and equipment …)
Auxiliary supplies (e.g. screws, nuts, bolts, glue, …)	Spare parts for production or for maintenance (e.g. drillers, cutting-disks, machine spare parts, lightbulbs …)
Consumables/operating supplies (e.g. oil/grease, gasoline, …)	
Purchased parts (e.g. sparks, valves, muffler parts, …)	Office supplies (e.g. paper, pens, staplers, …)
Purchased assembled modules (e.g. navigation system; bumper with grill and fog lights …)	Personnel (e.g. via recruiting-firms, hiring consultants or temporary staff, …)
	Information and business related services (e.g. competitor analysis, planning and conduction of exhibitions, events, business travel bookings, …)
Purchased developed systems (e.g. development and pre-assembly of the complete HVAC System fitted to the front module …)	Capital or financial services (obtaining loans, external financial support …)
Trade goods (e.g., bag for a notebook, DVDs for the camcorder…)	

own in-house suppliers, which are preparing certain modules or systems and present them to the assembly line once they are needed (this could be an exclusive steering wheel that is handmade for one car customer and which is presented to the assembly line). It could also be that propulsion components for the railway manufacturers are pre-assembled by in-house suppliers or internal wing components pre-assembled for an aircraft producer.

> ▶ **Practical Insights** For example, a car manufacturer keeps the creation of the tools to produce metal components such as fenders, doors, hoods, etc. inhouse in order to avoid characteristics regarding the outward appearance of the car being handed over to competitors in the very early stages of the design phase. This decision for the make is mainly driven by the aspect to avoid imitation of the car design.

Make or buy decisions have an impact on the overall level of the in-house value creation; respectively it is closely linked to the decisions around production strategy. When we talk about make or buy, the sourcing team will need to decide jointly with manufacturing experts whether external purchasing ("buy") might be the economically preferable solution or if the respective part should be produced inhouse ("make"). As detailed earlier, also for make or buy decisions a detailed analysis of the TCO (*total costs of ownership*) is highly recommended. Such a decision will also need to consider competitive factors regarding core competences or the fear of providing external parties with the knowledge that would offer the opportunity for imitations. In such cases the in-house "make" will be the preferred choice, even when external sourcing might be considered the economically more attractive alternative.

On the other hand, if the relevant value adding processes have historically been performed by an organizational unit's own people and the decision has been made to externalize certain processes (i.e., to buy), the so-called outsourcing takes place. That means that *outsourcing is* a result of a make or buy decision. Some of the common issues in the outsourcing analysis are as follows:

- lower production cost
- better use of available resources
- focusing on core competencies
- cost restructuring
- reduction of time-to-market
- risk sharing
- know-how sharing
- quality issues
- flexibility
- tax benefits.

> ▶ **Practical Insights** False outsourcing decision may ruin the company. A supplier for a ship building yard decided to outsource a welding process that was placed exactly in the middle of its technological process. However the order quantity was quite low (this was the reason for outsourcing) and new subcontractor always scheduled these orders as unimportant since it was not interested in maintaining high service level for such an unimportant customer. In the result, the lead time for deliveries at the ship building yards increased from 10 days to 35–40 days. The procurement manager needed to contact the subcontractor frequently and to ask to speed up. In a few months, the ship building yard cancelled the agreement. In the case of low machine utilization at a process step, it can be more sensible to try to in-source additional orders for this machine rather than outsource a part of technological processes, especially in the middle of the process.

Make or buy is not only connected to pure manufacturing processes. For example, raw materials or single loose parts can be evaluated; it could also be for modules or services, such as IT services, transportation logistics, management of facilities like cleaning, maintenance or security services. Furthermore, besides simply making, with complete buying mixed solutions are also possible in order to chime with market demands.

The following selection provides a summary based on Kummer et al. (2013) reflecting on possible parameters that might be considered when a company is going to decide about the "make" or the "buy":

- *Core competence/strategic fit*
  What are the unique capabilities that are very difficult to imitate?
  What are the strategic objectives the company needs to meet?

Does the focus on lean production require an adaptation of the production depth?

Is it necessary to buy more in new markets because of local content requirements?

- *Variety and/or stability on the demand side*

  What is the stable level of demand we can fulfil with our existing capacity and when is it recommended to increase peak capacity needs by temporary supplementary external sourcing?

- *Production capacity on the sourcing side*

  Are there existing contracts (e.g. purchasing agreements or sales orders) that need to be fulfilled and which will impact the make or buy decision?

- *Autonomy*

  Do we jeopardize our competitive position by providing external parties with confidential drawings, intellectual property rights, new research results, etc.?

  Is there a risk that we might even create a future competitor by going for a buy decision that will lead to a know-how transfer?

- *Dependency on suppliers*

  With the increasing level of external purchases, dependency on suppliers, their quality, reliability and also punctuality can significantly influence the organization's own reputation.

  Do we have a strong or weak market position and how does it look in the case of suppliers?

- *Evaluation of the cost structure*

  In the case of "make" decisions, the corresponding costs are linked to e.g., material and labour costs, salaries or the depreciation cost of the equipment in use. In the case of "buy", the decision will be related to the purchasing, transportation, handling, storage or transportation costs.

- *Financial shortage or need for capital*

  Especially at times of financial shortages, the decision to externally source parts, modules or services is an important factor, as it relieves the cost pressure.

In practice, decisions will, in addition to the qualitative criteria, be combined with quantitative methods to further substantiate the selection process.

5.2.4 Organization of Sourcing Processes

The last dimension in the management of the sourcing process is related to the *organization of the sourcing activities*. This dimension is focusing on the organizational set-up of the buying party or parties. A company can buy goods on its own individually, but it could also be that a few companies could jointly specify the goods that should be sourced from one supplier. That means that these few companies are organizationally creating a sourcing alliance.

In terms of the appropriate terminology, we could summarize, that in contrast to the individual sourcing process, collective sourcing might be a reasonable strategy. Heizer and Render (2013) give as examples small manufacturers of motorboats that formed such alliances in order to aggregate their demand for motorboat engines; or hospitals that ordered clinical supplies in a cooperative, thus benefiting from the effects of larger ordering volume because of this formation of a sourcing organization.

In the case of a global player in the telecommunications industry, the company is in a supplier–customer relationship with approximately 20,000 suppliers in 80 countries. Many different suppliers and different parts exhibit different characteristics, so that it is also important to stress that a company will need to define a sourcing strategy that will fit its individual purpose. Sourcing strategies will be considered in the next section.

5.3 Sourcing Strategies

Sourcing strategies can be classified according to three basic features:

- number of suppliers (single, dual, and multiple sourcing)
- geographical supplier distribution (local, national, international and global sourcing)
- sourcing principles (sourcing on-stock, JIT, particular sourcing).

Let us consider those strategies in detail.

5.3.1 Single vs. Dual and Multiple Sourcing

In this area, the task is to manage the supplier base with the objective of determining the right number of suppliers. By reducing the supplier base, larger volumes can be ordered from just one supplier (*single sourcing strategy*) with the objective of generating volume bundling (scale) effects. However, there might be a danger that dependence on just one supplier is considered to be a too high risk.

> ▶ **Practical Insights** Focusing on single sourcing provides many efficiency advantages. However, a number of recent disruptions force the SC managers to re-think this lean sourcing strategy since the cost savings can be overwhelmed by disruption impacts (Chopra and Sodhi 2014; Ivanov et al. 2014). Companies which used single sourcing with suppliers in Japan or Thailand, were drastically affected by tsunami and floods in 2011. Many production factories worldwide have been stopped for several months. Intel claimed to have lost $1 billion in sales during the fourth quarter of 2011. In 2010, eruption of a volcano in Iceland interrupted lots of time-sensitive air shipments in global SCs. A fire in the Phillips Semiconductor plant in Albuquerque, New Mexico in 2000 has caused its major customer, Ericsson, to lose $200 million in potential revenue. Nokia has also been affected by this disruption but could find alternative supply source within 3 days. However, it was very costly. Another risk of single sourcing is related to product standardization. If the sole supplier produces items which are used in

5.3 Sourcing Strategies

many different models of a product, the impacts of a disaster can ripple very fast in the SC like it was the case at Toyota in 2011. That is why many companies like Samsung tend to have at least two suppliers even if the second one provides only 20 % of the volume (Sodhi and Lee 2007).

Thus, it might also be a reasonable strategy to cooperate with a second or third source for a part or module. This supplier strategy is in contrast to the single sourcing strategy referred to as *dual sourcing* and might even increase to the *multiple sourcing strategy* to better balance the global flows of material and thus to reduce the risks. For example, ZARA produces their trendiest items in Europe close to highly dynamic and changing demand. Slow-moving items are on contrary produced in Turkey and Asia since lead-time is not crucial and cost reduction can be achieved in manufacturing. Li & Fung Ltd, a contract manufacturing company from Hong Kong, has a variety of supply plans that enable to flexibly shift production among the suppliers.

The discussion above allows us to formulate some critical issues to decide on single vs. dual or multiple sourcing. They include:

- volume
- product variety
- demand uncertainty
- lead time importance
- disruption and other risks
- transportation costs
- manufacturing complexity
- coordination complexity
- post-sales issues.

Some of the common *advantages of single sourcing* are as follows:

- long-term agreements
- price stability
- suppliers included in the product development process at a very early stage
- low transactional costs
- scale effects.

As *shortcomings* of the single sourcing strategy the following can be indicated:

- inefficient price policy
- lead time, quality and service issues
- lack of collaboration with many suppliers.

5.3.2 Local vs. Global Sourcing

Looking at the location of suppliers is another aspect of a sourcing strategy. This is related to the *geographic sourcing area strategy*. There are two extremes, starting from *local sourcing* (limited number of suppliers, but same norms, language, currency, shortest distance and thus fastest reaction time in case of changes) versus global sourcing (offering the broadest supplier base but suffering from e.g., long distances, different currencies, norms standards, etc.). In between there is also national or continental sourcing, which should be mentioned here.

In order to avoid wrong decisions that might be taken based only on the pure purchasing price, practice shows that a stringent focus on the TCO approach is highly recommended. Due to shrinking time-to-market and the need for agile management of the SC, the pure advantage of a low purchasing price can easily be eliminated by the need to order large lot sizes; these may be travelling around the globe for weeks, resulting in higher safety buffers, high inventory and high transportation cost. That means that TCO focus for the sourcing strategy also has to be considered.

> **Practical Insights** Of the 17 Louis Vuitton (LV) manufacturing shops for leather goods, 12 are located in France, three in Spain, and two in the United States. All manufacturing processes and development are handled at a central workshop in Italy. LV uses external manufacturers only to supplement its manufacturing segment and achieve production flexibility in terms of volume. It purchases its materials from suppliers located around the world, with which LV has established partnership relationships. The supplier strategy implemented over the last few years has enabled requirements to be fulfilled in terms of volume, quality and innovation (Heizer and Render 2013).

For *global sourcing*, items of high volume, steady demand, and low transportation costs are most preferable. However, different *chances and risks* in regard to costs, service, quality, and sustainability issues should be involved in the analysis.

- Costs: labour, taxes, transportation, insurance, transshipment, duties, and transactions.
- Quality: bill-of-materials, quality control, after-sales service, certifications.
- Service: on-time delivery, responsiveness, flexibility, technical equipment, image, reliability.
- Sustainability: political, economic, social issues.

Issues regarding global sourcing decision analysis are presented in Table 5.2. Global sourcing offers access to the broadest available range of suppliers (in contrast to local or national sourcing) and it provides many advantages. But at the same time efforts to establish a relationship with the global vendors or partners will increase, as they require certain language skills.

Global sourcing also requires longer time for travelling to suppliers and for the later transportation of goods. Also, aspects such as currency risk or political stability gain very high importance as do different cultures, norms or standards.

Table 5.2 indicates some advantages and disadvantages of the two extreme geographic sourcing strategies: local versus global sourcing. In between these

5.3 Sourcing Strategies

Table 5.2 Analysis of global sourcing decisions

	Local sourcing	Global sourcing
Advantages	• Same norms/standards • Easy to reach/short distances • Same culture, same currency, same political climate • Good basis for JIT deliveries • Lower disruption risks for overall SC	• Broadest variety of available vendors • Largest portfolio of products or services • Best opportunities to compare and negotiate with suppliers due to broadest supplier base
Disadvantages	• (Very) limited supplier base or there could be even no supplier base • Possibly limited bargaining power of buyer because of limitations on supplier side	• Longer travel and transportation time • Longer response time in case of changes • Possibly larger lot sizes • Potentially different norms/standards • Different cultures, currencies and political uncertainty • Higher disruption risks for overall SC

two extremes there are also opportunities to follow a national sourcing strategy; this would be related to an expansion of the sourcing radius, i.e., increasing the number of potential vendors but continuing to keep risks at a low level. The continental sourcing strategy would further enhance the accessible supplier base, but would still limit the risk of very long transportation times and related large volumes.

> ▶ **Practical Insights** In practice, per commodity and part the reasonable strategy has to be determined under evaluation of the corresponding opportunities and risks. In many cases, a mixed strategy with a combination of local and global sourcing elements can be a good choice. For example, Amazon prefers holding fast-moving items in distribution centres while slow-moving items tend to be stored centrally. Apple localized production in China but the distribution network is global. Such SC segmentation also helps to reduce disruption risk implications (Chopra and Sodhi 2014).

Case-Study "iPhone"
First the iPhone is developed in California. Then the engineering team creates a bill of materials for all the necessary components. Jointly with supply management, the engineering team finds the best combination of equipment and producability. Since Apple's SC is working globally it will require components from international suppliers. That is the reason why the camera is produced in the USA, high frequency components are made in Germany and the displays come from South Korea.

All the components are delivered to Shenzhen (China) where they are assembled in the Foxconn factories. Then the customer can order the iPhone via the Apple Online stores and UPS (United Parcel Service), and Fedex deliver directly to the customer. All remaining iPhones are shipped to the central warehouse in Elk Grove, California, after which they are distributed to Apple Stores and their designated partners.

The time from designing a product until actual production is usually 10 months. To accelerate the introduction of a new product, Apple acquires additional licences and if necessary also entire third-party businesses. In some cases Apple employs advanced payments to ensure access to strategically important raw materials. Furthermore Apple does not only build relationships with its suppliers, but also with the supplier to the supplier, to guarantee that the SC is not interrupted.

Generally speaking Apple relies on a few suppliers, which enables it to maintain efficient supplier management. Another advantage of focusing on a few suppliers is that Apple can concentrate on supplier development and also try to improve its performance. In addition, relevant key performance indicators (KPIs) support the impression that Apple's SC is highly efficient. The Gartner study (2014) shows that Apple's inventory turnover of 69.2 is significantly higher than that of Samsung's, which equals 18.1.

Discussion

Which KPIs could measure the efficiency of a SC?
What is the main procurement strategy followed by Apple?
What is a bill of materials?
What is your opinion of Apple's supplier management? What phases does it consist of?
What is your opinion of the product lifecycle of the iPhone? What is its influence on its SCM?

5.3.3 Just-in-Time

In order to have a sound understanding about the Just-in-Time (JIT) principles, let us first have a look at the definition that is provided by the American Production and Inventory Control Society (Lysons and Farrington 2012):

> JIT is a philosophy of manufacturing based on planned elimination of all waste and continuous improvement of productivity. It encompasses the successful execution of all manufacturing activities required to produce a final product from design engineering to delivery and including all stages of conversion from raw material onward. The primary elements include having only the required inventory when needed; to improve quality to zero defects; to reduce lead time by reducing set-up times, queue length and lot sizes; to incrementally revise the operations themselves; and to accomplish these things at minimum cost.

Making what the customer needs, when it is needed and in the quantity needed using the minimum resources of people, materials and machinery- this is the core idea of JIT. JIT was developed in the 1950s at Toyota in Japan. Along with the development of the Toyota Production System (TPS), JIT became a core element of the lean production concept. It is focused on meeting exact demands following a production-synchronous replenishment mode, which is activated by a customer order and it is linked to all predecessing value adding steps. JIT principle closely connects the functional disciplines of production, procurement/sourcing, logistics and sales. Furthermore, JIT requires the successful close cooperation between the internally and externally involved parties as it is based on the pull principle.

5.4 Supplier Relationship Management

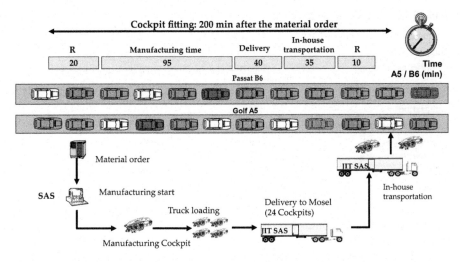

Fig. 5.3 Example of the JIT collaboration between the cockpit manufacturer SAS and VW [based on Olle and Ivanov (2009)]

JIT allows reduction of inventory at the production site, cutting lead times, increasing productivity and responsiveness. High-value materials with good demand predictability and quite steady demand especially can be recommended for JIT.

Case Study "Just-in-Time and Just in Sequence at Volkswagen Saxony"
The Volkswagen Saxony production plant is located in Mosel. The new plant was built as a "green-field" concept in the early 1990s looking back at a long car manufacturing tradition in Saxony. It was one of the largest construction sites in Europe. In the body plant, processes are highly automated with the help of robots. The painting is also automated and designed with environment considerations.

The plant produces VW Golf and Passat as well as car bodies for Bentley. The painted bodies receive a barcode for final vehicle assembly depending on the specification order by the customer. Assembly takes place on the assembly line. Readers scan the barcodes on the bodies. The material requirements are automatically generated and sent to the suppliers. They deliver the required modules JIT and JIS (just-in-sequence) for each individual vehicle. Consider an example of the JIT collaboration of the cockpit manufacturer SAS and VW (Fig. 5.3).

SAS manufactures the cockpits 3 km away from Mosel. Perfect timing is crucial for success. While SAS assembles the cockpits, production at VW continues in a parallel operation. This saves time and money. For this concept "synchronized production in partnership", VW Saxony received the German Logistics Prize. The completed modules arrive JIT at the assembly line.

5.4 Supplier Relationship Management

While selecting a sourcing strategy, the following aspects regarding SRM should be considered in practice (Geissbauer and D'heur 2010) (see Table 5.3)

Table 5.3 Sourcing strategy and SRM

Elements of the sourcing strategy	Corresponding sourcing activities
Supplier selection	Composition of an optimized supplier portfolio
Supplier evaluation	Systematic assessment of supplier capabilities and performance
Supplier development and integration	Increase supplier potential and capabilities
Supplier risk management	Prevention, reduction or elimination of supplier risks
Supplier phase-out	Optimization of supplier portfolio
Supplier relationship management	Sustainable activities to improve supplier performance
Supplier information management	Information systems for administration of supplier data
Supplier audit	Identification of performance and technology level

SRM can be divided into four areas:

- supplier analysis
- supplier selection
- supplier integration
- supplier development.

Let us consider these areas in detail.

5.4.1 Strategic Supplier Analysis

First, the sourcing department is obliged to perform a *spend analysis* in order to analyse which supplier for which sales volume is covered for what type of part or commodity. That means the number of purchased items requires careful analysis in order to generate the basis for developing improvement scenarios. Such scenarios could be related to adjusting (increasing or reducing) the number of suppliers or to transferring additional responsibilities to the supplier. In general, *the opportunities are assessed* in the first step of the strategic analysis phase.

The *second strategic step* is focusing on creating profiles for categories (e.g. paper, metal, rubber or seats, wheels, lamps, ...) and to cluster materials or services in order to identify repetitive sourcing patterns.

In order to develop a sourcing strategy in *step three*, the TCO has to be identified. This is important for developing comparable decision papers that will also be used to support make or buy decisions. The result is a condensed overview that points out which items will be externally sourced compared to the parts or components that will be produced internally.

In *strategic step four*, the potential suppliers need to be identified and screened. It might well be that new suppliers will be added after they have submitted a promising offer. Based upon defined supplier selection criteria, the supplier base will need to be critically evaluated. A set of pre-defined selection criteria captures and clarifies distinct attributes. These help to facilitate and speed up the assessment process (Baily et al. 2008).

When business experts are talking about a *spend analysis*, it is the objective to develop an understanding about the number of suppliers the monetary exchange per supplier. Bozarth and Handfield (2013) state that a *"spend analysis is the application of quantitative techniques to purchasing data in an effort to better understand spending patterns and identify opportunities for improvement."* Spend analysis can be used to answer the following questions:

- What categories of products or services significantly influence the company spending?
- How much are we spending with various suppliers?
- What are our spending patterns at different locations?

Thus the main idea behind this analysis is to obtain a good understanding about the spending behavior of a company with its suppliers or partners based on data analysis. Depending on the question that needs to be answered, a corresponding path needs to be taken for the review of the existing quantitative information. Practice shows that a company will for example spend a very high amount of their sourcing costs with only a very small number of supplying or service partners.

For the analysis of such a case, a Pareto analysis will be a good solution. In other cases, where a large number of data requires careful attention, a regression analysis might also be a good approach to choose. The teams elaborating such analyses therefore require correspondingly good skills and competences to enable them to run such data segregation.

Along with the spend analysis, some other methods are used in practice:

1. *Supplier industry analysis*—Review of the suppliers, their market shares, financial strengths, geographic coverage, to obtain a structured overview of the suppliers for certain goods and services including an understanding of the role these suppliers play in the SC (is it a local raw material provider or a globally acting partner to provide sub-assemblies?).
2. *Cost and performance analysis*—Examination of the cost drivers for the sourced goods and services as well as developing a solid key performance indicator (KPI) model. There is a recommendation to analyse the value adding steps on the supplier side and then to map cost drivers and performance drivers/influencers against the various transformation processes.
3. *Supplier role analysis*—Identification of the roles suppliers are playing in the design of the SC: which are the suppliers that will play an active role or that will coordinate parts of the SC versus the vendors that purely deliver their goods or services (e.g. diesel fuel refilling) in passive mode.
4. *Business process analysis*—Assessment of the business processes between the purchasing and the selling party. In practice that analysis will help answer the question of who from the customer side will exchange with whom how often and how with the suppliers of the corresponding commodity. This relates to the frequency of data exchange, processes of cooperation, documents to be transferred and also the tools (e. g. EDI, WebEDI or supplier portals) that need to be

used in order to facilitate the structured and harmonized exchange of information, so that the business process becomes practically alive.
5. *Business benefit analysis*—Quantification of the saving potential per commodity and usage of these identified benefits for transparent target setting purposes. Furthermore, such a substantiated business benefit analysis will also help senior management to make their decisions.
6. *Commodity plan implementation and execution*—Elaboration of a structured plan showing for what type of commodity with which supplier what type of strategy and tool should be implemented by whom of the organization and by when. That means the principles of project management are playing a significant role in converting the strategy into a plan with defined tasks and work packages.

Since a commodity sourcing strategy has a huge impact on the entire design of the SC, it is recommended that, in addition to the sourcing specialists, representatives from e.g. manufacturing, logistics/SC, quality, engineering and finance should be part of a cross-functional commodity sourcing strategy team. Of course, the individual composition of the team needs to be identified case by case depending on the enterprise, its global footprint and industry; but overall, a jointly developed strategy considering the inputs and contributions of multiple relevant functions should be the objective.

5.4.2 Supplier Selection

In this phase, the sourcing team will *create a supplier short list* based upon the identified supplier selection criteria. There are different approaches possible, but in principle, the task is to assess to which degree the capabilities of the suppliers meet the customer's selection criteria. Either they are completely fulfilled, or to a certain degree fulfilled, or they will not be fulfilled by the supplier. That means in order to identify the most appropriate vendor, commonly developed and accepted vendor selection attributes and processes will need to be defined and applied inside the organization.

The selection of vendors is a multi-criteria problem which will include qualitative and quantitative measures. According to Amid et al. (2011), the relative importance of the criteria, sub-criteria and in a lot of cases also the weighting factors are determined by top management and purchasing managers. It is important to emphasize that careful and proper selection of suppliers is a very crucial and thus important element in sourcing activities, because the performance of the overall SC significantly depends on every single party involved.

Once the short list is created, the detailed contractual discussions and *negotiations* will be initiated. Then, in this *step*, commercial conditions especially are on the agenda, but logistical requirements (e.g. packaging instructions, lot sizes, transportation devices, item identification tags or delivery notes) are also part of the agreements. When the contractual negotiations are finalized and the contracts are

5.4 Supplier Relationship Management

signed, these specified agreements will become part of the daily operational processes.

In practice, *weighted models* are frequently used in order to respect priorities or to focus on more important criteria. This might be quality, cost or sustainability related criteria for example. The factors of cost, quality, and delivery performance as well as capacity, experience, service, technical capability and financial status are used in practice. The consideration of these factors facilitates the long-term relationship with possible vendors or partners.

Task 5.1 Supplier Selection

To better understand the principle behind such systematic supplier selection, let's assume we are employees of a company and it is our task to evaluate two alternative suppliers against the list of supplier selection criteria for our company. In our example, we should have the following supplier selection criteria with the corresponding importance weighting next to it (see Table 5.4). The sourcing department will have created a standard containing the relevant selection criteria. This list of criteria will be used for all suppliers in order to ensure comparability of the supplier selection that has been made in the past and for the selection of future suppliers (Table 5.4).

Next to the company specific selection criteria are the individual weighting percentages. That means in total we will always have 100 %, split over the selection criteria. Also here, standard weighting factors will be used in practice to ensure the consistency and reproducibility of supplier selection.

Table 5.4 Scoring analysis for supplier selection

Criteria	Weight [%]	Scores for supplier A	Supplier A rating	Scores for supplier B *	Supplier B rating
Cost of purchased items	20	6	1,20	7	1,40
Quality of purchased items	20	4	0,80	6	1,20
On time delivery (OTD) performance	15	7	1,05	4	0,60
Sustainability standards compliance	25	6	1,50	8	2,00
Reputation of supplier in the market	10	3	0,30	4	0,40
References from other customers	5	8	0,40	4	0,20
Global footprint of supplier	5	9	0,45	6	0,30
Total	100		5,70		6,10

* The scale ranges from 0 points (very poor) up to 10 points (excellent).

In practice you will find that the relevant sourcing department has agreed requirements in order to assign points for each criterion. This will be multiplied line by line in order to calculate the overall supplier rating value. In our example, supplier A achieves in total a rating of 5.7 points, and for supplier B the total sum is 6.1 points. We would therefore in our team select supplier B.

As the ratings in the table above are quite close to each other, one might think about maintaining good relationships with supplier A, possibly for future second evaluation. Of course, it is not one supplier alone that is evaluated by the sourcing department; there are multiple companies that will be assessed.

Finally, since the usage of the factor-ranking method for supplier selection is very subjective, *sensitivity analysis* should be performed in the case of any quite similar evaluations of some suppliers. Such an analysis will help to identify the impact of changes in weights and scores on the overall supplier evaluation.

5.4.3 Supplier Integration and Development

In principle the repetitive process of sourcing execution and SC collaboration now starts. Practice has shown that traditional purchase orders tend to be considered inflexible, because quantities and delivery dates are fixed (simplified view). In contrast to purchase orders, *scheduling agreements* (flexible agreements) are preferred in business practice, because the exact demand date and quantity will be communicated from the ordering party to the supplier at a later stage. In this context of how to conduct sourcing execution and SC collaboration more practically, usage of IT should also be mentioned. *Supplier collaboration portals* (e.g., SupplyOn, see Chap. 3) enable communication between partnering companies and thus represent an intelligent platform in which to exchange necessary information to initiate the corresponding material flows.

Supplier development is focused on the one hand on improvement of the supplier's ability to implement production improvements, e.g. by practical problem solving or by establishing continuous improvement processes. The second issue is striving to improve supplier's cost, quality and delivery by having supplier development teams at the vendor's facility. As the details indicate, process- and results-oriented approaches are complementary.

Supplier development is related to active consulting support and to providing the necessary guidance in order to identify problems, to analyse them and to solve them practically. This might include the temporary provision of specialists or it might even be linked to financial support. Overall, the purpose is to secure, develop and maintain a solid and reliable supplier base.

Lysons and Farrington (2012) suggest a typical nine-step approach to systematically organizing structure and follow the supplier development process. These steps can be represented as follows:

1. *identify the critical products*
    (mainly strategic and bottleneck products);

2. *identify the critical suppliers*
    (assess their current and future capabilities; does it make sense to develop them?);
3. *appraise the performance of the suppliers*
    (usage of a standardized KPI framework, questionnaires, checklists or company specific assessment methodology);
4. *determine the gap between current and desired supplier performance*
    (identify the gaps from a supply point of view and also from a demand point of view, or combined gaps, such as the level of collaboration);
5. *form a cross-functional supplier development team*
    (who run the assessments, identify the gaps and also develop and negotiate a possible solution approach);
6. *meet with supplier's top management team*
    (to identify the required degree of collaboration relationship, it also helps mutually to better understand the improvement needs and to develop a relationship that is built on trust);
7. *agree how the identified gaps can be bridged*
    (e.g. to implement an IT solution, to form joint improvement teams, to execute a quality certification... develop a corresponding plan);
8. *set deadlines for the achievement of the improvements*
    (having an agreed action plan with defined actions, action owners, deliverables and due dates);
9. *monitor improvements*
    (during the implementation of the supplier development actions but also subsequently in order to ensure that the corrective measures are sustained).

In practice, such a development of a supplier is related to the establishment of a long lasting relationship which is based on mutual trust. Furthermore, the employees need to cooperate successfully together in order to align organizations and cultures. That means besides the theoretical nine steps summarized earlier, the soft human and cultural factors play in important role in order to achieve the objective of jointly improving supplier performance.

5.5 Key Points

In essence, in the sourcing activities, the following questions need to be assessed and answers have to be developed in principle for the articles of the commodity categories:

1. *What to source?*—These are the questions regarding the *sourcing objects* that need to be answered (e.g. single loose parts, modules, systems, services or non-product related objects?) It also refers to questions around Make or Buy, which respectively will consider outsourcing decisions.
2. *How to source?*—What is the *sourcing tool or process* that needs to be applied (e.g. do we consider manual sourcing or do we use IT tools such as portals, EDI?

How well are business processes aligned between the supplying and the buying parties?) What is the appropriate *sourcing organization*, i.e. whether to run the purchasing *individually* or to establish an alliance and thus follow the idea of *collaborative sourcing?*
3. *From whom to source?*—With *how many suppliers* or partners do we cooperate (do we focus on a *sole supplier*, do we prefer double sourcing or is our strategy to purchase the goods or services from multiple vendors?) Which supplier demonstrates good performance or has further potential—who should be developed and who should be substituted?
4. *From where to source?*—Do we focus on the *cooperation with local* suppliers, is our scope connected to national or continental vendors or is the strategy to aim for *global sourcing?*
5. *When to source?*—How to schedule the sourcing from a time perspective regarding the early supplier involvement already at the stage of product development in order to jointly develop the part or module and to agree on the most suitable delivery strategy *(e.g. JIT)* including the corresponding containers or stock keeping units (SKU). Alternatively the strategies of *stock sourcing or demand tailored sourcing* might be applied.

In parallel to these five dimensions, are other strategic aspects regarding long-term relationships with suppliers, their performance measurement and the steady analysis of spend patterns which need to be conducted in order to ensure continuous evaluation and the improvement of sourcing activities. Of course, the effort involved will differ from company to company and industry to industry; thus this chapter is intended to provide some guidance on the fundamental considerations with respect to the sourcing strategy, its related processes and how the relationship with suppliers is connected to the SCOM.

Bibliography

Amid A, Ghodsypour SH, O'Brien C (2011) A weighted max-min model for fuzzy multi-objective supplier selection in a supply chain. Int J Prod Econ 131(1):139–145
Baily P, Farmer D, Crocker B, Jessop D, Jones D (2008) Procurement principles and management, 10th edn. Pearson, Harlow
Bozarth C, Handfield RB (2013) Introduction to operations and supply chain management, 3rd edn. Pearson, Harlow
Chopra S, Meindl P (2012) Supply chain management. Strategy, planning and operation, 5th edn. Pearson, Harlow
Chopra S, Sodhi MS (2014) Reducing the risk of supply chain disruptions. MIT Sloan Manag Rev 55(3):73–80
Cohen S, Roussel J (2013) Strategic supply chain management: the five core disciplines for top performance, 2nd edn. McGraw-Hill, Boston
Geissbauer R, D'heur M (2010) 2010-2012 Global supply chain trends – are our supply chains able to support the recovery? Lessons Learned from the Global Recession. http://www.imperiallogistics.co.za/documents/Global-Supply-Chain-Trends-2010-2012.pdf. Accessed 15 Apr 2014

Heizer J, Render B (2013) Operations management: sustainability and supply chain management, 11th edn. Pearson, Harlow

Ivanov D, Sokolov B, Dolgui A (2014) The Ripple effect in supply chains: trade-off 'efficiency-flexibility-resilience' in disruption management. Int J Prod Res 52(7):2154–2172

Kummer S, Jammernegg W, Grün O (2013) Grundzüge der Beschaffung, Produktion und Logistik, 2nd edn. Pearson, Harlow

Lysons K, Farrington B (2012) Purchasing and supply chain management, 8th edn. Pearson, Harlow

Mangan J, Lalwani C, Butcher T (2008) Global logistics and supply chain management. Wiley, New York

Olle W, Ivanov D (2009) Just-in-time and just-in-sequence: example of Volkswagen Saxony. In: Ivanov D (ed) Supply chain management. St Petersburg Polytechnic University, St Petersburg (in Russian)

Sodhi MS, Lee S (2007) An analysis of sources of risk in the consumer electronics industry. J Oper Res Soc 58(11): 1430–1439

References for Sect. 5.1

Automobil-Produktion (2014) Taktgenau an die Linie – Logistik bei Volkswagen. http://www.automobil-produktion.de/2011/02/taktgenau-an-die-linie-logistik-bei-volkwagen/, Zugriff am 19.07.2014

Volkswagnis (2012) *Wirtschaftswoche*, 45

Wiberg Consulting (2014) [Online] Available at www.wiberg-consulting.com/files/admin/w5_nlk.pdf. Accessed 19 July 2014

Production Strategy

6

Learning Objectives for This Chapter

- Push and pull views of the supply chain
- Mass customization and modularization
- Order penetration point and postponement
- Basic production strategies in the supply chain
- Analysis of order penetration point location

6.1 Introductory Case-Study DELL vs. Lenovo

Dell

The company Dell was founded in 1984 by Michael Dell, at the age of 19. Starting off with only $1000 start-up capital borrowed from Dell's father, the company opened its first subsidiary in the UK only 3 years later. In 1995 Dell even became a global company and in 2001 was named the No. 1 computer systems provider. What is it about Dell that makes it so special?

Dell is well known for its direct-sales model and its ATO or "assemble to order" approach. This means manufacturing and delivering individual PCs configured to particular customer specifications. Instead of pre-assembling a complete PC, Michael Dell created a SC where inventory of components is hold in a few centralized locations, and as customer's placed their orders, a Dell computer would be assembled exactly to the customer's requirements. Distribution and shipping is made direct to the customer. Standard components are offered and

---

Find additional case-studies, Excel spreadsheet templates, and video streams in the *E-Supplement* to this book on www.global-supply-chain-management.de!

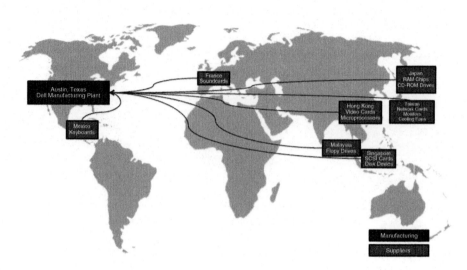

Fig. 6.1 DELL's supply chain

customers can choose the particular features they want to add to the technical device. Strong customer focus is an important part of the direct model. The online channel has proven very effective for the sale of computer hardware, and by 2009 represented about half of the sales in this category. In 2007 Dell expanded its sales channels and started to sell PCs through retail stores.

Most of Dell's suppliers come from Asian countries, such as Japan (RAM chips), Taiwan (monitors) and Singapore (disk devices). From there, all components are then delivered to manufacturing plants, for example in Austin, Texas (Fig. 6.1).

While using the ATO strategy, cycle times are reduced and inventory expenses are kept at a low level, as not all varieties of products need to be stored but only the standardized versions. Also, the assembly is quite easy because the features that can be chosen are rather independent from the outer appearance of the device. So after all Dell can offer high-quality products at comparatively low prices.

The customer is able to choose between what type of processor, software or storage they want in their device. However, the touch and feel experience of the device is lacking and there is little presence of Dell in retail stores. Customers might miss the presence of a sales expert during the purchasing process. Dell tried to overcome this obstacle by offering hotlines and live chat with sales representatives on their website.

Such a system allowed Dell to create more flexible SC and ensure efficiency. The lead time for shipping to the customer was initially from 4 to 6 weeks. With the ATO model, a PC could be fully assembled in 1–2 days, and the customer receives the order by the end of the week. This significantly reduces the inventory holding costs incurred during shipping as well as improves customer satisfaction. With this strategy, Dell commonly holds inventory for less than 4 days. By using a postponement assembly strategy, Dell is able to generate cash much faster and reinvest this cash into improving their SC model.

Even though Dell was a so-called rule-maker when they introduced the direct model, market changes were forcing the company to rethink the strategy. The model was mainly meant to be for mass production of personal computers for business customers. However, nowadays most sales are generated by laptops for end customers. For that reason Dell, needed to revise its strategy.

We discovered that only one in four of our customers were using the direct model anymore, says William Hutchinson, Dell's vice president of global logistics. While the direct model worked phenomenally well when Dell was aiming for a largely mature customer base, its customers today are just as likely to be from emerging markets with immature infrastructures.

During autumn 2013 the company went from being a public company to becoming private. The reason for that was mainly to regain more flexibility in decision making. Future product lines are now storage, networking (e.g. Dropbox) and cloud computing. For storage media, the direct model no longer applies to as there is little or no reasonable adaption to the product necessary. Hence, in this product area it is difficult for Dell to gain a competitive advantage. Most likely producing via a make-to-stock (MTS) strategy would be more reasonable. Additionally, with increasing demand, the risk of stock-outs due to low inventory is also increasing. Moreover, some customers are demanding more than low prices. To improve approaches to these high-end customers, the idea is to implement a "premium product line". In future Dell will most likely have a hybrid strategy using both MTO (make-to-order) and ATO.

Lenovo

The Lenovo brand appeared in 2004 but the company has a much longer history, starting in Beijing in 1984 as the New Technology Development Company (NTD Co.) of the Institute of Computing Technology (ICT) of the Chinese Academy of Sciences (CAS). In 1988 the company was expanded into Hong Kong and grew into the largest PC company in China. In 2004, it changed its name to Lenovo, and in 2005 it acquired the former IBM Personal Computing Division. Currently, Lenovo is one of the world's largest PC manufacturers. It has more than 33,000 employees in over 60 countries and operates in more than 160 countries worldwide.

A global SC at Lenovo was established in accordance with functional, geographic, and "internal customers" dimensions. In order to increase customer service in major markets, Lenovo established "strongholds' in Europe, America, Singapore and Shenzhen, China, to provide customers with business and financial services (see Fig. 6.2).

Lenovo's SC includes raw material procurement, production at three locations (Beijing, Shanghai, Huiyang), product distribution, transportation, warehousing (outsourcing) and payment. Lenovo's inventory cycle is now within 10 days, the cash cycle can be achieved within 10–20 days. These performance indicators contribute to relatively high profits for Lenovo China.

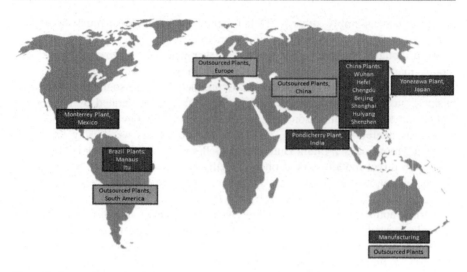

Fig. 6.2 Lenovo's supply chain

In October 2005, Lenovo announced a new organizational structure, composed of production, marketing and logistics. Lenovo sets product development and marketing in Hong Kong. This enables Lenovo's technical staff to receive timely market and technical information and understand the progress of market and technical aspects. This also shortens the company's product development cycle and the company products can keep up with international trends.

Production is mainly organized in Shenzhen and other production bases in China mainland. The labour costs and price of real estate in China mainland are much lower than in Hong Kong. Setting the production processes on the Chinese mainland helps reduce manufacturing costs. In addition to Lenovo's own investment in the construction of production factories in Shenzhen and other places, Lenovo also develops cooperative relations with other domestic manufacturers.

In procurement and inventory management, Lenovo integrates procurement, production, distribution and logistics into a unified system with over 300 suppliers. In addition, the company has more than 5000 customer channels in China. Purchase of raw materials such as monitors, hard drives, video cards and even the chassis and other parts is typically organized in collaboration with suppliers in Taiwan, which is one of the world's supply centres for IT components.

In production and inventory management, Lenovo takes a combination of MTS with a large margin of safety, and MTO production with a relatively low safety stock of finished goods to cover demand for only a couple of days. In mainland China, Lenovo's suppliers operate warehouses near Shanghai, Beijing and Huiyang so that these three factories can be delivered faster. Recently, Lenovo has opened production facilities in the United States to improve the relationship with its business customers and to be able to offer more flexible support.

Lenovo also uses a VMI purchasing pattern. In accordance with Lenovo's VMI project, its inventory manager, BAX Global Freight Logistics Ltd, as third-party logistics, is responsible for inventory control. The third-party logistics company is responsible for replenishing the production line at the right time with right items at the right quantity. VMI relies on sharing information between suppliers, third-party logistics and Lenovo and ensures timely delivery of materials needed for production. VMI brings considerable benefits to the production and inventory management at Lenovo. First, its internal business processes will be streamlined. Second, it places the inventory closer to production and enhances the elasticity of supply and better responds to changes in market demand. Third, it improves inventory liquidity. Fourth, through visual inventory management, Lenovo can monitor suppliers' delivery capabilities online. Eventually it accelerates Lenovo's logistics, shortens the lead time and ensures timely delivery of materials required for production; while the Lenovo SC is shortened, costs are reduced, and flexibility is enhanced.

In the distribution phase, Lenovo and partners form a closer relationship, with timely information sharing, and precise and efficient integration of operations. Lenovo's distribution channels are distributors, agents, distributors of contract and distributors of non-contract. Lenovo subdivides functions of different channels and uses two channel systems, i.e. one for home computers and one for business computers. Due to their different target customers, distributors can establish good relationships with their customers, which is helpful in opening up the market while avoiding strong competition between themselves. Lenovo adheres to the secondary distribution system, namely a maximum of two levels between Lenovo and consumers because excessive levels would reduce the efficiency of operations and increase Lenovo's management costs. Lenovo adopts a selective distribution strategy. On the one hand Lenovo can reach markets through the distributors. On the other hand by selecting and training core agents and distributors, Lenovo is able to provide users with better solutions. Through the development of secondary channels, Lenovo flattens the structure of its distribution channel. For MTO production, direct shipments are organized. As with Dell products, customers are able to order Lenovo's products online, but without any adaption tailored to customers.

To manage the complexity of the SC, Lenovo uses an ERP system from SAP. ERP helps Lenovo to run an effective SC execution by monitoring huge SC data in real time for more accurate information, helping to enable fast decision making in order to facilitate a responsive SC, and improving logistic efficiency. It also provides end-to-end visibility of the entire global SC, and increases transparency and efficiency with real-time access across the SC.

Discussion Questions
1. Identify basic stages in the value chain which are described in this case study.
2. Explain interconnections between production and distribution strategies at Dell and Lenovo.
3. Compare MTO and MTS strategies.
4. Describe advantages and possible limitation of VMI at Lenovo.

6.2 Postponement and Modularization

6.2.1 Problem: Mass Production or Product Customization

Henry Ford said: "A customer can have a car painted any colour that he wants so long as it is black". Till the 1970s, mass production dominated the industries and markets. The advantages were low unit costs because of rare machine setups, large batch material ordering, and use of standard technologies and materials. Since 1980s, customers play more and more important role in the SC. Products become individual and customized. This flexibility creates competitive advantage but is costly. Machines should be set up frequently, lot-sizes in manufacturing and procurement become smaller, the variety of technologies and materials rise.

In these settings, the problem is to determine right *production strategy* for the SC in order to combine advantages of mass production and customization.

6.2.2 Principles: Postponement and Modularization

In the era of a customer-oriented product individualization and global competition, companies are struggling to find ways to improve responsiveness without holding huge finished goods inventories. Postponement and modularization are useful tools in this area.

The *postponement* concept was first time introduced in the literature by Alderson (1950), where it was observed that products tend to become differentiated as they approach the point of purchase, and later further developed by Bucklin (1965). Apart from the postponed forward shipment of goods (time postponement) and maintaining goods at a central location in the channel (place postponement) certain manufacturing activities could also be postponed (Van Hoek 2001). Although this differentiation improves the marketability, the manufacturability of the products becomes more complex.

Van Hoek (2001) defines *postponement* as "an organizational concept whereby some of the activities in the SC are not performed until customer orders are received". Postponement is especially useful for:

- Significant number of variants of an end product with an uncertain split of demand on variants.
- Delivery time requested by customers must allow value-adding steps after receipt of customer orders (or reliable demand forecast).

Differentiation of the generic product into a specific end-product is shifted *closer to the consumer* by postponing identity changes, such as assembly or packaging, to the last possible SC location. This allows keeping *safety stock* of one generic product instead of multiple specific end-products. Especially in cases where the split of demand into specific end-products is uncertain, postponement with its *risk pooling* effect leads to less safety stock required and to a lower risk of obsolescence of end-products. Furthermore, as less value has been added to the generic product than to the specific end-product, *less capital* is bound in each stocked unit.

The concept of *modularization* implies a product design approach whereby the product is assembled from a set of standardized constituent units. It provides opportunities for exploiting economies of scope and scale from a product design perspective. The key issue here is to design for efficient linkage mechanisms in the constituent units so that any required combination can be conveniently assembled.

Baldwin and Clark (1997) describe modularity as "building a complex product or process from smaller subsystems that can be designed independently yet function together as a whole". The ideas of the integration the product and process modularity have been extensively investigated in the *mass customization* approach.

Ernst and Kamrad (2000) introduced a conceptual framework for evaluating different SC structures in the context of modularization and postponement. In the analysis, modularization is linked to postponement. The paper introduces taxonomy and develops a corresponding framework for the characterization of four SC structures, defined according to the combined levels of modularization and postponement: rigid, postponed, modularized and flexible.

6.2.3 Examples of Postponement Strategies

Asian Paints (Shah 2009)
Asian Paints is an Indian paint manufacturing firm that has employed the postponement strategy in its emulsions product category. Asian Paints offers four emulsion brands. In turn, each brand offers 150–250 shades. Offering a wide variety of colour shades is essential in the emulsions market. An emulsion comprises a "base" and a combination of "stainers". The base provides the functional aspects while the stainers provide the required shade. The base accounts for 99 % of the final emulsion volume. A wide range of shades is developed using just 10 stainers. At Asian Paints, the mixing of the base and the stainers, also known as "tinting", is carried out at the various sales points (SPs) distributed across the country. On average, there is one SP for every 400 retailers. At the retailer point, the customer chooses from a range of 150–250 shades.

The retailer immediately forwards this order to the SP. The effective time for tinting is about 10 min. The customer collects the shade of his choice within 1–2 days of placing his order. Except for certain fast-moving shades, the inventory at the SP is mainly bases and stainers. The SPs order these periodically from their designated regional distribution centres (RDCs). The factory warehouses replenish the RDC inventories periodically. The periodicity of ordering depends on the demand volumes. The RDC lead times (factory to RDC) are in the range of 2 weeks to 1 month while the SP lead times (RDC to SP) are in the range of 1–2 days. Thus, the delivery period will have been close to a month had the tinting operation taken place at the factory itself. Tinting is a low-technology operation due to low capital expenditure and simplicity. The delayed differentiation due to postponement of the tinting operation has reduced the inventory levels drastically. The customer service is high due to the reduced delivery period. Forecasting errors are also reduced considerably. There is no loss of scale economies owing to the postponement of the tinting operation. Being a simple operation, product quality is not diluted due to the transfer of the operations from the factory to the SPs.

Asian Paints revolutionized the postponement concept in the Indian paint industry. Asian Paints has been offering substantially higher number of shades and is maintaining its finished goods inventories at about 60 % of the industry average. This has helped them to maintain profitability that is consistently higher than the industry average, and has probably contributed to increasing its market share over a period of time.

Automotive Industry (Appelfeller and Buchholz 2011; Kagermann et al. 2011)
Modular design is an important method to control and reduce complexity. Using identical components and modules significantly reduces diversity and complexity. Limited and accurate defined number of components and modules, which are assembled to individualized final products, result in outward diversity and inward standardization. In the automotive industry this approach became known as platform strategy which can be used within or across product lines as well as across brands.

From the customer's perspective, postponement means being able to specify requirements as late as possible. Vehicle manufacturers are particularly well known for this practice. For example, BMW customers are able to modify their personalized vehicle up to 5 days before assembly begins. In turn, a gearbox or seat supplier has to defer production until the precise requirements are known.

While the implementation costs are significant, postponement in combination with JIT has many benefits:

- Lower inventory costs for finished goods but also for raw materials and work in process (WIP)
- Lower risk of product obsolescence
- Simpler forecasting and greater responsiveness
- Customized products can deliver competitive advantages such as time to market, as well as command a price premium

If a company shifts final assembly to a time and location close to the customer in time or space, it can supply more personalized solutions and avoid make-to-stock production, while still realizing economies of scale.

A good example of a case for successful implementation of the postponement strategy is the automobile manufacturer Toyota (Belson 2011). Building brands such as Toyota, Lexus and Scion in its own factories in Japan, Toyota ships the cars afterwards with the aim of selling them internationally. For this, Toyota employs port facilities, e.g. the 98-acre operation at Newark's port which is a scaled-down assembly plant. Cars, destined for sale from Virginia to Maine, are modified at the Newark's port according to a customer's special request at a very short notice.

A range of so-called port-installed options can added into 21 different models. The average length of time spent at Toyota's facility is 8 days for the up to 12,500 vehicles arriving by ship at any one time. Between 2 and 6 days are required for the necessary adjustments and it takes on average another 1.9 days for a car, once completed, to leave the facility.

By completing the modifications within 8 days and allowing a customer the possibility to adjust his/her order in regard to the car's configuration—including satellite radios, tyres, rims, bumper protectors, body mouldings and a variety of exterior items—until just 2 days before the car arrives in Newark, Toyota achieves better customer service and thus higher customer satisfaction. In addition, having established a close relationship with suppliers and ordering daily the accessory needs expected in just 2 days, the facility has refined its orders so finely that it has been able to reduce the amount of just-in-time inventory by 70 % within the last 4 years.

IKEA (Cheng et al. 2010; Kagermann et al. 2011)

With production in 41 different units worldwide, IKEA controls the SC with approximately 9500 finished products. The 'Range Strategy & Product Development Supply Chain' group is in charge of handling the SC as smoothly and efficiently as possible. IKEA developed the concept of 'design for logistics' (DFL). The DFL focuses on the design of the product not only from customer requirements, but also on efficient handling and transportation. This results in a more efficient stocking of items and the so-called flatpack approach, in which most items are being packaged in flat, easy to handle packages. IKEA ultimately aims for a fill rate of its trucks of 75 %. Due to vertical integration, IKEA produces 'make-to-stock', which means they follow a push strategy. This strategy comes with many advantages on the one hand, but also with some risks on the other hand. For once, the 'make-to-stock' approach requires accurate forecasting of demand to manage the trade-offs between costs (transportation cost/inventory cost) and service level (availability of items). Therefore, IKEA is engaging in risk when pooling activities such as:

- postponement (last step of the SC is the assembling of the product by the customer)
- material standardization (uniform screws, planks, colours, techniques)
- inventory pooling (at warehouse or in store)
- product pooling (similar kinds of products)

IKEA has taken the concept of manufacturing postponement to an extremely high level: final assembly of many furniture items occurs in people's houses. The company works closely with its suppliers to source and design attractive furniture that can be location-neutral and flat-packed whenever possible, making its products acceptable in many countries while keeping transportation and warehousing costs low. All products in IKEA retail stores are kept in semi-finished form (flat packs) and are assembled by customers or deliverymen after home delivery. In this way, truckload capacities can be utilized and configurations can be easily made at customer locations.

6.3 Push-Pull Views and Order Penetration Point

The push/pull view of the SC divides SC processes into two categories based on whether they are executed in response to a customer order (downstream part) or in anticipation of customer orders (make-to-stock, upstream part). Pull processes are initiated in response to a customer order. The advantages of the downstream part are responsiveness, and high degree of customer-oriented product individualization. Push processes are initiated and performed in anticipation of customer orders. The advantages of the upstream part are the economy of scale (low manufacturing and transportation costs), flexibility (high level of inventory), and the short supply times.

This view is very useful when considering strategic decisions relating to SC design, because it forces a more global consideration of SC processes as they relate to the customer.

The main idea behind the postponement is to delay product differentiation at a point closer to the customer. This point is also known as the order penetration point (OPP) (see Fig. 6.3).

In the case of a customer inquiry or order, the goods can be delivered from a general inventory holding unit (trajectory α) or customized according to the inquiry or order (trajectory β). Upstream of the OPP, the processes are designed to be lean. Downstream the processes are designed to be agile.

Three categories are primary relevant to the OPP location:

- Delay of product differentiation—postponement,
- Design and developing standard or generic configurable products that can be customized quickly—product modularization,
- Implementation of specific collaboration strategies, inventory strategies, buffers, etc. to fulfil service level objectives—agility.

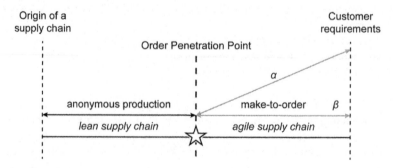

Fig. 6.3 Order penetration point

6.3 Push-Pull Views and Order Penetration Point

In practice, a selected postponement strategy determines the OPP location. The further upstream the OPP is located in the SC, the more manufacturing and logistics activities are postponed. In general, the aim is to postpone manufacturing and logistics as much as possible with maintaining high customer service standards.

The OPP location is dependent on a number of factors.

Factor 1. Costs of inventory holding. This factor has been highlighted in literature as one of the most important to analyse postponement strategies

Factor 2. Costs of modularization. High costs of modularization is the main drawback of postponements.

Factor 3. Costs of information systems installation and running. However, the introduction of new IT costs a lot of money.

Factor 4. Costs of replenishment. Practical case studies, i.e. of DELL, let draw the conclusion that SC responsiveness highly depends on the speed of replenishment of customer-individualized product units

OPP location depends on products.

Factor 1. How many variants of a product are possible?
Factor 2. What is customized (product, batch sizes, and package)?
Factor 3. Which part of the products can be customized from technological point of view?
Factor 4. Which part of the products can be modularized from technological point of view?
Factor 5. Price of products
Factor 6. What is the concurrency situation in the industry?
Factor 7. SC cycle for a product
Factor 8. Customization cycle of a product
Factor 9. Where strategic inventory is hold?

OPP location depends on customers.

Factor 1. Who launches orders (individual consumer, organization, retail or wholesaler)?
Factor 2. Who launches the customization (individual consumer or organization)?
Factor 3. Who is the end customer (individual consumer or organization)?
Factor 4. Number of customers.
Factor 5. Which contracts are used?

OPP location depends on suppliers.

Factor 1. How many alternative suppliers are available?
Factor 2. Possibility of strategic alliances under and with the suppliers
Factor 3. What contracts are used?

6.4 Selection of a Production Strategy

We already know the principles of postponement, push/pull views, and OPP. Now we can integrate this knowledge and consider some production strategies.

6.4.1 Types of Production Strategies

With pull processes, execution is initiated in response to a customer order. With push processes, execution is initiated in anticipation of customer orders. Therefore, at the time of execution of a pull process, customer demand is known with certainty, whereas at the time of execution of a push process, demand is not known and must be forecast (see Fig. 6.4).

The push/pull boundary is the place of the OPP that separates push processes from pull processes. A product is kept as long as possible in a generic state. Differentiation of the generic product into a specific end-product is shifted closer to the consumer by postponing identity changes, such as assembly or packaging, to the last possible SC location. According to the place of the OPP, the following *production strategies* can be determined:

- Make-to-stock (MTS)
- Distribute-to-order (DTO)/Configure-to-order (CTO)
- Assemble-to-order (ATO)
- Make-to-order (MTO)
- Engineer-to-order (ETO)

Make-to-stock strategy is typical for mass production of standard products like sugar, socks, etc. MTS advantages are low unit production costs and higher capacity utilization because of scale effect and quantity flexibility regarding demand fluctuations due to the product standardization. Disadvantage of MTS is higher inventory and lower production flexibility.

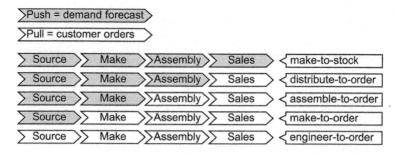

Fig. 6.4 Production strategies in the supply chain

6.4 Selection of a Production Strategy

Distribute-to-order (or *configure-to-order*) strategies allow a small grade of customer individualization. It can be customer-specific packaging (like in pharmaceutical industry) or some individual items added to a standard manufactured product. Advantages of DTO are higher flexibility regarding product structure and lower inventory.

Assemble-to-order presumes a higher degree of product individualization which happens directly within the manufacturing. A typical example of the ATO is car manufacturing or DELL in electronics industry. The assembly is performed individually for each customer from a set of standard modules. Advantages and shortcomings of the ATO are similar to the DTO/CTO, but with higher investments in the process and product flexibility and lower inventory.

Make-to-order strategy is similar to ATO but presumes also a possibility of customer individualization at the module/component level. This means that not only the final assembly from some standard modules can be individualized but also the modules and components can be manufactured individually for each particular customer. MTO can be recommended for customer-specific products with fluctuating demand. Advantages and shortcomings of the MTO are similar to the ATO, but with even higher investments in the flexibility and lower inventory.

Engineer-to-order declares the highest degree of customer individualization. An example can be production of an Airbus 380 or house building where customer is involved in the engineering and production processes right from the beginning and can select not only individual components but also materials and designs. ETO is reasonable for complex product of high value where customer individualization is crucial.

Case Study Airbus: Production Strategy and Strategic Supplier Collaboration with the Help of AirSupply
Taking aircraft manufacturing at Airbus as an example, the following case study describes how Airbus implements the ETO production strategy and collaborates with its suppliers using AirSupply. Each time an Airbus aircraft is made, it is the result of assembling a multitude of parts representing a very large volume of orders. And what's true for the Airbus assembly line is true for the whole aerospace industry where not only aircraft but also helicopters and satellites are built. Parts for manufacturing are coming from multiple suppliers from all over the world. Most of them are quite complex and need to fulfill highest quality standards. Each time delay can cause very high costs.

It is essential that all suppliers involved in the manufacture of an aircraft have a real-time visibility of the progress of demand and inventory to adapt to fluctuations and changes of customer requirements. If so, it is essential for customers and suppliers to have a common tool that will enable them to better collaborate and to gain visibility over demand as well as inventory.

In January 2009, EADS decided to initiate the development of a specific Aerospace & Defense industry solution to replace the current company individual SCM solution. EADS is one of the leading Aerospace & Defense companies

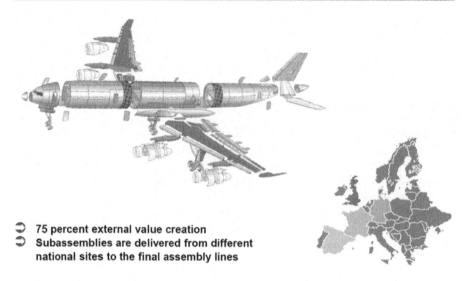

◌ 75 percent external value creation
◌ Subassemblies are delivered from different national sites to the final assembly lines

Fig. 6.5 Modular production strategy (based on SupplyOn video)

worldwide. The range of products includes aircraft from Airbus, helicopters from Eurocopter, and satellites from the Astrium division. Each aircraft is practically one of a kind. One of the reasons why commercial aircrafts are all configured differently is that the ordering airlines want to differentiate themselves from their competitors. The easiest way for passengers to spot these differences is by looking at the seats and entertainment systems.

With 75 %, the value added by external suppliers in aircraft manufacturing is relatively high. A single long-range aircraft is made up of around four million individual parts, supplied by companies of many countries. Even at the final assembly line, workers are putting together components originating in at least four different countries: fuselage sections and the vertical stabilizers come from Germany, the cockpit and central fuselage section from France, the wings from England, and the horizontal stabilizers from Spain (see Fig. 6.5).

Where the engines come from depends on the customer's preference. The task is made even more complex by the generous length of time Airbus gives its customers to submit their final wishes. Including lead-time, manufacturing takes around 2 years, and Airbus accepts customer change requests up to as late as 6 months before delivery (see Fig. 6.6).

Collaboration with suppliers begins only a few months after the order has been received. This is normal for the aerospace industry and is very different to the automotive industry for example. Delivery dates are coordinated with suppliers at weekly intervals, on both the capacity planning and order levels. The production of components begins before the date on which the customer is able to request the last modifications. Final assembly itself takes around 1 month. This intensive process of coordination with suppliers is managed via AirSupply.

6.4 Selection of a Production Strategy

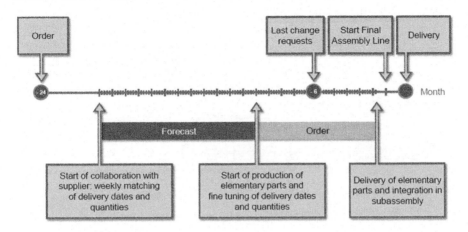

Fig. 6.6 Intense collaboration with suppliers throughout the whole production process of an aircraft

How the collaboration looks like in concrete terms? The first step is calculating future demands via the Airbus ERP system. This always takes place at the weekend. On the following Monday, the Airbus Order Officer checks the generated demand planning (see Fig. 6.7).

The next step is the approval of the requirements planning and transmission to the suppliers via AirSupply. The supplier now checks whether he can provide what is needed by Airbus. If the answer is yes, he sends his confirmation. If the answer is no, he can use AirSupply to propose alternative quantities and delivery dates. The Order Officer at Airbus then checks the supplier's proposal and accepts it. The collaboration process has now been successfully completed and the data is transferred back to the ERP system at Airbus.

It is evident that it would not have been possible to conduct this process by exchanging messages in conventional EDI format. The rules required to logically represent this collaboration are not provided by classical ERP systems. This is why the entire set of logical rules governing collaboration has been moved to the cloud. The ERP systems simply process the results of the collaboration. From the system architecture perspective, the solution is embedded in SupplyOn's cloud infrastructure. This is made up of central components that control registration of companies and users. At the current time, around 8000 companies from over 70 countries are using SupplyOn's solutions.

One of the most remarkable aspects of this project was that it created a solution for the entire European Aerospace &Defence industry and not just for the EADS group. To make this possible, the French aerospace industries association GIFAS formed the BoostAeroSpace initiative. SupplyOn designed the solution together with the lead partner EADS, and the companies Dassault Aviation, Safran and Thales. Up to 150 people were involved in the project in its most intensive phases, working a total of around 10,000 person days. After completion of design,

Collaboration via AirSupply

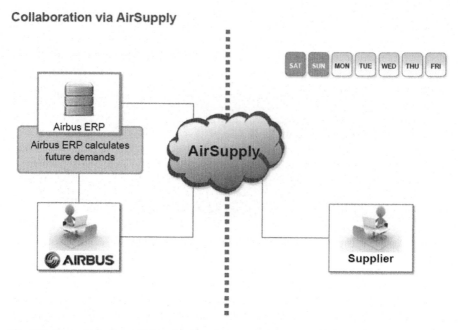

Fig. 6.7 Start of supplier collaboration

development and pilot phase the solution went live end of 2011. Shortly after that the integration of the suppliers began.

The strategic goal of EADS and Airbus is to maintain the competiveness of the European Aerospace & Defense industry in the long term. They are convinced that this can best be achieved by creating a common industry solution together with further leading companies in this sector. It was EADS's ambitious goal to build the best Aerospace & Defense industry SCM solution worldwide. This applies to the functionality of the solution as well as to the underlying business model. EADS and BoostAeroSpace opted for SupplyOn as implementation and operating partner due to its successful track record with a cloud-based solution for the automotive industry. Once AirSupply has been deployed at EADS, BoostAeroSpace partners and further customers, it will establish itself as the industry standard.

Discussion
- What benefits of AirSupply for supplier collaboration can you identify?
- Describe advantages and risks of ETO (engineer-to-order) production strategy!

Summarizing, the basic trade-off in selecting the right production strategy is between investments in flexibility and reduction of costs due to the scale effects or inventory reduction. Total flexibility, inventory, and unit costs should be balanced with customer satisfaction and service level. One possible approach to perform such an analysis is presented in the next paragraph.

6.4.2 Method: Lost-Sales Analysis

This task investigates the issue of how to determine right production strategy and OPP location in the SC. In the proposed model, we consider two strategies:

- MTS and delivering from a general inventory holding unit and
- introducing the MTO agile part downstream the general inventory holding unit.

We assume that the introduction of the agile SC part downstream the OPP leads to an increase in both flexibility and costs. As such, we propose the "lost-sales"-based treatment of the OPP location determination: OPP location can be determined through a comparison of financial results of the two strategies (with and without OPP). With regard to this treatment, a quantitative estimation of the OPP location can be found by relating the above-mentioned strategies to each other, i.e., an OPP location index can be calculated at different stages of the SC according to the model (**6.1**) (Ivanova et al. 2015):

$$D = \frac{R_a \cdot k_a - (C_u^a + C_d^a + P^a + L^a)}{R - (C + k \cdot P + k \cdot L)} \rightarrow \max[t_0; T] \qquad (6.1)$$

where

D is the index to characterize the efficiency of the OPP location,
R is the revenue in case of make-to-stock,
R_a is the revenue in case of introducing the agility part downstream the general inventory holding unit,
C are the SC costs in case of make-to-stock,
C_u^a are the SC costs upstream the OPP in case of introducing the agility part,
C_d^a are the SC costs downstream the OPP in case of introducing the agility part,
P are penalties of not-fulfilled contracts in case of make-to-stock,
P^a are penalties of not-fulfilled contracts in case of introducing the agility part,
L are looses of rejected customer's inquiries in case of make-to-stock,
L^a are looses of rejected customer's inquiries in case of introducing the agility,
k, k_a are correcting coefficients to take into account future increase in sales due to the increase of responsiveness in case of the introducing the agility part,
t is instants of time within the whole SC cycle $[t_0; T]$.

Different OPP locations can be investigated and the best one with the maximum value D > 1 is selected on the basis of the following formula (6.1).

Task 6.1 Selection of an OPP Location
We consider a SC where four potential OPP locations corresponds to the following strategies: MTO—Make-to-Order, ATO—Assembly-to-Order, CTO—Configure-to-Order and MTS—Make-to-Stock (Fig. 6.8).

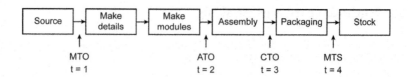

Fig. 6.8 Alternative OPP locations

Table 6.1 Comparison of OPP locations in the SC

t	1	2	3	4
R^a	160	180	200	220
R	220	220	220	220
C_u^a	40	40	40	40
C_d^a	160	160	160	160
C	192	192	192	192
P^a	3.5	3.5	3.5	3.5
P	7	7	7	7
L^a	2.5	2.5	2.5	2.5
L	11.2	11.2	11.2	11.2
k_a, k	1.15	1.15	1.15	1.15
D	−3.111739745	0.141442716	3.394625177	6.647807638

The following data is considered (Table 6.1):

Calculate the indexes D and propose the OPP location. $D_{max} = 6.65$ and corresponds to the OPP at $t = 4$.

Recommend a manufacturing strategy! We recommend to select the MTS strategy as there is no need for any OPP in this SC.

Explain the push/pull view of the processes within a SC.
The push/pull view of the SC divides SC processes into two categories based on whether they are executed in response to a customer order or in anticipation of customer orders. Pull processes are initiated in response to a customer order. Push processes are initiated and performed in anticipation of customer orders. The push/pull boundary separates push processes from pull processes.

Explain the basic trade-off between responsiveness and efficiency of the SCs regarding inventory. The fundamental trade-off when making inventory decisions is between responsiveness and efficiency. Increasing inventory will generally make the SC more responsive to the customer. This choice, however, comes at a cost as the added inventory decreases efficiency. Therefore, an SC manager can use inventory as one of the drivers for reaching the level of responsiveness and efficiency the competitive strategy targets.

Explain the meaning of the coefficients k! k, k_a are correcting coefficients to take into account future increase in sales due to the increase of responsiveness in case of the introducing the agility part.

6.5 Key Points

Customers play more and more important role in the SC. Products become individual and customized. This flexibility creates competitive advantage but is also costly. Right production strategy in the SC can combine advantages of efficient mass production and responsive product customization. The push/pull view of the SC divides SC processes into a downstream part (production in response to a customer order) and upstream part (production in anticipation of customer orders). Pull processes are initiated in response to a customer order. The advantages of the downstream part are responsiveness, and high degree of customer-oriented product individualization. Push processes are initiated and performed in anticipation of customer orders. The advantages of the upstream part are the economy of scale and flexibility (high level of inventory and the short supply times).

The first element of a production strategy from the push-pull point of view is postponement that is an organizational concept whereby some of the activities in the SC are not performed until customer orders are received. Postponement is especially useful for significant number of variants of an end product with an uncertain split of demand on variants. In addition, delivery time requested by customers must allow value-adding steps after receipt of customer orders (or forecast).

The second element of a production strategy is OPP which separates push and pull parts in the SC. In practice, selected postponement strategy determines the OPP location. The further upstream the OPP is located in the SC, the more manufacturing and logistics activities are postponed. In general, the aim is to postpone manufacturing and logistics as much as possible with maintaining high customer service standards.

According to the place of the OPP, the following production strategies can be determined:

- Make-to-stock (MTS)
- Distribute-to-order (DTO)/Configure-to-order (CTO)
- Assemble-to-order (ATO)
- Make-to-order (MTO)
- Engineer-to-order (ETO)

Acknowledgement The case-study is written with permission of SupplyOn and uses the materials and pictures from SupplyOn. We thank Mr. Arvid Holzwarth (MBA) for his help in preparing this case-study.

Bibliography

Alderson W (1950) Marketing efficiency and the principle of postponement. Cost Profit Outlook 3 (4):15–18

Appelfeller W, Buchholz W (2011) Supplier relationship management: strategie, organisation und IT des modernen Beschaffungsmanagements, 2nd edn. Gabler, Wiesbaden

Baldwin CY, Clark KB (1997) Managing in the age of modularity. Harvard Bus Rev 75:84–93
Belson K (23 Sep 2011) Far from the factory, adding final touches. The New York Times. http://www.nytimes.com/2011/09/25/automobiles/far-from-the-factory-adding-final-touches.html?pagewanted=all&_r=0. Accessed 10 May 2014
Bucklin LP (1965) Postponement, speculation, and the structure of distribution channels. J Market Res 2:26–31
Cheng TCE, Li J, Wan CLJ, Wang S (2010) Postponement strategies in supply chain management. International series in operations research and management science, vol 143. Springer, New York
Ernst R, Kamrad B (2000) Evaluation of supply chain structures through modularization and postponement. Eur J Oper Res 124(3):495–510
Gunasekaran A, Laib K-H, Cheng TCE (2008) Responsive supply chain: a competitive strategy in a networked economy. Omega 36(4):549–564
Kagermann H, Osterle H, Jordan JM (2011) IT-driven business models: global case studies in transformation. Wiley, Hoboken
Ivanova M, Kaeschel J, Ivanov D (2015) Analysis of the order recovery point location in the supply chain. Int J Integr Supply Manage 9(4):329–342
Olhager J (2003) Strategic positioning of the order penetration point. Int J Prod Econ 85(3):319–329
Shah J (2009) Supply chain management: text and cases. Pearson, Chennai
van Hoek RI (2001) The rediscovery of postponement a literature review and directions for research. J Oper Manag 19(2):161–184

Reference for Sect. 6.1

Chopra S, Meindl P (2012) Supply chain management: strategy, planning, and operations, 5th edn. Pearson, London
CNN (2013). http://edition.cnn.com/video/data/2.0/video/business/2013/12/13/world-biz--dell-brian-gladden.cnn.html
Dell (2014) http://www.dell.com
Global Integrated Supply Chain System (2006) Successful cases of SCM in China. http://tinyurl.com/p8rhuh8
Hirsh L. (2007) http://www.ecommercetimes.com/story/18779.html
http://www.it-times.de/news/nachricht/datum/2013/06/07/lenovo-eroeffnet-werkshallen-in-den-usa/
San Juan R (2013) http://www.gaebler.com/Dell-Direct-Model-to-Success.htm
Slack N, Brandon-Jones A, Johnston R (2011) Essentials of operations management. Pearson, London
Supply Chain Council (2012) Inside Lenovo's hybrid supply chain strategy. http://supply-chain.org/f/Zapko-Inside_Lenovos_Hybrid_Supply_Chain_Strategy.pdf
www.lenovo.com

Facility Location Planning and Network Design 7

We have already discussed the performance and the success as well as failures of SCs. Now it is time to discuss approaches to creating such a network. In particular, it is necessary to clarify important decisions that must be made in order to finally set up an SC. Such a network setup comprises both decisions about the usage and installation of network nodes (represented by factories and/or warehouses or any other immobile equipment such as supply regions or markets) as well as transportation links connecting different network nodes in order to enable the flow of materials as well as information between these nodes. In order to set up a supply network we have to cope with the challenge that long-lasting SC design (SCD) decisions (with several years of validity) have to be coordinated with mid-term network configuration decisions (commitments for some weeks or months) as well as with operational deployment decisions.

This chapter starts with an outline of a location planning problem in Sect. 7.1. Next, in Sect. 7.2, we analyse different decision tasks in a typical location planning scenario and reveal the interactions between individual decision situations of the three aforementioned categories (long-, mid- as well as short-term planning). The generic decision task regarding which regions should be incorporated into a supply network is addressed in Sect. 7.3. Section 7.4 is dedicated to the identification of explicit location proposals for those regions that contribute to SC cost efficiency. The multiple factor search for the right location for a facility in a region is addressed in Sect. 7.5.

Learning Objectives for This Chapter

- Understand the importance of selecting the right facility locations.
- Describe the main phases of location-related decision-making processes.

Find additional case-studies, Excel spreadsheet templates, and video streams in the *E-Supplement* to this book on www.global-supply-chain-management.de!

- Apply quantitative analysis techniques to solve SCD problems.
- Compute solutions to different settings of the warehouse location problem.
- Compute facility location with the help of Steiner-Weber model.
- Use centre-of-gravity methods and the Miehle algorithm.
- Understand the role of multiple factor analysis in locating facilities.
- Apply factor-ranking method to facility location decisions.

7.1 Introductory Case Study Power Pong Sports, China

In 1856 Alexander Parks produced the first celluloid, a plastic material that can be easily melted and brought into different shapes. Originally, Parks was looking for a material similar to ivory in order to make the production of billiard balls easier and cheaper. In the middle of the twentieth century celluloid was mainly used for film carriers and table tennis balls but it has also been an important ingredient of several explosive materials as well as weapons. It is a very dangerous material since it is harmful and is spontaneously inflammable.

One of the most commonly used products based on celluloid and sold in high quantities all over the world are table tennis balls. The majority of the annual overall production quantity originates from factories in China and Japan. However, table tennis balls are needed all over the world, so that significant quantities are exported. For example, in Germany, more than 20 million table tennis balls are sold annually.

The transporting of large quantities of products containing significant amounts of celluloid falls into the category of transporting dangerous goods. In 2001 a container loaded with 300,000 table tennis balls is reported to have exploded after being heated by the sun. Due to the aforementioned hazards more and more countries have banned celluloid in all forms from production, trading as well as handling. For these reasons, more and more products are replaced by celluloid-free substitutes.

While referring to the ongoing worldwide ban on celluloid, Mr. Adham Sharara, chairman of the International Table Tennis Federation (ITTF), announced in the year 2011 that the ITTF was going to change the international table tennis rules in order to allow the use of table tennis balls made without any celluloid. After that announcement, some manufacturers of table tennis balls started to redesign their corresponding production processes in SCs. It turns out that any waiver of celluloid requires a significant redesign of production processes; and investment into new production facilities as well as production technologies becomes necessary.

One of the major table tennis ball manufacturers is Power Pong Sport (PPS) headquartered in China. The most important markets for PPS in Europe (measured in goods sold) are France (FRA), Germany (GER) and the United Kingdom (UK). All other European countries are grouped into the markets of South-Eastern Europe (SEE), South-Western Europe (SWE) and Northern Europe (NEU). Because of the importance of the first three markets mentioned, PPS has already long-lasting exclusive import contracts with one retailer of sports equipment in France (TriColor Sportive), Germany (TT Profi) and the UK (Competitive Fitness).

7.1 Introductory Case Study Power Pong Sports, China

PPS has decided to build a new factory at Shanghai exclusively for the new table tennis balls manufactured without any celluloid. Mr. Xu Chen is head of the logistics department at PPS and is in charge of new contracts with resellers in Europe in order to supply the European markets with the new celluloid-free table tennis balls. Mr. Chen has already made two significant decisions, subject to PPS's SC strategy:

- A contract made with a European retailer will extend for 1 year in order to ensure that significant quantities can be sold.
- Only the most important markets in Europe will receive deliveries direct from PPS. This contributes to realizing significant economies of scale for the shipment of the table tennis balls from Shanghai to Marseille (TriColor Sportive), Bremerhaven (TT Profi) and Felixstowe (Competitive Fitness) by maritime container transportation in completely filled 20 ft containers.

Having monitored these settings Mr. Chen is now going to identify reasonable ways to ensure that besides the three major markets all European countries will have access to the new PPS balls. The basic idea is that PPS will extend the contracts made with TriColor Sportive, TT Profi and Competitive Fitness and distribute rights among these three resellers to deliver PPS balls into SEE, SWE and NEU countries.

Mr. Chen proposes his idea to the board of managers of PPS and gets a "go ahead", since his idea keeps the SC quite simple. However, Mr. Chen is instructed to keep the annual distribution costs as low as possible. At the same time, his distribution strategy has to ensure that the PPS balls are spread over the complete European market.

As a starting point for cost minimization, Mr. Chen contacts three resellers, invites their representatives to his office and explains his proposal. All three representatives are quite excited. In a few days they get the OK from their management. Contract negotiations are established.

Mr. Chen asks the local representatives of the three resellers to estimate their annual transportation costs from the corresponding warehouse to six markets. Since PPS wants to be the first to distribute celluloid-free table tennis balls in Europe, it will cover all transportation costs for the first-year contract. Table 7.1 contains aggregate costs per 1000 € for the first year. The forwarding costs from the selected European resellers to the rest of Europe are independently costed.

In order to make cooperation attractive for the three resellers PPS pays an annual fixed amount to a reseller used to redistribute balls into other European countries, as shown in Table 7.1. Furthermore, PPS does not allow conflicts of interest between the three indirect markets SEE, SEW and NEU. It guarantees that each of the six aforementioned markets is exclusively assigned to exactly one reseller.

Mr. Chen gets general agreement with the conditions from the three resellers. His next task is to decide about the way(s) in which the PPS balls can reach the six European markets.

Discuss the following issues as well as questions.

Table 7.1 Annual transportation costs between European resellers and markets as well as fixed annual payments to the European resellers (€thousand)

Reseller	Fixed annual costs	All markets					
		j=1 FRA	j=2 GER	j=3 UK	j=4 SEE	j=5 SWE	j=6 NEU
TriColor Sportive (FRA)	95	4	24	12	23	16	19
TT Profi (GER)	90	24	1	19	11	14	13
Competitive Fitness (UK)	70	30	16	3	24	21	17

- Which resellers should PPS use to distribute the celluloid-free table tennis balls over Europe?
- Which reseller(s) respectively should be assigned to SEE, SWE and NEU?
- Is it necessary to use more than one reseller to serve a market?
- What happens if one of the resellers is unable to handle the expected demand from SEE, SWE or NEU?
- Assume that a reseller has to open a new facility to handle the additional demand. Where should this facility be located?
- How can the annual costs be kept as low as possible?

7.2 Supply Chain Design Framework

The core decision to be made in the PPS case was the *selection of markets* (country) in which a base for the PPS operations should be installed. This decision was influenced by previous choices but also influences subsequent decisions. Strategic decisions made by the PPS board regarding the strategy for serving European markets through only a few entry gates were an implication of the strategic position of the PPS SC— to keep distribution costs as low, and as simple, as possible. These board decisions had to be considered by Mr. Chen during the selection of the gateway country being used to deliver PPS balls into the six European markets.

Mr. Chen has to consider these guidelines in order to ensure that the *strategic fit* of the PPS distribution system is achieved and preserved. On the other hand, as soon as the gateway markets have been determined, these decisions are binding and must be considered while making subsequent decisions. For example, if Germany were selected as the unique gateway country to serve the European markets, all transport operations and their planning must consider the available infrastructure, regulations and laws. Selection of the regions (countries) involved in SC operations is therefore an individual decision that is positioned in a sequence of other decision tasks which must be solved in order to set up and use the distribution network as part of the PPS SC.

In Fig. 7.1, a modified Chopra and Meindl (2012) SCD framework is presented in order to arrange all decision tasks required to setup and deploy the SC.

7.2 Supply Chain Design Framework

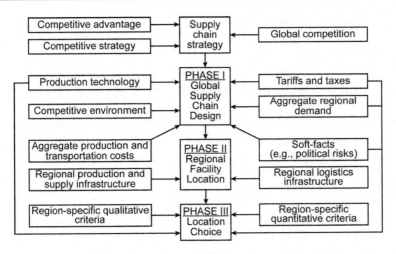

Fig. 7.1 Supply chain design framework (based on Chopra and Meindl 2012)

In this framework, the SC strategy is understood as the first decision phase. We refer to Chap. 4, Supply Chain Strategy, regarding this phase. Phase I addresses the compilation of those sourcing or supply regions/markets which are going to be considered subject to the long-term fulfilment of market demand. Such a region might cover a continent, a country, an area of cultivation or a fishing ground. Also the segmentation of the total (global) market varies from quite local areas to continents. Phase I provides a list of geographic regions that appear to be promising for consideration for setting up the SCD. In addition, suggestions for the installation of transportation links between supply and demand regions are provided by phase I.

In phase II all regions are processed individually. In each region, specific locations (expressed by coordinates) are identified at which a facility can be installed or from which supply quantities can infiltrate the SC. The output of phase II is a short list of candidates for locations (with existing facilities or with prospective facilities) which have been selected with regard to cost efficiency.

In phase III, final selection of the locations that will be considered in the SCD is carried out. Multiple criteria are considered at this stage and the analysis reaches far beyond cost minimization. Furthermore, capacities are allocated at all locations that are considered to contribute to the fulfilment of demand from the markets to be served.

Decisions associated with phases I–III fall into the category of strategic (long-term) SCD decisions. A revision of those decisions is hardly possible or implies significant costs. This chapter addresses these three decision phases of the location planning framework. We discuss and investigate tools to support the SC managers to identify the best decision alternatives. In Sect. 7.3 we introduce the *warehouse location problem* as a representative example of a core decision task in the selection of contributing regions (phase II). Tools for supporting the derivation of adequate location selection decisions are the focus of Sect. 7.4 (phase III). Decisions associated with phase III are considered in Sect. 7.5.

7.3 Global Supply Chain Design

Phase I of the location analysis framework addresses the selection of source regions that are incorporated into the overall SC. From the sourcing regions selected, markets are served so that the overall supply from the different sources covers the demand of each individual market. The PPS case is a typical representation of a phase I decision situation. By means of the PPS case presented in Sect. 7.1 we develop an appropriate mathematical optimization model (Sect. 7.3.1) as the starting point of rational decision making that incorporates computational resources to derive optimal location decisions.

For solving this so-called (uncapacitated) *warehouse location problem* (WLP) we explain the usage of a spreadsheet approach (Sect. 7.3.2) as well as the configuration of a general purpose decision support algorithm called *branch-&-bound* (Sect. 7.3.3). Finally, we investigate the consequences of scarceness, i.e. the limited availability of the quantities offered in source regions, leading to the definition of the *capacitated warehouse location problem* (CWLP). For the CWLP, we also propose an appropriate mathematical optimization model as well as a decision support technique (Sect. 7.3.4).

7.3.1 Warehouse Location Problem and Its Formalization

The case of PPS outlined is a representative example for a frequently appearing decision situation related to the SCD. First, a decision about regions (markets, countries) hosting a facility (factory, warehouse, partner) used as a network node is required ("location decision"). Second, a decision is made as to how those markets are supplied from a region with a facility so that the demand of each market is covered ("supply decision"). Such a problem comprising both location and supply decisions is called a *warehouse location problem* or WLP (Daskin 1995; Drezner 1995; Melo et al. 2009; Askin et al. 2014). The overall goal to be achieved in solving a WLP is to keep the total costs of supplying all regions as low as possible. Therefore, for each region it has to be decided if it is more beneficial to open a facility (creating fixed costs for running the facility) in comparison with using transportation links to supply a region (creating transportation costs).

Let S denote the set of all regions in which a facility/warehouse can be installed or used (e.g. $S = \{GER; FRA; UK\}$) and let M be the set of all markets (e.g. $M = \{GER; FRA; UK; SEE; SWE; NEU\}$). The set $T := S \times M$ contains all possible transportation links between a warehouse region and a market. If a facility is opened in region $s \in S$ then the annual costs rise by the amount f_s. The decision to use the transportation link $(s, m) \in T$ between the facility in region $s \in S$ and the market

7.3 Global Supply Chain Design

$m \in M$ increases the annual costs by the additional amount c_{sm}. Using the aforementioned sets, we are able to present the WLP in a formal way as follows.

First, the *objective function* (7.1) is formulated:

$$Z = \sum_{s \in S} f_s \cdot y_s + \sum_{s \in S} \sum_{m \in M} c_{sm} \cdot x_{sm} \qquad (7.1)$$

The sum of (annual) costs expressed in Eq. (7.1) has to be minimized by varying the values of the *decision variables* y_s as well as x_{sm}. The family y_s of binary decision variables represents the facility opening decisions. All these decision variables are allowed to be set to either 1 ("use this facility") or 0 ("do not use this facility"). Similarly, x_{sm} code the decisions whether to use the transportation links in T between warehouses and markets. Although the two decision categories introduced address different managerial decisions they fall into the same type of decisions: exactly one out of two options must be selected (binary decisions). Therefore, the WLP turns out to be a collection of interdependent binary decisions about the opening of the locations.

Each market has to be served from exactly one facility as is the case in the PPS example. In order to ensure this condition while fixing the values for the x-decision variables it is necessary to ensure that constraint (7.2) is respected.

$$\sum_{s \in S} x_{sm} = 1, \forall m \in M \qquad (7.2)$$

In a case where (7.2) remains unfilled then at least one market in M remains unserved. Since the overall sum of costs for supplying all markets must be minimized every solution in which a market $m \in M$ is connected with two or more facilities implies higher costs and selecting one of these facilities for serving the markets may reduce costs. In summary, in a cost optimal solution of the WLP each market is supplied from exactly one facility $s \in S$.

Obviously, it is useless to install a transport link between market m and facility s if s is not opened, e.g., if we set $x_{sm} = 1$ if, at the same time, $y_s = 0$ then we would end up with a useless and unrealizable solution of the WLP. In order to avoid such a failure, we introduce the constraints (7.3) and (7.4) that couple facility installation with transport link installation decisions and ensure that we install a transport link only if it has been decided to install the origin facility.

$$x_{sm} \leq y_s, \forall s \in S, \forall m \in M \qquad (7.3)$$

$$y_s \in \{0; 1\} \forall s \in S, x_{sm} \in \{0; 1\} \forall (s, m) \in T \qquad (7.4)$$

Using the mathematical model (7.1)–(7.4) we are now ready to state precisely the WLP problem as follows:

It is necessary to minimize the total costs for the installation of facilities and transportation links subject to Eq. (7.1) so that each market is served by exactly one facility (7.2). If we use a facility for supplying a market then this facility must be open *(7.3)*. *Each available facility is either opened or closed and each available transportation link is either used or not (7.4)*.

A pure formalized problem formulation is as follows: "minimize (7.1) while taking into account (7.2)–(7.4). The collection of mathematical expressions (7.1)–(7.4) is a mathematical model for the WLP. This model represents the underlying decision problem in a formal way. A solution to this model comprises a selection of values for each of the y-decision variables as well as each of the x-decision variables. Such a solution is called *feasible*, if and only if all constraints (7.2)–(7.4) are fulfilled, e.g., if the implementation of the selected values for the decision variables leads to logically true statements. Every feasible solution of the proposed WLP-model that leads to a non-dominated objective function value is called an optimal solution of the WLP-model. Such an optimal solution can be used to derive an optimal solution of the underlying real world WLP.

If we want to use the WLP model to represent Mr. Chen's problem in the PPS case, we first have to collect all relevant planning data. The set S of potential regions hosting a facility is compiled as $S = \{\text{GER; FRA; UK}\}$ and the set of markets M equals $\{\text{GER; FRA; UK; SEE; SWE; NEU}\}$. Consequently, the set of transportation links is formed as $T = \{(\text{GER;GER}); (\text{GER;FRA}); (\text{GER;UK}); (\text{GER;SEE}); (\text{GER;SWE}); (\text{GER;NEU});(\text{FRA;GER}); (\text{FRA;FRA}); (\text{FRA;UK}); (\text{FRA;SEE}); (\text{FRA;SWE}); (\text{FRA;NEU}); (\text{UK;GER}); (\text{UK;FRA}); (\text{UK;UK}); (\text{UK;SEE}); (\text{UK;SWE}); (\text{UK;NEU})\}$. The cost coefficients representing the annual running costs for an opened facility are $f_{GER} = 95$, $f_{FRA} = 90$ and $f_{UK} = 70$. Finally, the cost coefficients for the annual distribution costs in Europe are $c_{GER;GER} = 1$; $c_{GER;FRA} = 24$; $c_{GER;UK} = 19$; $c_{GER;SEE} = 11$; $c_{GER;SWE} = 14$; $c_{GER;NEU} = 13$; $c_{FRA;GER} = 24$; $c_{FRA;FRA} = 4$; $c_{FRA;UK} = 12$; $c_{FRA;SEE} = 23$; $c_{FRA;SWE} = 16$; $c_{FRA;NEU} = 19$; $c_{UK;GER} = 16$; $c_{UK;FRA} = 30$; $c_{UK;UK} = 3$; $c_{UK;SEE} = 24$; $c_{UK;SWE} = 21$; $c_{UK;NEU} = 17$.

Mr. Chen puts all the aforementioned data into the general WLP model and obtains the following mathematical optimization model that represents his SCD problem in Europe as mixed integer linear programming (MILP) model by (7.5)–(7.13):

$$\begin{aligned}\text{Minimize } Z = \ & 90y_{GER} + 95y_{FRA} + 70y_{UK} + 1x_{GER;GER} \\ & + 24x_{GER;FRA} + 19x_{GER;UK} + 11x_{GER;SEE} + 14x_{GER;SWE} \\ & + 13x_{GER;NEU} + 24x_{FRA;GER} + 4x_{FRA;FRA} + 12x_{FRA;UK} \\ & + 23x_{FRA;SEE} + 16x_{FRA;SWE} + 19x_{FRA;NEU} + 16x_{UK;GER} \\ & + 30x_{UK;FRA} + 3x_{UK;UK} + 24x_{UK;SEE} + 21x_{UK;SWE} + 17x_{UK;NEU}\end{aligned}$$

(7.5)

So that

$$x_{GER;GER} + x_{FRA;GER} + X_{UK;GER} = 1 \quad (7.6)$$

$$x_{GER;FRA} + x_{FRA;FRA} + X_{UK;FRA} = 1 \quad (7.7)$$

7.3 Global Supply Chain Design

$$x_{GER;UK} + x_{FRA;UK} + x_{UK;UK} = 1 \tag{7.8}$$

$$x_{GER;SEE} + x_{FRA;SEE} + x_{UK;SEE} = 1 \tag{7.9}$$

$$x_{GER;SWE} + x_{FRA;SWE} + x_{UK;SWE} = 1 \tag{7.10}$$

$$x_{GER;NEU} + x_{FRA;NEU} + x_{UK;NEU} = 1 \tag{7.11}$$

$$\begin{aligned}
&x_{GER;GER} \leq y_{GER},\ x_{GER;FRA} \leq y_{GER},\ x_{GER;FRA} \leq y_{GER}, \\
&x_{GER;UK} \leq y_{GER},\ x_{GER;SEE} \leq y_{GER}, x_{GER;SWE} \leq y_{GER}, \\
&x_{GER;NEU} \leq y_{GER}, x_{FRA;GER} \leq y_{FRA}, x_{FRA;FRA} \leq y_{FRA}, \\
&x_{FRA;UK} \leq y_{FRA}, x_{FRA;SEE} \leq y_{FRA},\ x_{FRA;SWE} \leq y_{FRA}, \\
&x_{FRA;NEU} \leq y_{FRA},\ x_{UK;GER} \leq y_{UK},\ x_{UK;FRA} \leq y_{UK}, x_{UK;UK} \leq y_{UK}, \\
&x_{UK;SEE} \leq y_{UK},\ x_{UK;SWE} \leq y_{UK},\ x_{UK;NEU} \leq y_{UK}
\end{aligned} \tag{7.12}$$

$$\begin{aligned}
&y_{GER} \in \{0;1\}, y_{FRA} \in \{0;1\},\ y_{UK} \in \{0;1\},\ x_{GER;GER} \in \{0;1\},\ x_{GER;FRA} \in \{0;1\}, \\
&x_{GER;UK} \in \{0;1\},\ x_{GER;SEE} \in \{0;1\},\ x_{GER;SWE} \in \{0;1\},\ x_{GER;NEU} \in \{0;1\}, \\
&x_{FRA;GER} \in \{0;1\},\ x_{FRA;FRA} \in \{0;1\},\ x_{FRA;UK} \in \{0;1\},\ x_{FRA;SEE} \in \{0;1\}, \\
&x_{FRA;SWE} \in \{0;1\},\ x_{FRA;NEU} \in \{0;1\},\ x_{UK;GER} \in \{0;1\},\ x_{UK;FRA} \in \{0;1\}, \\
&x_{UK;UK} \in \{0;1\},\ x_{UK;SEE} \in \{0;1\},\ x_{UK;SWE} \in \{0;1\},\ x_{UK;NEU} \in \{0;1\}
\end{aligned} \tag{7.13}$$

The fairly small SCD problem in the PPS case is represented by the mathematical model (7.5)–(7.13). Although only three potential facility sites as well as six markets are involved in the problem, the PPS case is quite a complex decision situation and the proposed model is so complex that it is impossible to solve it manually. We need to incorporate the support of a computer system.

7.3.2 A Spreadsheet Approach to the WLP

Even for a rather small WLP case such as the PPS scenario, it is hardly possible to identify a minimal cost instantiation of the y_i- as well as the x_{ij}-values. A spreadsheet calculation schema as shown in Fig. 7.2 is a first step to managing the problem's inherent complexity and to determine the costs of different decisions.

The upper part of this spreadsheet (rows 5–10) contain all relevant problem data, which are the annual fixed costs for each reseller (column C) and also the costs for installing a transportation link from a reseller into a market (column D–column I).

In the middle part of the calculation scheme (row 14–row 19) set-up decisions can be typed in the grey shaded cells. The area covering the cells C17 to C19 is used to code the decisions associated with the incorporation of a reseller. In case that a "1" is inserted then the corresponding reseller is considered, otherwise (if a "0" is typed in) this reseller remains unconsidered. For example, if TriColor Sportive is considered in the PPS European distribution system then cell C17 is filled with "1". Similarly, "1" and "0" values are typed in the cell area D17 to I19 in order to code

	A	B	C	D	E	F	G	H	I
1									
2									
3	PowerPong Sports – Distribution Costs								
4									
5			annual fixed costs	All markets					
6	i	re-sellers		j=1	j=2	j=3	j=4	j=5	j=6
7				FRA	GER	UK	SEE	SWE	NEU
8	1 (FRA)	TriColor Sportive (FRA)	95	4	24	12	23	16	19
9	2 (GER)	TT Profi (GER)	90	24	1	19	11	14	13
10	3 (UK)	Competitive Fitness (UK)	70	30	16	3	24	21	17
11									
12	Decisions about incorporated re-sellers and established delivery links from re-sellers into markets								
13									
14				delivery links (x_{ij})					
15	i	re-sellers	y_i	j=1	j=2	j=3	j=4	j=5	j=6
16				FRA	GER	UK	SEE	SWE	NEU
17	1 (FRA)	TriColor Sportive (FRA)							
18	2 (GER)	TT Profi (GER)							
19	3 (UK)	Competitive Fitness (UK)							
20	number of used sources			0	0	0	0	0	0
21									
22	Cost calculation (all values in thousand EUR)								
23									
24	annual fixed costs from selected re-sellers					0			
25	re-distribution costs					0			
26	total costs					0			

Fig. 7.2 Cost calculation sheet for the PPS-case

the decisions on the installed transportation links from the resellers into the six markets. For each market the number of selected resellers is calculated in row 20.

The costs for a coded collection of decisions are calculated in the lower part of the spreadsheet (row 24–row 26). The corresponding formulas are given in Table 7.2.

Theoretically, one might use the spreadsheet to test every possible combination of "0" and "1" values in the grey shaded cells. Unfortunately, there are $2^{21} = 2,097,152$ different combinations. First, each combination has to be checked for feasibility with respect to the constraints (7.6)–(7.13). Second, for each feasible combination the associated costs have to be calculated using Eq. (7.5). If we assume that these two steps can be executed within 1 s then it takes 2.5 days to find the best feasible solution for the PPS-WLP setting. Therefore, testing all combinations manually is somewhat impractical. Fortunately, spreadsheet calculation tools

7.3 Global Supply Chain Design

Table 7.2 Payments to the European resellers (€thousand)

Cell	Formulas	
F24	=SUMPRODUCT(C17:C19;C8:C10)	Sum of annual fixed costs
F25	=SUMPRODUCT(D17:I19;D8:I10)	Annual link costs
F26	=F24+F25	Total annual costs

(e.g. Microsoft Excel, Open Office) provide special purpose add-ins that assist a human user in testing different combinations. This add-in is called *"Solver"*.

The concept of the solver tool is as follows. The user declares those cells that are variable (here: the grey shaded cells) and the user also declares the cell in which the objective function value is contained (here: cell F26) and then the solver proposes a first set of values and inserts these values tentatively into the variable cells. After this, the solver reads the value in the objective function cell. Using optimization algorithms, the solver is now able to decide if the proposed values form an optimal solution or not. In the first case, the solver returns the current solution proposal by definitively inserting the current values into the variable cells. In the latter case, the solver iterates the recent proposal and re-evaluates this new proposal by reading the updated objective function cell. This iteration is repeated by the solver until an optimal combination of values for the decision variables is found or if it decides that there is no better solution available.

Note: An Excel file pre-configured with the PPS data and a suitable solver configuration can be found in the E-Supplement. The Excel solver is an add-in that comes with each Excel installation. In order to use this add-in it is necessary to activate it before first use. Open Office also includes a solver tool.

Before you can apply the solver add-in to the PPS case it is necessary to execute a careful configuration in order to provide the solver comprehensive problem information, e.g. to hand over the model parameter as well as decision variables to the solver. Figure 7.3 exhibits the necessary parameter settings.

First, the cell that contains the objective function value (or in which the objective function value is calculated) is inserted into the "set objective" input box. Here, cell $F$26 contains the target value that is the subject of optimization.

Second, the optimization goal is specified, e.g. it is established whether the objective function value is going to be minimized or maximized, or if a certain target value must be achieved. In the PPS case the totals calculated in cell $F$26 are minimized.

Third, those fields that should be modified by the solver ("variable cells") must be specified. Here, all cells in the area c17:$I$19 can be varied by the solver. The area $C$17:$C$19 represents the decision variable vector (y_{FRA}, y_{GER}, y_{UJ}) whereas the area $D$17 to $I$19 corresponds to the matrix of the x_{ij}-decision variables.

Fourth, you need to specify the constraints that must be considered/that belong to the model. Constraints are typed in one after another by clicking of the add button in the solver parameter window. Figure 7.4 shows an example of how the constraint $x_{GER;NEU} \leq y_{GER}$ from Eq. (7.12) is specified.

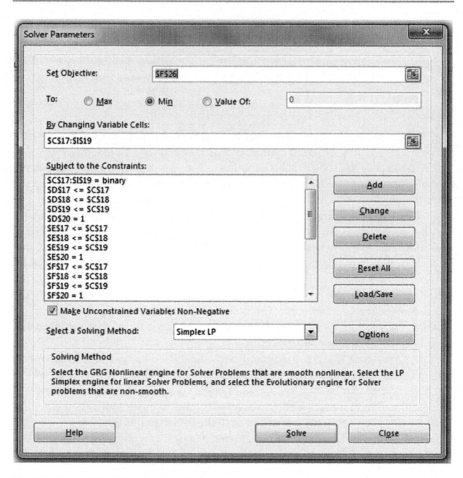

Fig. 7.3 Parameter settings for the solver

Fig. 7.4 Specification of constraints

For the declaration of the constraints (7.2), the solver refers to the cells D20 to I20 where the sum in the left side of Eq. (7.2) is calculated (Fig. 7.5).

If necessary, the decision variable domains must be restricted as shown in Fig. 7.6 for limiting the values of y_i as well as x_{ij} to either 0 or 1.

7.3 Global Supply Chain Design

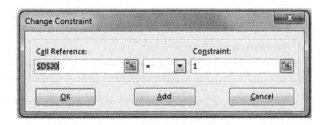

Fig. 7.5 Compilation of constraints

Fig. 7.6 Specification of the decision variable's domains

Finally, it is necessary to specify the optimization algorithm that the solver invokes to solve the specified mathematical model. For the PPS model we select the option simplex algorithm since the model (7.1)–(7.4) consists of a linear objective function and of linear constraints. The solver detects that the decision variables may only be instantiated with the values 0 or 1.

When the five steps mentioned above have been executed, the solving process is initiated by clicking on the "Solve" button. Now the optimization routines start the optimization process and write the final solution proposal into the variable cells.

In Fig. 7.7 the returned values for the PPS case have been written into the variable cells.

The optimal design of the PPS-network in Europe is to agree to the contract with the reseller in Germany ($y_2 = 1$) and to forward balls from Germany into the five remaining markets ($x_{2j} = 1$ for all $j = 1, \ldots, 6$). The annual costs for this design account to 172 TEUR (thousand Euro) p.a. and this sum includes the amount of 80 TEUR paid to TT Profi as a fixed annual amount to cover all the reseller's expenses for handling the intra-European orders, as well as the costs for the transportation links which account for 92 TEUR p.a. This proposal reduces the total annual costs so that Mr. Chen will go on to sign the contract with TT Profi but without signing the contracts with TriColor Sportive in France. Also no contract with Competitive Fitness in the UK will be signed.

From the methodological perspective we conducted three steps consecutively in order to solve the real world decision situation:

- The real world decision situation is coded into a mathematical decision model ("modelling step").
- The formalized decision representation (the mathematical decision model) is processed by an optimization algorithm which returns an optimal solution of the model ("model solving step").

PowerPong Sports – Distribution Costs

i	re-sellers	annual fixed costs	All markets					
			j=1 FRA	j=2 GER	j=3 UK	j=4 SEE	j=5 SWE	j=6 NEU
1 (FRA)	TriColor Sportive (FRA)	95	4	24	12	23	16	19
2 (GER)	TT Profi (GER)	90	24	1	19	11	14	13
3 (UK)	Competitive Fitness (UK)	70	30	16	3	24	21	17

Decisions about incorporated re-sellers and established delivery links from re-sellers into markets

i	re-sellers	y_i	delivery links (x_{ij})					
			j=1 FRA	j=2 GER	j=3 UK	j=4 SEE	j=5 SWE	j=6 NEU
1 (FRA)	TriColor Sportive (FRA)	0	0	0	0	0	0	0
2 (GER)	TT Profi (GER)	1	1	1	1	1	1	1
3 (UK)	Competitive Fitness (UK)	0	0	0	0	0	0	0
number of used sources			1	1	1	1	1	1

Cost calculation (all values in thousand EUR)

annual fixed costs from selected re-sellers	90
re-distribution costs	82
total costs	172

Fig. 7.7 Returned optimal solution for the PPS case

- The model solution is interpreted as a decision proposal for the real world problem ("model solution implementation step").

The problem solving approach reported here is a typical example of a *model-based decision approach*. The major challenge was to represent the WLP situation by a mathematical model. Due to the *linear* structure of the objective function as well as of the constraints we were able to apply a black-box model solving tool to derive the model solution.

Exercise

The management board of directors of PPS has decided to redesign the market segmentation in Europe. The former market region SWE has split into South-Western Europe I (SWE-I) and South-Western Europe II (SWE-II). SWE-I now

7.3 Global Supply Chain Design

demands one third of the former SWE-market. The annual costs for installing a transportation link are split correspondingly between SWE-I and SEW-II. Is it necessary to redesign the network in Europe?

Assume that SWE remains complete. However, due to the recent success of the Portuguese national table tennis teams, the Portuguese market grows rapidly. Situated in this emergent market, an additional potential reseller offers PPS the following conditions for cooperation: Annual costs are fixed at 60,000 € and for each of the six markets equal forwarding costs of 20 € per packaging unit are possible. Is there a benefit for PPS to consider this fourth reseller candidate for its European distribution network?

7.3.3 Branch-&-Bound: How the Solver Add-In Works

So far we have learned how to code a WLP into a mathematical optimization model. Furthermore, we have learned how we can deploy a black-box tool such as Excel Solver to derive a high quality (optimal) solution for the model.

Obviously, the knowledge of an appropriate decision model type is sufficient to solve the real world challenge of the WLP. However, so far, we do not have any knowledge about the way the black-box model solver processes the specified model neither do we have a chance to judge the optimality of the proposed model solution. In this section, we will learn the basic principles of a model solving algorithm that serves as a base for solvers of many kinds of decision models. This technique is called *branch-&-bound* (b&b).

As the name b&b suggests, there are two interdependent activities for processing the model. One activity is to split a problem into smaller problems (*branching*) and the second activity aims at estimating the best objective function value that may be achieved by solving a model of such a specific "branch" of the overall problem (*bounding*).

In this section we explain an efficient branching strategy for a WLP model as well as an efficient bounding scheme to determine a lower bound of the objective function associated with a model for each splitting up of a WLP sub-problem. Although the idea of b&b is applied to a fairly comprehensive collection of decision models for a quite large entirety of decision problems, both the branching strategy as well as the bounding scheme has to be adjusted for any specific model.

Let us start the motivation and explanation of b&b algorithms with a quite simple observation valid for the WLP model of PPS. Independently from the decisions on the reseller selection we can determine the least required transportation linkage costs in the following way. First, select a minimal value in each column associated with a target market in Table 7.1. Second, calculate the sum Z(---) of the six selected values, e.g. $Z(\text{---}) = 4 + 1 + 3 + 11 + 14 + 13 = 46$ TEUR. This value is needed to maintain the distribution network independently from the incorporated resellers. The fact that no reseller is selected is expressed by the three dashes "---" where the first dash represents the selection to incorporate the first reseller ("1") or the decision to refrain from cooperating with the first reseller ("0").

We start the configuration of a b&b algorithm for the WLP with the derivation of an adequate branching strategy. This strategy recursively splits the model M(---) of the given WLP model into two sub-models M(1--) and M(0--).

- In the model M(1--) we add the constraint that the first supplier must be incorporated ($y_1 = 1$).
- In the model M(0--) we postulate the constraint that the first supplier may not be considered ($y_1 = 0$).

Note that no solution of the WLP model remains unconsidered if we handle M(1--) and M(0--) instead of the initial WLP model, since y_1 equals either 1 or 0. However, one might now ask, what is the benefit of dealing with two models instead of one? In order to justify this model split, we analyse the consequences of the model replacement:

The recently generated models M(1--) as well as M(0--) are "smaller" than the original model M(---) since one of three requested decisions has already been made and only two decisions (about the second as well as the third reseller) must be solved.

The cost estimation value Z(1--) associated with M(1--) as well as the cost estimation value Z(0--) associated with M(0--) can be refined compared to the cost estimation Z(---) associated with M(---).

In the sub-problem represented by M(1--) the first reseller is incorporated and therefore the annual fixed cost amount of $f_1 = 95$ TEUR has definitely to be paid, in addition to the least transportation costs Z(---) = 46 TEUR so that we get Z(1--) = 46 TEUR + 95 TEUR = 141 TEUR: each decision alternative in which the first reseller is incorporated ($y_1 = y_{FRA} = 1$) creates annual costs of at least 141 TEUR.

In the sub-problem represented by M(0--) the first reseller is not incorporated. Therefore, no transportation link can originate from this reseller ($x_{ij} = x_{FRAj} = 1$, $\forall j \in \{FRA; GER; UK; SEE; SWE; NEU\}$). In particular, the link FRA to FRA cannot be used. The market FRA must be served from another reseller. Because of this, we cannot consider these transportation links for calculation of the least transport costs among the resellers and the markets. From the remaining links that can be used to serve FRA, we select the cheapest link, which is (GER;FRA). Since the linkage costs $c_{FRA;FRA} = 4$ but $c_{GER;FRA} = 24$, the least transportation cost sum increases by 20 TEUR p.a. so that we have Z(0--) = 46-4+24 = 46+20 = 66 TEUR p.a.

Having generated the two models M(1--) and M(0--) by deciding about the incorporation of reseller 1, we continue with the decision about consideration of reseller 2. Both sub-problems represented by M(1--) as well as M(0--) are therefore split into two smaller problems M(11-) and M(10-), respectively M(01-) and M(00-). Each of these four sub-problems is then split again in order to incorporate reseller 3 into the cost evaluation (Fig. 7.8).

The tree structure of all possible sub-problems in the PPS case is shown in Fig. 7.8. Each node in the tree represents one sub-problem determined by

7.3 Global Supply Chain Design

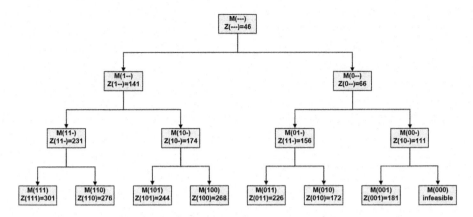

Fig. 7.8 Tree of sub-problems and cost estimations as well as solutions for the PPS case

combinations of involved/rejected/so far undecided resellers. A node represents an incomplete solution of the WLP where at least one reseller remains undecided. A node represents a solution of the WLP if there is a decision made for each reseller. The nodes in the first three upper levels of the tree in Fig. 7.8 represent incomplete solutions but the nodes in the lower level represent the different solutions of the WLP. The solution of the model M(000) is infeasible because no reseller is used and this is impossible. The remaining seven solutions are feasible and the solution of M(010) with the total costs of 172 is the cheapest solution available. Excel Solver has returned the same solution.

Overall, it was necessary to set up and evaluate 15 sub-problems to solve the PPS case. In general, WLPs come along with a significantly larger number of potential locations corresponding to resellers (or suppliers). Let N be the number of supply sources then the number of sub-problems equals $1 + 2 + 2^2 + 2^3 + \ldots + 2^N$. For example, let $N = 5$ then it requires the specification and evaluation (cost estimation) of $1 + 2 + 4 + 8 + 16 + 32 = 63$ sub-problems and if $N = 10$ then the number of sub-problems climbs up to $1 + 2 + 4 + 8 + 16 + 32 + 64 + 128 + 256 + 512 + 1024 = 2047$. The time needed to solve all these sub-problems is prohibitively high. However, we can use the objective function value of the first found solution during a b&b execution to reduce the number of sub-problems that must be set up and evaluated. For this reason, we analyse the sequence in which the sub-problems are generated (Figs. 7.9–7.13).

After the first branching step on the decision about the incorporation of reseller 1 we have two sub-problems. We now select the sub-problem with the lower cost estimation and assume that the first reseller remains unconsidered (Fig. 7.10).

The right-hand sub-problem represented by M(0--) has a lower cost estimation value and will be split up next. For this reason, we generate the sub-problems 01- and 00- and determine the lower bound of the costs (Fig. 7.11).

Figure 7.11 contains the current stage of the decision tree. The right-hand sub-problem represented by M(000) is infeasible but the left-hand sub-problem corresponds to a first complete and feasible solution with costs 181. We set the

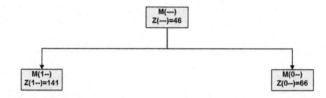

Fig. 7.9 Tree after first branching step

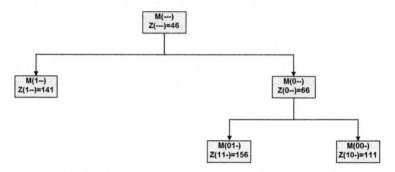

Fig. 7.10 Tree after second branching step

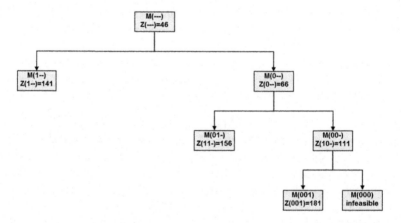

Fig. 7.11 Tree after third branching step

current least cost to $Z^{least}:=181$ TEUR. Since both sub-problems 001 and 000 cannot be split up further, it is necessary to go back to the previous level and to investigate the open sub-problem represented by M(01-). Such a step back into a higher level is called a backtracking step (Fig. 7.12).

After backtracking has been done, we expand the sub-problem 01- and obtain two new solutions for the WLP. The costs from solution 011 account for 226 TEUR and do not improve the least cost Z^{least} of the best solution found so far. Solution 010 creates costs of 172 TEUR which improves Z^{least} so that we may update Z^{least}

7.3 Global Supply Chain Design

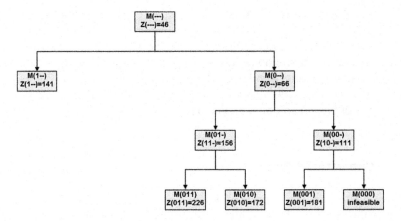

Fig. 7.12 Tree after backtracking and fourth branching step

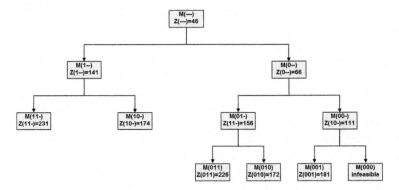

Fig. 7.13 Tree after double backtracking and fifth branching step

and set $Z^{least} := 172$ TEUR, tracking back to level three. Since there are no open sub-problems left in level three which have not been processed we track back into level 2 and process the open sub-problem 1-- (Fig. 7.13).

We generate the sub-problem 11- as well as sub-problem 10- and determine the lower bound of the costs (Fig. 7.13). For both sub-problems, the lower bounds 231 and 174 exceed the costs 172 of the least cost solution found so far. Therefore, it is not necessary to analyse these two sub-problems any further since it is impossible to find an improved solution for the WLP model.

As we see from the final tree in Fig. 7.13 it is not necessary to generate all possible sub-problems if we save the best found solution so far.

▶ **Practical Insights** For small instances, b&b is a suitable method. However, the solution of real-life problems involves a higher complexity. This makes it necessary to solve the WLP by different heuristic methods (offering no guarantee to find the best available solution) rather than exact algorithms. The reason for that is the high number of integer variables. However, heuristic procedures offer no guarantee of finding an optimal solution.

7.3.4 Capacitated WLP

We investigate now the impacts of limited capacities on SCD. Therefore, it is necessary that we know the quantities q_s (s $\in$ S) that can be handled by each reseller per year. Furthermore, in order to assign a sufficient quantity to each reseller we need to have the demand quantity d_m of each market (m $\in$ M). For the PPS case the maximal quantities that can be handled by a reseller are summarized in Table 7.3. Table 7.4 shows the expected annual demand from the six markets. All values are expressed in number of packing units (parcels).

Obviously, there is no reseller solely able to serve the total demand of 23,300 packing units. Therefore, it is necessary that at least two resellers are incorporated. Consequently, at least a second annual fixed handling amount has to be paid. In contrast to the uncapacitated WLP, an optimal solution to the case investigated here, called the CWLP or Capacitated Plant Location Model (CPLM) differs from a WLP solution, because more than one reseller is considered in an optimal solution.

Again, we have to decide about the incorporation of resellers, so the corresponding decision is coded again by the binary decision variables y_s (s $\in$ S). In the WLP we use the binary decision variable family x_{sm} in order to represent decisions about the installation of a transportation link connection supplier (reseller) s with market m. In the context of the CWLP it is also necessary to determine the quantity shipped along a transportation link. Therefore, we use the

Table 7.3 Annual handling quantities (packing units) of the reseller/market

s	q_s
TriColor Sportive (FRA)	20,000
TT Profi (GER)	20,000
Competitive Fitness (UK)	15,000

Table 7.4 Annual demand of six markets packing units

m	d_m
FRA	5000
GER	8500
UK	3200
SEE	2800
SWE	2100
NEU	1700

7.3 Global Supply Chain Design

family of non-negative decision variables z_{sm} in order to represent decisions about the installation and usage of transportation links. If z_{sm} equals 0 then there is no link installed to connect supplier s with market m. If z_{sm} is larger than 0 then the value of z_{sm} is interpreted as the quantity shipped along the transportation link originating from supplier s and terminating in market m.

We have used the annual fixed cost value c_{sm} to determine the annual costs for the incorporation of the transportation link between supply location s and market m. This parameter determines the annual costs for moving the complete demand of the target market m from the supply source s. In the CWLP, we aim at distributing the total demand of a market among different transportation links; it is necessary to know the costs c'_{sm} for moving one package unit along the transportation link, connecting supply source s with market m. We can calculate the values for c'_{sm} from the values contained in Table 7.1. We explain this for an example of the transportation link between the UK reseller and the market SEE. Here, the total costs to deliver the market's demand of 2800 package units are 24,000 € per year, so that each package unit accounts for transportation costs of 24,000 €/2800 package units ≈ 8.57 € for each package unit shipped between the supplier in the UK and the market SEE. Table 7.5 summarizes the shipment costs c'_{sm} per package unit.

Using the transportation cost coefficients per package unit as well as the decision variables z_{sm} for the shipped quantities, we can determine the overall distribution costs Z^{CWLP} per year according to Eq. (7.14).

$$Z^{CWLP} = \sum_{s \in S} f_s \cdot y_s + \sum_{s \in S} \sum_{m \in M} c'_{sm} \cdot z_{sm} \qquad (7.14)$$

Using the flow quantity variables z_{sm}, we can re-formulate the demand covering constraint (7.2) so that a supply of a market from more than one supplier (reseller) also becomes possible [Eq. (7.15)].

$$\sum_{s \in S} z_{sm} \geq d_m, \forall m \in M \qquad (7.15)$$

Similarly, we have to ensure that no supplier (reseller) intends to deliver more quantities to all markets together than the available quantity. Such a constraint is not contained in the model of the uncapacitated WLP. The left side of constraint (7.16) calculates the actual supply quantities delivered from supplier s into all other markets and this quantity must not exceed the available quantity q_s.

Table 7.5 Shipment costs c'_{sm} between European resellers and markets per package unit

Reseller	All markets					
$i = 1, \ldots, 3$	j=1 FRA	j=2 GER	j=3 UK	j=4 SEE	j=5 SWE	j=6 NEU
TriColor Sportive (FRA)	0.80	2.82	3.75	8.21	7.62	11.18
TT Profi (GER)	4.80	0.12	5.94	3.93	6.67	7.65
Competitive Fitness (UK)	6.00	1.88	0.94	8.57	10.00	10.00

$$\sum_{m \in M} z_{sm} \leq q_s, \forall s \in S \qquad (7.16)$$

Again, it is necessary to ensure that a supplier (reseller) s sends out quantities only if this reseller s is unconsidered, i.e. it is necessary to code the implication $z_{sm} \geq 0 \Rightarrow y_s = 1$ in a linear constraint. We can adjust the corresponding constraint (7.3) and obtain constraint (7.17). In this constraint, K represents a "sufficiently large" number, e.g. K can be set to 1,000.000 in the PSS-case scenario. If $z_{sm} > 0$ for a certain market m and if Eq. (7.17) should be valid then it is necessary that $K \cdot y_s > 0$, which is equivalent to the fact that $y_s > 0$ and this means that supplier s is considered. This technique to model logical implications between non-binary and binary decision variables is called the "big-K-method" or "big-M-method". It is necessary to select an appropriate value for K for each scenario that is modelled.

$$\sum_{s \in S} z_{sm} \leq K \cdot y_s, \forall s \in S, \forall m \in M \qquad (7.17)$$

Finally, the domains of the incorporated decision variables are declared by constraint (7.18).

$$y_s \in \{0; 1\} \forall s \in S, z_{sm} \geq 0 \quad \forall (s, m) \in T \qquad (7.18)$$

Using the aforementioned mathematical expressions we are now ready to state the CWLP challenge precisely:

It is necessary to minimize the total costs for the installation of facilities and the shipment of packages as expressed in (7.14), so that the each market's demand is covered (7.15) but no supplier distributes more than its local stock quantity (7.16). If we use a facility for supplying a market then this facility must be open (7.17). Each available facility is either opened or closed and the number of packages to be shipped between each pair of supplier and market must be determined (7.18).

A pure formalized problem formulation of the CWLP is: minimize (7.14) while the constraints (7.15)–(7.18) are respected. Figure 7.14 represents the CWLP problem in Excel spreadsheet form. The necessity to consider the limited availabilities of supply quantities at the different suppliers (resellers) allows the CWLP solving process to become more challenging compared to the solving of the WLP. In particular, it becomes necessary to redefine the components of the b&b algorithm used for the WLP. A major difficulty is to decide whether a sub-problem has a feasible solution, i.e., to find out if suppliers already considered and still untreated can provide enough capacity to cover the demand from all markets. The evaluation of a single sub-problem becomes quite complicated and requires huge computational effort. Therefore, we refer the reader to the scientific literature (Daskin 1995; Drezner 1995; Melo et al. 2009; Benyoucef et al. 2013; Askin et al. 2014) and report only a spreadsheet approach for the CWLP.

Figure 7.14 depicts a spreadsheet model that is used to provide all problem data to the Excel Solver. Special attention is paid to the preparation of the handling of

7.3 Global Supply Chain Design

	A	B	C	D	E	F	G	H	I	J	K	L
2												
3	PowerPong Sports – Distribution Costs, Demand and Availability											
4												
5	Distribution costs per loading unit in EUR											
6			max. handling quantities S_i	annual fixed costs	All markets							
7	i	re-sellers			j=1	j=2	j=3	j=4	j=5	j=6		
8					FRA	GER	UK	SEE	SWE	NEU		
9	1 (FRA)	TriColor Sportive (FRA)	20000	95000	0,80	2,82	3,75	8,21	7,62	11,18		
10	2 (GER)	TT Profi (GER)	20000	90000	4,80	0,12	5,34	3,93	6,67	7,65		
11	3 (UK)	Competitive Fitness (UK)	15000	70000	6,00	1,88	0,34	8,57	10,00	10,00		
12	demanded packages D_j		55000		5000	8500	3200	2800	2100	1700	23300	
13												
14	Decisions about incorporated re-sellers and established delivery links from re-sellers into markets											
15												
16					delivery quantities (z_{ij})							
17	i	re-sellers		y_i	j=1	j=2	j=3	j=4	j=5	j=6	delivered quantities	excess quantities
18					FRA	GER	UK	SEE	SWE	NEU		
19	1 (FRA)	TriColor Sportive (FRA)									0	-20000
20	2 (GER)	TT Profi (GER)									0	-20000
21	3 (UK)	Competitive Fitness (UK)									0	-15000
22	fulfilled demand				0	0	0	0	0	0		
23	uncovered deman				5000	8500	3200	2800	2100	1700		
24												
25	Cost calculation (all values in EUR)											
26												
27	annual fixed costs from selected re-sellers						0					
28	re-distribution costs						0					
29	total costs						0					

Fig. 7.14 A spreadsheet model of the CWLP

the quantity constraints on the maximal supply quantities (7.15) as well as of the least provided quantities to cover the demand of the individual markets (7.16).

The upper part of the spreadsheet from row 1 to row 12 contains the problem parameter now including the locally available stock (column C) as well as the demand expressed from the individual markets (row 12). The cost matrix (E9:J11) contains the costs for shipping a single package unit instead of the annual costs for serving a complete market (the annual costs for the installation of a transportation link in the WLP).

The middle part of the spreadsheet from row 14 to row 23 contains the variable cells (D19:J21). In addition, we calculate the fulfilled demand (row 22) as well as the open (uncovered) demand for each market (row 23). The last mentioned values are used later in the formulation of the constraints propagated towards the solver. Furthermore, we can calculate the total sum of deliveries from each supplier (column K) as well as the excess of local stock (column L). We are going to incorporate the stock excess values into the constraints. The lower part of the spreadsheet contains the costs calculated from the parameters as well as from the variable cells (rows 27–29).

In Figs. 7.15, 7.16, 7.17, and 7.18, we describe the building of the constraint system [Eqs. (7.15–7.18)] for CWLP.

Fig. 7.15 Representation of the demand covering constraint (7.15) in the Excel Solver add-in

Fig. 7.16 Representation of the limited stock constraint (7.16) in the Excel Solver add-in

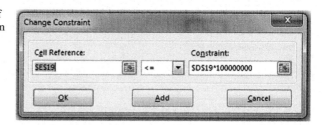

Fig. 7.17 Representation of the constraint family (7.17) in the Excel Solver add-in

Fig. 7.18 Representation of the constraint family (7.18) in the Excel Solver add-in

According to the constraint shown in Fig. 7.15 we enforce the solver add-in to avoid uncovered demand. According to the constraint shown in Fig. 7.16, the solver add-in is instructed to prevent any excess of stock at the suppliers. The Big-K-method to represent the logical dependencies between the usage of a supplier and the delivery quantities coded in constraint (7.17) is shown in Fig. 7.17, where $K = 1,000,000,000$. Finally, Fig. 7.18 shows the domain specification for the shipped quantities represented by the decision variable family z_{sm}. In Fig. 7.19, the solution to CWLP is presented.

In order to test this model, we first use it to solve the WLP scenario. We assumed that each supplier (reseller) is able to handle the overall demand from all markets.

7.3 Global Supply Chain Design

	A	B	C	D	E	F	G	H	I	J	K	L
2												
3	PowerPong Sports – Distribution Costs, Demand and Availability											
4												
5	Distribution costs per loading unit in EUR											
6			max. handling quantities S_i	annual fixed costs	All markets							
7	i	re-sellers			j=1	j=2	j=3	j=4	j=5	j=6		
8					FRA	GER	UK	SEE	SWE	NEU		
9	1 (FRA)	TriColor Sportive (FRA)	25000	95000	0,80	2,92	3,75	8,21	7,62	11,18		
10	2 (GER)	TT Profi (GER)	25000	90000	4,80	0,12	5,94	3,93	6,67	7,65		
11	3 (UK)	Competitive Fitness (UK)	25000	70000	6,00	1,88	0,94	8,57	10,00	10,00		
12	demanded packages D_j		75000		5000	8500	3200	2800	2100	1700	23300	
13												
14	Decisions about incorporated re-sellers and established delivery links from re-sellers into markets											
15												
16					delivery quantities (z_{ij})							
17	i	re-sellers		y_i	j=1	j=2	j=3	j=4	j=5	j=6	delivered quantities	excess quantities
18					FRA	GER	UK	SEE	SWE	NEU		
19	1 (FRA)	TriColor Sportive (FRA)		0	0	0	0	0	0	0	0	-25000
20	2 (GER)	TT Profi (GER)		1	5000	8500	3200	2800	2100	1700	23300	-1700
21	3 (UK)	Competitive Fitness (UK)		0	0	0	0	0	0	0	0	-25000
22	fulfilled demand				5000	8500	3200	2800	2100	1700		
23	uncovered deman				0	0	0	0	0	0		
24												
25	Cost calculation (all values in EUR)											
26												
27	annual fixed costs from selected re-sellers						90000					
28	re-distribution costs						82000					
29	total costs						172000					

Fig. 7.19 Returned optimal solution to the CWLP scenario in the PPS case

Sufficiently high quantities of stock have been specified in the cells C9, C10 and C11. The returned optimal solution is the same as shown in Fig. 7.7. Only reseller #2 is used and the total costs equal 172,000 €.

In the second experiment, we limit the stock size (max. handling quantity for each reseller) by the values compiled in Table 7.3. The optimal solution is shown in Fig. 7.20.

In this case it is necessary to consider a second reseller since TT Profi is unable to handle to total annual demand of the six markets. In the new solution, the model suggests also considering reseller #3. It contributes 100 packages for delivery to market FRA and fulfils the completed UK market demand. The total costs have increased from 172,000 € to 226,120 €. This is an increase of 54,120 €. The consideration of the second reseller creates 70,000 € costs per year. Furthermore, the limited handling quantity requires the inclusion of the UK to save the GER market at increased transportation costs of 120 € but we can profit from cheaper transportation costs into the UK which saves 16,000 €. Therefore, we obtain a total saving of 16,000 €−120 € = 15,880 € of shipment costs but we have to pay an additional 70,000 € annual fixed charges to the second reseller.

	A	B	C	D	E	F	G	H	I	J	K	L
2												
3	PowerPong Sports – Distribution Costs, Demand and Availability											
4												
5	Distribution costs per loading unit in EUR											
6			max.	annual fixed costs	All markets							
7	i	re-sellers	handling quantities S_i		j=1	j=2	j=3	j=4	j=5	j=6		
8					FRA	GER	UK	SEE	SWE	NEU		
9	1 (FRA)	TriColor Sportive (FRA)	20000	95000	0,80	2,82	3,75	8,21	7,62	11,18		
10	2 (GER)	TT Profi (GER)	20000	90000	4,80	0,12	5,94	3,93	6,87	7,65		
11	3 (UK)	Competitive Fitness (UK)	15000	70000	6,00	1,88	0,94	8,57	10,00	10,00		
12	demanded packages D_j		55000		5000	8500	3200	2800	2100	1700	23300	
13												
14	Decisions about incorporated re-sellers and established delivery links from re-sellers into markets											
15												
16					delivery quantities (z_{ij})							
17	i	re-sellers	y_i		j=1	j=2	j=3	j=4	j=5	j=6	delivered quantities	excess quantities
18					FRA	GER	UK	SEE	SWE	NEU		
19	1 (FRA)	TriColor Sportive (FRA)	0		0	0	0	0	0	0	0	-20000
20	2 (GER)	TT Profi (GER)	1		4900	8500	0	2800	2100	1700	20000	0
21	3 (UK)	Competitive Fitness (UK)	1		100	0	3200	0	0	0	3300	-11700
22	fulfilled demand				5000	8500	3200	2800	2100	1700		
23	uncovered demand				0	0	0	0	0	0		
24												
25	Cost calculation (all values in EUR)											
26												
27	annual fixed costs from selected re-sellers						160000					
28	re-distribution costs						66120					
29	total costs						226120					

Fig. 7.20 Returned optimal solution for the CWLP scenario in the PPS case

7.4 Regional Facility Location

The WLP-based approach supports the identification of regions that should be considered for setting up an SC. These regions might be continents, countries, states or even farms or growing areas or plantations supplying or consuming products. According to the location planning scheme outlined in Sect. 7.2, the outcome of phase I (the regions to be considered in the prospective SCD) are forwarded into phase II where one or several locations have to be identified for each region as network node.

In the context of the PPS case the regions are the countries that host the resellers or the markets. A typical phase II decision is now to select a warehouse to which the packages are shipped from China and from where customers in the market receive their deliveries. We can now assume that the regional reseller's existing facilities are too small to handle the additional freight flow associated with the celluloid-free balls and the reseller is looking for a new location in the associated country to build or rent a new warehouse. This section addresses the particular problem of identifying promising candidates for establishing a new facility that can handle incoming and outgoing materials as part of the global SC. In particular, we will

7.4 Regional Facility Location

- become familiar with typical phase II decision problems related to location planning
- introduce a simple model of *centre-of-gravity* representing a phase II decision situation
- develop simple mathematical calculations for the identification and determination of the coordinates of an optimal location
- consider available demand knowledge while deriving such an optimal location by solving the so-called Steiner-Weber model
- learn how the *Miehle algorithm* can be used to solve the *Steiner-Weber model*.

We start in Sect. 7.4.1 with the verbal description of the typical phase II decision problem. Next, in Sect. 7.4.2, we propose a modelling approach for a phase II decision problem. In Sect. 7.4.3, we discuss a mathematical calculus for the derivation of the optimal solution of the location model.

7.4.1 Management Problem Description

We consider the phase II decision situation of TT Profi, the German reseller selected by PPS as part of its global SC. TT Profi is looking for a new warehouse in Germany to receive the inbound material flow from the PPS factory in Shanghai. From this facility the five major local retail partners in Germany, shown in Table 7.6, receive their deliveries.

Each delivery is executed by a small forwarding company which is paid according to the distance between the pickup point and the delivery point of a shipment. In order to keep the distribution costs as low as possible TT Profi wants to open its new warehouse at a location that leads to the smallest annual transportation distance to be bridged. The chairman of TT Profi wants to know at which coordinates the new warehouse should be placed in order to minimize total transportation costs from the warehouse to all customers.

7.4.2 A Mathematical Model of the Decision Situation

All relevant issues in this decision problem are customer locations, distances from the warehouse to customers, and customer demands. Each customer location is

Table 7.6 German customers of TT Profi

i	Name	Coordinates x_i	y_i	Annual demand $D(x_i; y_i)$
1	Sport 1-2-3 KG	10	−80	3 t
2	TT direct	−45	−30	1 t
3	Sports and fun	60	50	1.5 t
4	Leisure outlet	45	−75	3.5 t
5	Raquets & more	−75	80	2 t

represented by the ordered pair of (x;y)-coordinates. The (x;y)-coordinates of the five locations are given in the third as well as fourth column of Table 7.6. These data cannot be modified; they are input data or problem *parameters*. The coordinates of customer *i* are named $(x_i;y_i)$, e.g. $(x_1;y_1) = (10;-80)$ and so on. Demand for each customer is also given and denoted as $D(x_i;y_i)$.

In contrast, the (x;y)-coordinates $(p_x;p_y)$ of the new warehouse are variable and have to be determined. Consequently, p_x as well as p_y are the *decision variables* in the investigated decision scenario.

We *assume* that the total transportation cost sum is proportional to the distance and the transportation volume (i.e., the demand). This leads us to the formulation of *objective function* as Eq. (7.19):

$$Z(p_x;p_y) = \sum_{i-1}^{N} d\big((p_x,p_y);(x_i,y_i)\big) \cdot D(x_i,y_i) \to \min \qquad (7.19)$$

We can observe that the total transportation costs depend on the coordinates p_x and p_y of the prospective warehouses and distances. We assume that total transportation cost sum from the prospective warehouse location $(p_x;p_y)$ to a customer location $(x_i;y_i)$ is more or less equivalent to the distance and demand. Therefore, the distance $d((p_x;p_y); (x_i;y_i))$ between the *i*-th customer location and the warehouse should be determined in order to calculate transportation costs.

In order to minimize the payments to the forwarding company it is necessary to vary p_x as well as p_y as long as $Z(p_x;p_y)$ becomes minimal. The minimization of (7.19) represents the decision situation to identify the lowest cost facility for TT Profi, so that it can be understood as a model for the decision situation outlined in Sect. 7.4.1.

7.4.3 Solving the Mathematical Model: Centre-of-Gravity Approach

We call each pair $(p_x;p_y)$ that minimizes (7.19) an optimal solution of the model (7.19). Since there are no further limitations to be considered that restrict the selection of values of p_x or p_y, the decision problem represented by (7.19) falls into the category of *global optimization* problems. All possible values of p_x and p_y represent a feasible solution of (7.19) and are therefore candidates to become the optimal solution.

There are two options for calculating the distances. The first option is to use *direct line distance* (Euclidean distance) and the second one is the *orthographic (square)* distance calculation. According to the first option, distance equals the Euclidean distance between these two points in the plane. This value can be determined according to Pythagoras' Theorem leading to Eq. (7.20).

7.4 Regional Facility Location

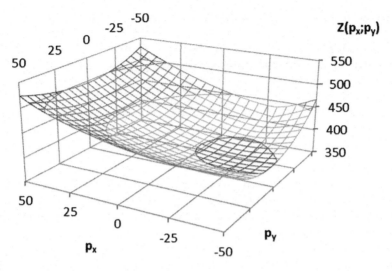

Fig. 7.21 Total distance to all customers (objective function value) in dependence of the values of p_x as well as p_y (all values given in kilometres)

$$d\big((p_x;p_y);(x_i;y_i)\big) = \sqrt{(x_i - p_x)^2 + (y_i - p_y)^2} \qquad (7.20)$$

Figure 7.21 depicts the total distance from the warehouse to all customers in dependence of the warehouse coordinates $(p_x;p_y)$ (*without demand considerations*). We observe that the function Z shows exactly one minimum, that means there is exactly one pair $(p_x;p_y)$ that minimizes Z. Reading the exact values of this optimal pair is hardly possible. Furthermore, if the number of customers N is quite high then drawing a similar picture requires huge computational efforts. For these reasons, a quicker and more reliable method for the determination of the pair of optimal warehouse coordinates is required.

The function Z is continuous and differentiable and the decision variables are unrestricted. Hence, we can determine the optimal point of Z by differential calculus. The following consecutive steps have to be executed in the given order.

(i) The first derivative Z' of Z is determined and
(ii) The zero of Z' is determined.

$$\frac{dZ}{dp_x} = \frac{Np_x}{\sqrt{(x_i - p_x)^2 + (y_i - p_y)^2}} - \sum_{i=1}^{N} \frac{x_i}{\sqrt{(x_i - p_x)^2 + (y_i - p_y)^2}} \qquad (7.21)$$

$$\frac{dZ}{dp_y} = \frac{Np_y}{\sqrt{(x_i - p_x)^2 + (y_i - p_y)^2}} - \sum_{i=1}^{N} \frac{y_i}{\sqrt{(x_i - p_x)^2 + (y_i - p_y)^2}} \qquad (7.22)$$

We start with the situation in which we do not consider individual demand, i.e. $D(x_i;y_i) = 1$ for all i. Since Z is a function of the two decision variables p_x as well as p_y the derivative Z' consists of the two partial derivatives (7.21) and (7.22). They can be determined by considering p_y respectively p_x as invariant.

$$p_x = \frac{\sum_{i=1}^{N} x_i}{N} \qquad (7.23)$$

$$p_y = \frac{\sum_{i=1}^{N} y_i}{N} \qquad (7.24)$$

Setting the right-hand part of Eq. (7.21) equal to 0 leads to the formula (7.23) and setting the right-hand side of Eq. (7.22) equal to 0 gives the formula (7.24). These two formulas (7.23) and (7.24) can be used to determine the optimal values of the coordinates of the warehouse.

Application of the developed formulas determines the optimal location of the warehouse for TT Profi. We get the optimal coordinates $p_x = \frac{10-45+60+45}{5} = -1$ and $p_y = \frac{-80-80+50-75+80}{5} = -11$. Using these two formulas enables us to derive an optimal solution of the model (7.19) (without demand considerations) from the problem parameters provided.

We now incorporate the *demand* associated with each customer subject of the model (7.19). This is necessary since a forwarding company is typically paid according to the bridged distance but also to the quantity moved. The product of distance (measured in km) and weight (measured in tons) is called the transport performance. It is expressed in ton kilometres (tkm).

The model (7.19) is called the *centre-of-gravity model* of location analysis (Chopra and Meindl 2012) or the *Steiner-Weber model* (Domschke and Drexl 1985). Using demand data, formulas (7.25) and (7.26) are used to calculate optimal coordinates.

direct line method.

$$p_x = \frac{\sum_{j=1}^{N} \frac{D(x_j;y_j) \cdot x_j}{\sqrt{(p_x-x_j)^2 + (p_y-y_j)^2}}}{\sum_{j=1}^{N} \frac{D(x_j;y_j)}{\sqrt{(p_x-x_j)^2 + (p_y-y_j)^2}}} \qquad (7.25)$$

$$p_y = \frac{\sum_{j=1}^{N} \frac{D(x_j;y_j) \cdot y_j}{\sqrt{(p_x-x_j)^2 + (p_y-y_j)^2}}}{\sum_{j=1}^{N} \frac{D(x_j;y_j)}{\sqrt{(p_x-x_j)^2 + (p_y-y_j)^2}}} \qquad (7.26)$$

The determination of an optimal pair of coordinates for the warehouse again requires the determination of the directional derivatives. These two functions are then set equal to 0 and we get the expressions (7.25) and (7.26) respectively to express p_x and p_y. Unfortunately, these characterizations of p_x and p_y are recursive,

7.4 Regional Facility Location

which means that we need p_x (on the right-hand side of the equation) to calculate p_x. The same problem is observed for the determination of p_y. It is impossible to transform the two equations so that the recursion is avoided. We cannot determine the values of $(p_x;p_y)$ as we did in the case without demand data. Another approach is required.

In order to break the circulation in the formulas (7.25) and (7.26), Miehle (1958) proposes an approximation approach. The basic idea of the *Miehle algorithm* comprises the consecutive calculation of a sequence of solutions $(a_0;b_0)$, $(a_1;b_1)$, $(a_2;b_2)$, ... of (7.19). The values of $(a_{i-1};b_{i-1})$ are used as p_x- and p_y-values in the right-hand part of the Eqs. (7.25) and (7.26) and they are used to calculate the next solution $(a_i;b_i)$. This approach represents an example of a recursive calculation. If we calculate the coordinate pairs in this way then the sequence of objective function values $Z(a_0;b_0)$, $Z(a_1;b_1)$, $Z(a_2;b_2)$, ... is decreasing and converges towards the minimal possible performance value. Therefore, the sequence of calculated coordinates approximates the optimal pair of coordinates of the new warehouse with respect to the minimization of the overall required transport performance.

We demonstrate the application of the Miehle algorithm and apply it to the example data given in Table 7.6. Ignoring customer demand we can determine a first coordinate pair $(a_0;b_0)$ by means of the application of the formulas (7.23)–(7.24) so that we start with $(a_0;b_0) := (-1;-11)$. The required performance is $Z(-1;11) = 89{,}738$ tkm.

If we set $p_x = a_0 = -1$ and $p_y = b_0 = -11$ in the right-hand sides of (7.25) and (7.26) then we get the updated solution $(a_1;b_1) = (8{,}78;-36{,}16)$ with a reduced required performance value $Z(8{,}78;-36{,}16) = 80{,}837$ tkm. The next iterations are repeated similarly and an existing solution is replaced by an updated one, re-applying the formulas (7.25) and (7.26) (see Table 7.7).

Unfortunately, there is no guarantee that the iterative process terminates after a particular number of repetitions. For this reason, we stop the solution update as soon as we observe that the original solution $(a_i;b_i)$ and its update $(a_{i+1};b_{i+1})$ have become similar. Here, we call two solutions similar if the distance between the

Table 7.7 Iterations of the Miehle algorithm applied to the TT Profi data

Iteration	Old solution		Updated solution			Costs
i	a_i	b_i	a_{i+1}	b_{i+1}	Distance	$Z(a_i;b_i)$
0	−1.00	−11.00	8.78	−36.16	26.99	897.38
1	8.78	−36.16	14.69	−50.10	15.14	808.37
2	14.69	−50.10	18.05	−58.14	8.71	771.93
3	18.05	−58.14	19.64	−62.48	4.62	757.29
4	19.64	−62.48	20.28	−64.57	2.18	752.67
5	20.28	−64.57	20.49	−65.48	0.94	751.58
6	20.49	−65.48	20.53	−65.87	0.39	751.37
7	20.53	−65.87	20.52	−66.03	0.16	751.33
8	20.52	−66.03	20.50	−66.10	0.07	751.32
9	20.50	−66.10	20.49	−66.14	0.04	751.32

two represented points is less than 0.05 km. In the TT Profi example, we stop the Miehle algorithm after ten iterations since the tenth solution proposal (20.50;−66.10) and its update (20.49;−66.14) are less than 0.05 km away from each other (column 6 in Table 7.7). Letting the coordinates for the warehouse be (20.49;+66.14), the total transportation cost is 751.32 € subject to (7.19).

We have seen in the example application of the Miehle algorithm that the Z-objective function value decreases after each executed update and the original point and its update become more and more similar. Now, we summarize the steps of the Miehle approach:

Start: determine an initial pair of coordinates $(a_0;b_0)$ by applying (7.21) to determine a_0 and (7.22) for determining b_0.

Iteration: as long as the distance between the point $(a_i;b_i)$ and its update $(a_{i+1}; b_{i+1})$ exceeds a given threshold then start another update cycle. Otherwise return $(a_{i+1};b_{i+1})$ as approximation of the (unknown) optimal solution of the gravity-location model (7.19).

The evolution of the intermediate solutions during the execution of the Miehle algorithm is shown in Fig. 7.22. We can observe that the original proposal (the dark triangle) is far away from the final proposal (the diamond). Since Leisure Outlet

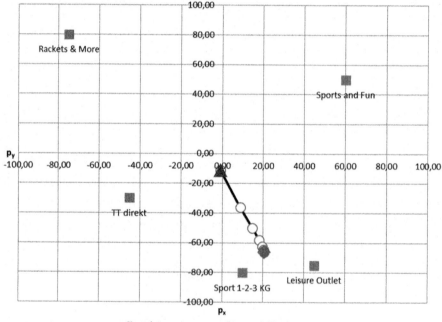

Fig. 7.22 Graphic representation of the progress of the Miehle algorithm

7.4 Regional Facility Location

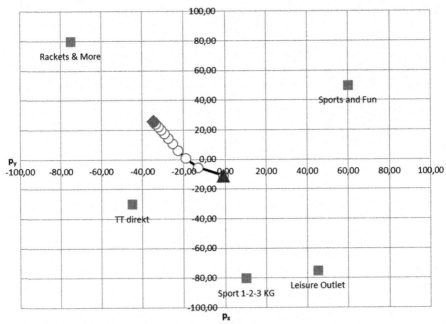

Fig. 7.23 Graphic representation of the progress of the Miehle algorithm if Rackets & More should demand 8 tons

requests the largest quantity from TT Profi it is reasonable to position the warehouse close to this important customer.

If the customer Rackets & More increases its annual demand quantity up to 8 tons, then it is beneficial to place the new warehouse in the upper left-hand area of the operations field. This shows that the selection of the right warehouse location is responsive to the demand data. It is therefore very important to take trustworthy and stable demand estimations for selecting the right warehouse (see Fig. 7.23).

Note: An Excel file containing a spreadsheet model of the Miehle approach to the TT Profi setting can be found in the E-Supplement.

In a second option for distance calculation, we use the formula (7.27), followed by (7.28)–(7.29) to determine $p_x; p_y$:

$$d((p_x; p_y); (x_i; y_i)) = |x_i - p_x| + |y_i - p_y| \qquad (7.27)$$

Table 7.8 German customers of TT Profi

i	Name	Coordinates		Distances from (8,25; −29,75)	Demand
		x_i	y_i	$d(x_i;y_i)$	D_i
1	Sport 1-2-3 KG	10	−80	52	3 t
2	TT direct	−45	−30	37	1 t
3	Sports and Fun	60	50	72	1.5 t
4	Leisure Outlet	45	−75	82	3.5 t
5	Racquets & More	−75	80	117	2 t

$$p_x = \frac{\sum_{i=1}^{N} D_i \cdot x_i}{\sum_{i=1}^{N} D_i} \quad (7.28)$$

$$p_y = \frac{\sum_{i=1}^{N} D_i \cdot y_i}{\sum_{i=1}^{N} D_i} \quad (7.29)$$

Using data from Table 7.6, we get $p_x = \frac{30-40+90+157.5-150}{10} = 8.25$ and $p_y = \frac{-240-30+75-262.5+160}{10} = -29.75$.

The calculation of distances is shown in Table 7.8.

Subject to Eq. (7.19), total cost is calculated as follows:

$$Z = 52 \cdot 3 + 37 \cdot 1 + 72 \cdot 1.5 + 82 \cdot 3.5 + 117 \cdot 2 = 822 €$$

We can observe that total costs in the second case are higher than the result of the Miehle algorithm. This can first be explained by the larger distances in the square method compared to the Euclidian distances. Second, we used a simplified procedure for coordinate calculations without improving them with the Miehle algorithm. Using the Excel file in the E-Supplement to this book, you can prove that letting initial coordinates from Table 7.7 be (8.25;−29.75), then the Miehle algorithm would provide the same coordinate solution as for the initial case with coordinates (-1;−11). Setting these optimal coordinates (20.49;−66.14) into (7.19) and using square distance metrics, calculate total transportation costs and compare to the solution with Euclidian distances!

7.5 Factor-Ranking Analysis

7.5.1 Case-Study OTLG Germany

Volkswagen Original Teile Logistik GmbH & Co. KG (OTLG) is a service partner for spare parts of Volkswagen, Volkswagen Nutzfahrzeuge, Audi, Seat and Škoda. OTLG is the wholesale level in the SC and responsible for sales and marketing in Germany. At present, OTLG operates in seven locations in Germany.

The company's annual revenue is almost 2.5 billion euros; it serves almost 5000 partners in Germany and occupies a total warehouse area of more than 300,000 m^2 (equivalent to 47 football pitches). Annually 45,000,000 materials call-off, pick-up and delivery actions take place, corresponding to approximately 200,000 daily operations.

During the logistics optimization project DNO D (distribution network optimization), OTLG's distribution network was redesigned. Eleven distribution centres (DC) were consolidated into eight as shown in Fig. 7.24.

Among them, a new DC VZ Brandenburg in Ludwigsfelde, was established (see Fig. 7.25). The first step consisted of selecting a location for the new DC. Initially, many potential locations and selection criteria were identified, as shown in Fig. 7.26. Next, a short list of favoured locations was established (Fig. 7.27).

After evaluation, the location Preußenpark was selected because it had the best scores for the listed criteria. In Fig. 7.28, the new DC is shown.

First, excellent rail and road connections favoured the selected location. These criteria are crucial for OTLG because of highly dynamic logistics. Daily, 250 trucks are used for regular supplies and 200 small vans are used for day-to-day supplies. This ensures that 98 % of orders are fulfilled within 24 h. The total SKU number reaches almost 100,000 positions with an inventory value of 43.2 million euros. Daily, in excess of 30,000 positions are delivered, making it possible to supply 402 VW/Audi and 476 SEAT/Škoda customers with original spare parts.

Discussion
1. Analyse the redesign of the OTLG distribution network. Which type of logistics network has been implemented? What could be the reasons for looking for a new location in Brandenburg?
2. Describe on the basis of this case study example the basic steps in facility selection decisions! Why were the logistics criteria so important for OTLG? Which criteria would be important, e.g., for the case of a new hotel?

7.5.2 Factor-Rating Method

Having seen how OTLG GmbH & Co. KG has conducted the analysis to identify the right location for their distribution centre, we need to take a deeper look into the related decision criteria and decision-making procedure. The OTLG case study has demonstrated that the region around Berlin in combination with an excellent

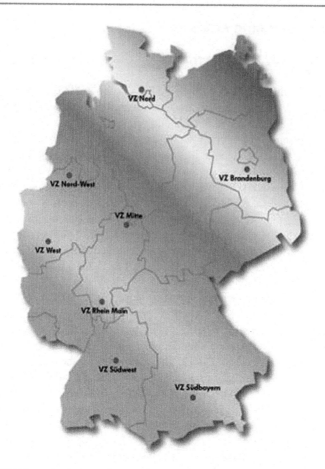

Fig. 7.24 OTLG footprint in Germany (© OTLG GmbH & Co. KG)

infrastructure (road/rail connection) highly influenced their particular decision. In other words, the availability of infrastructure was the factor with the highest priority for OTLG GmbH & Co. KG.

As you can imagine, not all companies will rate the criterion "infrastructure" as the most important one, as they will prioritize other factors to decide upon a location. That means that different companies will select different location criteria or location factors which have different priorities. Therefore we need to take a closer look at the generic list of possible *plant location criteria*.

Location criteria can be divided into *quantitative* and *qualitative* areas which are summarized in Table 7.9.

7.5 Factor-Ranking Analysis

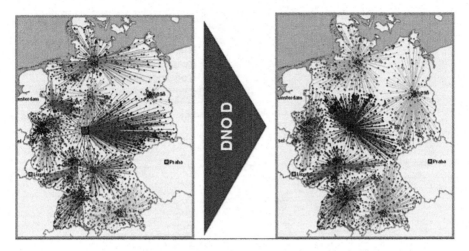

Fig. 7.25 Distribution network re-design at OTLG (© OTLG GmbH & Co. KG)

> **Practical Insights** In practice, the list of location selection criteria is the first step in facility location planning. On the one hand, this list can very quickly become quite long. That is why it is a common practice to build main and sub-groups of criteria to facilitate a clear understanding of the list structure. On the other hand, many experts from different departments are involved with setting up this list. It may take quite a long time to find the compromise on which criteria should be included.

The next step is to evaluate different potential locations according to the defined factors. The *factor-rating method* is a very easy method. The team in charge of identifying the new location selects the relevant criteria. As we will see later, this depends on the industry specifics, i.e., each company in a certain industry will compose an individual company-centred list of site location factors.

To make the process very tangible, let's assume that we would be consultants and we would need to support another company like OTLG GmbH & Co. KG in their decision-making process. Then imagine that in our consulting team, we would have compiled the following list with six criteria, as shown in Table 7.10. According to importance, the team decides the maximum amount of points that can be obtained per location factor. For the criterion "Infrastructure" this might hypothetically be 300 points at maximal. Then the team assigns the points for each of the options and per factor.

> **Practical Insights** It might be a reasonable variant to let the team members individually make their rating and then to calculate the

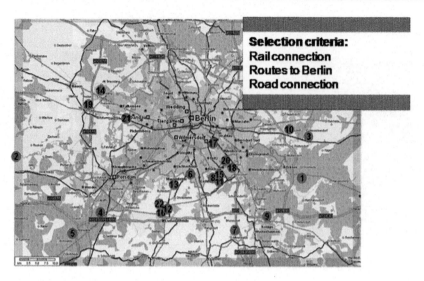

Fig. 7.26 Facility location planning at OTLG (© OTLG GmbH & Co. KG)

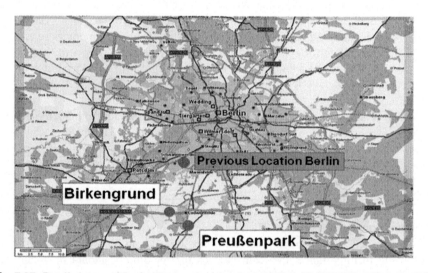

Fig. 7.27 Detailed stage of the facility location planning at OTLG (© OTLG GmbH & Co. KG)

averages per factor and option. The individual score sheets are archived so that the pathway of decision making is fully transparent and also reproducible for later reviews.

7.5 Factor-Ranking Analysis

Fig. 7.28 New distribution center in Ludwigsfelde (© OTLG GmbH & Co. KG)

6. Compute weighted average if many experts are involved
7. Choose the option with the highest "total utility value"

Table 7.9 Facility location selection criteria

Quantitative criteria	Qualitative criteria
Transportation costs	Infrastructure
Building and construction costs	Quality of labour
Rental costs	Transportation development
Labour costs	Purchasing power
Material costs	Options for financing (free trade zones, etc.)
Taxes	Suppliers
Financial support from local governments	Political risks
	Natural disaster risks
	Proximity to customers and suppliers
	Business climate
	Environmental regulations
	Competitive advantage
	Government and trading barriers

1. Identify location options.
2. Determine decision criteria (location factors) and their measurement
3. Determine weighting totaling 100% for the different criteria
4. Evaluate every location option on a normalized scale to achieve "partial utility values", e.g. usage of a scale from 1-10
5. Calculate the "total utility value" of a location option by multiplying "partial utility values" with weights and adding these values

Table 7.10 Factor-rating model

Location factor	Range min-max	Location A	Location B	Location C
Infrastructure	0–300 pts	213	232	204
Proximity to suppliers	0–200 pts	170	182	186
Proximity to customers	0–200 pts	180	171	192
Other facilities	0–150 pts	113	156	78
Quality of labour	0–100 pts	72	65	85
Cost of energy	0–50 pts	42	48	32
Sum	0–1000 pts	790	854	777

If the operations management team consists for example of five members and each individual scores the first factor of the first option, the resulting scores might look like this:

Member 1: scores 210
Member 2: scores 230
Member 3: scores 220
Member 4: scores 200
Member 5: scores 205.

On average, this will result in $1065/5 = 213$ points for the first factor "Infrastructure" for option A. For all other criteria a similar exercise will need to be done in practice so that a completely transparent rating can be presented to senior management.

The option that receives the highest score is the one that is suggested as the most suitable new location. In our example it would be location B. If the scores of different options are very close to each other, *sensitivity analysis* is mandatory.

Shortcomings of the factor-rating method include the fact that the weighting percentages assigned per factor are not clearly visible. Another useful method to overcome this criticism is the so-called *utility value analysis*.

7.5.3 Utility Value Analysis

We will elaborate the principle approach followed by the *utility value analysis* (see Günther and Tempelmeier, 2009) in connection with a theoretical case, in which a global player developed a strategy to produce and distribute its goods in Asia.

Just imagine that the top management of a globally functioning firm has asked the SCOM team to look for a suitable location to create a new factory in Asia. The sales department of that hypothetical global firm might have assessed that the market for the firm's products is growing significantly in, for example, India. As a consequence, the SCOM team will run an assessment on potential locations there.

The following list provides an overview for location of a new production facility depending on the different levels of the location decision problem.

7.5 Factor-Ranking Analysis

Step 1. Selection of the Economic Region First of all, the respective continent for the economic region or trade-zone needs to be specified, where the search for an appropriate location has to be conducted.

For the first step, the following criteria are extremely important:

- attractiveness of the economic region
- expected sales potential and/or market development
- political stability of the region
- legal requirements regarding the establishment of a production facility, etc.

Step 2. Selection of a Country Within the Economic Region Our theoretical case also shows that the options need to be further streamlined, i.e., the search for a site has to be narrowed down (here it is focused on India). That means in the continent of Asia (step 1); the sub-continent India has been identified in step 2 for the execution of the location planning and location analysis. Besides the expected market development already mentioned, there are also such location factors as:

- labour availability
- quality of human resources, for example, education levels
- salary and/or wage levels
- local/regional support for the location of a new facility
- local/regional support regarding business development
- availability of appropriate suppliers
- availability of transport-technology and/or infrastructure which play an important role.

Step 3. Selection of a Region Within the Country in the Economic Region In the third step, the sub-continent or maybe country identified has to be further assessed by the SCOM team. That means a certain kind of county or district will be identified for the placement of the new production facility. In reality there will be most probably multiple options available and it will be the task of the experts to identify the best location for the company. To do this, further criteria have to be taken into consideration, which will be presented next.

When we refer back to our example, the decision-making operations team for the identification of the new facility in India will need to evaluate different alternatives. That means a long list of alternative sites is drawn up and different options then need to be critically assessed. This critical assessment has to be reproducible and needs to be compiled in such a way that the top management can trace back the different steps that led to the identification of the preferred location(s). In practice, a table will be compiled that shows the different alternatives, which are then mapped and rated against a defined list of location factors (criteria). This is the fundamental principle of the utility value analysis. These criteria can be:

- connection to available infrastructure (e.g. roads, rail, ports, airports)
- availability of utilities (such as electricity or water for cooling)
- availability of raw-material (e.g. iron for steel production)
- availability of green-field properties or existing objects/facilities
- subsidies or taxation benefits, etc.

Step 4. Selection of the Facility Location In step four, the final decision for the selected location has to be substantiated, in case there are multiple possible properties available on the same pieces of land. Just imagine, for example, that there might be a newly created industrial park, where the home community offers different properties for sale. Therefore, the above mentioned location factor table will provide evidence for identification of the most suitable plot of land for the new facility. Final decision factors could therefore be:

- geographic dimensioning of the land (either more longitudinal or rectangular or maybe triangular shape of the property)
- topographic suitability or existing constraints (e.g. hilly grounds or existing electrical pylons)
- cost of the property and later options for enlargement/expansion
- opportunities for suppliers to locate nearby
- environmental constraints (e.g. regarding emissions)
- connection to existing infrastructure (accessibility for inbound flows and also shipment of finished goods outbound).

The principle *sequence of the activities* that need to be performed by the SCOM team to conduct such a utility value analysis is as follows:

1. Identify location options.
2. Determine decision criteria (location factors) and their measurement.
3. Determine weighting totalling 100 % for the different criteria.
4. Evaluate every location option on a normalized scale to achieve "partial utility values", usage of a scale from 1 to 10 points (in which 10 = best).
5. Calculate the "total utility value" of a location option by multiplying "partial utility values" with weights and adding these values.
6. Choose the option with the highest "total utility value".

Table 7.11 depicts a simplified example of the potential application of the utility value analysis.

The possible location factors presented above are just respective indications of inspirations for the SCOM team. In practice the location criteria will be different depending on the respective industry and will have different priorities. For example, for a chemical company, ecological restrictions are expected to be extremely important and for heavy industry, the availability of required resources will most probably have a significant influence on the decision-making process. Also factors

7.5 Factor-Ranking Analysis

Table 7.11 Utility value analysis

Location factor	Weight	Option X		Option Y		Option Z	
		Points	Partial value	Points	Partial value	Points	Partial value
Infrastructure	35 %	7	2.45	8	2.80	6	2.10
Proximity to suppliers	20 %	6	1.20	7	1.40	8	1.60
Proximity to existing sites	20 %	8	1.60	4	0.80	9	1.80
Expansion potential	10 %	6	0.60	7	0.70	7	0.70
Quality of labour	10 %	8	0.80	3	0.30	8	0.80
Topography	5 %	10	0.50	8	0.40	9	0.45
Sum	100 %						
Total utility value			7.15		6.40		7.45

such as the company's other existing facilities in the region researched might influence the decision for a new site.

> **Practical Insights** Facility location planning decisions imply the usage of both quantitative and qualitative methods. Despite of rigor and technical power, the simulation and optimization methods are not the dominating techniques in decision-making on facility location planning and SCD. In practice, these decisions are typically driven by corporate policies and are analysed with the help of business cases and empirical data.

Case Study "Niedersachsen Park" (Based on www.niedersachsenpark.de)
The objective of this case study is to find out why the Adidas Group selected the Niedersachsenpark as a location for its new distribution centre. The Adidas Group is the world's second-biggest sports goods manufacturer and is headquartered in Herzogenaurach, Germany. In Germany, the Adidas Group has three distribution centres. Two of them are in the area of the group's headquarter in Bavaria and the third one, which opened in 2013, is located in the Niedersachsenpark, the largest industrial and commercial area in Lower Saxony. This newly established distribution centre is the group's largest in terms of throughput. In 2015, the Adidas Group expects a throughput of 100 million pieces per year at this distribution centre. In comparison, the two distribution centres in Bavaria (in Uffenheim and Scheinfeld) together achieve a total throughput of 80 million pieces.

Besides the expected throughput, the new distribution centre in the Niedersachsenpark indicates further advantages such as its location. In contrast to the locations in Bavaria, this one is directly located on highway A1 and the main harbours are easily accessible from this location. This is extremely important for the Adidas Group as the main components of its products arrive in Germany by sea

Table 7.12 Factor-rating and utility value analysis

Key success factor	Weight	Scores (out of 100)		Weighted scores	
		N-Park	Bavaria	N-Park	Bavaria
Total scores					

(Hamburg, Bremen, Bremerhaven). Therefore, the group can decrease its transportation costs from the harbours to the distribution centres. Furthermore, since the Niedersachsenpark is quite a newly established industrial and commercial park, it can be highly flexible in terms of construction and development plans to fulfil the Adidas Group's requirements.

Additionally, the construction rights for the whole area are advised. There will be no possibility of public disputes that might cause long waiting times or potential reputation damages before one can start operating at this location. Since there are no residential areas in the immediate vicinity of the Niedersachsenpark, the distribution centre is allowed to operate 24/7 compared to 17 h per day in Uffenheim and Scheinfeld. This allows for highly efficient processes at the Niedersachsenpark. Another significant advantage of Niedersachsenpark is the chance to reserve opportunity areas for potential future expansion. Companies can reserve these areas in case they do not want to exclude possible future expansion but as yet do not have any concrete plans. This advantage creates a valuable degree of flexibility for the organizations located at the Niedersachsenpark.

To sum up, the advantages outlined indicate that the Niedersachsenpark is a favourable location for the Adidas Group's new distribution centre. In many aspects it surpasses the distribution centres in Bavaria. According to Lars Mangels (Corporate Communication Manager at Adidas Group), the Niedersachsenpark meets all the requirements that they expect from a location for a distribution centre.

The case study reveals that the Niedersachsenpark is the optimal location for the Adidas Group's new distribution centre. Do you agree? Apply the factor-rating and utility value analysis methods to this case (N-Park = Niedersachsenpark; Bavaria = Uffenheim&Scheinfeld) (use Table 7.12).

7.6 Key Points

This chapter introduced the problems, models and techniques for managing location decisions in the context of a supply network set-up. We received insights into location analysis processes and understand the importance of selecting the right location for facilities during the formation of a supply network. There are several different important decision tasks to be solved before the network can be set up. We

7.6 Key Points

have introduced an SCD framework for aligning these decisions. Finally, we have become familiar with the tools for supporting SCD decisions. The selection of an approach mainly depends on the problem data we want to consider to obtain optimal decisions.

Section 7.3 provided an introduction into an important decision problem of location planning. The WLP addresses the challenge to research markets and suppliers, and to forge transportation links between markets and suppliers from a longer term perspective. The goal of warehouse location planning is the minimization of the total costs for SCD. With the help of the PPS example we analysed a typical WLP setting as well as the relevant planning data.

We investigated a model-based approach to identify the best SCD. First, we proposed a mathematical optimization model for the WLP. Second, we configured and applied a spreadsheet decision support tool using the Excel Solver add-in. Third, we learned the technique of branch-&-bound as a general approach to deriving optimal design options for the WLP model. Finally, we analysed the impacts of limited product availability at certain suppliers for the SCD and introduced the CWLP model for which we configured a spreadsheet-based tool to derive optimal solutions.

It can be concluded that mathematical programming techniques are useful and powerful tools for improving decisions for SCD. They allow for consideration of demand, capacity and costs to determine global SCD. At the same time, the application of these tools in real life should be considered subject to numerous limitations such as assumptions on linear functions, deterministic parameter values, and computational complexity. A solution to the mathematical model is not automatically a managerial decision! Up-to-date research trends are involved in consideration of non-deterministic parameters (Lim et al. 2013); reliable SCD (Snyder and Daskin 2005; Klibi et al. 2010; Li et al. 2013); and the ripple-effect in SCs (Ivanov et al. 2014).

Section 7.4 considered the next stage in the SCD, where all regions are processed individually. In each region, specific locations (expressed by coordinates) are identified at which a facility can be installed or from which supply quantities can infiltrate the SC. The output of this phase is a suggestion for locations for opening facilities with regard to cost efficiency. We learned how to apply the centre-of-gravity method to facility location decisions and how to determine optimal location coordinated with the help of a simple average method and the Miehle algorithm. The centre-of-gravity method can help to determine the location of one warehouse subject to minimal transportation costs. It is a simple method which is easy to implement. The shortcomings are linear assumptions, impossibility of considering multiple locations, deterministic data, and poor consideration of geographic and road infrastructure reality.

In Sect. 7.5, multiple criteria analysis was considered reaching beyond cost minimization. We learned factor-rating and utility value analysis methods, their advantages and limitations in practice. Factor rating and utility value analysis methods allow for consideration of different qualitative and quantitative factors for location decisions which are easily understood by managers. Some shortcomings are the subjectivity of these methods regarding the selection of factors and their scoring and weighting. Sensitivity analysis is important for practical application of factor rating and utility value analysis methods.

Recall Chap. 4, Supply Chain Strategy, and analyse the PPS case with regard to the following:

- Discuss the SC strategy of PPS with respect to Europe and the celluloid-free table tennis balls. What is the market to be served? Is there a reactive strategy preferred or is there a push strategy intended?
- What are the limitations given to Mr. Chen for the set-up of the SCD in Europe?
- Assume that PPS wants to offer a 72 h delivery time to all customers in Europe when they order a packaging unit via a retail website. Discuss whether the SCD as intended by Mr. Chen can be used again or whether significant redesign efforts are required.

Acknowledgement The authors thanks the OTLG GmbH & Co. KG for the permission to use the company materials in this textbook.

Bibliography

Askin RG, Baffo I, Xia M (2014) Multi-commodity warehouse location and distribution planning with inventory consideration. Int J Prod Res 52(7):1897–1910

Baker KR (2015) Optimization modeling with spreadsheets, 3rd edn. Wiley, New York

Baron O, Milner J, Naseraldin H (2011) Facility location: a robust optimization approach. Prod Oper Manage 20(5):772–785

Benyoucef L, Xie X, Tanonkou GA (2013) Supply chain network design with unreliable suppliers: A Lagrangian relaxation-based approach. Int J Prod Res 51(21):6435–6454

Bierwirth C (2000) Adaptive search and management of logistics systems: base models for learning agents. Kluwer, Alphen aan den Rijn

Chopra S, Meindl P (2012) Supply chain management. Strategy, planning and operation, 5th edn. Pearson, Harlow

Cousins PD (2002) A conceptual model for managing long-term inter-organisational relationships. Eur J Purch Supply Manage 8(2):71–82

Cousins PD, Lamming R, Lawson B, Squire B (2012) Strategic supply management – principles, theories and practice, 2nd edn. Pearson, Harlow

Daskin MS (1995) Network and discrete location: models, algorithms, and applications. Wiley, Hoboken

Domschke W, Drexl A (1985) Logistik: Standorte, 2nd edn. Oldenbourg Wissenschaftsverlag, Munich

Drezner Z (ed) (1995) Facility location: a survey of applications and methods. Springer, New York

Geoffrion AM, Graves GW (1974) Multicommodity distribution system design by benders decomposition. Manage Sci 20(5):822–844

Günther H-O, Tempelmeier H (2009) Produktion und Logistik, 8th edn. Springer, Heidelberg

http://www.truckinginfo.com/channel/fleet-management/news/story/2014/04/amazon-testing-delivery-fleet.aspx, November, 9, 2014

Ivanov D, Sokolov B, Pavlov A (2014) Optimal distribution (re)planning in a centralized multi-stage network under conditions of ripple effect and structure dynamics. Eur J Oper Res 237(2):758–770

Klibi W, Martel A, Guitouni A (2010) The design of robust value-creating supply chain networks: a critical review. Eur J Oper Res 203(2):283–293

Li Q, Zeng B, Savachkin A (2013) Reliable facility location design under disruptions. Comput Oper Res 40(4):901–909

Lim MK, Bassamboo A, Chopra S, Daskin MS (2013) Facility location decisions with random disruptions and imperfect estimation. Manuf Serv Oper Manage 15(2):239–249

Manzini R, Bindi F (2009) Strategic design and operational management optimization of a multistage physical distribution system. Transport Res E Log Transport Rev 45(6):915–936

Melo MT, Nickel S, Saldanha-da-Gama F (2009) Facility location and supply chain management – a review. Eur J Oper Res 196(2):401–412

Miehle W (1958) Link-length minimization in networks. Oper Res 6(2):232–243

Schönberger J (2011) Model-based control of logistics processes in volatile environments: decision support for operations planning in supply consortia. Springer, New York

Snyder LV, Daskin MS (2005) Reliability models for facility location: the expected failure cost case. Transport Sci 39(3):400–416

Stadtler H, Kilger C (2008) Supply chain management and advanced planning, 4th edn. Springer, Berlin

Vidal CJ, Goetschalckx M (1997) Strategic production-distribution models: a critical review with emphasis on global supply chain models. Eur J Oper Res 98(1):1–18

Wernerfelt B (1984) A resource-based view of the firm. Strategic Manage J 5(2):171–180

8. Distribution and Transportation Network Design

In Chap. 7, we discussed the identification of appropriate facility locations. The SCOM theory states that the interactions of several facilities and their common activities have a crucial impact on the success of a supply network. Therefore, the linkage of several facilities plays an important role in the SC configuration phase. In this phase, key decisions related to the availability of facilities have already been made but their physical connections by the installation of appropriate transportation links are not addressed so far.

In this chapter, we will discuss basic strategies to configure distribution and transportation networks so that given supply locations are physically connected with demand locations. In Sect. 8.1, we introduce a case study to discuss the challenges related to the installation of transportation links. Section 8.2 introduces generic types of transportation network set-ups as a starting point to more sophisticated network layouts. Section 8.3 introduces the concept of shipment consolidation as the key approach to the realization of economies of scale in transportation. Section 8.4 is dedicated to the presentation of different transport network configuration objectives and their balancing so that efficient and profitable network layouts can be set up. Section 8.5 surveys the optimization of the incorporation of transport service providers (freight carriers). Section 8.6 is devoted to different case studies of distribution network design.

Learning Objectives for This Chapter
Within this chapter you will become familiar with the most important aspects of configuring transportation networks. In particular, you will:

- learn typical aspects and decision problems of configuring today's distribution and transportation networks

---

Find additional case studies and videos on information technology for SCOM in the *E-Supplement* to this book on www.global-supply-chain-management.de!

- become familiar with generic types of distribution and transportation network structures
- understand the basic trade-offs in distribution and transportation network design with regard to costs and responsiveness
- understand what consolidation is and how consolidation can be used to achieve economies of scale in the context of distribution and transportation
- optimize the engagement of a logistics service provider by assigning different shipping quantities to appropriate transportation links.

8.1 Introductory Case Study: Bavarian Wood

Bavarian Wood is a manufacturer of high quality furniture. The product portfolio mainly comprises all types of furniture made from natural wood. A typical customer of Bavarian Wood is willing to pay quite a high price in order to get a fairly high quality product. Figure 8.1 depicts the supply network for Bavarian Wood.

Since wood is the main ingredient of Bavarian Wood products, the procurement of different kinds of this natural ingredient is critical to the performance and success of Bavarian Wood operations. A large amount of the wood is bought from Asian suppliers. After having seen the trees, deputies from Bavarian Wood's procurement department select those trees that will be used as raw material "suppliers". Local farm workers chop the trees, clean them roughly and load them on containers. These containers are forwarded to the nearest container port from where they are shipped directly or with transshipments from different carriers to the container ports of Hamburg, Bremerhaven or Wilhelmshaven in northern Germany. Due to weather conditions in the Asian supply regions and the incorporation of different container vessel lines, it is impossible to even out and balance the quantity of containers bringing supplies for Bavarian Wood.

After a container for Bavarian Wood has arrived in one of the three container terminals, a wood expert inspects the raw material and sometimes rejects a container due to low quality or vermin infestation. After a container load has passed quality control, the wood is transshipped on hired trucks which bring it to the Bavarian Wood manufacturing site close to Munich, which is approx. 800 km away from the coast (see Fig. 8.1).

Bavarian Wood was founded in 1875, and since then has grown continuously with stable economic success. However, during the economic crisis, between 2008 and 2010, Bavarian Wood was in danger of becoming bankrupt. It was able to survive only with the help of additional investments. Recently, the new stakeholders have been analysing and evaluating all of Bavarian Wood's processes in order to protect their investments and achieve long-term profitability. These evaluations are executed by external consultants. In their final evaluation report they mention that transportation costs for the raw materials are quite high. They recognize that the imported woods are not available in Europe so that the international procurement strategy is necessary but they recommend reconsidering the

8.1 Introductory Case Study: Bavarian Wood

Fig. 8.1 The European procurement network of Bavarian Wood (© 2015 Basarsoft, Geobasis-DE/BKG (© 2009), Google, basado en BCN IGN Espana)

process of bringing the imported woods from the ports in northern Germany to the manufacturing site in Bavaria.

Having received the evaluation reports from the stakeholders the management board of Bavarian Wood discusses the implications. Regarding the "transportation problem", they admit that they have not enough logistical knowledge for assessing and potentially restructuring the transportation processes. They discuss the situation with stakeholder representatives and get the OK to extend the management board with another member who will be in charge of transportation and logistics processes. After a careful application and candidate selection procedure, Bavarian Wood hires Mike as the responsible transportation and logistics manager. Mike has worked for several years as a transport consulting engineer and has worked on several development and restructuring projects for national and international transport networks.

His first duty with Bavarian Wood is to check the current setup of the transportation process system between the ports and the manufacturing site of Bavarian Woods.

(a) Mike discovers that Bavarian Wood does not possess its own trucks. Whenever a certain transport quantity has to be moved, Bavarian Wood hires a truck from a freight forwarding company at a fixed daily rate. Is this a good idea? Please discuss the pros and cons of this set-up.

Having managed the critical years, Bavarian Wood wants to start growing again. Currently, they are preparing the integration of two other furniture factories into their company. One of these production facilities is located close to Prague, capital of the Czech Republic. The second additional production site is in Austria, close to Salzburg, directly beside the Austrian–German border. After the integration of these two additional production sites has been completed, imported quantities of wood will increase by approx. 150 %. In order to ensure availability of sufficient quantities of wood, imports will also be processed via the Dutch port of Rotterdam.

(b) Should the previous method of transport be retained? What are the possible modifications required for hinterland transportation? Should Bavarian Wood buy its own trucks and set up its own transport department? Which production site should be supplied from which port in order to keep transportation costs to a minimum? Should all necessary transport services be given away to a transport service provider?

8.2 Generic Transport Network Structures

Mike prepares a short summary about the generic *transport network* structures from the perspective of the so-called origin-to-destination (OD) demand. The OD demand expresses the need to move a given quantity of goods from a location of supply (the origin) to a location of demand (the destination).

In the simplest set-up the supply quantities are available at a single location (the origin) and the available supply quantity is requested completely or partially from a single location (the destination) as outlined in Fig. 8.2. There is no opportunity to optimize (reduce) the transportation efforts if the destination wants to receive the requested quantity immediately. If a split delivery is allowed it is possible to divide up the total quantity into smaller shipments which can be picked up and delivered one after another. Time of delivery of individual shipments can be arranged.

Decisions about the distribution network set-up outlined in Fig. 8.3 are the same as in the link set-up described previously. Only the time of delivery can be decided.

Only the destination requests a certain supply quantity but the demand quantity is distributed over several origin locations (Fig. 8.4). In general, the total available quantity exceeds the quantity demanded. Besides responding to the question of when to deliver, another important decision needs to be made. It is necessary to decide which origin provides which supply quantity. It is important to take care that the cheapest transportation links are used. But if the relevant origin does not offer sufficient quantities it is necessary to use a second (and maybe further) transportation links in order to satisfy demand from the destination. From the perspective of the location planning framework introduced in Chap. 7, answering the question as to which supply location contributes which quantity to fulfil the total demand would be the fourth phase decision; this is called the capacity allocation decision.

8.2 Generic Transport Network Structures

Fig. 8.2 Transportation link

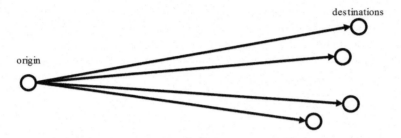

Fig. 8.3 Distribution network

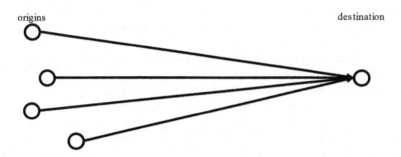

Fig. 8.4 Supply network

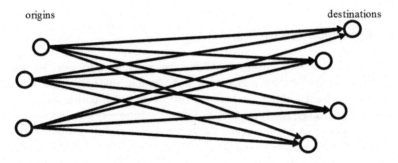

Fig. 8.5 Many-to-many network structure

The most complex situation is represented by the *many-to-many network* structure shown in Fig. 8.5. Here, several origins provide supply quantities but there are also several demanding destination locations. Beside the decisions about delivery times it is necessary to make two additional decisions. First, it is necessary to decide from which location(s) an individual destination location is supplied. Second, for each origin location there is a decision required about the quantities and destinations that are supplied. Finally, the decision becomes even more complex if the costs for moving goods along the available transportation links are different.

Mike concludes his introduction into generic transportation network structures by applying the new vocabulary to the Bavarian Wood case. Currently, there is a supply network structure available with the three ports Wilhelmshaven, Bremerhaven and Hamburg forming the set of origins and a single destination in Munich. However, as soon as the second manufacturing facility (either in the Czech Republic or in Austria) is integrated into the wood supply network, the network type changes to a many-to-many network structure.

8.3 Realizing Economies of Scale in Transportation

Walter, who is Bavarian Wood's finance officer, is very interested in Mike's statements. He is the first one to ask Mike a question. He wants to know how money can be saved in the transportation business and how the process efficiency can be improved. From his daily business he knows that economies of scale are typically realized if large quantities of a product are bought or if unnecessary set-ups of machines can be avoided. Walter wants to know from Mike if there are similar principles that can be exploited in transportation.

Mike is happy about this question since it offers an entry point for his explanations about the way money can be saved through sophisticatly organized transportation systems and elaborated transportation processes. Manager Walter (finance officer): What is the general logic behind reducing costs in transportation? What are the general issues to be considered here for a "good transportation" system configuration?

8.3.1 Consolidation of Shipments

Mike wants to hire trucks from a trucking company to carry out the necessary transportation services between Hamburg and Munich, since Bavarian Wood does not run its own trucks. After a telephone call to an old friend in the forwarding company TransRoad he receives an offer for forwarding services. According to the offer, the provision of a truck costs 850 € per day including all mileage and the costs for the driver, insurances, etc. The truck provides a payload of at most 25 tons and the aforementioned amount is due independently from the actual loaded weight. If Mike wants to ship more than 25 tons a day he is obliged to hire and pay for a second truck. The rental conditions for the second and a conditional third truck are identical to the conditions already outlined.

An evaluation of this offer reveals the following interesting cost structures and properties. If a truck is hired for the first ton payload then the remaining 24 tons can be transported without any additional costs. This means that the proposed tariff

8.3 Realizing Economies of Scale in Transportation

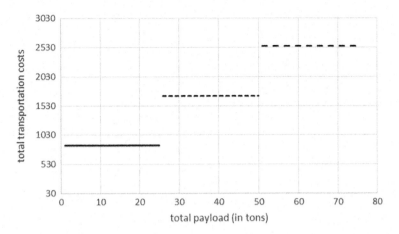

Fig. 8.6 Piece-wise constant function of the total transportation costs for given payload quantity

contains a "bounded flat rate" up to 25 tons (see Fig. 8.6). The continuous line represents the costs if one truck is hired, the dotted line represents the situation with two hired trucks and the dashed line applies to the costs if the payload is so high that a third trucks must be hired. There are discontinuities of the total costs whenever another truck is needed.

The aforementioned conclusions can be formulated after some basic name conventions have been introduced. Let F be the price for hiring a truck and Q be the payload of the hired truck. Let d_R be the corresponding OD demand for $\left\lceil \frac{d_R}{Q} \right\rceil$ the considered OD relation R. The number of required trucks N(R; Q) equals then and the total transportation costs for this relation R sum up to $C(R; Q; F) := F \cdot N(R; Q)$.

If the costs for the truck are equally split over the complete payload assigned to this truck then the average costs per ton decrease with increasing payload as long as the total payload does not exceed 25 tons (the payload capacity provided by the truck). The carriage of 1 ton leads to a cost factor of 850 € per ton, while the carriage of 10 tons reduces this cost down to 85 € per ton (Fig. 8.7). If the payload exceeds 25 tons it becomes necessary to hire an additional truck which causes a discontinuity in the total costs C leading to an implied increase in the costs $c(d_R;F;Q)$ per ton payload.

> ▶ **Practical Insights** Transportation costs typically comprise 6–8 % of the company's costs. In most cases, transportation costs can be reduced by 10–15 %. For example, a company with total costs of 1 billion euros can cut its transport costs by around 8 million euros.

Mike concludes from the aforementioned facts that he should attempt to fill a hired truck completely in order minimize the costs per moved ton of payload. Furthermore, a potentially necessary second hired truck should also be filled as much as possible in order to reduce transportation costs.

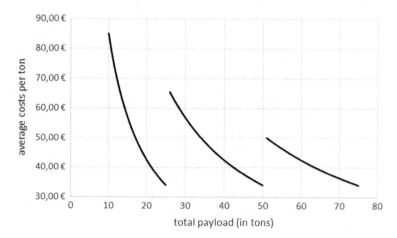

Fig. 8.7 Costs per ton of payload (the cost-per-ton-values for fewer than 10 tons of payload are not shown in order to preserve the readability of the graphs)

Consolidation is the term for the combination of two or even more quantities to be shipped between a given origin and a given destination. Mike thinks about ways to consolidate several quantities in order to fill up a partially filled truck. In the selected week shown in Table 8.1, Mike detects that the stated demand for Monday (the production output from the concrete factory) is 32 tons so that two trucks are needed in order to carry the complete production output to Munich. This results in total truck hiring costs of 1700 € which leads to 1700 €/32 tons = 53.13 €/ton costs for each carried ton but the average fill rate is only 64 %. The immediate transport of the total quantity without the postponement of any quantities requires to hire 15 trucks, so that the weekly transportation costs account for 15 × 850 € = 12.750 € at an average fill rate of 71.5 %.

8.3.2 Postponement

Analysing the daily transport demand for a week as shown in Table 8.1 Mike comes up with the idea to postpone the transfer of a fraction of the daily transportation demand in order to avoid the inclusion of a truck that is only partially filled. Mike knows that there is no urgency related to the shipment of demand as long as at least one truck travels from Hamburg to Munich each day. His idea is now to send out only completely filled trucks (except on Sunday, when the residual quantity of the weekly demand must be moved to Munich).

Table 8.2 shows the resulting transport activities. The incoming demand is merged with postponed quantities to the recent available demand. *Full truck loads* (FTL) are derived from the available demand quantities but residual quantities are postponed until a later day of the week. This strategy results in completely filled trucks for Mon to Sat but on Sun the average fill rate falls to 90 %.

8.3 Realizing Economies of Scale in Transportation

Table 8.1 Daily transportation demand within a week without consolidation

	Mon	Tue	Wed	Thu	Fri	Sat	Sun	Sums
OD-demand d_R (in tons)	32	53	18	34	43	60	30	270
Fulfilled demand	32	53	18	34	43	60	30	270
Hired trucks	2	3	1	2	2	3	2	15
Costs C	1700 €	2550 €	850 €	1700 €	1700 €	2550 €	1700 €	12,750 €
Costs c (per ton)	53.13 €	48.11 €	47.22 €	50.00 €	39.53 €	42.50 €	56.67 €	

Table 8.2 Daily transportation demand within a week with postponement of fractional truck loadings

	Mon	Tue	Wed	Thu	Fri	Sat	Sun	Sums
Incoming OD-demand d_R	32	53	18	34	43	60	30	270
Postponed demand	0	7	10	3	12	5	15	
Available demand	32	60	28	37	55	65	45	
Now fulfilled demand	25	50	25	25	50	50	45	270
Hired trucks	1	2	1	1	2	2	2	11
Costs C	850 €	1700 €	850 €	850 €	1700 €	1700 €	1700 €	9350 €
Costs c (per ton)	34.00 €	34.00 €	34.00 €	34.00 €	34.00 €	34.00 €	37.78 €	

However, only 11 trucks are needed costing 9350 €, representing a saving of transportation costs of 26.67 % and an average capacity utilization rate greater than 98 %.

Mike is very surprised how much money he can save if he performs the postponement strategy with the goal of sending out only fully loaded trucks in order to realize the largest possible economies of scale. However, Mike is aware that this postponement strategy is fragile. In the event that the demanding construction site requests immediate transportation of the produced quantities produced, this strategy can no longer be applied. Therefore, Mike is looking for other opportunities to increase the fill rate of the hired trucks.

8.3.3 Milk-Runs

Mike analyses the daily supply quantities from the three ports of Hamburg, Bremerhaven and Wilhelmshaven, all located close together in the northern part

Table 8.3 Daily transportation demand within the three German ports

	Mon	Tue	Wed	Thu	Fri	Sat	Sun	Sums
Demand waiting in Hamburg								
OD-demand d_R (in tons)	32	53	18	34	43	60	30	270
Fulfilled demand	32	53	18	34	43	60	30	270
Hired trucks	2	3	1	2	2	3	2	15
Costs C	1700 €	2550 €	850 €	1700 €	1700 €	2550 €	1700 €	12,750 €
Costs c (per ton)	53.13 €	48.11 €	47.22 €	50.00 €	39.53 €	42.50 €	56.67 €	48.17 €
Utilization	64 %	71 %	72 %	68 %	86 %	80 %	60 %	72 %
Demand waiting in Bremerhaven								
OD-demand d_R (in tons)	23	42	31	28	38	50	20	232
Fulfilled demand	23	42	31	28	38	50	20	232
Hired trucks	1	2	2	2	2	2	1	12
Costs C	850 €	1700 €	1700 €	1700 €	1700 €	1700 €	850 €	10,200 €
Costs c (per ton)	36.96 €	40.48 €	54.84 €	60.71 €	44.74 €	34.00 €	42.50 €	44.89 €
Utilization	92 %	84 %	62 %	56 %	76 %	100 %	80 %	79 %
Demand waiting in Wilhelmshaven								
OD-demand d_R (in tons)	13	12	25	13	26	38	11	138
Fulfilled demand	13	12	25	13	26	38	11	138
Hired trucks	1	1	1	1	2	2	1	9
Costs C	850 €	850 €	850 €	850 €	1700 €	1700 €	850 €	7650 €
Costs c (per ton)	65.38 €	70.83 €	34.00 €	65.38 €	65.38 €	44.74 €	77.27 €	60.43 €
Utilization	52 %	48 %	100 %	52 %	52 %	76 %	44 %	61 %

of Germany. Currently, Bavarian Wood hires trucks for all three links, Hamburg-Munich, Bremerhaven-Munich and Wilhelmshaven-Munich. Each of these trucks picks up the assigned payload quantity at the selected port and brings it directly to the Munich area. For the example week given in Table 8.3, this approach leads to a total number of 36 hired trucks. The costs to be paid to the forwarding companies add up to 30,600 €. Average capacity utilizations between 61 % and 79 % are observed and the average costs per moved ton vary between 44.89 € and 60.43 €.

8.3 Realizing Economies of Scale in Transportation

The first analysis of the data from Table 8.3 reveals that only 17 of the 36 hired trucks are fully loaded. More than half of the hired trucks are operated only partially loaded. In addition, the quantities carried by the partially loaded trucks are often quite small. Mike analyses the situation on Thursday. From Hamburg, the second hired truck carries only 9 tons. The second truck hired for the Bremerhaven to Munich service picks up only 3 tons while the only truck going from Wilhelmshaven loads only 13 tons. Mike recognizes that these three "excess" quantities add up to 25 tons so that one truck is able to move all three shipments. For this reason, Mike decides to evaluate a so-called milk-run service (Chopra and Meindl 2009) from the ports to Munich. In a milk-run, one truck visits two or even more pickup locations before bringing the complete load to the common destination.

In the Bavarian Wood set-up there are four different milk-runs possible: (1) Hamburg, Bremerhaven and Wilhelmshaven are served as pickup locations by the same truck; (2) Hamburg and Bremerhaven are served in one milk-run; (3) demand quantities waiting in Hamburg as well as in Wilhelmshaven are consolidated; (4) one truck loads demand quantities in Bremerhaven as well as in Wilhelmshaven. The visiting sequence depends on the initial position of the truck as well as on the pickup locations and the common drop-off location (see Chap. 14). Milk-runs represent the location-based consolidation of shipments.

In order to achieve the largest cost reduction by milk-runs Mike employs the following approach. He starts determining the minimal number of fully loaded trucks for each day and port. As an example, Mike considers Monday. Hamburg expresses a demand of 32 tons so that one full truck load of 25 tons can be achieved. Mike puts the remaining 7 tons in the "milk-run quantity". From Bremerhaven, 23 tons must be carried away but no full truck load can be generated so that Mike puts all 23 tons into the milk-run quantity. From Wilhelmshaven, Mike puts 13 tons into the milk-run quantity. Overall, 43 tons have been selected for being fulfilled by a milk-run service.

One option (Table 8.4) is to hire two trucks for milk-runs. The first truck among them starts in Hamburg, picking up 7 tons. It proceeds to Bremerhaven where it loads an additional 13 tons; next it continues to Wilhelmshaven where 5 tons are picked up. The second hired milk-run truck starts in Bremerhaven and loads 10 trucks and, additionally, picks up 8 tons in Wilhelmshaven. The incorporation of the milk-run services needs two trucks instead of three if no milk-run is used, so that one truck is saved on Monday. Similarly, Mike compiles milk-runs for the remaining days (see Table 8.4). The daily saving of trucks for hire finally leads to a reduction of trucks required down to 28 (compared to 36 trucks without milk-runs). This implies a reduction of hiring costs by 22.2 % down to 23,800 €. The average capacity utilization rate climbs up to 92 % and the average costs for moving a 1-ton payload falls to 37.38 € when milk-run operations are performed.

Table 8.4 Daily transportation with milk-runs

	Mon	Tue	Wed	Thu	Fri	Sat	Sun	Sums
Demand waiting in Hamburg								
OD-demand d_R (in tons)	32	53	18	34	43	60	30	270
Fulfilled demand	25	50	0	25	25	50	25	200
Hired trucks	1	2	0	1	1	2	1	8
Costs C	850 €	1700 €	- €	850 €	850 €	1700 €	850 €	6.800 €
Utilization	100 %	100 %	0 %	100 %	100 %	100 %	100 %	86 %
Demand waiting in Bremerhaven								
OD-demand d_R (in tons)	23	42	31	28	38	50	20	232
Fulfilled demand	0	25	25	25	25	50	0	150
Hired trucks	0	1	1	1	1	2	0	6
Costs C	- €	850 €	850 €	850 €	850 €	1700 €	- €	5100 €
Utilization	0 %	100 %	100 %	100 %	100 %	100 %	0 %	71 %
Demand waiting in Wilhelmshaven								
OD-demand d_R (in tons)	13	12	25	13	26	38	11	138
Fulfilled demand	0	7	25	0	25	25	11	93
Hired trucks	0	1	1	0	1	1	1	5
Costs C	- €	850 €	850 €	- €	850 €	850 €	850 €	4250 €
Utilization	0 %	28 %	100 %	0 %	100 %	100 %	44 %	53 %
Remaining demand fulfilled in milkruns								
Milkrun demand in Hamburg (HH)	7	3	18	9	18	10	5	70
Milkrun demand in Bremerhaven (BHV)	23	17	6	3	13	0	20	82
Milkrun demand in Wilhelmshaven (WHV)	13	5	0	13	1	13	0	45
Total demand	43	25	24	25	32	23	25	
Milkrun HH-BHV-WHV	25	25		25			25	
Milkrun HH-BHV			24		25			

8.3 Realizing Economies of Scale in Transportation

								Total
Milkrun HH-WHV	18					23		
Milkrun BHV-WHV		25	24	25	7		25	
Fulfilled demand	43	25	24	25	32	23	25	
Hired trucks	2	1	1	1	2	1	1	9
Costs C	1700 €	850 €	850 €	850 €	1700 €	850 €	850 €	7650 €
Utilization	86 %	100 %	96 %	100 %	64 %	92 %	100 %	91 %
Overall number of hired trucks	3	5	3	3	5	6	3	28
Costs C	2550 €	4250 €	2550 €	2550 €	4250 €	5100 €	2550 €	23,800 €
Moved quantity	68	107	74	75	107	148	61	640
Costs per ton	38 €	40 €	34 €	34 €	40 €	34 €	42 €	37.38 €
Utilization	91 %	86 %	99 %	100 %	86 %	99 %	81 %	92 %

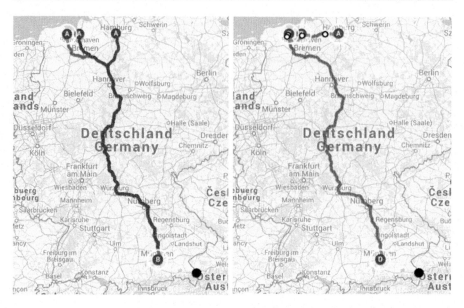

Fig. 8.8 Direkt delivery network for Bavarian Wood (*left*) and milk-run service-based network (*right*) (© 2015 Basarsoft, Geobasis-DE/BKG (© 2009), Google, basado en BCN IGN Espana)

8.3.4 Transshipment

Mike has explained the benefits of the milk-run services. However, he also mentions the shortcomings and deficiencies. The major challenge is to ensure that the milk-run services fit to daily demand. From day to day the milk-runs implemented have to be adapted to recent demand. This makes milk-run planning quite complicated. If the total quantities from the milk-run locations are slightly above the full truck load quantity, then the incorporation of an almost empty truck cannot be avoided. Furthermore, in the case of the prospective inclusion of the port of Rotterdam as well as the two manufacturing sites in Austria and the Czech Republic, milk-runs seem to become less attractive due to the long distances involved. Because of these challenges, Mike proposes a third consolidation approach to the management board of Bavarian Wood.

As it can be observed from the left-hand map in Fig. 8.8 the major part of the three truck routes from the sea ports to the production site is the same. All three pickup locations Wilhelmshaven, Bremerhaven and Hamburg "share" a large part of their connection path to their common destination Munich. In order to increase the fill rate of trucks travelling long distances, Mike proposes to install a transshipment facility in Hanover, where trucks coming from the

8.3 Realizing Economies of Scale in Transportation

Fig. 8.9 Transportation network with transshipment point in Hanover (© 2015 Basarsoft, Geobasis-DE/BKG (© 2009), Google, Mapa GISrael, ORION-ME, basado en BCN IGN Espana)

three seaports enter the same major north-to-south motorway A7. In this transshipment facility, the inbound trucks are unloaded and sent back to the ports in order to bring further quantities to this facility. Other trucks are then loaded with the quantities recently arrived, and these trucks travel then to Munich (Fig. 8.9).

Mike outlines two major benefits of this type of shipment consolidation. First, the trucks travelling from the ports to the transshipment facility travel relatively short distances, between 150 and 200 km. Therefore, they can shuttle twice or even three times between their pickup port and Hanover so that one truck is enough to forward all quantities from the port to the transshipment facility in the port hinterland. Second, due to the consolidation of the inbound flow of quantities originating from the three sea ports there are huge opportunities to compile full truck loads for the main-haul service between Hanover and Munich. Both aspects contribute to the reduction of the transportation costs.

Mike explains the idea of transshipment-based consolidation by means of the following set-up. A hired truck is available and paid for 24 h. Within this period it can execute three feeder cycles between a port and the transshipment facility and a subsequent main-haul trip from Hanover to Munich (type-A service pattern). Alternatively, it can complete six feeder cycles and no main-haul trip (type-B service pattern); or, as the third option, it can execute one main-haul trip only (type-C service pattern). A truck that is operated only in the feeder service in northern Germany can be hired for a reduced tariff of 750 € since the truck operator incurs fewer costs for overnight stays for the vehicle and crew. The reduced tariff of 700 € applies to a truck executing one main haul only due to reduced travel distances as in the type-C-pattern. In the first two consolidation approaches (postponement and milk-runs) Mike was unable to exploit the reduced tariffs since each hired truck is assigned to a long haul operation. The separation of feeder operations from main-haul operations results in the possibility of agreeing different tariffs for trucks assigned to different service patterns.

Table 8.5 and model (Eqs. (8.1)–(8.4)) contain calculations for the number of trucks needed as well as the associated costs. Determining the least cost number of trucks operating type-A, type-B or type-C patterns per day is an optimization problem with constraints. The least cost number of hired trucks for the three patterns should be found but it must also be ensured that the minimal number of required feeder cycles as well as the minimal number of main-haul services is provided. However, this problem can be modelled as an integer linear program as follows. Let y_A be the integer decision variable representing the number of trucks hired for executing a type-A service pattern. For the number of hired type-B pattern trucks and type-C pattern trucks, the integer decision variables y_B as well as y_C are used. Let k^{feed} denote the minimal feeder service number required and let k^{mh} denote the minimal main-haul services required.

$$Z = 850 y_A + 750 y_B + 700 y_C \tag{8.1}$$

$$3 y_A + 6 y_B \geq k^{feed} \tag{8.2}$$

$$1 y_A + 1 y_C \geq k^{mk} \tag{8.3}$$

$$y_A, y_B, y_C \in \{0; 1; 2; \ldots\} \tag{8.4}$$

The goal is to minimize the total hiring charges [Eq. (8.1)] but the minimal number of required feeder services [Eq. (8.2)] and main-haul services [Eq. (8.3)] must be respected. Only complete trucks can be hired [Eq. (8.4)]. This model can easily be solved using Excel Solver or any other solver software.

Mike has determined the best number of trucks as shown in Table 8.5. The incorporation of trucks assigned to main-hauls only (type-C pattern) realizes costs reductions of more than 6 % compared to the milk-run situation although the number of incorporated trucks remains the same.

Although the transshipment strategy requires the least weekly transportation costs if no postponement is possible, Mike is aware of some shortcoming. First, the transshipment facility must be constructed, hired or rented. The transshipment activities and the necessary storage processes cause costs. As long as the additional

8.3 Realizing Economies of Scale in Transportation

Table 8.5 Daily transportation with trans-shipments

	Mon	Tue	Wed	Thu	Fri	Sat	Sun	Sums
Demand waiting in Hamburg								
OD-demand d_R (in tons)	32	53	18	34	43	60	30	270
Fulfilled demand	32	53	18	34	43	60	30	270
Required feeder services	2	3	1	2	2	3	2	15
Demand waiting in Bremerhaven								
OD-demand d_R (in tons)	23	42	31	28	38	50	20	232
Fulfilled demand	23	42	31	28	38	50	20	232
Required feeder services	1	2	2	2	2	2	1	12
Demand waiting in Wilhelmshaven								
OD-demand d_R (in tons)	13	12	25	13	26	38	11	138
Fulfilled demand	13	12	25	13	26	38	11	138
Required feeder services	1	1	1	1	2	2	1	9
Total demand Hanover to Munich	68	107	74	75	107	148	61	640
Required feeder cycles	4	6	4	5	6	7	4	36
Required feeder cycles	3	5	3	3	5	6	3	28
Hired trucks for type-A-pattern	2	5	2	2	2	3	2	18
Hired trucks for type-B-pattern	0	0	0	0	0	0	0	0
Hired trucks for type-C-pattern	1	0	1	1	3	3	1	10
Available feeder cycles	6	15	6	6	6	9	6	54
Available main-haul services	3	5	3	3	5	6	3	28
Hiring costs	2400 €	4250 €	2400 €	2400 €	3800 €	4650 €	2400 €	22,300 €
Hired trucks	3	5	3	3	5	6	3	28

costs are less than the transportation costs savings, Mike would suggest using a transshipment facility. However, Mike also warns managers that the complexity of the transport network configuration increases.

So far, Mike has introduced the concept of shipment consolidation as a strategy to avoid partially filled truck trips. The intention of consolidation is to achieve economies of scale during transportation. Three consolidation strategies have been proposed. Postponement compiles shipments from different time slots together.

Milk-runs aim at loading shipments from different pickup operations on one truck in order to lift the fill rate of this truck. Transshipment exploits different hiring tariffs for different kinds of truck operations (depending on regional services).

Mike concludes that the ideas presented here apply in general also for other means of transport like trains, plans, vessels or barges. In case of transshipment consolidation, feeder services as well as main-haul operations can be assigned to resources from different means of transport (see Sect. 8.6).

8.4 Trade-Off-Based Transportation Network Design

After Mike has finished his presentation, a discussion is initiated about the right distribution network strategy for Bavarian Wood. The board members like the idea of redesigning the supply network based on transshipment. However, they do not feel comfortable with the necessary investment nor with the annual costs for running a transshipment point. With respect to the prospective extension by the inclusion of Rotterdam, Salzburg and Prague they cannot estimate the associated costs and benefits. Therefore, they ask Mike to deliver further explanations about this issue.

Mike expected such a question. He has prepared an executive summary of the section "Factors Influencing Distribution Network Design" from Chopra and Meindl's (2009) SCM book, where the aforementioned topic is discussed in detail. He distributes these copies and provides an oral survey.

There are two general directions for designing and evaluating transportation networks. First, *customer needs* must be identified. These needs will be the starting point for the set-up of the transportation network. Second, *costs* of the installation and deployment of the transportation network have to be determined. Both of these are compromised by the uncertainty of the future circumstances under which the transport network is used. On the one hand, customer needs are unknown, hidden or will change. On the other hand, the costs for running a certain network are subject to external impacts maybe from oscillating customer demand, varying fuel prices, labour costs and so on. Therefore, only a rough estimation of benefits with regard to customer satisfaction and costs is possible.

The major driver of customer satisfaction is the ability to react immediately and with high reliability to an expressed customer demand. If a customer recognizes the need for transportation, this customer wants to have the associated services as soon as possible. Here, the urgency is related to either the quickest possible pickup time or the earliest delivery time. With respect to the Bavarian Wood situation the following might occur. A manufacturing site (Munich, Salzburg or Prague) recognizes that additional material is needed as soon as possible. If the material is stocked (even for a short time but regularly) in one of the import or transshipment facilities contained in the Bavarian Wood supply network, the average re-supply time tends to decrease with the increasing number of network nodes. Depending on

8.4 Trade-Off-Based Transportation Network Design

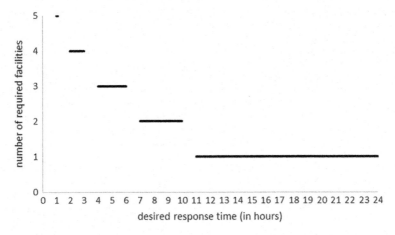

Fig. 8.10 Relation between desired customer response time (x-axis) and the number of facilities required to ensure this response time

the spatial distribution of the nodes where materials are stocked, the re-supply time (which equals the difference between the time of arrival of the additional material and the time when the need is expressed) decreases proportionally, degressively or progressively (see Fig. 8.10).

Figure 8.10 clearly shows that there is a strong relationship between the *number of facilities* for storing supply materials and the customer *service level*. In the Bavarian Wood case each transshipment point will hold some quantities of different types of wood which is in transit from the import ports in Germany and (prospectively) in the Netherlands to the manufacturing sites. Mike emphasizes that storing even small quantities in a transshipment yard can contribute to ensuring a quick re-supply. The major reason is the reduced distance from a transshipment yard to the factories compared to the average distance from the seaport to the manufacturing sites. However, Mike also explains that the number of facilities play a higher role in the distribution of goods with late customer orders.

In order to achieve a higher level of material availability and a quicker re-supply time, Mike proposes to discuss the installation of two transshipment points. Besides the one in Hanover he proposes to establish a transshipment facility in the region of Wuerzburg which lies just between Hanover and Munich, close to the major motorway A7. In this transshipment facility the inbound flow of wood from the German seaport can be merged with the inbound flow from Rotterdam. Furthermore, from the Wuerzburg facility it is possible to send materials to all three manufacturing sites. A small warehouse here can be used to maintain a centralized safety stock of all material for all three production sites at each transshipment yard. Of course, costs for keeping all facilities running increases if the number of operated facilities is increased.

Fig. 8.11 Relation between desired customer response time (x-axis) and the number of facilities required to ensure this response time

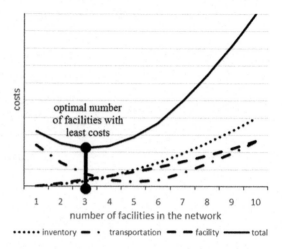

After Mike has clarified the interrelations between the number of considered network nodes and the service to be offered to the customer he continues to explain the main cost drivers in a transportation network. Mike points out that there are three major cost drivers to be considered during the determination of the right network design (Fig. 8.11). First, there are *inventory costs*. Inventory costs tend to grow if the number of networked facilities is increased because each facility holds a certain quantity of inventory. Besides the fact that there is planned inventory already stocked, there might also be inventory just waiting to be forwarded. Second, the costs directly associated with the *usage of the facilities* have to be considered. Obviously, these costs increase if the number of facilities is increased. Third, there are the *transportation costs* that contribute to the overall expenditures.

In Fig. 8.11, the typical development of the transportation costs is represented by the dashed-dotted graph. Up to a certain number of maintained transshipment facilities, additional economies of scale can be realized by consolidation, as discussed in Sect. 8.3. If more transshipment facilities are incorporated into the network then the number of transport connections exceeds a threshold value. Beyond this threshold value, it is no longer possible to completely fill a truck. The average quantity to be moved by a truck decreases, since total transport demand is distributed over a higher number of transport options so that the costs per moved ton increase further. Totalling two increasing cost functions for facility costs as well as inventory costs and of the convex transportation cost function leads to a convex function for the total costs. Such a function has an optimal number of facilities with minimal total costs. Incorporating this optimal number of facilities minimizes the total costs of the transportation system and thus contributes to balancing costs and customer satisfaction.

8.5 Capacity Allocation in a Many-to-Many Network

After Mike has completed the outline of the scheme to find the appropriate transportation network, another discussion among the board members of Bavarian Wood is initiated. Robert, who is the responsible human resource manager, wants to know if it is possible to establish and operate a highly sophisticated transportation network without well-trained and educated staff members. Mike is sure that this is impossible since transportation management requires in-depth knowledge about transport technologies, transport processes and transport regulations as well as laws.

This clear statement is considered by the board members in the subsequent discussions. Since it seems impossible to operate a complex transportation network efficiently without a well-trained group of transportation managers there are two options left: either a well-trained highly specialized group of transportation managers must be established (hired or trained); or transportation activities must be outsourced.

Robert wants to know from Mike about his own opinion. Mike replies as follows. So far, Bavarian Wood follows a strategy somewhere in between the two options. Since Bavarian Wood has no trucks of its own, these vehicles are hired. However, the risk of failing to achieve the required high fill rate in order to gain economies of scale is completely with Bavarian Wood. If no economies of scale can be realized for any reason, the transportation costs are quite high, as seen in the examples in Sect. 8.3. For this reason, Mike agrees to think about outsourcing the complete transportation. In this context, it can be useful to look for transport service providers who are paid only for an executed transport service, as in the letter and parcel service industry. From calculations similar to those conducted in Sect. 8.3, Bavarian Wood knows the costs per ton in case the hiring approach followed so far is used again.

Mike suggests contacting several forwarding companies to collect information about their tariffs for all possible import connections between Bavarian Wood's four seaports and three manufacturing facilities. One week later, there is another meeting between Mike and the board members. Mike wants to use this meeting to explain how the transportation costs can be minimized if the transport service providers are paid by carried tons only.

During the last week Mike had contacted several freight carriage companies and he had asked for their tariffs to move freight between the seaports and the manufacturing sites. More specifically, he had asked for the price per ton moved between a given seaport as the loading location and a given factory as the unloading location. Mike had collected all the information. For each of the 12 possible transportation links, he had selected the cheapest freight carrier. The associated tariffs (per ton) are given in Fig. 8.12. Additionally, Mike has indicated the supply quantities available at each seaport and the quantities ordered by each factory per week.

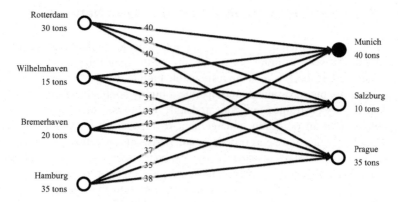

Fig. 8.12 Data of the transportation analysis for Bavarian Wood

8.5.1 The Transportation Problem

The *transportation problem* [or the Hitchcock distribution problem (Hitchcock 1941)] addresses the situation outlined in Fig. 8.12 and aims at minimizing the total sum of transport expenses while the individual demand from each receiving node is fulfilled and no supply node aims to supply more quantities than it has in stock. As can be seen from the example in Fig. 8.12, solving the transportation problem is not a trivial task. For each supply node it has to be decided which quantity is assigned to which receiving node; and vice-versa for each receiving node, as it has to be decided which quantity is ordered from which supply node.

The core to solving the transportation problem is to assign the shipped quantities to each available transport link connecting a seaport (supply node) with a manufacturing site (receiving node). If zero quantity is assigned to a link, then this link is not used. It is necessary to select those shipment quantities for each link where the sum of costs over all transportation links is minimal, but where the demand for each receiving node is fulfilled (restriction A) and no supply node stock is exceeded (restriction B). Obviously, all assigned quantities must be zero or larger than zero (restriction C).

8.5.2 Decision Model

Similar to the warehouse location problem (WLP) in Chap. 7, it is possible to represent (to "model") the decision situation associated with the Hitchcock distribution problem in terms of a *linear optimization model*. The parameters of this model (Eqs. (8.5)–(8.8)) are as follows. The set S contains all of the supply nodes and for each element $s \in S$ the available (stored) supply quantity q_s is known. All receiving nodes are collected in the set R and node $r \in R$ requests the quantity d_r. All quantities are expressed in tons per week. The costs for moving one ton from

8.5 Capacity Allocation in a Many-to-Many Network

supply node $s \in S$ to the receiving node $r \in R$ is written over the corresponding arc in Fig. 8.12 and this cost factor is c_{sr}. There are no discounts available if the transported quantity is increased.

The decision variables are x_{sr} representing the transport quantity assigned to the transportation link originating from the supply node s and terminating in the receiving node r. All non-negative real values are allowed for x_{sr}.

$$\min Z = \sum_{s \in S} \sum_{r \in R} c_{sr} \cdot x_{sr} \tag{8.5}$$

$$\sum_{s \in S} x_{sr} \geq d_r \forall r \in R \tag{8.6}$$

$$\sum_{r \in R} x_{sr} \leq q_s \forall s \in S \tag{8.7}$$

$$x_{sr} \geq 0 \forall s \in S, r \in R \tag{8.8}$$

It is necessary to minimize the total transportation costs (8.5). The individual demand of all receiving nodes must be covered (8.6) but the available stock is to be considered (8.7). All quantities assigned to a transportation link must be non-negative (8.8). This linear programme formulation of the Hitchcock distribution problem was originally introduced by Dantzig (1951), who has also proposed an elegant algorithm to determine optimal transport quantities for each link. This method is known today as the modified distribution *(MODI) method*. However, the MODI method presumes that a feasible initial solution for the model (8.5)–(8.8) is already available. Therefore, such a construction procedure is discussed first in Sect. 8.5.3, before the MODI methodology is introduced. The MODI algorithm is then used to iterate and improve the initial solution, taking care that for each iteration feasibility is maintained and the costs are reduced. This two-phase concept, comprising a construction phase and a subsequently processed improvement phase processed subsequently, is an important and well-investigated approach to the identification of optimal or sub-optimal solutions of an optimization model. Mike is going to explain the computation of the cost of the minimal transport quantity assignment using the MODI approach. He uses the example data given in Fig. 8.12.

> ▶ **Practical Insights** In practice, the transportation problem can also be solved for cases with capacity bottlenecks. In this situation, the capacity can be extended by the so-called over-costs. In addition, the transportation problem can be extended to the multi-stage SC setting such as cross-docking or hub-and-spoke systems. This form is called a transshipment problem.

8.5.3 Finding the First Feasible Model Solution

Mike starts the construction of a first feasible assignment by analysing the total quantities demanded as well as the total available quantities. In order to apply the MODI approach it is necessary that these two sums are equal ("balanced transportation problem"). Since the equality is not observed in our example (the sum of supply quantities are 100 tons but total demand is only 85 tons) Mike introduces an artificial customer ("dummy demand node") that requests the residual supply quantity. The artificial transportation costs towards this artificial demand node are set to 0. With this modification, the transportation problem is now "*balanced*" with respect to demand and supply in the SC (Fig. 8.13).

In order to keep the description of the construction algorithm as compact as possible, Mike presents all data in the so-called *transportation matrix* shown in Fig. 8.14. The heads of the rows contain the seaport names and the available supply quantities but the column heads carry the names of the demanding nodes (factories) and the quantities demanded. The spanned matrix consists of 4×4 cells. In the upper left corner of the cell in row i and column j Mike writes the costs c_{ij} for shipping 1 ton along the link originating from i and terminating in j.

Currently, all cells are empty but Mike is going to fill them consecutively with the quantities that are forwarded along the corresponding transportation links. Mike starts with the upper left cell that represents the transportation link from Rotterdam to Munich $(1 \rightarrow 1)$. This cell (connection) is labelled by the bold frame. Mike assigns as much quantity to this link as possible. The maximal quantity is 30 tons since Rotterdam does not offer a larger quantity. Mike assigns 30 tons to the labelled link and writes this quantity in the marked cell. After this assignment, Mike concludes two issues. First, the demand from Munich is partially unsatisfied (10 tons have to be carried there from another seaport) but Rotterdam cannot be

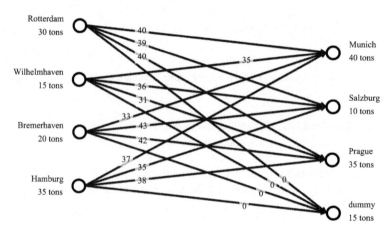

Fig. 8.13 The transportation problem data for Bavarian Wood including the dummy customer ("balanced transportation problem")

Fig. 8.14 Empty transportation matrix (start of construction)

	Munich 40	Salzburg 10	Prague 35	dummy 15
Rotterdam 30				
Wilhelmshaven 15	35	36	31	0
Bremerhaven 20	33	43	42	0
Hamburg 35	37	35	38	0

Fig. 8.15 Partially filled transportation matrix after assignment of first quantity to the transportation link Rotterdam to Munich

	Munich 40	Salzburg 10	Prague 35	dummy 15
Rotterdam 30	40 / 30	39 / -	40 / -	0 / -
Wilhelmshaven 15	35	36	31	0
Bremerhaven 20	33	43	42	0
Hamburg 35	37	35	38	0

used to supply any other location. Therefore, Mike can close all remaining connections starting in Rotterdam. He indicates this closure by writing a "-" into the affected cells (Fig. 8.15).

Mike is going to fill the next cells. He tries to satisfy the demand of the only partially served site in Munich. This means that he assigns 10 tons to the link Wilhelmshaven to Munich with a cost factor of 35 €/ton. Now the demand from Munich is completely satisfied and Mike closes all connections terminating here. These cannot be used further (Fig. 8.16).

Wilhelmshaven has still some quantity available and the remaining 5 tons are now assigned to the next available demand location after Munich. This is Salzburg (see Fig. 8.17).

The stock size at Wilhelmshaven is exhausted but demand from Salzburg is not yet completely fulfilled. Mike selects Bremerhaven as the next available supply node after Wilhelmshaven (Fig. 8.18). Bremerhaven provides the remaining 5 tons for Salzburg.

Fig. 8.16 Partially filled transportation matrix after assignment of quantity to the transportation link Wilhelmshaven to Munich

	Munich 40	Salzburg 10	Prague 35	dummy 15
Rotterdam 30	40 / 30	39 / -	40 / -	0 / -
Wilhelmshaven 15	35 / 10	36	31	0
Bremerhaven 20	33 / -	43	42	0
Hamburg 35	37 / -	35	38	0

Fig. 8.17 Partially filled transportation matrix after assignment of quantity 5 to the transportation link Wilhelmshaven to Salzburg (*3rd step*)

	Munich 40	Salzburg 10	Prague 35	dummy 15
Rotterdam 30	40 / 30	39 / -	40 / -	0 / -
Wilhelmshaven 15	35 / 10	36 / 5	31 / -	0 / -
Bremerhaven 20	33 / -	43	42	0
Hamburg 35	37 / -	35	38	0

The demand from Salzburg is completely fulfilled but Bremerhaven still has 15 tons available. This quantity is given to the next demand location which is Prague (Fig. 8.19).

However, Bremerhaven is unable to completely fulfil the demand from Prague. The remaining quantity of 20 tons is provided by the next supply location after Bremerhaven, which is Hamburg (Fig. 8.20).

Figure 8.21 shows the completed first transportation matrix which represents the first constructed feasible solution of the transportation model. The residual supply quantity of 15 tons is assigned to the link originating from Hamburg and heading to the dummy demand node. All used transportation links are shaded in grey.

This construction scheme is called the north-west corner rule (Gass 2003). Mike determines the costs associated with the instantiated transport quantities by totalling products of assigned quantities and the cost coefficients. Here, Mike gets 40 €/t_0 ·30 t_0 + 35 €/t_0 ·10 t_0 + 36 €/t_0 ·5 t_0 + 43 €/t_0 ·5 t_0 + 42 €/t_0 ·15 t_0 + 38 €/t_0 ·20 t_0 + 0 €/t_0 ·15 t_0 = 3335 € as total forwarding costs.

8.5 Capacity Allocation in a Many-to-Many Network

Fig. 8.18 Partially filled transportation matrix after assignment of quantity 205 to the transportation link Bremerhaven to Salzburg (*4th step*)

		Munich 40	Salzburg 10	Prague 35	dummy 15
Rotterdam	30	40 / 30	39 / -	40 / -	0 / -
Wilhelmshaven	15	35 / 10	36 / 5	31 / -	0 / -
Bremerhaven	20	33 / -	43 / 5	42	0
Hamburg	35	37 / -	35 / -	38	0

Fig. 8.19 Partially filled transportation matrix after assignment of quantity 15 to the transportation link Bremerhaven to Prague (*5th step*)

		Munich 40	Salzburg 10	Prague 35	dummy 15
Rotterdam	30	40 / 30	39 / -	40 / -	0 / -
Wilhelmshaven	15	35 / 10	36 / 5	31 / -	0 / -
Bremerhaven	20	33 / -	43 / 5	42 / 15	0 / -
Hamburg	35	37 / -	35 / -	38	0

Fig. 8.20 Partially filled transportation matrix after assignment of quantity 20 to the transportation link Hamburg to Prague (*6th step*)

		Munich 40	Salzburg 10	Prague 35	dummy 15
Rotterdam	30	40 / 30	39 / -	40 / -	0 / -
Wilhelmshaven	15	35 / 10	36 / 5	31 / -	0 / -
Bremerhaven	20	33 / -	43 / 5	42 / 15	0 / -
Hamburg	35	37 / -	35 / -	38 / 20	0

Fig. 8.21 Completely filled transportation matrix after assignment of the residual quantity of 15 tons to the transportation link Hamburg to the dummy demand node (*7th step*)

		Munich 40	Salzburg 10	Prague 35	dummy 15
Rotterdam	30	40 / 30	39 / -	40 / -	0 / -
Wilhelmshaven	15	35 / 10	36 / 5	31 / -	0 / -
Bremerhaven	20	33 / -	43 / 5	42 / 15	0 / -
Hamburg	35	37 / -	35 / -	38 / 20	0 / 15

8.5.4 Optimality Check

After the presentation of the construction procedure, Mike is asked by Walter if the proposed solution is optimal and how Mike can check if it is optimal. In general, the application of the matrix minimum method does not lead to the optimal solution of the model, Mike replies. However, there is an intuitive way to check if and how the assignment can be modified so that costs are reduced.

The basic idea is to find out whether shifting some of the quantities between the transportation links will lead to a cost reduction. If such a shifting is impossible then the available solution is optimal, as no further cost reductions are possible. On the other hand, the cost-reducing shifting is identified and applied immediately, leading to a new and updated assignment with lower total costs.

Total costs of 3335 € are associated with the used transportation links so far. The used transportation link is called a base link and a currently unused link is called a non-base link. Mike is going to check whether the usage so far of a non-base line will lead to a cost reduction. Therefore, Mike first distributes the current cost amount over all network nodes.

$$u_1 + v_1 = 40 \tag{8.9}$$

$$u_2 + v_1 = 35 \tag{8.10}$$

$$u_2 + v_2 = 36 \tag{8.11}$$

$$u_3 + v_2 = 43 \tag{8.12}$$

$$u_3 + v_3 = 42 \tag{8.13}$$

$$u_4 + v_3 = 38 \tag{8.14}$$

$$u_4 + v_4 = 0 \tag{8.15}$$

Fig. 8.22 Initial solution proposal with potential values and savings per ton

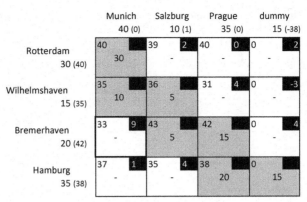

Therefore, he introduces the so-called potential values u_i for supply node $i \in S$ and v_j for receiving node $j \in R$ and splits the costs c_{ij} for all currently used transportation links $i \rightarrow j$ so that $c_{ij} = u_i + v_j$. This leads to the system of linear equalities shown in Eqs. (8.9)–(8.15). It has a unique solution if we set $v_1 = 0$ (without this setting there would be more than one solution). This solution can be derived by the application of the Gaussian elimination method. In the example considered here, we get the potential values $u_1 = 40$, $u_2 = 35$, $u_3 = 42$, $u_4 = 38$, $v_1 = 0$, $v_2 = 1$, $v_3 = 0$ and $v_4 = -38$. These values are written in brackets (see Fig. 8.22).

Mike is now able to calculate imputed cost factors c'_{ij} per ton for the currently unused links by adding the potential u_i for the starting location i and the potential v_j for the terminating location j ($c'_{ij} := u_i + v_j$). If he compares the imputed current costs with the real costs computing $c'_{ij} - c_{ij}$ which apply if a currently unused link is used, he can see if the incorporation of this leads to savings. These savings/values are written in the upper right corners of the cells representing the recently unused cells (small black rectangles). All connections with the exceptions of Rotterdam–Prague and Wilhelmshaven–dummy will lead to a cost reduction. Therefore, the initial solution is not an optimal solution.

If Mike finds out for a given solution that there is no non-base connection associated with a positive (>0) saving $c'_{ij} - c_{ij}$ per ton, then the solution currently available is optimal. Therefore, Mike can use the implied savings $c'_{ij} - c_{ij}$ associated with non-base connections as a general optimality criterion in order to check whether a given feasible solution is optimal or not.

8.5.5 Solution Improvement

Since Mike has found out that the constructed solution is not optimal he has to modify it. Therefore, he first identifies the non-base connection with the highest saving per ton. This is the link Bremerhaven to Munich with a saving of 9 € per assigned ton (3 → 1). Mike indicates this link by a black bold frame (see Fig. 8.22).

Fig. 8.23 First solution with zig-zag-path (costs are 3335 €)

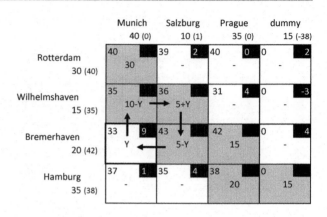

Since each ton assigned to this link reduces the total transportation costs by 9 €, Mike wants to assign the highest possible quantity Y to this link. Therefore, he has to move some quantities between the links already used. When Mike assigns Y tons to the delivery from Bremerhaven to Munich then Munich receives Y tons above the quantity demanded. Therefore, the quantity associated with another used link terminating in Munich must be reduced by Y tons. In the example shown in Fig. 8.23 the quantity to be shipped from Wilhelmshaven to Munich is reduced by Y tons. However, the reduction of the quantity to be shipped from Wilhelmshaven reduces the total outbound quantity by Y tons. This implies the need to increase the quantity to be shipped from Wilhelmshaven to another location by Y tons in order to prevent the reduction of the total outbound quantity associated with Wilhelmshaven. Here, it is only possible to increase the quantity assigned to the link Wilhelmshaven to Salzburg by Y units. Now, Salzburg receives a too large quantity so that the inbound quantity provided by another supply node must be reduced by Y tons. Here, only the quantity assigned to the link Bremerhaven to Salzburg is reduced by 5 tons. After this reduction all inconsistencies related to the assigned quantities are solved. The sequence of the arcs shown in Fig. 8.23 represents the sequence of modified shipment quantities. This is known as the "zig-zag path". For its construction, only base connections are allowed to be modified.

Following the zig-zag path, Mike can determine the maximal feasible value that can be assigned to Y. Therefore, he records all original quantities from which he has subtracted Y. Since the updated quantities must not become negative, Mike assigns the minimal recorded value to Y. In the example, it is $Y := \min\{10; 5\} = 5$. The resulting updated solution is shown in Fig. 8.24. The costs associated with this new solution are 3335 € $- 5\ t_0 \cdot 9$ €/$t_0 = 3290$ €.

Mike summarizes the steps to update the solution for the transportation problem.

1. Determine the potential values u_i and v_j for all involved locations.
2. Determine the imputed costs $c'_{ij} = u_i + v_j$ for all current non-base links. (connections).

8.5 Capacity Allocation in a Many-to-Many Network

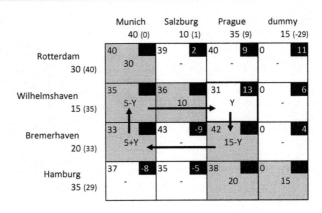

Fig. 8.24 Second transportation matrix with costs = 3290 € and Y = min {10;5} = 5

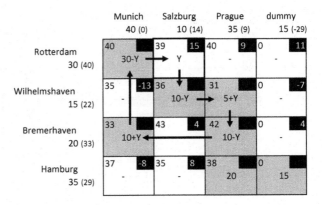

Fig. 8.25 Third transportation matrix with costs = 3225 € and Y = min {10;10;30} = 10

3. Compare the imputed costs with the real costs. If $u_i + v_j - c_{ij} > 0$ for at least one non-base link the given solution is not optimal (otherwise it is an optimal solution).
4. Select the non-base link $i^* - j^*$ with the maximal savings value $u_i + v_j - c_{ij}$ per ton.
5. Determine the quantity Y to be assigned to the link originating from i^* and termination in j^* by the determination of a zig-zag-path through the current base links.

These five steps are repeated until in step (3) it is recognized that there is no non-base link whose incorporation will reduce the total cost. Figs. 8.24, 8.25, 8.26, 8.27, 8.28, 8.29, and 8.30 contain the intermediate transportation matrices that are consecutively generated by the repeated application of steps (1)–(5).

The third transportation matrix is non-optimal, so that a zig-zag-path is determined (Fig. 8.25). Here, both base links Wilhelmshaven to Salzburg and Bremerhaven to Prague carry the same minimal quantity of 10 tons. The first of

Fig. 8.26 Fourth transportation matrix with costs = 3075 € and Y = min {15;0;20} = 0

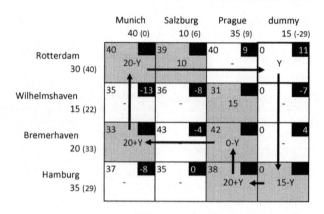

Fig. 8.27 Fifth transportation matrix with costs = 3075 € and Y = min {10;15} = 10

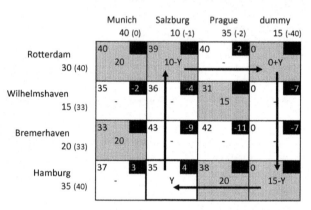

Fig. 8.28 Sixth transportation matrix with costs = 3035 € and Y = min {20;5} = 5

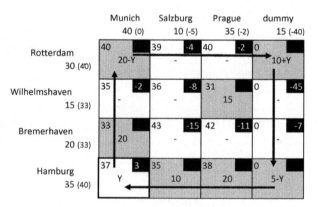

both base links Wilhelmhaven to Salzburg becomes a non-base link ("-") while the other link remains a base link and the quantity is set to 0 (Fig. 8.26).

The MODI method can be used to optimize the assignment of quantities to different transportation links in a many-to-many-network set-up. Besides this

8.6 Distribution Network Design

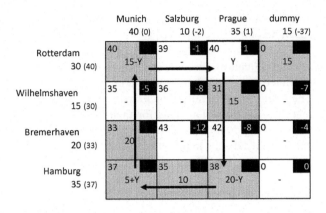

Fig. 8.29 Seventh transportation matrix with costs = 3020 € and Y = min {15;20} = 15

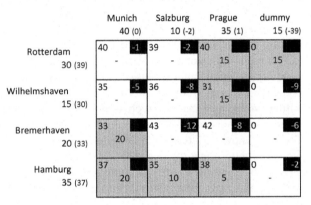

Fig. 8.30 Eighth transportation matrix with costs = 3005 € (optimal)

north-west-corner algorithm there are other procedures to generate an initial solution: the matrix-minimum algorithm as described in Vahrenkamp and Mattfeld (2007) and Vogel's approximation algorithm as described in Domschke (2007). Also, alternative improvement algorithms like stepping-stone algorithms (Charnes and Cooper 1954) can be used to identify optimal solutions for a transportation model.

8.6 Distribution Network Design

8.6.1 Case Study: ALDI vs. Homeplus

The learning objectives of this case study are to (1) identify basic trade-offs between facility, inventory, transportation costs, and distribution network design; and (2) understand an alignment between SC responsiveness and efficiency.

ALDI stands for Albrecht Discount, and is a supermarket founded in Germany in 1913. The chain has expanded immensely and can nowadays be found all over the world. ALDI's strategy is to sell very reasonable quality at discount prices. The unique combination of being efficient but yet selling high quality products gives ALDI a competitive advantage.

The company has a purchasing power that makes it simple to use economies of scale and quantity discounts to buy in products. The variety of products is rather restricted compared to other supermarkets. This allows inventory cost reduction. The stores are generally rather small and standardized. Moreover, ALDI chooses relatively low-cost locations for their supermarkets. This also cuts down facility costs. Transportation costs are rather low as this is typically planned using large batches. ALDI sells mainly their own brands and keeps marketing and advertising to a minimum, enabling them to reduce overhead costs. Additionally, profit margins are quite small compared to ALDI's competitors. These operational decisions enable ALDI to sell at low prices while holding a large market share. This strategy works extremely well for price-conscious customers. However, some consumers might miss their favourite branded product or a wider variety of products to choose from. Additionally, other supermarkets offer more non-food products and services, making them attractive to customers. ALDI has improved in this sector offering for example photo or travel services on their web page.

Shopping on the internet has become very popular in recent years. At first people bought only books and electronics, nowadays basically everything is available online. Many supermarkets such as Wal-Mart and Tesco have developed concepts where customers can order on line and have groceries delivered to their homes. Tesco is known by the name Homeplus in South Korea and adapts its business model to better meet the needs and preferences of its local customers. While they did also offer online grocery shopping, Homeplus was considering a better way of reaching their customers, the "virtual store" concept. The virtual store is based on m-commerce technology in which shoppers can browse through pictures of available products in a public place, in this case a subway station. Products can be selected by scanning the QR-code with a smartphone which uses a mobile application to directly order products. The products are then sent to the customer's home within the same day. Deliveries are arranged to arrive quickly, so the groceries will be in the shopper's kitchen that night and there is no need to wait in to receive them.

The virtual store fits perfectly with the expectations of local customers; sales increased 130 % in 3 months, and the number of registered users went up by 76 %. The virtual m-commerce store might be more suitable for the Korean market than most other markets. Yet the benefits, such as shorter shopping times, convenient order and payment services and home delivery may also become more and more appreciated around the world, just as more and more countries will reach smartphone acceptance rates similar to those of South Korea. From an SCM perspective, additional benefits can be achieved. Most notably, physical stores can be eliminated, leading to a more cost-effective SC with direct shipping as a distribution strategy. The entire purchasing process can be automated without any human intervention from the retailer's side. With fewer centralized distribution centres, higher customer service (product availability) rates and reduced safety stock can be achieved. However, delivery costs for very small quantities could become a serious issue, depending on customers' order behaviour and stores' delivery pricing policy.

Homeplus displays its goods at public transportation hubs, such as metro stations. Customers can observe the products on posters just like on a real shelf and can scan them with their smartphone. What is the premise for the big hit? Korea is an early adopter when it comes to technology. In 2011 40 % of the entire South Korean population was using smartphones. So scanning the items via QR codes makes it easy for customers to shop while they are waiting. Homeplus was rewarded for its creativity. The application was downloaded 900,000 times in the first year and the company was even nominated for multiple design awards. Sales increased tremendously and Homeplus is now the number one retailer on-line. The company is expanding its virtual stores to bus stops and train stations.

From the operational point of view there are, as always, up- and downsides to the virtual store. Delivering goods directly to the customer reduces the number of goods sold in the store. As a result, less stock is needed and inventory costs are reduced. Moreover, online ordering makes it easier to track items and potentially fewer goods are lost through theft, miscounting or other human intervention. Also, with direct shipping, the FIFO method is fairly easy to apply, as customers are not able to pick between the same types of goods from the shelf. This way the products that are closer to being out-of-date can be sold prior to the longer lasting goods. Moreover, customer service is improved when the availability of items is higher, since they are delivered from central warehouses. This again reduces costs for warehousing along with personnel costs. In short, having online ordering and direct deliveries makes it easy to design a more cost-efficient SC compared to traditional selling in stores.

Most importantly, customers benefit immensely from the innovation. They can use their waiting time at the bus stop or metro station to do their grocery shopping. Time is a precious good in today's society which is perhaps why buying food after work may be more of a hassle to most people than a pleasure. With the highly developed technology in South Korea the virtual store concept becomes easy to use. Moreover, stores are less crowded, which is another benefit passively affecting offline shoppers. Increased customer service improves the reputation of Homeplus compared to their competitors. It is important that Homeplus pays great attention to this service level so that they continue to please their potential consumers. This concerns for example the functionality of the smartphone application as well as on-time deliveries and the quality of products. A disadvantage of the concept can arise with delivery costs. As all goods are delivered directly, the shipping costs may be higher. Homeplus can design an efficient delivery system while using milk-run truck deliveries to multiple customers in a nearby area.

Additionally, making goods and prices available on line improves comparability. There are already many applications helping the customer to find the cheapest goods at each of the stores. This trend is most likely to increase. This makes it necessary for vendors to focus on unique selling points so they do not find themselves exposed to selling at drop-down prices.

Discussion

Consider trade-offs between inventory costs, number of warehouses, and transportation costs at ALDI and Homeplus. Explain the efficiency and responsiveness issues in the case study based on these trade-offs.
Which factors of efficiency and responsiveness can you identify at ALDI and Homeplus?
Which distribution strategy is used by Homeplus in South Korea?
Which transportation strategy is used by Homeplus in South Korea?
Which factors facilitated the Homeplus concept in South Korea?
Is it possible to implement a virtual store in your country? What challenges might be encountered?

8.6.2 Types of Distribution Networks

According to the transportation network design, different *distribution network structures* can be distinguished (Fig. 8.31).

In the case of direct shipments, distribution is organized as a direct network, with storage on the manufacturing side. Alternatively, if the production strategy is assemble-to-order (ATO) or make-to-order (MTO), the products can be delivered directly to customers (for example, this has been DELL's strategy).

In the retailing business, most distribution networks are organized as multi-stage systems with intermediate warehouses, distribution centres, cross-docking centres, and hub terminals. Such complex systems are typically managed by logistics service providers. Consider as examples cross-docking and hub-and-spoke networks.

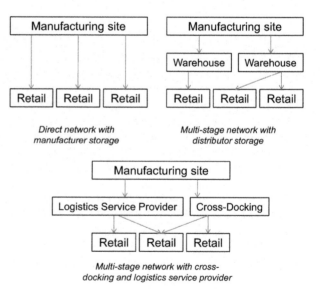

Fig. 8.31 Types of distribution networks

8.6 Distribution Network Design

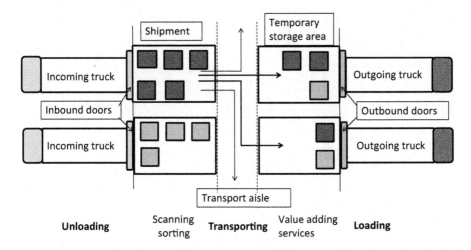

Fig. 8.32 Cross-docking terminal [based on Stephan and Boysen (2011)]

Cross-docking implements the idea of the consolidation of goods from inbound trucks to outbound trucks via an intermediate transit point (i.e. the cross-docking centre). The special feature of cross-docking is that the goods do not remain in the warehouse longer than 24 h (see Fig. 8.32).

Some *advantages* of cross-docking are the realization of economies of scale in transportation, frequent bundled deliveries, inventory reduction, faster product flow, reduction of errors, savings in material handling and labour costs, increase in fleet capacity utilization, and mitigation of the bullwhip effect. At the same time, high investment is required to establish a cross-docking terminal. The coordination complexity and risks of stock-out/disruptions in the SC also increase. Finally, data security issues become crucial. Examples of successful cross-docking realization can be found in many retailing companies, e.g., Wal-Mart, E. LeClerc, etc.

Hub-and-spoke network also implements the idea of consolidation (Fig. 8.33).

A hub represents the consolidation element in the distribution network. Spokes are the regional warehouses and customers. This concept is used for shipment consolidation with similar advantages and disadvantages as cross-docking. For example, the airport Leipzig-Halle is DHL's largest hub in Germany. In further course of the chapter, you will find case studies on different distribution networks.

8.6.3 Case Study: Seven-Eleven Japan

The Seven-Eleven Japan Co. Ltd was founded in 1974 and grew to be one of the largest retail networks, with more than 50,000 stores worldwide with an average area of 100–150 m^2 per store. At first, the company's SC was straightforward oriented, from producers to the stores (Fig. 8.34).

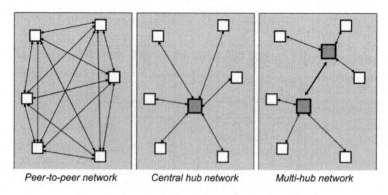

Fig. 8.33 Types of hub-and-spoke networks

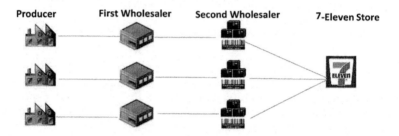

Fig. 8.34 Straightforward oriented supply chain

This type of structure resulted in significant shortcomings. Due to the high number of facilities, high total facility/handling, inventory and logistics costs (more than 70 deliveries a day to the stores) were encountered. The information line was too long which negatively impacted the service level because of low response times and inventory turnover (about 25 turns a year in 1970s).

In redesigning the distribution network, Seven-Eleven Japan (SEJ) undertook some crucial changes. The key objectives of the redesign were to further enhance customer satisfaction and profitability. The opportunities for doing this were seen in reducing costs, preventing stock-outs and ensuring high quality of the products. The company launched several actions, such as high investment information and communication systems, identification of an adequate partner for each region, and assurance of long-term relationships. In addition, a combined delivery system (CDS) was developed which was based on absence of direct store delivery (Fig. 8.35).

Different manufacturers and distributors from the same geographical regions consolidate their shipments in order to minimize the number of trucks going to the combined distribution centres (CDC). The five CDCs (i.e., frozen products, chilled products, fresh foods, drinks and noodles, and magazines) are sorted by product category and required storage temperature. From here different suppliers' products are delivered to the shops. For some products (e.g., fresh boxed products),

8.6 Distribution Network Design

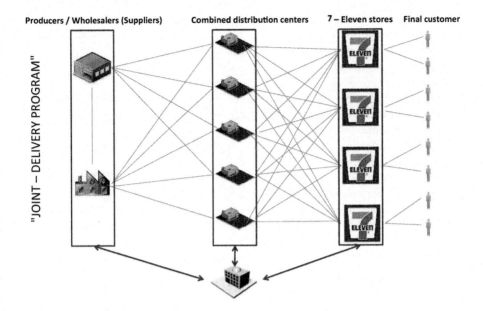

Fig. 8.35 Redesigned supply chain

deliveries happen several times a day. For frozen products, three deliveries a week are enough. Each truck's tour covers more than one store, preferably during off-peak hours. By omitting the need for inspection of incoming goods the costs of the whole SC operations can be further decreased.

Changed distribution network design affects all stages in the SC and the SC costs (inventory, transportation, facilities and information). Stores have to reconfigure store shelves at least three times daily and storefronts cater to different consumer segments and demands at different times. SEJ headquarters should design and manage location, transportation, inventory and information systems to support their objectives. They are also responsible for planning where to open new stores to ensure a strong presence. On-time delivery is now the supplier's responsibility In the event of non-compliance with agreed delivery dates the supplier has to pay a penalty equivalent to the gross margin of the product being delivered. In return for this, suppliers are rewarded with long-term business relationships and adoption in new projects, such as the e-commerce project "7dream.com". In conclusion, awareness of customer needs and management's ability to react and respond to market preferences by simultaneously considering costs, ensure the long-term economic success of SEJ.

Redesigning SEJ could achieve improvements in many areas, e.g. growth in sales (+11.29 %), store numbers (+5.84 %) and profit margins (+30 %); higher sales per square metre; higher average per store day sale (66,900 yen/51,500 yen), daily number of customers (1059 in SEJ/industry average 880), remarkably low stock-out rate, an increase in SC efficiency, a decreasing inventory relative to sales, a reduction in the number of stock keeping units (SKUs) to 2500, a decrease in inventory turnover (45 turns instead of 14 in 1974), and a decrease in the average number of deliveries to each store.

Discussion
Identify impacts on different actors in the SC of redesigning the distribution system.
Why has Seven-Eleven chosen off-site preparation of fresh foods and subsequent delivery to stores?
How did the following SC costs change: inventories/transportation/facilities and handling/information?
What is the name of the transportation strategy when the tour of each truck starts from a distribution centre and covers more than one store?
Which transportation network design is used in the SEJ case? What are the advantages and limitations of this network type?

8.6.4 Transportation Modes

Case Study: Transportation of Shoes from China to Austria via Hamburg
Diary of a container full of shoes from the company Deichmann (see Fig. 8.36).

In the following, the journey of a container from Wenzhou to Vienna is described, based on the article "Schuhe unterwegs" in HHLA-Messe-Magazine, 2011.

Ningbo, China, 7 November, 11:30: One of the largest container ships is loaded with different containers. One of them is container CMAU 146090-0, which is

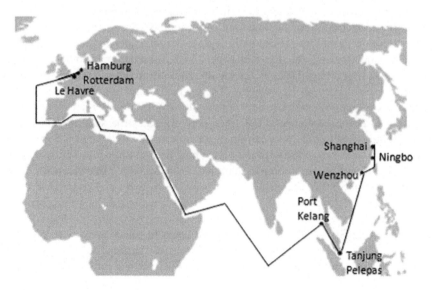

Fig. 8.36 Deichmann's transportation chain

loaded with the Deichmann shoe collection. The shoes are produced in Whenzou and transported to Ningbo, where the container is loaded onto a container ship.

Suez Canal, 28 November, 0:57: The container ship sails the 160 km-long Suez Canal at 7.5 knots. The Suez Canal is one of the most important shipping routes in the world.

Hamburg, Burchardkai, 29 November, 8:00: The container ship has capacity for 14,000 standard boxes. This means that good planning of the loading process is essential in the different ports. At the HHLA Container Terminal Burchardkai loading preparations for the port of Le Havre are under way, overseen by a responsible ship planner.

Le Havre, 7 December, 6:00: The container ship is leaving Le Havre after a short stop. The ship planner is organizing the dispatching and loading of the ship in Hamburg. The ship planner uses planning software to decide where each container will be stacked.

Hamburg, Burchardkai, 10 December, 8:45: Tugboats are helping the container ship to dock. Giant, detailed planned dispatching machinery starts.

9:00: The responsible ship planner decides together with the container ship's officer when the planned loading and reloading is going to be done.

12:14: From 9 o'clock dispatching starts. Several thousands of containers have to be reloaded.

12:15: For such cases, the HHLA has invested in berths and efficient bridges.

12:16: The bridge driver has an inside monitor so he can see which containers he has to take. At the same time another ship planner controls the number of unloaded containers.

12:17: The driver of the van-carrier gets an automatic message when the containers have been put down on the quay side.

12:20: The driver of the van-carrier is putting down the container full of shoes. The cranes are computer-assisted and they move the container into an optimal position for interim storage.

Hamburg, Burchardkai, 11 December, 10:50: The container is loaded onto the train by the company Metrans going towards Prague. The train is fully loaded with 60 containers.

11:25: Loading from interim storage and the train is done by ten van-carriers. The van-carrier drivers obtain their information about the loading process from the computerized networks. The goal is to achieve a smooth loading and unloading.

14:31: Metrans employees are organizing processes for the 1781 Metrans trains, which are transporting the goods from Prague to Hamburg. The container with the shoes is loaded onto the first section of the train.

15:48: The 600 m-long train is leaving the port of Hamburg. The computerized network informs the Metrans dispatcher in Prague and the logistics experts from Deichmann that the container is on the way to Prague.

Decin, goods rail depot, 12 December, 6:10: A change of locomotive drivers. Metrans has a special logistic plan of their capacity utilization so that they are able to transport more containers than their competitors. Of the international traffic overseas on the rail networks, 75 % is done by Metrans.

Mode of transport	Typical usage	Advantages	Disadvantages
Road	Door-to-door. Ideal for mixed cargo. Typically used for first and final leg	Most flexible for door-to-door, cheap	Limited to continental transport. Urban congestion. Damage to roads
Rail	For domestic, continental and inter-continental transport	Ideal for heavy goods and long distances. Environmental-friendly	Connection to rail system required. Complete trains require large volumes (thus low frequency), otherwise handling in yards (low transport speed)
Air	To ensure fast transport	Fast and safe	Expensive. Limits for size and weight. Typically as part of multi-modal transport
Sea	bulk shipments, where long lead time is ok	Ideal for bulky and heavy goods. Highly standardized sea containers worldwide. Less costly than air for inter-continental transports	inflexible routes. Long lead time. Inflexible timetables (ship will not wait for missing container)

Fig. 8.37 Comparison of different transportation modes (based on SupplyOn)

Prague, 12 December, 8:57: The train is arriving at one of the largest trans-shipment centres in Europe. A total of 15,000 containers can be stored and ten trains can be loaded and reloaded at the same time.

Dunajska Streda, 13 December, 9:11: The company Deichmann opened their new distribution centre next to the terminal area. The terminal area offers space for 25,000 containers. The shoes arrive at the distribution centre where they are arranged into various transport units for the different cities.

Vienna, permanent establishment of Schenker, 14 December, 13:45: The container destined for Vienna is leaving the distribution centre. The container arrives at the warehouse in the Gottfried-Schenkerstreet at 13:45.

Vienna, Mariahilfer Street 41, 15 December, 8:12: The trip from China to Austria ends at Deichmann's subsidiary company, in the old Vienna shopping street. The journey from Ningbo to Vienna has taken 37 days, 20 h and 42 min.

As we can see from this example, the modern transportation chains comprise different transportation modes (i.e., the *intermodal transportation*). The main transportation modes, their advantages and disadvantages are summarized in Fig. 8.37.

It can be observed from Fig. 8.37 that no single transportation mode provides the ideal solution. The selection of the transportation mode is based on prioritizing such criteria as speed, costs, networking, security, schedules, etc.

8.7 Key Points

The fundamental questions in distribution and transportation network design are as follows:

- When and where do goods in required quantity and quality need to be picked up and consolidated in order to have them in time at the destination?
- Which service levels have to be respected (on-time delivery, tolerances)?
- Which mode of transport and means of transport are possible and the right choice for the whole or a defined part of the transport?
- Who organizes and who executes (which part of) the transport?
- Who pays for which part of the transport?
- How can the promised cost for an efficient and reliable transport be minimized?

We have discussed typical aspects and decision problems of configuring distribution and transportation networks as they appear today. Thereby, we have discussed general challenges associated with the set-up of the right and appropriate transportation network; in addition we have provided an in-depth presentation of particular decision tasks.

At the end of this chapter, we have become familiar with several generic types of distribution and transportation network structures. Starting from quite simple direct delivery layouts we are able to extend these structures by postponement strategies, milk-runs and transshipments in order to achieve economies of scale in the context of transportation planning through consolidation. However, we have seen that the success of consolidation depends on the availability of adequate shipments that can be grouped together to make full truckloads. The risk associated with shipment consolidation is quite high if the transportation demand varies over time. In such a situation, the incorporation of a logistics service provider can be beneficial if it is paid only per shipped quantities. The assignment of quantities to be shipped to different links in a many-to-many transport network is a quite complicated decision problem, known as the Hitchcock distribution problem. We have discussed and applied procedures to solve this important decision task in the context of configuring a transportation network.

Bibliography

Akkermann R, Farahani P, Grunow M (2010) Quality, safety and sustainability in food distribution: a review of quantitative operations management approaches and challenges. OR Spectr 32:863–904

Amiri A (2006) Designing a distribution network in a supply chain system: formulation and efficient solution procedure. Eur J Oper Res 171(2):567–576

Barnhart C, Laporte G (eds) (2007) Transportation. In: Handbooks in operations research and management science, vol 14. Elsevier, Amsterdam

Button K (2010) Transport economics, 3rd edn. Edward Elgar, Cheltenham

Charnes A, Cooper WW (1954) The stepping-stone method for explaining linear programming: calculation in transportation problems. Manage Sci 1(1):49–69

Chen Z-L (2010) Integrated production and outbound distribution scheduling: review and extensions. Oper Res 58(1):130–148

Chopra S, Meindl P (2009) Supply chain management. Strategy, planning and operation, 4th edn. Pearson, Harlow

Dantzig GB (1951) Application of the simplex method to a transportation problem. In: Koopmans TC (ed) Activity analysis of production and allocation. Wiley, New York, pp 359–373

de Palma A, Lindsey R, Quinet E, Vickerman R (eds) (2011) A handbook of transport economics. Edward Elgar, Cheltenham

Domschke W (2007) Logistik: transport, 5th edn. Oldenbourg Wissenschaftsverlag, München

Gass SI (2003) Linear programming: methods and applications. Dover, New York

Hitchcock FL (1941) The distribution of a product from several sources to numerous localities. J Math Phys 20:224–230

Ivanov D, Sokolov B, Pavlov A (2014) Optimal distribution (re)planning in a centralized multistage network under conditions of ripple effect and structure dynamics. Eur J Oper Res 237(2):758–770

Konrad S, Boysen N (2011) Cross-docking. J Manag Control 22:129–137

Kunnumkal S, Topaloglu H (2011) Linear programming based decomposition methods for inventory distribution systems. Eur J Oper Res 211(2):282–297

Li J, Chu F, Chen H (2011) A solution approach to the inventory routing problem in a three-level distribution system. Eur J Oper Res 210:736–744

Manzini R, Bindi D (2009) Strategic design and operational management optimization of a multistage physical distribution system. Transport Res E Log 45(6):915–936

Vahrenkamp R, Mattfeld DC (2007) Logistiknetzwerke: Modelle für Standortwahl und Tourenplanung. Gabler, Wiesbaden

References for Sect. 8.6.1

BBC (2011) Shopping by phone at South Korea's virtual grocery. http://www.bbc.co.uk/news/business-15341910, accessed 10 May 2014

Coe NM, Lee Y-S (2006) The strategic localization of transnational retailers: the case of Samsung-Tesco in South Korea. Econ Geogr 82(1):61–88

Kumar N (2006) Strategies to fight low cost rivals. Harv Bus Rev 84:104–112

Park N, Kim Y-C, Shon HY, Shim H (2013) Factors influencing smartphone use and dependency in South Korea. Comput Hum Behav 29:1763–1770

Slack N, Chambers S, Johnston R (2010) Operations management, 6th edn. Pearson Education, London

Strother J (2011) BBC news – shopping by phone at South Korea's virtual grocery

The Telegraph (2011) Tesco builds virtual shops for Korean commuters

TESCO PLC (2012) Tesco Homeplus expands number of virtual stores. http://www.tescoplc.com/index.asp?pageid=17&newsid=593, accessed 10 May 2014

References for Sect. 8.6.3

Bensaou B (1996) 7-Eleven Japan: creating the virtual corporation. In: Proceedings of the 4th European conference on information systems, Lisbon, Portugal, pp 1275–1289

Chopra S, Meindl P (2013) Supply chain management – strategy, planning, and operation, 5th edn. Pearson, Boston, MA

Zentes J, Morschett D, Schlramm-Klein H (2012) Strategic retail management: text and international cases. Gabler Verlag, Springer Fachmedien, Wiesbaden

Factory Planning and Process Design 9

Learning Objectives for This Chapter

- role of factory planning in SCOM
- factory planning processes
- role and methods of capacity planning
- options for process flow design
- lean production systems
- modern trends: Industry 4.0

9.1 Introductory Case-Study "Factory Planning at Tesla"

The location of a new factory can provide competitive advantage and has strategic relevance for every company. For once, location influences cost structures. For example, producing in a low-wage country influences the production price of the product. Risks are constituted by politics, exchange rates and currency swings. Many companies operate in various countries making use of the advantages in each location.

On the other hand, innovation plays another important role for business success. Proximity to universities, research areas or other enterprises operating in the business can enhance innovation incentives. Here, qualified employees are also easier to reach, for example through recruiting from universities. Much of the time governments will support particular areas with tax advantages to trigger the development of innovation clusters. In these areas the infrastructure is well developed. Therefore, supplies are easily delivered to the area and finished products to the

---

Find additional case-studies, Excel spreadsheet templates, and video streams in the *E-Supplement* to this book on www.global-supply-chain-management.de!

retailer or end customer. The location of the market, where the customer is located, is also relevant.

E-mobility is the new trend in the car industry. With decreasing amounts of fossil fuel electricity is an attractive option to pursue while helping to protect the environment. But there is criticism that some factories are not zero emission producers but simply reallocate the emissions elsewhere. Batteries need to be charged by power plants and batteries are difficult to produce. Nevertheless, researchers found that electric cars still save energy and are more environmentally friendly than gasoline or diesel operated vehicles. According to experts, e-mobility could reduce CO_2 emissions by 47 % by 2030. Companies have discovered this trend and have been trying to find the most efficient versions of e-mobility. The biggest obstacle is still presented by batteries. Many are expensive to produce or do not last very long. Moreover, safety issues have to be resolved. Development of lithium-ion batteries has brought major advancement. Many governments support the implementation of non-fuel systems. The so-called original equipment manufacturers (OEM) are constantly developing new electric vehicles.

Tesla is one of the new generation enterprises on the e-mobility scene. Recently, Tesla Roadster and Tesla S presented models for the mass audience. A third one is planned—a sports version. The cars have a relatively low noise level, zero emission and cost approximately $35,000. This constitutes serious competition for long established OEMs.

Tesla's production plant is located in Fremont, California. The city is located right in the heart of the prestigious Silicon Valley research area. Here many companies have settled, producing basically everything technology has to offer. Silicon Valley became popular in the 1980s and 1990s, and is called a post-fordistic complex with special dynamics. There are various advantages to this location. Its proximity to technology-savvy Stanford University is just one of them. So-called knowledge dynamics and well-educated, highly qualified employees along with a fiscal friendly policy attract enterprises. Additionally, military and aircraft industries are close by, which support location factors which are already beneficial. A supplier network has been developed and established. Moreover, Silicon Valley is located near San Francisco, which offers a good working atmosphere for its employees.

There are also downsides to the technology cluster. The infrastructure is highly overloaded. While people have continuously moved to the area, the infrastructure has not kept pace with demand. Additionally, rent prices have exploded, making it especially difficult for smaller companies to rent office space. Very often, small start-ups turned out to be the most successful enterprises.

Tesla purchased a dormant production plant in Silicon Valley from Toyota, which uses relatively little of the huge factory space. Various suppliers deliver lightweight components to the plant by trucks. The long waiting time for Tesla S' customers, currently around 4 months, is especially problematic. This is mainly due to the shortage of lithium-ion batteries supplied by Panasonic.

In the plant there are eight robots in each assembly line. Usually, a robot is able to fulfil only one task; however, Tesla's robots are able to handle four at once.

Tesla S is the model currently on the production line. Processing time at each station (so-called *takt time*) is 5 min and the *total production lead time* (PLT) (so called *cycle time*) takes 3–5 days. This is still quite long compared to large car manufacturers. Eighty Tesla S cars are built on the site every day. In the first year 20,000 cars were planned, which is rather a small number compared to Tesla's big competitors such as Hyundai and Beijing Motors. Tesla started its business around 10 years ago and is still working on a much smaller scale. Nevertheless, it is fairly successful. Currently, Tesla is upgrading the factory for the assembly of an SUC model or a sports car. The assembly line will remain the same; only the robots have to be reprogrammed. This factory concept is extremely flexible and saves enormous investment costs compared to building a new production line or plant.

Questions
What are advantages of the factory location in Silicon Valley?
What are the general advantages of Tesla's production layout?
How could the lead-time problems be resolved?
What problems could Tesla potentially face in the future?
How many cars could be produced in 8 h by Tesla if the takt time could be reduced to 3 min?

9.2 Factory Planning

9.2.1 Role of Factory Planning in SCOM

Factory planning and *process design* problems occur when, for example, an existing factory requires adaptation in order to make sure that new products can be produced using the existing infrastructure. Planning and design could also be required to implement new technology into the production process so that throughput times can be reduced. These are just two typical problems when the factory has to be modified to generate competitive advantage.

But there are also problems related to the creation of completely new factories. The erection of a completely new manufacturing facility is also considered the "green-field approach", compared to the "brown-field approach" when modifying existing plants.

Sometimes it might also be necessary to centralize the so-called *production footprint*, which means that factories might be adjusted in their size (expanded or reduced) in a case where factories might be closed or parts of old ones might be reactivated. Current challenges in the business demand dynamic, adaptable, scalable and modular factories (Wiendahl et al. 2005; Schenk et al. 2014). This is related—among many other influencing factors—to shorter product life cycles and shorter time-to-market requirements as well as improvement in production technology. Additionally, a fast reaction to changing market needs and technological conditions requires the design of new and modular factories. Grundig (2015) provides a very structured and systematic approach on the processes and steps in factory planning.

A new, *modular factory* is the one that BMW created in Leipzig, Germany. This facility covered the three main production areas of the car—body shop, paint shop and final assembly. The important aspect is the scalability and the expansion potential the factory has in order to enable adjustments to its layout in accordance with market development. Recently the Leipzig plant has been expanded in order to produce BMW's electrical vehicles as well.

It becomes evident that the spectrum of "factory planning and process design" covers a broad variety of practical problems that are approached in a structured way. It is the purpose of this chapter to elaborate on the approach and steps taken to solve the challenges summarized above.

9.2.2 Processes of Factory Planning

Systematic factory planning is related to a planning cascade, also referred to as a "*planning pyramid*", from the initial idea, through the process of the ideal factory, to the detailed elaboration, to when the factory finally operates. In general, one will need to consider the steps of target planning, concept development, elaboration and evaluation of alternatives and execution of the selected alternative leading to the final factory building.

Three basic *processes in factory planning* can be classified as in Table 9.1.

Table 9.1 Factory planning processes

Phase	Main contents or results to be achieved
Planning	Collection of requirements (e.g. production programme); Analysis of tasks that need to be performed; Health, Safety and Environment (HSE) /feasibility studies that need to be considered; Description of functional areas and expected output, layout alternatives; Layout models/site layout plans to be presented; Required documents to obtain authority approval.
Realization	Statements of work (e. g. also for subcontracting purposes); Screening of quotations/offers to be evaluated; Detailed project plans and related information on realization and capacity planning (who/which company is going to work when on what to be finalized by when (this is a very challenging task for the project management team); Purchasing plans for heavy equipment (e.g. robots, transportation devices, machines, logistical equipment, cranes...); Plans for the IT installations such as terminals for shop-floor management, etc.; Plans for departmental commuting; Plans for the training or hiring workforce.
Operation	Plans on the final approval and commissioning of the factory and its functional areas to make sure it can be operated; Documents to be obtained from external approval bodies, quality certificates, HSE and construction approval; Planning of the ramp-up phase including training and education of the workforce, Preparation for start of volume production.

Consider these processes in more detail.

Planning pre-requisites and factory planning preparation consists of the collection of the relevant short-, medium- and long-term inputs for the factory planning project. This *target planning* is the input for structuring the process and for creating the planning documentation. The results from this first block create the precise formulation of the tasks and targets/objectives of the factory planning process and have contributed to a first or pre-feasibility study.

9.2.2.1 Factory Structure Planning

This complex deals with the creation of the first high-level factory layout designs which support the evaluation of alternative concepts for the factory. It is important to mention that in this case an ideal view is taken, which means that potential constraints regarding the available infrastructure or pieces of land are not considered. The reason for this disconnected view is to develop the most appropriate structure (*principle planning*), the identification of the main production areas, the necessary assembly processes and also the required logistical flows and set up.

In other words, this planning complex has the objective to evaluate and select the most appropriate structure under the best conditions and it also aims at dimensioning the functional areas. Furthermore the connection and logistical linkages as well as the process sequencing are advanced by the factory planning team so that an *ideal layout* of the factory can be presented. Once this has been agreed to, adaptation to the real existing or available conditions is made. This transfer from the ideal scenario to what can be achieved is leading to the generation of the so-called *realistic layout*. The different variants presented (scenarios) can be mentioned as well as the related *feasibility study*.

Still, it might be necessary to de-couple functional areas due to vibrations (e. g., a press shop), and to separate buildings in order to comply with local construction rules and regulations (e.g., fire protection, noise emission, pollution) or to consider a special foundation. These aspects differ from case to case and from country to country so that this will need to be investigated in detail once a decision for a new factory is made in practice.

9.2.2.2 Detail Planning and Project Preparation for Realization

After management has decided on the preferred factory layout variant, the detailed planning (fine planning) takes place. Starting with the block layouts (rough layouts) that were described earlier, the exact allocation and space for machines, positioning of supporting equipment, planning of additional space and office infrastructure (locker rooms, medical support, offices, sanitary space), but also planning of media (gas, water, electricity, information technology...) have to take place. One could say that the "empty facility" of the rough planning is now filled in with its exact functional content (fine planning) so that the factory can finally be created.

The deliverable of this process is the factory planning project including all detailed plans.

9.2.2.3 Project Realization
When details are defined, the suppliers and partners will need to be involved in line with the project plan specified. In parallel to all these planning complexes a team will need to make the necessary cost calculations (business case development and validation) followed by running stringent cost controlling. Additionally, the planning needs to be properly set up by a project management team to track progress, to visualize it and to alert in case of deviations. These could be cost, time or quality related deviations. These are typical tasks that will be run under the guidance of the factory planning project management team.

In order to make the factory planning process with typical use case scenarios more transparent for the reader, the short cases are presented as follows:

- An existing factory is regularly adjusted to current production needs.
- An existing factory is completely redesigned to meet strategic objectives.
- A new factory is completely built from scratch in order to generate competitive advantage in a new market.
- Temporary factory with a partner.

9.2.2.4 An Existing Factory Is Regularly Adjusted to Current Production Needs
The factories are planned from a layout and process point of view in a way to ensure flawless execution of all necessary production and assembly steps. This is also done in consideration with the corresponding production system and its underlying Lean principles. The company needs to adjust its production and thus the layout of the factory whenever there is a new product launched. That means the team dealing with factory planning reviews the existing factory, the material flow from the incoming area over the storage area, considers the involvement and allocation of suppliers into the production process, and deals with questions as to how to test the product and how to ship it to the customer. As we can see, factory planning is linked to layout planning, production sequencing and also recognizing the importance of a streamlined material flow. If there are new production or assembly steps, if there are more suppliers that need to be involved, if the existing buildings need to be adjusted or if there is a need to create a new building, this is all done by the factory planning department. As this first case shows, even without creating a completely new factory, the aspect of factory planning plays a crucial role during the normal production of the product portfolio and thus represents a regular task to ensure continuous improvement.

9.2.2.5 An Existing Factory Is Completely Redesigned in Order to Meet Strategic Objectives
In contrast to the above summarized continuous adjustment of the factory to meet current production needs, a complete factory makeover is a task where the location

of the factory on the plot of land remains the same, but where fundamental changes are implemented. Such a complete factory makeover is furthermore based on a strategic decision as it involves significant investment.

Based on inputs from the sales team regarding the expected production programme for the next few years, the resulting capacity needs are derived. That means an understanding is required of what type of product and in what quantity is expected to be placed on the market. This information is provided to the factory planning team on an aggregated level. The factory planners then review the existing setup of the facility and determine which production steps are necessary, what kind of technology is required and what it means in terms of manufacturing hours, stations and number of buildings.

For example, a strategic decision was made to almost double the production volume to satisfy global markets. This would require a complete redesign of the layout, allowing, for example, mixed-model lines with shortened set-up times; it was also strongly linked to the set-up of a completely new logistics concept to feed the assembly lines continuously with material from the warehouse. The warehouse would be completely newly built and so-called logistics trains to be installed to provide the parts and components to the assembly stations. That means that the shape of the building remains the same, but the internal allocations of the stations, the material flow and the allocation of the warehouse have to be completely made over to satisfy the demands of growing markets.

9.2.2.6 A New Factory Is Completely Built from Scratch in Order to Generate Competitive Advantage in a New Market

Factory planning also plays a significant strategic role with respect to the generation of competitive advantage. For example, the Indian market might require new products (e.g., investment goods). To win the corresponding commercial bid, it would be necessary to ensure that the products are made to a very high degree locally in India itself. This is also referred to as "local content". That means a location needs to be identified to set up a completely new factory, in which local staff would create the final product with a high proportion of locally sourced materials. For this case of factory planning, the aspect of location planning would also be important because the company needs to identify a region in which to create the new factory on green-field site. Under consideration of site selection criteria (e.g., existing infrastructure, availability of potential workforce, appropriate suppliers or capable logistics service providers) a location for the factory has to be identified. The plot of land also has to provide for possible later expansion of the factory. Finally, a completely new facility with internal suppliers on site would need to be created in India.

9.2.2.7 Temporary Factory with a Partner

This is a special case of factory planning, where local content requirements have to be met, but where no new factory has to be created. Imagine that investment goods have to be made for a customer in Romania. Assume that this would be related to a one-time contract (products are produced, but then no further products have to be made for that customer), there was no business case for a new factory. In such a situation, there would be no business case justifying the creation of a new factory. In order to produce in Romania with local staff for the local customer, the existing infrastructure would be analysed to find already existing facilities that need to meet the necessary requirements (such as infrastructure, size and height of buildings, handling equipment, floor density, etc...). In a traditional industrial zone, appropriate facilities could be identified. The available alternatives will be reviewed regarding their strategic and operational fit. Finally, the investment goods might be produced in a factory that originally generated, for example, heavy power plant transformers. Of course, that factory will need to be replanned with consideration for the assembly and logistical processes required to ensure on-time and on-quality delivery of products to the final customer. This example shows that factory planning has to be considered as a strategic decision to be responsive and flexible when it comes to customer focus.

9.2.2.8 Health, Safety and Environment

It is important to emphasize, that in all examples and activities around factory planning, the aspect of HSE has highest priority. HSE deals with the proper working conditions that have to be ensured by the company so that employees can contribute to value adding under safe and healthy conditions. Thus, the workforce has to be provided with personal protection accessories, such as safety shoes, gloves, hard hats, ear plugs, etc. Furthermore, the ergonomic aspects need to be considered and corresponding tools (e. g. lifting or transportation devices) have to be made available. People need to be safe when they perform their work. Safety trainings and education is a mandatory objective. Also, safety and work instructions need to be available for all employees, including instructions on how to proceed in case of an injury.

Factory planning and HSE are strongly connected, as HSE is also related to ensuring proper daylight or illumination, as well as to keeping working areas free from dust (e.g., from welding); smells (e.g., from glues) or from the noise of machines or processing. Also emissions have to be avoided when for example fork lift trucks are charging the batteries: proper emission or smoke evacuation technology has to be installed. A safe workplace means also that emergency exits need to be clearly marked, fire extinguishers are available within easy reach and corresponding visual aids show the shortest path to extinguishers or to the emergency exit. Therefore HSE related topics always have to be on top of the agendas in running operations but also when new operations are planned.

9.3 Capacity Planning

Under *capacity*, we understand the throughput, or the quantity of units a facility can hold, receive, store, or produce in a period of time (Heizer and Render 2014). That means there is a constraint or a limit on production to satisfy demand. This limit can be theoretical and effective.

9.3 Capacity Planning

The theoretical limit is called *design capacity* which is the maximum theoretical output of a system. *Effective capacity* is the capacity a firm expects to achieve given current operating constraints (Heizer and Render 2014). In practice, effective capacity is usually lower than design capacity.

Let us look at capacity using a very simple example. Assume that we have a small bakery shop in a big railway station. If it takes a single person 2 min to prepare a sandwich, then that person can produce 30 sandwiches (60 min per hour/ 2 min preparation time per sandwich = 30 sandwiches) per hour. So, looking at the aforementioned definition, the total amount that can be produced per hour is 30 sandwiches, in other words the capacity is equal to 30 sandwiches per hour. In this theoretical example, we might have analysed that there are peak demands in the morning hours (8.00 o'clock), during lunchtime (12.00 o'clock) and in the evening (at 17.00 o'clock), when people are travelling back to their homes. During these three peak times, the demand might be 90 sandwiches per hour. That shows two typical operational problems: first we have a capacity issue at the peak times; and second we need to *balance capacity according to demand*. What we could do, for example, is to increase the workforce during times of high demand; or we might use technology to shorten the time to create one product; or we might pre-produce the components of our sandwiches (this could be pre-slicing of the bread or slicing the cheese). This simple example indicates that a company needs to know its existing capacity, so what it is able to perform per period. The company also needs to adjust its capacity respectively and needs to clearly know where the *constraints or bottlenecks* are.

Now, let us translate this way of thinking into the operational world. In order to determine the capacity, it is necessary to know the products that have to be placed on the market. This understanding of demand could be order-driven, and/or it could be forecast driven. In our bakery example, it could be that there is a bank building nearby which placed a fixed order of 50 sandwiches every day. That means that there is an existing contract that specifies exactly the quantity and the composition of the goods. On top of that we know the regular daily demand patterns including the three peaks per day explained at the beginning of this section. The forecasting aspect plays a role when we consider vacation periods or other seasonal aspects. It can also happen that we recognize that daily demand increases about a certain percentage when there is a football game nearby.

All this is very important information for us to understand the demand of products per time unit and how to balance that against our existing capacity. This also tells us that we need to be able to adjust our capacity to cope with swings on the demand side. As a consequence, we need to have the space, the workforce and the machinery and tools to meet the demand. Of course this information on future demand is not only required to determine capacities, but it is also relevant to managing the SC, as the corresponding need for materials needs to be communicated to suppliers. In the simplified bakery example for better illustration purposes, this might be bread, butter, cheese, etc. In real large factory operations, raw materials, urchased parts and components need to be in line with foreseen demand as well as with the required technical and human capacities.

9.3.1 Little's Law

In 1961, John D.C. Little provided the mathematical evidence for the rule that puts the inventory L (= average number of objects in a system) in relation to the throughput rate λ (= average arrival rate of objects) and the waiting time W (= average time an object spends in the system). Little's Law says "that, under steady state conditions, the average number of items in a queuing system equals the average rate at which items arrive multiplied by the average time that an item spends in the system." (Little and Graves 2008). Letting

L = average number of items in the queuing system (e.g., work-in-progress inventory in the system)
W = average waiting time in the system for an item
λ = average number of items arriving per unit time
the law can be represented as Eq. (9.1):

$$L = \lambda \cdot W \qquad (9.1)$$

Little's Law demonstrates that when we reach a steady state, the average number of objects arriving in the system during a time period (e.g. 1 h or 1 day) are equal to the ones that are leaving the system during that time period. Elegant in its simplicity, Little's Law represents one of the basics in capacity analysis. The following adapted example is related to the application of Little's Law in a manufacturing plant described by Bozarth and Handfield (2013).

Task 9.1. Little's Law
Let us assume that in a car garage, two standard repairs are offered in a special express service zone at extremely competitive prices. Batteries can be exchanged in workstation 1 and oil is changed in workstation 2. Prior to this, customers need to register and they also receive a general car inspection. Then they are assigned to either station 1 or 2 depending on the repair that is required (either battery or oil service). As shown in Fig. 9.1, 200 customers per day arrive at that garage:

- As stated, all customers are passing through the general inspection where in average 20 cars are in the system for inspection.

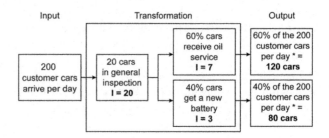

Fig. 9.1 Little's Law—example of usage in a car garage

- Sixty percent of clients request an oil service, and the average inventory is seven cars.
- The other 40 % want their batteries to be exchanged, and the average inventory is three cars.

Looking at this scenario, we can calculate the following metrics:
The waiting time W for the general inspection is
$W = L/\lambda =$ (20 cars inventory in inspection)/(200 customer cars per day) = ·0.1 day in general inspection = 48 min waiting time, if we assume that the company operates 8 h (= 480 min) per day.

We can observe that 120 cars receive an oil service per day, and on average there are seven cars in the oil service area. Applying the same calculation principle as before, this leads us to the waiting time for the oil service of:
$W = L/\lambda =$ (7 cars inventory in oil service)/(120 cars per day) = 0.0583 per day = 28 min waiting time for a day with 480 min working time.

But we also have a total of 80 cars per day that will receive a new battery. On average, there are just three cars in the inventory. Taking the formula according to Little's Law, this leads us to the waiting time for the battery exchange of:
$W = L/\lambda = 3$ cars inventory in oil service)/(80 cars per day) = 0.0375 per day = 18 min of waiting time for a day with 480 min working time.

What is the waiting time for the cars receiving either an oil service or a new battery? In total, the cars require 48 min for the general inspection + 28 min for the oil service = 76 min of waiting time. In the case of the general inspection plus installation of a new battery, it is 48 min + 18 min = 66 min of waiting time.

As we have learned from that example, the simple but powerful "Little's Law" formula can be used for just one single process, but can also be applied for a multi-process-step transformation system.

Learning take away on Little's law

One can also use that simple formula for the quick assessment of a manufacturing facility, for example in connection with a *rapid plant assessment* (RPA). During a plant tour, simply consider Eq. (9.1). If you ask during a visit to the factory what is the average throughput rate per day and what is the throughput time, you can simply calculate the average inventory that is carried. On the other hand, if you are an operations manager in a factory and you know Little's Law, you should try to identify the key drivers for the throughput time, i.e. the key processes with their durations that cause delays or prolong the throughput time. Try to understand these and try to identify actions to reduce these delaying factors. The overall idea is to keep the same output throughput rate, but to reduce the throughput time in order to bring down the inventory carried. If inventory is not a concern for the company, but the achievement of a higher output per day is the priority, a throughput time reduction will also help here. If inventory remains stable and throughput time can be reduced as a consequence, the throughput rate will increase. That means we can produce more, and that is the reason why Little's Law is also connected to management of capacity.

Discussion Points
- Where else could you think about applying the simple formula of "Little's Law"? Think about usage in a manufacturing environment but also in a service environment.
- Consider yourself being in the position of manager of an insurance company and you would like to increase customer satisfaction by promising to all customers that everyone would be served within 15 min of arrival. How could "Little's Law" help you?
- If you would like to increase performance of the value added system, thus reducing the throughput time, where would you prioritize your observations?

9.3.2 Bottleneck Analysis/Theory of Constraints

The *bottleneck* determines the capacity of the transformation system. To make it more transparent, just assume that there is a product (e.g. a chair) that requires for example four simple production steps (see Fig. 9.2):

In this simplified production process, painting and drying requires the longest duration as it requires 10 min per chair (10 min per chair/60 min per hour = 0.167 h per chair). Or putting it more simply, six chairs per hour can be painted and thus the system capacity is six chairs as this is determined by the bottleneck. After the identification of the bottleneck (step 1), the operations manager's tasks would be to seek opportunities as to how this bottleneck time could be reduced.

Another frequently used term for bottleneck is *constraint*, as it is the process that prevents the enterprise from achieving its objectives (Goldratt 1990). If we want to produce ten chairs per hour, something needs to be done in order to limit the impact of that constraint or bottleneck, the performance manager needs to find a way (most probably with the help of a manufacturing engineer) to reduce the bottleneck time from 10 to just 6 min per chair. A possible solution might be to improve the spray process or to use a different type of paint or to increase the temperature for the paint to dry faster. That means a plan has to be created to mitigate the impact of the constraint and to reduce the bottleneck time (step 2). The operations manager and the manufacturing engineer are the dedicated resources that will need to work on the implementation of the identified measures (step 3).

Furthermore, one should try to better balance the work and maybe try to do some necessary preparatory work required for the painting, such as cleaning after the back of the body of the chair was installed. If this is also done, we are trying to spread the work from the bottleneck as well as to try to increase capability in related production processes (step 4). If this has been successfully implemented, the

Fig. 9.2 Process chain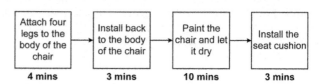

performance manager will start again to identify new constraints and bottlenecks as part of this continuous search for improvements (step 5).

9.3.3 Drum, Buffer, Rope

The drum is the instrument responsible for the *beat* (beat rate or *takt time*) of the production system. This can also be considered as the pace or production schedule and thus provides information regarding the items that need to be produced per time unit.

The buffer can also be considered as the *inventory* (or another type of resource) of the system which allows the bottleneck to perform at the beat of the drum. The last symbol is the rope. This is the means to exchange information or it enables necessary communication between the different parties. It refers to the need to synchronize the different elements or workstations in the system to operate in alignment and thus has the function of sending signals.

Assume there is a motorway that has five lanes and at a particular location (e. g., a bridge) it is narrowed to three lanes, then this is the capacity limitation or constraint, as cars could only use these three lanes. According to the theory of constraints (ToC), you only *achieve an improvement or advantage when it is possible to increase the capacity of the bottleneck*. That means for our example that you can only improve the system by creating a broader bridge with four or even five lanes.

The second principle of the ToC is that *it does not improve the performance of the system if you try to work on a non-bottleneck area*. For our example, if you create a better motorway with six lanes but you keep the old bridge with three lanes, this will not improve the system, as the bottleneck remains the same.

The third principle says that the *time that you spent at the bottleneck*, the bridge in our case, *is lost*. In real operations, you could try to mitigate the impact of the bottleneck by using well trained staff or by putting in a strict management system to lower the impact of the bottleneck. In a real factory the paint shop or a crane might be a bottleneck. In the case of the crane, you might schedule its usage tightly and should use a skilled crane operator who can maneuver goods with the highest precision, so that the time consumed for picking the goods, moving them and to position them at their destination is strictly limited.

We can summarize that bottleneck management and dealing with constraints is a daily task for operations managers. Furthermore, a constraint will always exist and due to expected or unexpected occurrences, new bottlenecks will arise (key people leave the company, workers are sick or on strike, a machine breaks down, a supplier cannot provide the parts...). Other drivers for bottlenecks could also be changing product mixes, usage of a new technology and the training of people to create new products using a new technology. Knowing and dealing with such constraints is part of the day-to-day business in SCOM.

9.3.4 Break-Even Analysis

In the previous sections dealing with Little's Law or the ToC, we looked only at capacity without consideration of profit and loss aspects. The break-even analysis is an approach that also looks at costs, respectively revenues. Slack et al. (2010) summarize that the break-even analysis is "the technique of comparing revenues and costs at increasing levels of output in order to establish the point at which revenue exceeds cost, that is, the point at which it 'breaks even'".

The *break-even point* is the point at which the total costs of the number of units that need to be produced are equal to the total revenues that are generated (Krajewski et al., 2013). That means that from a capacity point of view a firm needs to operate above the break-even point, or graphically speaking on the right-hand side of that point, as Fig. 9.3 depicts.

With the number of units that lead to a surplus on the revenue side, i.e., where the revenues are higher than the cost, the company will enter the profit zone. Below that production volume, graphically speaking, the firm is running left from the break-even point and thus is only generating losses, as the costs are higher than the revenues.

Task 9.2. Break-Even-Point

Put yourself in the position of a production manager who needs to evaluate if it is reasonable to purchase a new machine for the production of certain goods. The underlying assumptions are that costs and revenues are linear functions and that we know these exact costs. Furthermore, interest rates or cost of inventory is excluded from our break-even analysis model. It will be your task to calculate the break-even point in the number of units but also in terms of money, i.e., in $US.

Consider the following notations:

BP_x represents the *break-even point in units x*
$BP_\$$ represents the *break-even point in $US*
p represents the *price per unit*

Fig. 9.3 Break-Even-Point

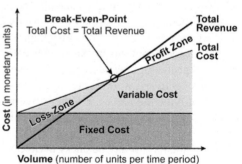

9.3 Capacity Planning

x represents the *number of units produced*
vc represents the *variable costs*
fc represents the *fixed costs*.

Equation (9.2) is used to determine the total revenues (TR):

$$TR = p \cdot x \qquad (9.2)$$

Equation (9.3) is applied to determine the total cost (TC):

$$TC = fc + vc \cdot x \qquad (9.3)$$

According to the definition of the break-even analysis, the *break-even point* is reached when TRs are equal to TC. That means for you as the production manager, you will need to set:
TR = TC or considering the details from above we can use Eq. (9.4)

$$p \cdot x = fc + vc \cdot x \qquad (9.4)$$

to identify the *break-even point in units*.
The *break-even point in units* thus equals [see Eq. (9.5)]:

$$BP_x = fc/(p\text{-}vc) \qquad (9.5)$$

To convert this into monetary values (e.g. $US), the result BP_x needs to be multiplied by the price per unit, i.e.

$$BP_\$ = BP_x \cdot p = [fc/(p\text{-}vc)] \cdot p = fc \cdot p/(p\text{-}vc) \qquad (9.6)$$

Based upon Eq. (9.6), the profit can also be calculated, because profit (simplified) equals TR−TC, which translates in Eq. (9.7):

$$\text{Profit } P = TR - TC = p \cdot x - (fc + vc \cdot x) \qquad (9.7)$$

Consider a numerical example. You received the following annual values from your controlling department (see Table 9.2):

In order to calculate the break-even point in $US $BP_\$$, you will need to use formula (9.6):
$BP_\$ = 20{,}000 \cdot 5/[5 - (1+2)] = 100{,}000/2 = 50{,}000\$/\text{year}$.

Table 9.2 Initial data for break-even point analysis

Fixed Cost (FC)	$20,000
Material cost per unit	1 $ per unit
Direct labour per unit	2 $ per unit
Selling price per unit	5 $ per unit

That means the break-even point in $US BP$_\$$ is reached, once the value of $50,000 is exceeded. As a production manager, you would like to know the quantity in units that needs to be produced to reach the break-even point in units BP$_x$. Therefore you now need to use formula (9.4):

$BP_x = 20,000/[5 - (1 + 2)] = 20.000/2 = 10,000$ units/year.

Of course, the break-even point in $US is directly linked by the sales price per unit with the break-even point in units, as you can easily see in the example above. You can simply test the result by taking the BP$_x$ (which is equal to 10,000 units in our task) and multiply it by the selling price (which is here equal to $5/unit). The result is 10,000 units · $5/unit = $50,000, as calculated above.

> ▶ **Practical Insights** In practice, the break-even point in $US is more relevant for the sales or the controlling department, whereas the break-even point in units "talks" more appropriately to the managers responsible for production, purchasing or logistics. This is because of the fact that production or logistics managers need to consider not only the size or weight of the products in order to determine space requirements on the production floor or in the warehouse, but also to identify the correct lifting or transportation devices. That means that the break-even analysis is a simple calculation method that provides a rich variety of people inside the organization with information essential for their purposes.

9.3.5 Decision Trees

In practice, *market uncertainty* and such factors as production cost, demand, prices, inflation or exchange rates influences managerial decisions. Should we expand our production or not, is it a profitable choice to redevelop the old distribution centre if demand for the following years is uncertain or should we sign the long-term contract with our supplier if we do not know if customers like our new product?

Decision tree analysis helps to make decisions in uncertain environments. A decision tree helps to build a graphic overview of possible strategies and to calculate in simple steps the revenue, cost and expected monetary value of several opportunities. Decision tree analysis offers a combination of strategic decisions, such as expanding a production site or not, and financial planning. It evaluates strategic decisions by its profitability to support the decision-making process. For that reason it can help to make decisions and aid design of processes and networks.

Task 9.3 Decision Tree Analysis
A company thinks about expanding their production site because they assume a favourable market development. To calculate *expected monetary value (EMV)* we have to consider probability P for both a favourable (0.35) and an unfavourable (0.65) market development. Option A means a large expansion, option B—a

Fig. 9.4 Decision tree expansion production site

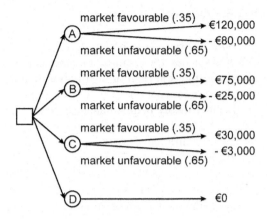

medium expansion, option C—a small expansion, and option D—no expansion. At the end of the tree you can see the cost or gain of each opportunity (Fig. 9.4).

To calculate the EMV we have to use Eq. (9.8):

$$EMV = P(favorable) \cdot gain + P(infavorable) \cdot losses \qquad (9.8)$$

Using Eq. (9.8) it becomes possible to decide which expansion would be the most profitable:

$EMV(A) = 0.35 \cdot 100,000 \text{ €} + 0.65 \cdot (-80,000 \text{ €}) = -10,000 \text{ €}$
$EMV(B) = 0.35 \cdot 75,000 \text{ €} + 0.65 \cdot (-25,000 \text{€}) = 10,000 \text{€}$
$EMV(C) = 0.35 \cdot 30,000 \text{ €} + 0.65 \cdot (-3000 \text{ €}) = 8550 \text{ €}$
$EMV(D) = 0 \text{ €}$

We can observe that medium expansion would be the best decision from the financial point of view, in a case where market development will be similarly predicted. Option D, no expansion, would lead to no difference because the company would not be changing anything.

▶ **Practical Insights** It is important in decision tree analysis to identify all factors that influence cost and to decide which factors are uncertain in the calculation. The critical issue is how to assess probability for relevant uncertain factors and consider their influence. Moreover, a company should not focus only on financial analysis. Other factors may also be important and the financial part can only be a fraction of the decision-making process. In practice, decision tree analysis is frequently supported by the development of *business cases* for possible future expansion.

9.3.6 Queuing Theory

Queuing theory is an important tool in many situations in normal life or industry. We find queues for example in supermarkets or in waiting rooms; or there are queues of trucks in front of distribution centres or of several orders that have to be processed in production.

Queuing theory helps to analyse *performance of a process* such as that of the temporal arrival of goods in a distribution centre. Performance generally can be measured in different dimensions such as capacity, time, cost, quality or flexibility and these factors can influence each other. The queuing model is a good tool for analysis of time dimension in a process. In Fig. 9.5, a simple queuing model (one-channel model) is presented.

A queuing model comprises the following elements:

- *input* (e.g., patients)
- *queue* (e.g., patients in the waiting room)
- *processing station* (e.g., a doctor)
- *output* (patients after the treatment).

In queuing theory, different options exist to describe these four elements. To describe the queues we use the notation

$$a/b/c,$$

where
  a is probability distribution of arrival rate, e.g.:

- D = degenerate distribution (deterministic)
- M = Markovian distribution (Poisson process)
- G = general distribution;

  b is probability distribution of service time

- D = degenerate distribution
- M = exponential distribution
- G = general distribution;

  c is number of servers (processing stations)

In regard to the number of servers, there are two basic kinds of models. A *one-channel model* considers only one queue and one server that process the input.

Fig. 9.5 Queuing model

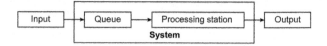

Fig. 9.6 Notations for queuing theory

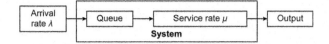

A *multiple-channel model* is involved with one queue and several servers or several queues and several servers.

Consider a system where there is no constraint in the queue and we follow the rule "first come first serve" for defining the processing sequence. To analyse this case, we introduce some notations that describe the system components (Fig. 9.6).

We consider the so-called M/M/1 queue. We determine mean number of arrivals per time period as λ and mean number of people or items served per time period (i.e., average service rate) as μ. It means that the arrival rate is Markovian distributed, service time exponentially distributed and there is one server. We can find this queue, for example, in post offices or small supermarkets with only one cashier or in waiting rooms for only one doctor's surgery.

Consider the following formulas to understand how to analyse the performance of the queuing process. To determine the time between the arrivals of two customers, e.g. patients, we use Eq. (9.9):

$$\text{Estimated } \textit{inter-arrival time} = \frac{1}{\lambda} \tag{9.9}$$

To analyse the service time we use Eq. (9.10):

$$\text{Estimated } \textit{service time} = \frac{1}{\mu} \tag{9.10}$$

To analyse the *utilization* factor for the system we use Eq. (9.11):

$$\rho = \frac{\lambda}{\mu}; \rho \leq 1 \tag{9.11}$$

To calculate the *probability* of more than *n*-units in the system, we can use Eq. (9.12):

$$P_n = \rho^n \cdot (1-\rho) \tag{9.12}$$

To find out the *length of the queue* (e.g., the estimated number of patients in the waiting room), we use Eq. (9.13):

$$L_Q = \frac{\rho^2}{1-\rho} \tag{9.13}$$

The *length of the system* (e.g., the estimated number of patients in the waiting room *and* in the doctor's surgery) is determined with the help of Eq. (9.14):

$$L_s = L_Q + \rho = \frac{\rho}{1-p} \tag{9.14}$$

Waiting time in the queue (e.g., time spent in the waiting room) can be found using Eq. (9.15):

$$T_Q = \frac{\rho^2}{\lambda \cdot (1-\rho)} \tag{9.15}$$

Waiting time in the whole system (e.g., time spent in waiting room and doctor's surgery) is calculated with the help of Eq. (9.16):

$$T_s = T_Q + \frac{1}{\mu} = \frac{\rho}{\mu \cdot (1-p)} \tag{9.16}$$

Task 9.4 Queuing Theory M/M/1 System

In a bookshop in the city centre there is only one cashier because the other two are off with influenza. Normally the cashier is able to cash up an average of 70 customers per hour. But on average there are only 55 customers per hour in the bookshop. Next to cashing up customers the cashier also has to unpack deliveries. Analyse the performance of the queue, and check if there is enough time to unpack deliveries.

$$\text{Inter-arrival time} = \frac{1}{55} = 0.018\,\text{h} = 1.08\,\text{min} = 64.8\,\text{s}$$

Every 65 s there is a new customer who wants to buy books.

$$\text{Service time} = \frac{1}{70} = 0.0143\,\text{h} = 0.86\,\text{min} = 51.4\,s$$

$$\frac{1}{70} = 0.86\,\text{min} \cdot 55 \ \textit{customers} = 47.3\,\text{min}$$

The cashier needs at average 51.5 s to cash up one customer and 47.3 min for all 55 customers per hour which means the cashier has 12.7 min per hour to unpack deliveries.

$$\rho = \frac{55}{70} = 78.6\,\%$$

And so the cashier is occupied 78.6 % of the time.

Now we want to analyse the queue as seen from the customer's perspective.

9.3 Capacity Planning

$$L_Q = \frac{0.786^2}{1-0.786} = 2.89; \ L_s = 2.89 + 0.786 = 3.68$$

There are on average around three people waiting in the queue and approximately four people in the system.

$$T_Q = \frac{0.786^2}{55 \cdot (1-0.786)} = 0.0525\,\text{h} = 3.15\,\text{min}$$

$$T_s = 0.0525 + \frac{1}{70} = 0.0668\,\text{h} = 4.01\,\text{min}$$

Customers are waiting 3.15 min on average in the queue and 4.01 min in the bookshop in total before they can leave the shop with their purchase.

Task 9.5 Queuing Theory M/M/c System

In the case of an M/M/c queue, formulas are different. We can find M/M/c queues for example in a distribution centre. There are several trucks waiting in waiting zones to unload their goods onto loading docks or to get loaded. In the case of M/M/c queues we have a Markovian distribution of arrival rate, an exponential distribution of service time and c servers (>1).

Consider the following example for M/M/c queues. On average there are 40 trucks arriving per hour and one loading dock is able to unload and load 12 trucks/h. Furthermore there are four loading docks. Assume that every loading dock has the same capacity and needs the same time. There is only one waiting queue.

To calculate the occupancy rate of the system we use Eq. (9.17):

$$\rho = \frac{\lambda}{c \cdot \mu} = \frac{40}{4 \cdot 12} = 83.3\,\% \tag{9.17}$$

The distribution centre loading docks are occupied for 83.3 % of the time.

To calculate the estimated number of trucks waiting in the queue we need to find the probability that the system is completely empty [Eq. (9.18)].

$$P_0 = \frac{1}{\sum_{i=0}^{c-1} \frac{(c \cdot \rho)^i}{i!} + \frac{(c \cdot \rho)^c}{c!} \cdot \frac{1}{(1-\rho)}} \tag{9.18}$$

$$P_0 \frac{1}{\frac{(4 \cdot 0.833)^0}{0!} + \frac{(4 \cdot 0.833)^1}{1!} + \frac{(4 \cdot 0.833)^2}{2!} + \frac{(4 \cdot 0.833)^3}{3!} + \frac{(4 \cdot 0.833)^4}{4!} \cdot \frac{1}{(1-0.833)}} = 2.14\,\%$$

The probability that the system is empty is 2.14 %. Now it is possible to calculate the number of trucks in the queue [Eq. (9.19)].

$$L_Q = \frac{c^c \cdot \rho^{c+1}}{c! \cdot (1-\rho)^2} \cdot P_0 = \frac{4^4 \cdot 0.833^{4+1}}{4! \cdot (1-0.833)^2} \cdot 0.0214 = 2.183 \quad (9.19)$$

In case of four loading docks and 40 estimated trucks per hour, 2.2 trucks are waiting in the queue.

The estimated number of trucks in the whole system is calculated using Eq. (9.20):

$$L_s = L_Q + c \cdot \rho = 2.183 + 4 \cdot 0.833 = 5.515 \quad (9.20)$$

On average there are 5.5 trucks in the system.

Waiting time in the queue is defined using Eq. (9.21):

$$T_Q = \frac{L_Q}{\lambda} = \frac{2.183}{40} = 0.0546\,\text{h} = 3.276\,\text{min} \quad (9.21)$$

Waiting time in the whole system is defined using Eq. (9.22):

$$T_s = T_Q + \frac{1}{\mu} = 0.0546 + \frac{1}{12} = 0.1379\,\text{h} = 8.274\,\text{min} \quad (9.22)$$

As you can see, waiting time in the system is 8.3 min.

Discussion Questions
- Why do you think capacity management is important for globally active companies that have a large production network with multiple production sites?
- Why is capacity management very important from a strategic point of view?
- What are the consequences when it is identified that the existing capacity of a firm is too high as opposed to when it is too low? What are the corrective measures that you would suggest to adjust the existing available capacity so that it can meet future demand?
- Is it the right strategy to aim for almost 100 % capacity utilization, or do you think one should also consider some idle capacity for the unpredictable?

9.3.7 Simulation: Case Study AnyLogic

Problem Description
Centrotherm Photovoltaics AG is a global supplier of technology and equipment for the photovoltaics, semiconductor and microelectronics industries. The company needed to identify the best automated production line and factory configuration to minimize costs and maximize throughput and reliability. Special focus was to:

- determine the type and amount of equipment required to fulfil production plans;
- evaluate layout alternatives to improve the throughput and utilization rate;

9.3 Capacity Planning

- inspect possible bottlenecks in the material flow;
- evaluate the impact of operator behaviour on factory output;
- test the consequences of maintenance within various time frames;
- identify system behaviour in case of breakdowns;
- identify scrap probability;
- evaluate change of performance during planned downtimes.

Model Development
The consultants used AnyLogic simulation and modelling technology to provide the answers to these problems. Using AnyLogic Professional's ability to create and save custom object libraries, the consultants encapsulated their vast simulation experience in the photovoltaic and semiconductor manufacturing industries and created their own libraries, which they reused in many projects, including this one.

Solution Development
These libraries featured elements built on top of the AnyLogic model development environment and allowed the consultants to easily model different kinds of equipment, material handling systems inside factories, personnel, and production control systems, all specific to the photovoltaic and semiconductor industries. In the Centrotherm project, this solution helped modellers quickly reproduce various aspects of the client's production system behaviour.

Testing the Solution
Once the model was built, the experimental phase of the project began. The consultants tested many parameters to find the best solutions. The input data, which included layout configurations and various parameters, was taken directly from Excel and Access files. Each simulation run reproduced 1 year of factory operation.

First, the consultants experimented with the overall production line design, using parameter variation and optimization. They tested many parameters, including those concerning capacity and the number of various pieces of equipment, cassettes, bins, etc., to see which configurations would work best in terms of throughput, reliability and scrap rate. Then the consultants worked to optimize transportation policies, buffer zone allocation, and watermark control processes.

Analysing the Results
Some of the proposed layout variants were rejected during this stage due to their poor performance. Finally, the few resulting solutions were tested manually to investigate the benefits and drawbacks of each one, and to find out how they could be further improved.

Implementation
The solutions proposed provided Centrotherm Photovoltaics AG with the opportunity to significantly improve the production line design and choose the best solution in terms of throughput, reliability and scrap rate at a low cost. Additionally, at the end

of the project, the model was released to the client so that it could be used for analysis of future changes in the factory. The model allows the customer to carry out their own experiments, playing with parameters and layout, changing input data, etc. This manufacturing facility simulation model will serve as a decision support tool at the factory for a long time to come.

9.4 Process Flow Structures

It is intuitively clear that not all products are produced in the same way. In order to enlarge on this for you, we need to think through another hypothetical case, in which you would be the producer and the product would be a chair. It is a very simple example, but makes it easy to grasp the underlying ideas and concepts.

9.4.1 Job Shop

Just put yourself into the situation that you plan to produce your own little chair for your room or for your apartment. You would go to the closest do-it-yourself centre, would buy some pieces of wood, some nails and your favourite colour of paint (e.g. red). These are the materials you would need for the chair. Furthermore, you need some tools, maybe a brush, a saw and a hammer. These standard tools and your materials plus your creativity and manual work are everything that you require in order to build your own, fully individualized piece of furniture (maybe you would produce and assemble it in your kitchen or in the garage).

The result would be an absolutely unique product and nobody else would have the same one! Maybe one of your friends will ask you to produce a second one, but with some changes regarding the size and also regarding the colour (your friend wants to have a bigger chair, painted in green). With your equipment, you would also be able to create such a product for your friend.

What we have just described is a typical set-up of the so-called "*job shop*" process flow structure. The secret behind it is that with such a process flow structure, absolutely unique products are made under the usage of standard tools in very low quantities. Also, the manual effort is quite high, in respect of the automation level, which is in general very low.

As you produced it manually and bought only a small amount of material, the unit price is quite high, but so is the flexibility to adjust your production set-up and to meet changing requirements. If you followed carefully the hypothetical wooden chair example from above, you will now understand that a job shop is a process flow structure that is used in order to create products at very low volume (just this one chair for you and the adjusted one for your friend). At the same time, we can understand that the job shop is suitable for creating products with great variation.

It is obvious that, even with this very unusual and hypothetical example, we still have developed the concept of the "job shop". In reality, this is used for the creation of e.g. replacement teeth, medical eye-glasses or maybe exclusively styled motorcycles or exclusively tuned cars. Another example is the traditional tailor who produces a dress or suit exclusively for you. These are all individual products with great variety and very low volume.

9.4.2 Batch Shop

Now let us continue with the hypothetical example of our chair, made out of wood. Let us assume that you would go to a market in order to sell your products. While you are selling and people come to you stating that they would like to have the small chair and the big one with arm rests in various colours, the result would be increasing the volume of similar types of products that need to be created.

Most probably, the best idea would be that you would offer two standard chairs (a small one and a big one) that could be painted in five different colours, for example. Because of that selected product portfolio, the natural reaction would be that you would produce a certain lot size of the small and then another lot size of the bigger one. As products are processed in *lots or batches*, this flow structure is called batch processing or batch production (i.e., products are produced in a batch shop). In the last production step, you would then do the customization, i.e., the individual painting on the market using a spray can.

Again, right now let us switch back to reality. Of course, not only exclusive suits are produced as you know, but also other exclusive products in small series like agricultural or construction machines respectively, helicopters or ambulances. In these cases, batches of similar products would be created. For example, the producer of special construction equipment would produce a small series of 20 excavators, which would all have the same communication equipment on board and would all be painted in blue for a specific customer and bearing the company's logo. The idea is to reduce the impact of set-up times and set-up cost and also to introduce stability into the value creation process.

9.4.3 Assembly Line

Let us continue the hypothetical chair journey. Your chairs are superb, everyone in your neighbourhood loves them and now even shops ask you to produce them in higher quantities. That means the required volume is significantly increasing and the consequence is, that for example manually cutting the wood for the chairs and running a manual assembly would no longer be efficient.

The consequence then might be to look at the possible usage of more machines for cutting the wood, drilling holes, putting the parts together, painting and even packaging them. So we would consider higher machine utilization and even think about more automation. Furthermore, we would think about the definition of work packages or focus on work specialization (cutting, drilling...), leading to the identification of work stations in the *value creation process*. In order to ensure the constant *product flow*, the different stations would also need to be balanced to avoid *idle times*. The product being created moves at a defined *takt time* from station to station. This is also referred to as the product following a defined *pacing* through the work stations. In an ideal case, one would employ a *conveyor belt* or similar for the movement of the product throughout the production facility.

And this is what is applied in the real world. *Assembly lines* are used for mass production of articles with relatively high volumes and a well defined level of variants. The most known examples of products created on an assembly line are cars (e. g., Henry Ford's assembly line for mass produced automobiles of the famous T-Model). Other examples produced on assembly lines are household devices such as washing machines, refrigerators or microwave ovens, but also consumer goods electronics like TVs or computers. All these have in common that the item produced is made in *large volume* and is moving at a constant speed through the factory from work station to *work station*. This makes the production quite efficient, but it is also vulnerable if a station may not be working or the wrong (or no) parts have been supplied to the station. The result could be a stopping line.

Task 9.6. Assembly Line Balancing

The planner in charge of assembly line balancing requires some inputs. One fundamental input is the manufacturing bill of materials (BoM) that provides the necessary information regarding the composition of the single parts that will be assembled in order to create the final product. To ensure this, the logical sequence of the different steps (so called *precedence relation*) also needs to be known (just imagine the sequence in which a pizza is created: first comes the dough, then the tomato sauce, followed by mushrooms, then the cheese, then it is placed in the oven, etc.). Additionally, the *task times* for different activities have to be known along with demand and available capacity per period of time.

Let us look at the example of how to assemble a simple manual scooter. You are in charge of balancing the assembly line according to the following inputs from the manufacturing engineers (Table 9.3):

Step 1: Precedence Diagram

The first step is to create the so-called "precedence diagram" based upon the inputs received. Table 9.3 indicates the precedence relationships and the corresponding diagram can be created. A simplified illustration is shown in Fig. 9.7:

Table 9.3 Initial data for assembly line balancing

Activity	Task	Predecessor	Task time (minutes)
A	Install brake in board	None	1.5
B	Install rear wheel in board	A	1.0
C	Glue anti-slip covering on top of the board	B	1.8
D	Pre-assemble Front Fork-Module	None	2.5
E	Install Front wheel in Fork-Module	D	0.6
F	Insert Front Fork-Module into Board	C, E	1.3
G	Install Steering Bar-Module	F	1.5
H	Test the correct functionality	G	1.4
	Sum of total Task Times		11.6

Fig. 9.7 Precedence diagram for the scooter assembly

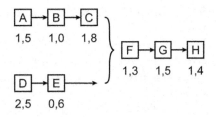

Step 2: Identify the Number of Followers
According to the precedence diagram, we can identify the number of the following activities. Just count the respective following tasks. This is needed to apply heuristics for the later assignment of the tasks to workstations (WS).

- Activity A has 5 followers.
- Activities B and D have 4 followers.
- Activities C and E have 3 followers.
- Activity F has 2 followers.
- Activity G has 1 follower.
- Activity H has 0 followers.

Step 3. Defining the Assignment Heuristic
We will apply the heuristic to start the loading of the assembly line beginning with the activity that has the highest number of the following activities. The precedence diagram needs to be respected. If there are activities that have the same number of the followers, the one with the higher number of task times will be used.

> ▶ **Practical Insights** Heuristics can be applied to obtain a reasonable result, but sometimes it might be required to review and re-do the exercise in case that the heuristic might not lead to a satisfactory result. In addition to the heuristic presented here (Jacobs and Aquilano 2014), Heizer and Render (2014) suggest further heuristics, but these are not considered for our example. In real business, more sophisticated mathematical methods are used which are supported by software. These methods allow considering different cases with parallel machines, uncertain processing times, etc. (Dolgui and Proth 2010)

Step 4: Identify the Bottleneck Activity and Determine Maximal Production Rate

In our example, the activity "D" has the longest processing time of 2.5 min. This activity is also considered as the bottleneck and determines maximal production rate. Let's assume that we work 8 h per day in our scooter manufacturing facility. Considering 60 min per hour, we get

available production time per day of 8 h/day · 60 min/h = 480 min/day

In order to identify maximal production rate per day, we need to divide the available production time per day by the bottleneck time. In our example, this is calculated as follows

Max. production rate = (480 min/day)/(2.5 min/product) = 192 products/day

Step 5: Calculate the Takt Time Based on the Required Output

Let's assume, that we have to balance our assembly line for a production rate per day of 150 scooters. In this case, we need to divide the available production time per day by the required output. We get:

Takt time = (480 min/day)/(150 scooters/day) = 3.2 min/scooter

Step 6: Calculate Theoretical Minimal Number of Workstations

As it can be observed from Table 9.3, the sum of the task times equals 11.6 min. Takt time is 3.2 min/scooter. That means we need to distribute the total task time over several workstations. This is exactly the task right now. In order to identify the minimum number of WS, we divide the total task time by the identified takt time:

Min number of WS = (11.6 min/scooter)/(3.2 min/scooter/WS) = 3.63 WS

As we cannot have fragments of WS, we need to round up. That means for our example that at least four WSs will need to be considered.

Step 7: Loading the Workstations According to Step 3

Workstation 1
3.2 min − A (1.5 min) = 1.7 min
1.7 min − B (1.0 min) = 0.7 min (= remaining idle time)
Workstation 2
3.2 min − D (2.5 min) = 0.7 min
0.7 min − E (0.6 min) = 0.1 min (= remaining idle time)
Workstation 3
3.2 min − C (1.8 min) = 1.4 min
1.4 min − F (1.3 min) = 0.1 min (= remaining idle time)
Workstation 4
3.2 min − G (1.5 min) = 1.7 min
1.7 min − H (1.4 min) = 0.3 min (= remaining idle time)

The clustering of the activities per workstations (WS) is shown in Fig. 9.8.

Figure 9.8 illustrates the clustering of the tasks per workstations well, but it does not provide a good overview on the takt time and efficiency of the assembly line. Therefore, *stacked bar charts* are used in practice which demonstrate the loading per station including the corresponding idle time. In Fig. 9.9, the corresponding

9.4 Process Flow Structures

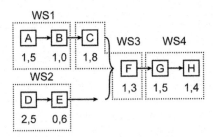

Fig. 9.8 Precedence diagram with indication of workstations

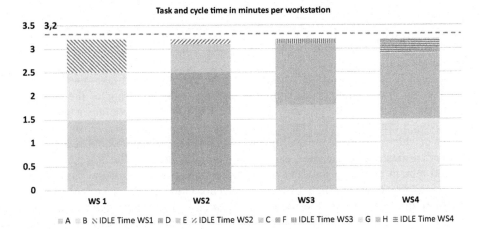

Fig. 9.9 Yamazumi Chart for the balanced assembly line

stacked bar chart is presented. In practice this is also called *Yamazumi chart* ("*Yama*" means *mountain* and "*zumi*" means to *pile up* in Japanese). Thus it is a graphical interpretation of the piled up work per station.

Step 8: Calculate the Efficiency of the Assembly Line
In the last step, the efficiency of the newly balanced assembly line will need to be determined. As the stacked bar chart (Yamazumi) shows (Fig. 9.9), there are idle times on each of the WSs, which results in inefficiency. The planners of the assembly line will try to find the ways to reduce these inefficiencies in numerous iterations. If we consider the loading of our assembly line for the scooters, we can calculate the efficiency using Eq. (9.23):

$$\text{Efficiency } [\%] = \text{total task times}/(\text{takt time} \cdot \text{number of workstations}) \quad (9.23)$$

For our example, efficiency $[\%] = 11.6$ min$/(3.2$ min $\cdot 4) = 11.6$ min$/12.8$ min $= 0.906$ which means 91 %.

The planners would now try to break down the individual tasks into smaller portions in order to reduce the idle times and increase efficiency.

9.4.4 Continuous Flow

Now should demand for chairs be very high, i.e., many thousand items per day required, one would even rethink the chair's design and materials. The questions are how could we simplify the design in order to reduce the number of parts and as well as the *throughput time* of assembly? That means, one could argue, that the product should no longer be made out of wood, but maybe out of plastics. Instead of cutting pieces of wood, putting them together on the assembly line and then painting them, one could suggest that the chair is done in one continuous outflow of plastics in various colours. Production would take place following the plastics moulding process.

Instead of having multiple workstations, the process would take place in one continuous flow, a value-added process starting with the filling of the plastics granulate, heating it up, pressing it into the form required, cooling it and then removing it from the mould. Human intervention would be involved for supervision of the machines and to ensure quality, but creation of the product would be achieved through utilization of machines, using the highest automation. The cost per product would remain relatively low, but on the other hand, the cost for the facility and machines would be very high, because of the enormously high level of automation. Furthermore, complete customization is not possible because the moulds are especially designed to create one product and thus are very expensive. This will result in very low flexibility for adjusting the product to possible changes from the customer side.

9.4.5 Product-Process Matrix

In essence, the considered product flow structures have different advantages as well as disadvantages. The relationship between products and processes can be summarized in the form of a so-called *product-process matrix* (see Fig. 9.10).

Let us get back to the initial hypothetical example of our chair. If you want to produce your chair exclusively and in small quantities, you will select the job shop; if on the other hand the task is to produce the chair in the highest quantities, the continuous flow would be a recommended structure. Overall, the question of

9.5 Lean Production Systems

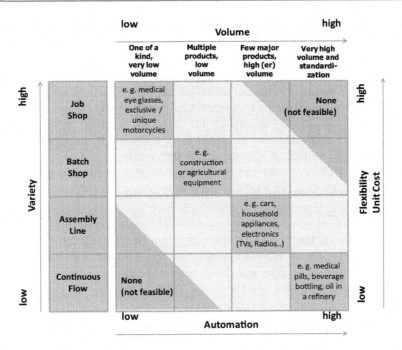

Fig. 9.10 Product-process matrix [based on Chase et al. (2006)]

volume and variety are the factors that will drive your decision towards the most appropriate process flow structure.

9.5 Lean Production Systems

9.5.1 Lean Thinking

"Lean" means the continuous process of increasing efficiency and improvements in the organization, which requires teamwork, respect and taking over responsibility. Team members are also responsible for detecting defects and striving for their root cause, plus identifying a solution for future avoidance. Lean also requires a good relationship with the unions accompanied by the trust.

The lean organization is characterized by a set of the following five key principles (Womack and Jones, 1996; Bicheno and Holweg, 2008):

- *value* from the customer point of view
- *value stream* and waste (*"muda"*) elimination
- smooth *flow* throughput in production
- *pull*-control policies, e.g., *Kanban*
- perfection and *continuous improvement (Kaizen)*.

The underlying philosophy of all above mentioned principles is the *respect* for people and *learning* from mistakes.

9.5.1.1 Value

Identifying the *'value'* of a product or service means understanding and specifying what the customer is expecting to receive. Understanding what the customer wants and does not want are key aspects in lean thinking. Womack and Jones (2005) described value as a capability provided for a customer at the right time at an appropriate price, as defined in each case by the customer.

9.5.1.2 Value Stream and Value Stream Mapping

The *value stream* presents the specific activities required to design, order and provide a specific product, from concept to launch, order to delivery, raw materials into the hands of the customer. The most effective process is achieved by performing the minimal required number of value-added steps and no waste steps. This is the ideal goal that is almost impossible to achieve in practice. A method to maximize the volume of the value-added steps in lean practice is called value stream mapping and analysis.

VSA (*value stream analysis*) is a tool to connect process flow and costs analysis. It is a suitable tool for redesigning the value creation systems. The availability of a well-trained team is essential as a key success factor. In VSA, different process steps in the value creation process are identified, listed, sequenced and visualized. Then the value-added times are measured. For comparison the non-value added times are also measured.

Value stream mapping (VSM) provides understanding of the current process by:

- visualizing multiple process levels
- highlighting waste and its sources,
- rendering "hidden" decision points apparent.

VSM also provides a communication tool for stimulating ideas by capturing critical organizational knowledge and identifying locations for data gathering and process measurement.

9.5.1.3 Flow

Womack and Jones (2005) described *flow* as "the progressive achievement of tasks along the value stream so that a product proceeds from design to launch, order to delivery, and raw materials into the hands of the customer with no stoppages, scrap or backflows". The concept of flow is focused on the movement and value adding processes of the product as such but also involves the material, information and financial flow. The flow principle can also be extended to the non-production area where it is related to information flow. The flow of information among the parties involved in a value creation network is as important as the physical flow of the materials.

9.5.1.4 Pull

The *"pull"* principle considers a system from downstream to upstream activities in which nothing is produced by the upstream supplier until the downstream customer signals a need. Pull means that one should start the creation of a product or service when the customer asks for it.

9.5.1.5 Seek Perfection

Seeking perfection is the element of *continuous improvement* in the lean philosophy. Perfection does not only mean quality. Perfection should be considered as being able to create exactly what the customer wants, when it is needed and at an acceptable, fair price with a minimum of waste. It is important to understand that a process will not be perfect and that there is a need for continuous re-examination of the process to remain competitive and lean. It is required to repeat this optimization cycle to get closer to the optimum with every loop taken. Womack and Jones (2005) summarized perfection as "the complete elimination of *muda* so that all activities along the value stream create value".

9.5.2 Lean Production Principles

For an all-embracing view on the origin of Lean, please consider "The Machine that Changed the World" by Womack et al. (2007). Insights on the important Just-in-Time (JIT) principle are provided in 5.3.3 and various practical Lean shop-floor examples are presented in section 10.2. of this book.

In 1950, Eiji Toyoda, a member of the Toyoda family who founded the Toyota Motor Company, visited Ford's Rouge factory in Detroit. From 1937 to 1950, i.e. over a period of 13 years, Toyota produced in total 2685 cars in contrast to 7000 automobiles that Ford produced at the Rouge site in a single day (Womack et al. 1990). Eiji Toyoda assessed in detail the mass production principles applied in Detroit and concluded that the performance of the Toyota facilities could also be improved and he exchanged information on that with Taiichi Ohno, Toyota's leading production engineer in Nagoya. Even the Japanese considered the Toyota staff as "a bunch of farmers", initially producing looms, then military trucks and some hand-crafted automobiles—but today, the company is recognized as being one of the most efficient and highest-quality producers of motor vehicles in the world.

9.5.2.1 Lean Production/Toyota Production System

As a result of the research at the MIT International Motor Vehicle Program (IMVP) the expression 'lean production' was coined and Holweg (2007, p. 426) points out, that: "The term 'lean production' was first used by Krafcik in 1988, and subsequently, Womack et al. of course used the term 'lean production' to contrast Toyota with the Western 'mass production' system in the 'Machine' book."

Ohno (1988) identified that the U.S. mass production principles would not be applicable for the craft production oriented Japanese industry. Thus he created a new approach. In the western industries, multiple machines were used, and each one had to produce enormous amounts of the same pressed parts, as the changeover required specialists and took a lot of time.

Taiichi Ohno developed presses, in which the dies were slid in (every couple of hours instead of months) via rollers and fixed by simple quick mechanisms to use few machines to press with multiple dies. This saved *time, cost, and space*. Also instead of using specialist changeover teams, Taiichi Ohno suggested that the workers should be capable of and responsible for running the exchange of dies; after continuous efforts on improvement, changeover times were reduced down to just 3 min by the end of the 1950s. He also identified that it was more cost efficient to press small lot sizes of parts instead of running press batches of large quantities, resulting in (a) a reduction in carried inventories and (b) immediate identification of defective pressed metal sheets.

The result was an increased awareness regarding quality and early identification of flaws. It also avoided large quantities of wrongly produced parts that would have needed to be repaired, reworked or even scrapped—if they had followed the system of producing *large batches* according to the mass production philosophy. In order to further perfect this approach, no stupid exchangeable de-humanized workers would be required but instead a set of highly skilled, motivated and pro-active workforce!

Toyota also suffered from the financial crisis when it was subject to post-war American occupation. Toyota intended to lay off 25 % of their workforce, which resulted in turmoil leading to the strengthened rights of employees and strong unions. The compromise was that the workforce was reduced by a quarter, but President Kiichiro Toyoda resigned and the remaining workers received a life-time working guarantee at Toyota accompanied by seniority-based wages and receipt of bonus payments. In other words, the *employees became part of the Toyota community* with the right to use the available facilities.

Ohno understood that because of this agreement, workers could remain at Toyota for life. Toyota and the workers became 'one community'. So he intended to strive for *continuous improvement* of their skills and competencies as they became part of the "human assets". This needs to be seen in contrast to Ford's perception of using the workers as "human equipment" to perform one or two tasks repeatedly, supervised by a foreman, managed by industrial engineers and so on along the hierarchy. This also contributes to the establishment of a lean culture (Mann 2010).

One striking finding for Ohno was that in Ford's approach, cars would be moved along the line, even when there were defects, because these were corrected in an especially dedicated rework area before being shipped to dealers. Back in Japan, Taiichi Ohno formed teams of skilled workers, led by a capable team leader. The team leader was manager and worker at the same time and was also utilized as a "jumper" to fill in the gap of an absent team colleague. These teams were furthermore autonomously responsible for numerous assembly processes and for a certain area in the plant, so to say, their working domain. They were also responsible for quality control, housekeeping and cleaning as well as conducting small repairs. A key element of the teams was *continuous process optimization*—the teams were at the frontline, so they felt the pain and knew how to improve things.

9.5.2.2 Kaizen

This approach of *continuous improvement* is called "*Kaizen*" in Japanese (Imai 1993). MacDuffie et al. (1996) summarized that "under the philosophy of continuous improvement that characterized lean production, problems identified through the minimization of buffers are seen as opportunities for organizational learning". In contrast to mass production in the western world, where mistakes or parts installed incorrectly would move throughout the entire line and by the time mistakes had possibly been identified, many faulty cars would have been created, Taiichi Ohno did something completely different. Ohno made another simple, but revolutionary, invention. He attached a cord to the assembly line and workers were encouraged to pull the cord, thus stopping the entire assembly line if a mistake was identified by a worker (Ohno 1988). Then the workers in their community looked for a solution to the problem, which gave them a lot of responsibility in making sure to do it right the first time.

9.5.2.3 Waste Reduction

In order to convert to lean principles in other functions of the organization, such a process can also be implemented in non-production processes: the cord or *andon*[1] sign is there to highlight mistakes when they appear (Dennis 2010).

Ohno also tried to assess the reason for mistakes occurring by asking the "Five Whys", which is a structured approach to get to the so-called "root cause" of problems (Ohno 1988). Initially the assembly lines stopped very often, but the more mature this error analysis and prevention attitude became, the more failure rates dropped significantly to almost no defects: this is a 100 % yield at Toyota compared to 90 % in the mass production plants. This is the reason why in today's Toyota plants there is almost no space planned for rework, because there is almost no rework compared to today's mass production plants which devote 20 % of their space to quality corrections. Close to the waste reduction idea is also the Six Sigma concept that set up special requirements on quality management and control (Chiarini 2012).

Waste, or *muda*, can be classified in two ways.

- Type I Muda is found in activities that add no value for the customer, but are necessary, to deliver the product.
- Type II Muda is found in activities that do not create value and can be eliminated immediately, such as waiting and unnecessary transport.

Type 1 muda needs to be reduced to the minimum and type II muda needs to be eliminated.

This list of *7 + 1 wastes* is one of the key elements in Lean Thinking. Womack and Jones (2005) stated that Taiichi Ohno's original enumeration of the wastes was commonly found in production. The term *"seven plus one"* wastes comes from the fact that initially, seven wastes were identified, but then it became obvious that not meeting the requirements of the customer was also waste, hence "7+1":

---

[1] Andon is Japanese and means "lantern" and thus is a visual, such as a traffic light that highlights in the production process anything going according to plan (green = OK) or if there are problems/disturbances (red = NOK) that would require immediate intervention and mitigation.

- *Over-production* ahead of demand
- *Waiting* for the next processing step
- *Unnecessary transport* of materials (for example between villages, suppliers, facilities etc.)
- *Over-processing* of parts due to e.g. poor tool and/or product design
- *Inventory* that exceeds what is required
- *Unnecessary motion and movement* by the employees during the performance of their work (for example looking for parts, tools, documentation etc.)
- Production of *defective parts plus*
- *Not meeting customer requirements*

Recently, wasted *ideas or knowledge* waste has been added to "7+1" (Dennis 2010). The Toyota's case clearly demonstrates how aspects of the process flow structures, layout and factory planning and the evolution from craft to lean production are connected. Furthermore, it has shown that the principles of continuous improvement and thinking in terms of quality are all closely connected. It has also shown its initial limitations, for example the need for a total system view regarding the lean enterprise and the intensive need for cooperation with the SC partners involved (no matter if they are internal or external).

To summarize the principles of lean production, it can be stated that *lean* strives for the combination of the advantages of both craft and mass production, trying to avoid the high unit cost of craftsmanship and at the same time avoiding the rigid, boring and inflexible processes of mass production. This has led to the ability to reduce costs per unit and has dramatically improved quality while at the same time being able to provide a wider range of products to the customer and more challenging work for the staff. Regarding composition of workers' teams, lean production is striving for the creation of flexible teams consisting of multi-skilled staff that operates highly flexible machines to produce volumes of products in high variety. These principles are applied to the tiers of suppliers, but are also looking at an integration of dealers and buyers into the lean concept.

To summarize, the *Toyota Production System* covers in principle the following key areas (see also Heizer and Render, 2014[2], p. 661):

1. *Pull-System*: Parts are only produced, when they are needed for further production. This is the contrary to a Push-System, in which material is fed into the production area or warehouse. The purpose of the pull principle is, e.g., to increase efficiency and to avoid overproduction, unnecessary transportation and too high levels of inventory.
2. *Just in Time (JIT)*: Following the Pull-System, parts and modules are delivered to the station in the right quantity and at the right time (thus just in time), when they are needed. It is to avoid, that the facility is flooded with unnecessary material.

---

[2] Heizer J, Render B (2014) Principles of operations management: sustainability and supply chain management, 9th edn. Pearson, Boston

3. *Kanban*: Kanban means a "sign" or a "card". A Kanban signal is used to indicate that a small batch of components needs to be produced. It is a practical approach based on real material consumption that initiates the replenishment process (unlike as material requirements planning (MRP) that presumes the planned replenishments).
4. *Standard Work Practices*: These are agreed upon documented procedures for the production process. This is to secure that everyone follows the same steps and sequence in the value creation. Thus, the timing per operation will be met and the quality to complete the work will be the same for all similar products.
5. *Minimal Machines*: Proprietary machines are designed for specific Toyota applications. It might also be a good idea to use general multi-purpose machines with certain adapters to simplify the usage and to ease the maintenance.
6. *Respect for People*: The employees are treated and are also respected as capable workers with knowledge and they are empowered to use their capabilities.
7. *Empowered employees*: The employees have responsibility. For example, they can stop the production in urgent cases, might evaluate improvement ideas and are also actively involved in quality control circles.
8. *Kaizen Area*: This is an area, where the employees are involved in order to make suggestions. Furthermore, the ideas or suggestions are tested, discussed and evaluated.
9. *Jidoka*: Machines are equipped with built-in devices for the monitoring of performance and to "make judgements". If a problem occurs, the machine will interrupt the process, that's why Jidoka is also considered as machines or automation with "human touch". This avoids a processing of defective components and allows to analyse the root causes of the defects.
10. *Andon System*: Initially, in case of a problem a cord was pulled or a light was flashing at a station. Nowadays, problems are also openly displayed on a board or a screen in order to highlight deviations from the standard. It is part of the idea to visualize problems.
11. *Level schedules*: Models on the assembly line are mixed in order to meet customer demands and to avoid huge variation in the loading of the assembly line. The work needs to be balanced or levelled, focussing on the processing of smaller batches.
12. *Assembly components*: Parts or modules may be placed inside the car for an easier access instead of placing the parts in shelves next to the assembly line. Bigger modules are pre-assembled close to the main assembly line and are then fed into the main assembly line ("fishbone line feeding").

9.5.3 Lean Supply Chain

9.5.3.1 Lean Thinking in the Supply Chain

Anker (2013) pointed out that a car can comprise 25,000 single parts and the related material cost represents approximately 70 % of the total production cost. In relation to the price, the customer pays, the material cost accounts is in a range of 50 %. The level of supplies provided by external parties is at approximately 75 %, that means the in-house production roughly 25 % (Anker 2013). In the case of the Smart production facility in Hambach (France), the external contribution is close to 90 %, which shows that in that case the production depth is mainly with the suppliers and the original equipment manufacturer (OEM) accounts for approximately 10 %.

If we compare this with the examples given earlier, Ford initially strived for 100 % at the Rouge Complex, but reduced it back to 50 % after World War II. For Taiichi Ohno the question was how suppliers and producers could in the efficient way work together in order to jointly reduce cost and increase quality.

The principle process from design to production in Ford's or GM's approach was that their own engineers designed the parts (previously purchased externally) completely on their own. Then the blueprints were sent to potential part suppliers who were supposed to submit their tenders. Following that, the supplier was selected in principle on price, but also considering quality and delivery reliability—with the side effect that suppliers were often switched, when others made better offers. Also here one can see the change in mindset regarding the criteria to select suppliers.

Lean SCM recognizes that there was a lack of cooperation from suppliers and their integration into the value chain. The potential of continuous improvement and their contribution regarding best practices remained unutilized in the mass production approach. Also suppliers followed the principle of producing large batch sizes that were shipped to the car producers. If a defect was discovered, many faulty parts had already been installed in cars and at the same time a high number of defective parts (inventory) were produced that required rework or scrapping.

Lean SCM identifies the potential of the suppliers that was—comparable to the knowledge capabilities of the shop floor workers—not utilized. Therefore lean SCM encourages suppliers to contribute their own expertise, meaning that Toyota specified the technical requirements that the part needed to fulfil, but the detailed design was developed by the suppliers (who were able to optimize the components they offered according to their own manufacturing).

Then, Ohno classified suppliers into multiple tiers. The *tier 1 suppliers* were the ones who autonomously developed parts based on key requirements (e.g. deceleration parameters, diameters and measures for brake systems. The suppliers created prototypes that became the serial components when they successfully passed functionality tests. The tier 1 suppliers were in principle not in competition with each other, thus they openly shared their information at supplier level. Taiichi Ohno also requested that the tier 1 suppliers should on their own establish a second line of suppliers for themselves according to a similar principle. These fabricating suppliers were in principle manufacturing specialists but not engineering experts.

These *second tier* suppliers were clustered and organized in non-competitor supplier associations which also contributed to openly sharing information among suppliers. As a side effect, "Toyota spun its in-house supply operations off into quasi-independent first-tier supplier companies in which Toyota retained a fraction of the equity and developed similar relationships with other suppliers who had been completely independent" (Womack et al. 2007, p. 60). Toyota also supported its suppliers with financial loans but also with workforce and encouraged the supplier base to offer their products to other companies and industries.

9.5.3.2 Kanban

Presently, Lean thinking in the SC has been frequently considered in light of SC risk management. It has been recognized that typical lean techniques such as single sourcing or low inventory make the SC fragile in the case of disruptions at factories and suppliers due to man-made and natural catastrophes (see Chap. 4, Ripple effect).

The next idea of the lean SCM is the simplification of the logistical processes and material call-offs. In principle, a connected chain as in a huge factory has to be created, in which the previous production process feeds material in limited quantities to the following process step after the material has been called off.

The idea was to employ *circulating containers or boxes*. Each container or box was equipped with a *card* which signals the need for another container or material. This card was called "*kanban*". The containers and boxes were filled with parts and then sent to the next production step and—when completely empty—returned to their origin and thus acted as a call-off sign. The advantage was that inventory was reduced throughout this SC. In an unfavorable situation in which one container carried defective parts, the entire system would stop as soon as the defective part was detected, since the circulation of the boxes would also be interrupted.

In essence, the following five elements are crucial for a lean SC.

- *Perfect first-time quality* is achieved through the objective of creating zero defects, revealing and solving problems at their ultimate source (e. g. the shop floor), achieving higher quality and productivity simultaneously through teamwork or worker empowerment.
- *Waste minimization* is achieved by removing all non-value-added activities and by making the most efficient use of scarce resources (e. g. capital, people and space) and by applying JIT deliveries as well as eliminating any safety buffers for inventory reduction.
- *Continuous improvement* (reducing costs, improving quality and increasing productivity) is achieved through a dynamic process of change, simultaneous and integrated product/process development, rapid takt time and time-to-market, openness and information sharing.
- *Flexibility* is achieved through producing different mixes or greater diversity of products quickly, without sacrificing efficiency at lower volumes of production, through rapid set-up and manufacturing in small lot sizes.
- *Long-term relationships* between suppliers and primary producers (assemblers, system integrators) are established through collaborative risk sharing, costs haring and information sharing arrangements.

9.6 Modern Trends: Industry 4.0

Industry 4.0—what does this mean? This new expression sounds very much like new software or it could be considered as a fourth release from a computer application. Indeed that is not that wrong, it is actually related to the fourth revolution in the industrial environment.

What it means is that *the first industrial revolution is related to the mechanization of the production processes*. Here, predominantly steam- and water-power was used to increase efficiency during the creation of goods.

After that, the principles of Taylor and the *electrification of the production* floors took place, which is considered as the *second revolution*. A combination of the separation of work packages and electrical power to operate machines helped the industry to produce goods in large quantities and also to use moving production lines. One well known result from that era was the production of cars, such as the Ford T-Model, on an assembly line. The flow principle and product creation in well planned work packages led to the final move from craft to mass production.

The era starting with the 1970s was characterized by the increased usage of computer technology during the value creation processes. This *information orientation of production represented the third industrial revolution*. This means that electronics, information technology and the ambition for automation were the dominant objectives leading to e. g., *computer integrated manufacturing* (CIM).

During all these three industrial revolutions, significant improvements regarding productivity and efficiency were made. But the improvements do not stop here. We are now in the middle of the next industrial revolution.

Because of that, we do talk about the *fourth industrial revolution now, or in other words it is the decade of Industry 4.0*. The main idea is that companies will in future intensively utilize and connect their machines, materials, tools, warehouses, transportation technology, etc. in an intelligent way. The keyword here is related to the formation of *Cyber-Physical-Systems (CPS)*. Materials, machines or devices can exchange information mutually, can set priorities, can trigger action and can also help to schedule and sequence the work in process, which will result in the achievement of a new level of "Lean" (see "Leandustry 4.0"; Tsipoulanidis, 2015).

According to the BMBF (German Federal Ministry of Education and Research 2014): "Industry is on the threshold of the fourth industrial revolution. Driven by the Internet, the real and virtual worlds are growing closer and closer together to form the Internet of Things. Industrial production of the future will be characterized by the strong individualization of products under the conditions of highly flexible (large series) production, the extensive integration of customers and business partners in business and value-added processes, and the linking of production and high quality services leading to so-called hybrid products."

Value-adding processes will improve themselves, and that means the fundamental idea of continuous improvement is no longer connected to the human being. Operational process, material movement, production flow and SC activities will lead to the so-called *smart factory*. "The focus regarding the topic of 'Smart Factories' is on intelligent production systems and processes and the realization of distributed and networked production sites. At the same time, strategic funding measures in the field of the Internet of Things will also address the 'Industry 4.0' project. Under the heading 'Smart Production', there will be a stronger focus on areas such as intra-company production logistics, human-machine interaction and the use of 3D printing in industrial applications. The close involvement of small and medium-sized enterprises as both providers and users of 'smart' production methods is of key significance in this context" (BMBF 2014).

Now one might ask how this is going to work and what is the foundation of that additional intelligence in production? The basic technology behind it is the above mentioned so-called *internet of things* which means that no longer will human beings be communicating, but also the non-human beings—the things—will communicate via information technology. In order to better explain that, a short case study should help.

Case Study "Industry 4.0"
Imagine that you are loading a truck with fresh strawberries. In order to ensure product quality, the cold chain needs to be permanently monitored. The temperature in the truck with the cooler is constantly monitored. We also know via GPS where the truck is at each point in time. With the *machine-to-machine (M2M)* technology all this collected data can be transmitted in real time, because the M2M technology is comparable to a mobile phone. Just imagine that the truck is calling a central monitoring centre and on a regular basis submits to a computer in the monitoring facility the data that are measured during the journey.

In other words, the machine (truck) is communicating with the other machine (computer in the monitoring centre). Following that process, the cold chain can be permanently documented. Furthermore, if the truck has a technical problem and the cooling device does not ensure the proper temperature, the driver will be notified. From a logistical perspective, it does not make sense to continue the journey with perished good. Based upon the GPS data, the next appropriate waste deposit and recycling station should be identified and the driver should be instructed to go there. Furthermore, the next repair facility can be contacted for maintenance of the defective truck.

Assuming that the truck was bringing strawberries from the field to a yoghurt factory, the factory will need to be informed that the truck was damaged so that the replenishment with new strawberries cannot take place. Although this is an unfavourable situation, the producing factory might be able to change the production volume to produce alternative yoghurt, perhaps one with a nuts or vanilla flavour instead of strawberry.

In essence, Industry 4.0 will involve the technical integration of CPS into manufacturing and logistics and the use of the Internet of Things and Services in industrial processes. This will have implications for value creation, business models, downstream services and work organization. In the U.S., a similar project (to the German "Industry 4.0" initiative) has been launched; this is called *SMLC—smart manufacturing leadership coalition.*

9.7 Key Points and Discussion Questions

The decision on building a new or modifying an existing factory is of strategic importance and needs to contribute to the generation of competitive advantage. The role of factory planning is also to consider a successful partnership with the involved parties in the SC and it is also aiming at the efficient operations management. It is recommended to consider the following questions in factory planning activities in order to elaborate a successful approach to place a well operating facility with the appropriate process flow structures and capacity at the right location.

How to Plan a Factory in a Structured Way?

Factory planning is in general related to significant investments. That is the reason why the planning needs to take place in a structured and systematic way. A wrong approach can result in an enormous loss of capital. Thus, a logical connection between the initial planning phase of the facility, the realization of the new or adjusted factory and the later operation (running the factory) needs to be established. Between these different steps, careful milestone checks need to be made in order to obtain the approval by the decision makers to move into the next phase.

Which Different Options Could Be Considered?

In factory planning it is not always necessary to create a completely new facility. It is part of the general, regular tasks of the planners to re-design existing facilities in order to ensure that new models can be produced at existing sites. Furthermore, the existing plants can be expanded because of increasing demands. They can also be reduced (or even closed) when the markets show decreasing demands. Another option is the complete new creation of a factory on the "green field" to be close to the new market or local temporary production partnerships might also be an option to meet possible local content requirements.

How to Support the Factory Capacity Planning Process?

In order to ensure the appropriate output of the facility, the demand needs to be known or estimated in a substantiated way, so that the (design and effective) capacity can be determined. Useful tools that help to identify the capacity aspects are for example related to the application of Little's Law, to run a bottleneck analysis (theory of constraints) or to apply the principles of a systematic break-even-analysis, decision trees, and waiting line theory.

What Are the Generic Process Flow Structures that Need to Be Considered?

When we talk about process flow design, the immediate relation to the aspect of volume of demand and the variety of the goods that will be produced needs to be made. When products with very low volume and a significant variety have to be produced, the principle of the "job shop" will be the right decision. If products need to be produced in small lot sizes, for example 10 exactly same fire trucks for the regional fire brigade, these 10 products will most probably be produced following the "batch shop" approach, as these items are periodically produced in small batches or lots. Assuming that for example 700 cars or 2000 microwave ovens will need to be created per day, the "assembly line" is a suitable process flow structure as it allows mass production of standard goods following a regular pace while moving the item from work station to work station. Finally for the production of very large volumes of standard products such as medical pills, bottles of mineral water or sugar, the production following the concept of a "continuous flow" will be the fitting strategy.

How Do We Identify Non Value Adding Activities and What to Focus On?

One of the fundamental principles in running the operations is the application of the "lean thinking". According the idea of "lean", a clear statement of what the customer expects and what is considered as "value" is needed. Therefore, the value stream has to be mapped and value adding respectively non-value adding processes has to be analysed, so that unnecessary efforts or activities, such as waiting, over production, defects etc. can be identified. This results in the identification and elimination of the so-called 7+1 wastes. Recently also wasted talent or knowledge has been added to the 7+x wastes. Another aspect of "lean" is the smooth flow of the value adding processes without obstacles or buffers according to the so-called "pull" principle. Lean thinking also emphasizes to seek perfection by continuous improvement. A fundamental lean consideration is the respect for people.

What Will Be Necessary for the Future?

Besides the focus on operational factors such as the design or the application of Lean principles, also the rapid development of intelligence and internet technology requires recognition. One modern trend is called Industry 4.0 which is related to the fourth industrial revolution following firstly mechanization, secondly electrification and thirdly the use of information technology in the production domain. Using the *Internet of Things*, machines and materials can exchange information in so-called cyber-physical-systems. It is expected to gain additional efficiency potentials of approximately 30 % due to the intelligent combination of machines, materials and the human being (Lemmer, 2014).

Discussion Points
- Discuss in groups which external factors might influence companies to search for new manufacturing or service sites
- Elaborate on the advantages and disadvantages but also which types of risks and opportunities you can see when firms are regularly adjusting their industrial footprint
- Analyse the impact of lean thinking on SC risk and vulnerability
- What are new requirements for the human being in the production environment considering the development towards Industry 4.0?
- Will the new additive manufacturing technologies such as 3D printing in combination with new lightweight materials such as carbon composites impact the process design and flows structures in future?

Bibliography

Anker S (2013) Wie viel Luft ist noch im Autopreis?. VDI nachrichten, 01 Jun 2013, p 4
Belekoukias I, Garza-Reyes JA, Kumar V (2014) The impact of lean methods and tools on the operational performance of manufacturing organisations. Int J Prod Res 52(18):5346–5366
Bicheno J, Holweg M (2008) The lean toolbox: the essential guide to lean transformation, 4th edn. Picsie Books, Buckingham

BMBF - Federal Ministry of Education and Research (2014) Project of the future: industry 4.0. http://www.bmbf.de/en/19955.php?hilite=industry+4.0. Accessed 16 Jun 2014

Bozarth CC, Handfield RB (2013) Introduction to operations and supply chain management, 3rd edn. Pearson, Harlow

Chase RB, Jacobs FR, Aquilano NJ (2006) Operations management for competitive advantage, 11th edn. McGraw-Hill, Boston

Chiarini A (2012) From total quality control to lean six sigma: evolution of the most important management systems for the excellence. Springer, Milan

Dennis P (2010) The remedy: bringing lean thinking out of the factory to transform the entire organization. Wiley, New Jersey

Dolgui A, Proth J-M (2010) Supply chain engineering: useful methods and techniques. Springer, Berlin

Goldratt EM (1990) What is this thing called Theory of Constraints and how should it be implemented? North River Press, Croton-on-Hudson

Grundig CG (2015) Fabrikplanung: Planungssystematik – Methoden – Anwendungen, 5th edn. Carl Hanser Verlag, München

Heizer J, Render B (2014) Principles of operations management: sustainability and supply chain management, 9th edn. Pearson, Boston

Holweg M (2007) The genealogy of lean production. J Oper Manage 25:420–437

Jacobs FR, Aquilano RB (2014) Operations and supply chain management, 14th edn. McGraw-Hill, Berkshire

Jasti NVK, Kodali R (2015) Lean production: literature review and trends. Int J Prod Res 53(3): 867–885

Krajewski LJ, Ritzman LP, Malhotra MK (2013) Operations management – processes and supply chains, 10th edn. Pearson, Harlow

Lemmer R (2014) Inselhopping in der Werkshalle. WirtschaftsWoche, 13 Oct 2014, pp 94–96

Little JDC, Graves SC (2008) Little's law. In: Chhajed D, Lowe TJ (eds) Building intuition: insights from basic operations management models and principles. Springer, New York, pp 81–100

MacDuffie JP, Sethuraman K, Fisher ML (1996) Product variety and manufacturing performance: evidence from the international automotive assembly plant survey. Manag Sci 42(3):350–369

Mann D (2010) Creating a lean culture: tools to sustain lean conversions, 2nd edn. Productivity Press, New York

Marodin GA, Saurin TA (2013) Implementing lean production systems: research areas and opportunities for future studies. Int J Prod Res 51(22):6663–6680

Ohno T (1988) Toyota production system: beyond large-scale production. Productivity Press, New York

Schenk M, Wirth S, Müller E (2014) Fabrikplanung und Fabrikbetrieb* Methoden für die wandlungsfähige, vernetzte und ressourceneffiziente Fabrik, 2nd edn. Springer, Berlin

Slack N, Chambers S, Johnston R (2010) Operations management, 6th edn. Pearson, Harlow

Tsipoulanidis A (2015) Von Lean Thinking zu Supply Chain & Operational Excellence durch die digitale Transformation, Der Tagesspiegel, http://www.tagesspiegel.de/themen/digital-businesses-und-services/prof-dr-alexander-tsipoulanidis-von-lean-thinking-zu-supply-chain-und-operational-excellence-durch-die-digitale-transformation/12530142.html

Wiendahl H-P, Nofen D, Klußmann JH, Breitenbach F (eds) (2005) Planung modularer Fabriken – Vorgehen und Beispiele aus der Praxis. Carl Hanser Verlag, München

Wilson JM (2014) Henry Ford vs. assembly line balancing. Int J Prod Res 52(3):757–765

Womack JP, Jones DT (1996) Lean thinking – banish waste and create wealth in your corporation. Touchstone Books, London

Womack JP, Jones DT (2005) Lean solutions: how companies and customer can create wealth together. Simon & Schuster, New York

Womack JP, Jones DT, Roos D (1990) The machine that changed the world – the story of lean production. HarperCollins, New York

Womack JP, Jones DT, Roos D (2007) The machine that changed the world: the story of lean production - toyota's secret weapon in the global car wars that is revolutionizing world industry. Simon & Schuster, New York

References for Sect. 9.1

Bresnahan T, Gambardella A (2004) Building high-tech clusters. Cambridge University Press, Cambridge

Dickerman L, Harrison J (2010) A new car, a new grid. IEEE Power and Energy Magazine 10: 55–61

Eberhard M, Tarpenning M (2006) The 21st Century Electric Car Tesla Motors. http://idc-online.com/technical_references/pdfs/electrical_engineering/Tesla_Motors.pdf, Accessed 4 Aug 2014

Husmann N (2014) Mitten im Strom. http://www.focus.de/magazin/archiv/fotoreportage-mitten-im-strom_id_3969468.html, Accessed 4 Aug 2014

Markoff J (2012) Skilled work, without the worker. *The New York Times*, p 18

Layout Planning 10

Learning Objectives for This Chapter

- role of layout planning in SCOM
- layout planning in manufacturing
- layout planning in warehouses
- methods of layout planning.

10.1 Introductory Case-Study "OTLG Ludwigsfelde"

Volkswagen Original Teile Logistik GmbH & Co. KG (OTLG) is a service partner for spare parts of Volkswagen, Volkswagen Nutzfahrzeuge, Audi, Seat and Škoda. OTLG is the wholesale level in the SC and responsible for sales and marketing in Germany. At present, OTLG operates in seven distribution centers in Germany. After locating new distribution center, layout planning has been done as follows (Fig. 10.1).

The warehouse layout comprises an incoming area for the receipt and inspection of goods. If an order for the supplied item already exists, the item is moved via the cross-docking area directly to the outbound area. Otherwise, the items are first stocked and then put away, and picked up after an order is received. Such a layout ensures the shortest transportation routes and the efficient placement, put away and pick up of items with the help of sophisticated software and automated material handling technologies.

Describe on the basis of this case study example the basic processes and areas in warehouse logistics layout!

Find additional case-studies, Excel spreadsheet templates, and video streams in the *E-Supplement* to this book on www.global-supply-chain-management.de!

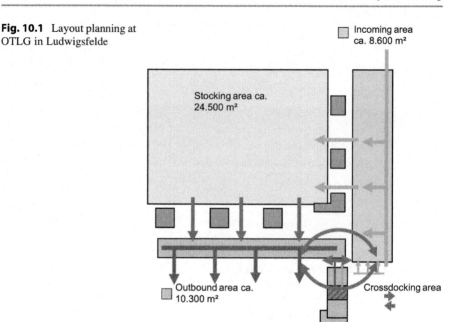

Fig. 10.1 Layout planning at OTLG in Ludwigsfelde

10.2 Layout Planning in Manufacturing

In Chap. 9 the process flow structures were presented and it became evident, that the underlying parameters determining process flow structures are volume and variety. The process flow structures do not as such indicate what type of manufacturing layout is best suited, but the layout types are closely linked to the processes applied to create a product.

A layout is the physical arrangement of objects in space. Fundamental objectives related to that are as follows:

- to limit the travel distances between machines or departments
- to allocate departments or functional areas/main production areas in a reasonable pattern
- to avoid crossing flows (material, transportation devices, human beings, etc.)
- to prepare for later adaptation or expansion.

In general, there are four basic types of layouts in manufacturing and these are:

- fixed position layout
- process flow layout
- product flow layout
- cell-based layout.

10.2.1 Fixed Position Layout

We start with the *fixed position layout*. As the name indicates, the product or object where the value adding takes place remains in a fixed position. Just imagine that there are construction works going on in a city, all workers, tools, machines and parts are brought and placed at the location where the work is performed. The same is also valid for a movie set, where the technicians, actors, cameramen, directors, etc. are coming to the location where the movie is shot.

Now that we have this understanding about the meaning of a fixed position layout, we can refer to the manufacturing environment. A similar approach as in the movie example can also be applied in operations where the volume of goods produced is rather low and where the product is extremely heavy or bulky, i.e., difficult to move around. Examples could be locomotives/trains, airplanes or electrical power windmills. In all of these cases, the product would remain at the same location for a very long period of time and the materials would need to be brought close to the point of value creation.

On the *production floor*, certain designated areas will need to be defined, where the parts or components would be placed by logistics/material movement staff. The defined footprints (= marked areas on the factory floor) need to be defined, where the necessary material would be buffered. The workers would need to walk from the material buffer to the product back and forth to move material to the product. The same transportation effort also applies to the tools, machines or media (such as electricity, gas or water).

To give it a practical example: imagine the assembly of a locomotive in a factory facility and all necessary parts are buffered outside, so that the workers need to pick them up and carry them inside the locomotive in order to conduct the final assembly, which is inside the locomotive. As this example implies, the flexibility to e.g. change the sequence of assembly work packages is quite high in such a fixed position layout set-up.

Also the impact of defective tools or machines is not that intense, as the layout provides an opportunity to replace the machine and then to continue working. At the same time, aspects of motion and movement, walking, waiting, searching or the relatively high possible levels of buffered inventories need also to be mentioned as disadvantages. The symbolic illustration below shows the motion and movement of the media, workers, tools, etc. in a simplified way (see Fig. 10.2).

> ▶ **Practical Insights** *In essence*: For the production of few heavy, bulky products, the fixed position layout might be a good choice, as it provides the advantages of flexibility and adaptability. The disadvantage needs to be seen in the high amount of unnecessary motion and movement.

Fig. 10.2 Principles of the fixed position layout

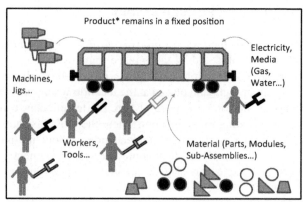

*Useful for heavy, bulky products such a a locomotive, forexample

10.2.2 Process Flow Layout

In the case of further processing of e. g. metal parts or metal products, the process flow layout is another basic type of layout to consider. The key principle here is that the operational environment will be split into specialized functional areas, for example a department where metal is cut, another department which is specialized in drilling, another one specialized in milling, etc.

Such a layout of specialized functional areas in manufacturing is quite similar to the layout of a hospital, where you have the first aid, and the ophthalmologist, internist or cardiologist departments.

In metal manufacturing, product 1 might first require a drilling operation, then some milling and finally some welding. Product 2 might first require bending, then drilling, milling and then welding. What becomes obvious is that the sequence of processes that need to be performed determines the product flow between departments. This is also the reason why this layout type is called "process flow layout". The big advantages are that the layout is quite flexible, as it allows the production of a very high number of very different products (of course they need to be created under usage of similar production technologies and machines, as explained above) also in relatively high numbers.

The disadvantages are production in certain lot sizes, the high transportation effort and the danger of having quite a high number of crossing/contradicting material flows. As the departments are in principle specialized, multiple machines will also most probably be available in e.g. the drilling department (see Fig. 10.3).

The process flow layout is not very vulnerable to the breakdown of machines. If drilling machine 4 breaks down, maybe the parts can alternatively be produced using drilling machine 5, for example, as Fig. 10.3 depicts. In order to understand Fig. 10.3, the following short explanation regarding the hypothetical case above should be given. Product A would first be processed on drilling machine D2, then it would be moved to milling machine M4 and would then be welded on W2. After that the product would be painted in paint shop P1. Finally the packaging and shipping preparation would take place. Product B would be moved through the

10.2 Layout Planning in Manufacturing

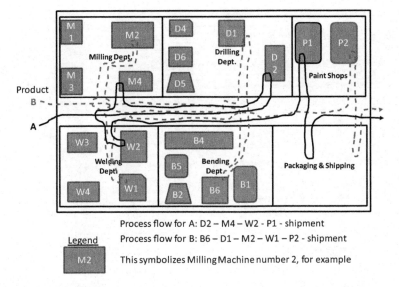

Fig. 10.3 Principles of the process flow layout

facility, being processed on machines B6, D1, M2, W1 and P2. As indicated above, the products A and B would flow through the manufacturing department according to the relevant process steps.

As illustrated in Fig. 10.3, the flow might become almost chaotic, referred to as a kind of "spaghetti flow illustrated as a spaghetti diagram" in the lean thinking terminology.

> ▶ **Practical Insights** *In essence*: For the production of hundreds or thousands of similar (metal) parts, the process flow layout might be a good choice, as it provides the advantages of flexibility, its general usability and relatively low level of vulnerability. The disadvantages need to be seen in the high amount of unnecessary motion and movement and also crossing material flows.

Process-Flow Layout: A Practical View

Figure 10.4 shows a bay of the factory where machine-centres for the creation of high-tech break disks are installed. Minimization of the transportation distances between the machines has been the fundamental principle for the layout planning. The machine allocation ensures a flow to perform series of specialized processes. In this specific case, the flow is structured in the following way: turning—milling—drilling. The non-destructive testing is also part of the processes that can be performed along with in-process removal of burrs or the balancing of the break disks.

The criterion of "high flexibility" is integrated into the layout design. The production processes that are performed on multiple machines require the object movement from one machine-centre to other centres. This can be implemented in the developed layout. All the product flows according to the production processes are in principle possible.

Fig. 10.4 Machine-centres for turning, milling and drilling (© Knorr-Bremse Berlin SfS GmbH)

Figure 10.4 also depicts the major lean principles. For example, visualization boards showing material availability, Pareto charts on quality KPIs, check sheets or charts showing adherence to the production progress are placed on the shop floor. The objective is to obtain transparency regarding the planned and actual production progress, to respect *5S principles* (sort, systemize, sweep, standardize, sustain—in Japanese *seiri, seiton, seiso, seiketsu* and *shitsuke*) and to secure TPM (*Total Productive Maintenance*). Furthermore, the standardized colour-coding clearly indicates the footprints for raw-material and finished goods.

The break disks are produced in specified lot-sizes (batches) (see also Chap. 13) and subject to the storage capacity of the shelves on the shop floor that define the respective batch sizes. For example, if the storage capacity of a shelf equals 20 units, the batch-size of 30 units would be impossible.

The set-up of the manufacturing area in Fig. 10.4 is very flexible. It makes it possible to implement alternative flow patterns according to the required processes for the creation of the respective product. This is a very good example of a "process-flow layout".

10.2.3 Product Flow Layout

The key idea of this type of layout is that the product being created is moving through a series of especially designed and equipped workstations. It could be that the product will be moved under usage of a conveying system (such as an assembly line for the production of cars or household devices), but it could also be that the

10.2 Layout Planning in Manufacturing

Fig. 10.5 Principles of the product flow layout

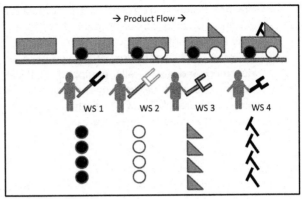

product is moved through the defined workstation manually (e. g. production of converter boxes for the railway industry).

Usually, this type of layout is considered when a very high number of quite similar products are produced, for example 1000 cars per day. It is important for a properly working product flow layout that the product is moving through a facility with the same speed (see Fig. 10.5).

To give an example, it might be that the product is moving at a beat (or pace) of e.g. 90 s from workstation to workstation. In principle, the different stations are equipped with all necessary machinery and media, and the material required to be installed into the product at that station is also buffered at the station. That means each and every station is especially designed for a special purpose. If you think about car assembly, you have an early station where the cable harnesses are placed into the car, after which the carpets are installed, followed by the seats, and so on. The sequence is important, but also the duration of the work that needs to be performed, as well as supporting technology and the necessary space for the material that is required at the respective station. With respect to the logistics and the placement of materials, the exact number of parts needs to be identified prior to planning the layout as they must be buffered exactly next to the assembly station at the line, so that everything (the product, the parts to be installed, the tools and media) is within easy reach. These parameters, parts, processes, tools, media, etc. have a significant influence regarding the dimensioning of the layout.

The product flow layout can also be applied to the creation of household appliances such as washing machines, fridges or microwave ovens, or for sport shoes, etc. and the production volume needs to justify the special arrangements of the workstations and the necessary tooling. The advantage is that the products can be assembled in a very efficient way; the product flow is longitudinal and the timing is very well balanced, respecting the defined pace (beat rate) of the product that is moving through the production facility in a one-piece single flow mode. Besides these obvious advantages, there are also disadvantages to mention: if parts are missing or are defective, the product flow will most probably be interrupted, also when a machine or tool breaks down, which results in high efficiency but also shows the high vulnerability of the product flow layout.

▶ **Practical Insights** *In essence*: For the production of thousands of similar products (such as cars or household appliances) per day, the product flow layout might be a good choice, as it provides the advantages of efficiency and smooth flow at a given pace along especially defined, designed and technically equipped workstations. The product is flowing over these workstations at a constant cycle time. The disadvantage is the probability of interruptions or stoppages in case of missing parts or defective machines, for example.

Product-Flow Layout: A Practical View

In the labour-intensive after sales and services business areas with their rather low production volumes and high variety, the fundamental manufacturing layout considerations of a steady *product-flow layout* combined with lean principles can also be implemented (see Fig. 10.6).

Fig. 10.6 Product—Flow Layout/Assembly Line for Refurbishment Processes [front view](© Knorr-Bremse Berlin SfS GmbH)

10.2 Layout Planning in Manufacturing

In the specific case, the used break systems are refurbished in a special area of the factory. Although there is no conveyor belt, the general assembly line principles (see Chap. 9) have been applied when the layout was designed. Figure 10.6 depicts the final assembly of the refurbished break systems as the product moves through a set of especially designed workstations following a steady timing. This is also called *takt time* (see also Chap. 9), which "is the rate (time per unit) at which the system must produce a product to meet external customer demand" (Martin 2007).

Prior to the final assembly, the received used break systems are checked in the initial goods reception processes. Following that, the disassembly and cleaning of the received systems take place (Fig. 10.7).

Pre-kitted sets of new replacement parts and other required assembly material are provided to the assembly line along with the cleaned and disassembled components on trolleys. Visual media and footprints on the floor mark the individual positions for the trolleys, as shown in Fig. 10.7. Furthermore, tools and jigs are placed within easy reach respecting the *best point philosophy* for an *ergonomic workplace*. Figure 10.7 clearly shows that for smaller series with high manual efforts, the fundamental principles of the "product-flow layout" can also be effectively applied.

Fig. 10.7 Product—Flow Layout/Assembly line for refurbishment processes [top view] (© Knorr-Bremse Berlin SfS GmbH)

10.2.4 Cell-Based Layout

In the case of the *cell-based layout*, the advantages of the product flow layout (smooth flow) and process flow layout (flexibility) are combined. This type of layout is also called hybrid layout or is referred to as grouping of technology. The main idea is to group the required machines, tools and equipment in the exact sequence of the production steps so that there will be no crossing of the materials and the transportation distances are minimized.

In such a case the product will be created by moving through the cell. Most probably the movement of the pallets with the products in production process (semi-finished goods) is moved from one machine to another manually, i.e. in most cases there will be batches of products produced per machine and when they are finished on that particular machine, the lot is moved to the next machine or station (see Fig. 10.8).

That will in most cases not be a one-piece single flow, but most probably the movement of the respective batch. Besides this inefficiency, there will still be a kind of smooth flow. In contrast to a real assembly line, the alignment of the machines in the cell is cheaper, and with reasonable effort the cells can be rearranged for other products that will need to be produced.

Figure 10.8 refers to the products A and B and their production sequence as it was introduced for the process flow layout. The following illustration considers the generation of two cells. One for the creation of product A and the second one for product B: as one can see, the flow of products became almost one directional and the crossing of the material flows is significantly reduced due to the rearrangement of the required machines, now installed in the before mentioned two cells.

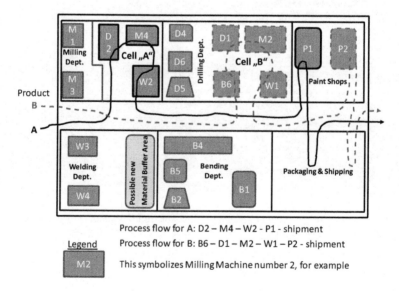

Fig. 10.8 Principles of the cell-based layout

▶ **Practical Insights** Please note, that for some machining such as welding also exhaust evacuation systems might be required. Therefore space constraints or certain media connections will need to be assessed.

In essence: For the production of similar products (such as computer chips, sub-assemblies, lamps, etc.), the cell-based layout might be a good choice, as it provides the advantages of the smooth flow of the product flow layout and the flexibility of the process flow layout.

Cell-Based Layout: A Practical View

In Fig. 10.9, the assembly of valves in a *cell-based layout* is depicted. The developed layout considers a balanced one-piece-single-flow that runs in a counter-clock-wise manner. The operational processes start on the upper left-hand side. It can be observed that the cell has a typical "*U-shape*". After the product has moved through the cell and reached the upper right-hand point, all necessary production steps are finalized and the handover to the inspection department takes place.

The applied layout design strictly separates the operators and their value-adding working environment inside the very well illuminated U-shape from the material replenishment processes which take place outside the cell. The workers continue their work in the centre of the cell while new material is fed into the cell and empty

Fig. 10.9 Assembly of valves in a Cell (© Knorr-Bremse Berlin SfS GmbH)

bins are collected from the outside. This ensures disturbance-free operation on the process side and the secured material availability.

All tools, machinery and material can be easily reached. *Lean ergonomics* criteria, adjustable best point locations and positions as well as *5S principles* have also been considered for the creation of the cell-based layout. Furthermore, the screens show the standard operating instructions. The torques of the machines and the usage of lubricants are automatically supervised in order to secure the *zero defects* throughout all the production steps.

Such a concept allows eliminating non-value adding times, securing highest quality outputs while the operating processes are balanced and conducted in the most ergonomic way all at the same time. The manufacturing area shown in Fig. 10.9 is a very good example of a *"cell-based layout"*.

10.3 Layout Planning in Warehouses

The processes in warehouses can be done manually or automated. Automation is not always the best option. Automation requires investments in software. Manual process organization can be the more flexible option. However, automation can help in increasing efficiency and lead time reduction.

The basic warehouse processes are represented in Fig. 10.10. Consider these processes in detail.

10.3.1 Incoming Area

After the receipt and control of goods in the incoming area, items can be either moved to storage or directly to the outbound area if, e.g., customer orders already exist or due to a cross-docking principle which means in-transit merging of different incoming bins to some outgoing bins without intermediate storage.

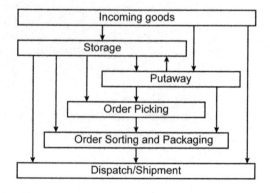

Fig. 10.10 Warehouse processes

10.3 Layout Planning in Warehouses

In many cases, the returns are also processed in the incoming area. For example, in the warehouses of E-Commerce retailers, the return rate can be up to 70 % of the sales.

10.3.2 Storage Area

Next, in the storage area, some storage strategies can be applied, for example:

- dedicated storage
- cluster storage and class-based storage
- random storage.

In the case of *dedicated storage*, each item is assigned exactly to a predetermined storage place. *Cluster storage* presumes building some zones foritems with some common features, e.g., items which are frequently ordered together; or items from the same supplier. *Class-based storage* means that items are stored on the basis of ABC classification (see Chap. 13). In random storage, a chaotic warehouse policy is applied.

The advantages and shortcomings of each strategy are summarized in Table 10.1.

10.3.3 Put-Away and Order Pick-Up

FIFO (first-in-first-out) and LIFO (last-in-first-out) are two basic strategies for put-away organization. For order picking, "man-to-goods" and "goods-to-man" strategies exist. In "man-to-goods" strategy, the following options exist: Printed pick-up list, Electronic messaging, Pick by Light, Pick by Voice.

It should be noted that even if new technologies like pick by voice may have some advantages, many logistics managers consider them to have some shortcomings from an ergonomic point of view.

Table 10.1 Advantages and shortcomings of storage strategies

Strategy	Advantages	Shortcomings	Applications
Dedicated storage	Item positions are exactly known	Low capacity utilization	Spare part warehouse Workforce fluctuations
Cluster storage/ class-based storage	Productivity increase Transportation reduction	Decrease in capacity utilization	Retail warehouses
Random storage	High capacity utilization	Control complexity; investments in IT	Automated high-level warehouse

10.3.4 Layout Concepts

Basically, straightforward and L-shaped layout can be distinguished. In the introductory case-study, we considered OTLG distribution centre. They apply the L-shaped layout. In Fig. 10.11, an L-shaped layout of the OTLG warehouse is presented.

Consider another example, company REWE, which is active in the food retailing industry. Specific for the food retailing industry are fast processing times for fresh goods. That is why a straightforward layout has been selected (Fig. 10.12).

According to this layout, the warehouse is divided into four temperature zones: dry assortment, fruits and vegetables area, fresh meat area (0 °C), and deep-freezing area (−24 °C). The work in the deep-freezing area is very hard since in summer the difference between the outside and inside temperatures can be higher than 60 °C. The trucks from suppliers arrive at the gates and are unloaded. The pallets (mostly plastic pallets because of hygiene and weight reasons) are moved to the storage area. The random storage principle is applied to the placement of pallets on the shelves. With the help of lift trucks, the pallets are picked up and delivered to the outbound area. The plastic pallets are used to simplify the handling at the stores since their weight is only 6 kg. In addition, heavier items are typically located on the bottom of the pallet while light items come on the top. The warehouse operates

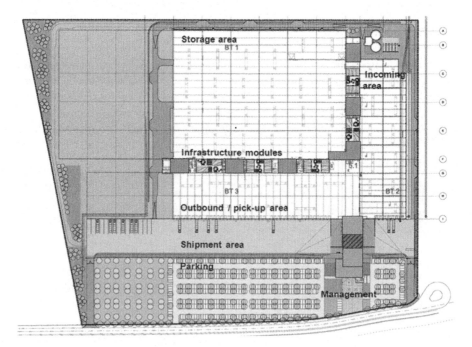

Fig. 10.11 L-shaped layout of a warehouse

10.4 Methods of Layout Planning

Fig. 10.12 Straightforward layout form of a warehouse

from Sunday 4:00 am to Saturday 6:00 pm. Since demand constantly increases, automation can reduce lead time and adjust process capacity.

About 380 employees in Oranienburg (Germany) ensure the replenishment of REWE supermarkets with about 11,000 SKU (Stock Keeping Units). One hundred trucks deliver products to 330 supermarkets from Sassnitz to Jüterbog daily. This means optimization of 240 routes daily. With the help of modern software using a scientific methodology of vehicle routing and advanced navigation information technology, 95 % capacity utilization for trucks is achieved. In the first half of 2012, 35 million incoming items of freight which arrived on 958,398 euro-pallets were processed in the incoming area. Thirty-six million items of freight were delivered to markets. The average inventory in warehouse is valued at about 30.6 million euros. The inventory turnover for dry assortment is about 12; for fresh meat—2100 (on average, a package of fresh meat is processed at the warehouse within 4 h).

10.4 Methods of Layout Planning

Methods of layout planning can be divided into qualitative and quantitative. We consider in this chapter a qualitative method "REL-charts" and a quantitative method "quadratic assignment problem".

10.4.1 REL-Charts

10.4.1.1 Problem Statement

REL stands for relationship. With the help of this chart, the activities are illustrated according to their relationship (activity relationship charts, ARC). Now let us consider a specific problem. A layout for a retail warehouse has to be developed

Fig. 10.13 Warehouse process

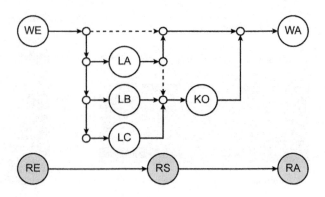

with considerations of desirable/undesirable proximity of some areas. The process is presented in Fig. 10.13.

The following notations are used:

- WE—incoming and inspection area
- LA, LB, LC—storage areas for A-items, B-items, and C-items respectively
- WA—shipment area
- KO—pick-up area
- RE—receiving area for returns
- RS—storage area for returns
- RA—shipment area for returns

10.4.1.2 Solution Method

The REL-chart method is based on the identification of desirable/undesirable proximity relations for each pair of warehouse areas. This identification is subjective and based on expert estimations. For our case, the following REL-chart can be developed (Fig. 10.14).

The following notations are used:

- A—proximity is absolutely mandatory
- E—proximity is very desirable
- I—proximity is important
- O—proximity is possible
- U—proximity is undesirable

For example, the relation between the pick-up area and the shipment area is set up as "A" since these areas are to be located close to each other according to the process flow in Fig. 10.10.

Taking into account the process flow from the problem statement and the developed REL-matrix, the following layout can be suggested (Fig. 10.15).

Note that since REL-chart is a qualitative method on the basis of expert estimations, the suggested solution is only one possible option.

10.4 Methods of Layout Planning

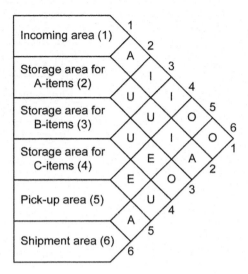

Fig. 10.14 REL-Chart matrix

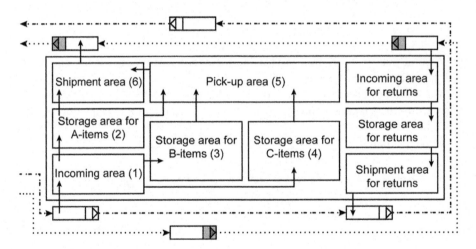

Fig. 10.15 Warehouse layout

10.4.2 Quadratic Assignment Problem

10.4.2.1 Problem Statement

Some machines have to be assigned to some available locations. For each pair of locations, a *distance* is known. Similarly, for each pair of facilities a *material flow* is specified (Fig. 10.16).

Fig. 10.16 Problem statement for assignment problem

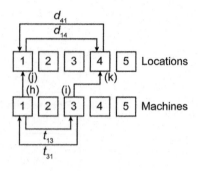

Assign machines to locations so that total transportation cost is minimized.

10.4.2.2 Model
Consider the following notations according to Fig. 10.16.

$M = \{M_j, j, k \in M, j, k = (1, \ldots M)\}$ is a set of locations
$N = \{N_h, h, i \in N, h, i = (1, \ldots N)\}$ is a set of machines
$d_{j,k}$ is a distance between two locations
$t_{h,i}$ is material flow intensity between two machines

Assume that transportation costs is linear and therefore proportional to $d_{j,k} \times t_{h,i}$ fort he assignment $h \to j$ and $i \to k$.

We introduce an auxiliary variable x_{hj} which is equal to 1 if the h-machine is assigned to the j-location and $x_{hj} = 0$ otherwise. Then the model can be defined in the following way:

Objective function

$$F(x) = \sum_{h=1}^{P} \sum_{\substack{i=1, j=1 \\ i \neq h}}^{P} \sum_{\substack{k=1, \\ k \neq j}}^{P} t_{hi} \cdot d_{jk} \cdot x_{hj} \cdot x_{ik} \Rightarrow \text{Min!} \quad (10.1)$$

Constraints

$$\sum_{j=1}^{P} x_{hj} = 1 \sum_{h=1}^{P} x_{hj} = 1 \quad (10.2)$$

$$x_{hi} \in \{0, 1\} \quad (10.3)$$

Constraints (10.2) define that each machine should be assigned to only one location. Constraint (10.3) defines that auxiliary variable x_{hj} is a Boolean variable. In reality, additional constraints of a technological and technical nature may exist which are difficult to formalize.

10.4.2.3 Model Analysis and Solution Methods

The model (10.1)–(10.3) is a linear integer programming model. Such a class of model is NP-hard. That means the optimal solution for reasonable problem size and in reasonable time is difficult to obtain with the help of classical methods for solving such problems (e.g., branch&bound). That is why different heuristics are used in practice for such solutions.

10.4.3 Simulation: Modeling Operations at Pharmaceutical Distribution Warehouses with AnyLogic

Problem Description

Cardinal Health, a billion dollar pharmaceutical distribution and logistics firm, manages multiple products, from brand name pharmaceuticals and generic drugs to over the counter drugs, health and beauty items and their own private label. They face a multitude of typical distribution warehouse challenges that are further complicated by the nature of pharmaceutical products, which are smaller in size, consumable, expensive, and possibly life critical. Cardinal Health is an essential link in the healthcare SC, offering next day delivery to over 30,000 locations including hospitals, retail pharmacies, physicians' offices, and direct to consumer.

Other value added services include efficiency and demand management, working capital management and contract credit management. These services along with poor manufacturing reliability and supply disruptions in the market due to Food and Drug Administration (FDA) and Disability Discrimination Act (DDA) regulations add complexity to decision making. Cardinal Health must keep up with the variability in pharmaceutical distribution management. Cardinal Health considers facility layout, flow of product, order picking, labour planning and scheduling, customer order requirements and day-to-day operations management.

Model Development

Traditional analysis tools such as empirical trial and error are risky, expensive and difficult to use for making changes. Industrial engineering and operations researchers suggested mathematical models which were inexpensive but do not capture unexpected dynamics. If anything is open or has emergent behaviours such as congestion, a standard mathematical model would be unable to solve the problem. Process driven or discrete event modelling is not advantageous due to its inability to represent a facility naturally. This led Brian Heath (Director of Advanced Analytics at Cardinal Health) and Cardinal Health to explore alternative analysis options. Agent Based Modeling (ABM) with AnyLogic Simulation and Modeling software gave Cardinal Health the tools required to tackle many distribution warehouse issues without the restrictions of traditional tools.

Solution Development
ABM represents abstraction of distributed autonomous entities that can interact with each other and their environment through space and time, allowing Cardinal Health to capture work time allocation, congestion waiting time, cycle times, distance travelled, worker variability and other important metrics.

Testing the Solution
The model built was ultimately concerned with the activities of employees and their interaction with each other during the day, making it necessary to import such data as picking time and performance standards into the model.

Analysing the Results
Cardinal Health can gather congestion waiting time data and see how much of a problem it is causing in the warehouse since "agents" are modelled as individuals with special relationships to each other. Additional parameters included in the model are several worker speeds, worker behaviour, learning curves, cycle times, product turn-around and distance covered walking or driving. The ability to import Excel files was also imperative as Cardinal Health has numerous warehouses, and it is mandatory to test multiple layouts. Using AnyLogic, a change is as simple as updating the Excel file, importing it into the model and running the model again.

Implementation
The ABM built with AnyLogic software allows Cardinal Health to compare layouts, picking technology and product slotting strategies. In addition, they can evaluate different methods of picking to update staffing models and for on-the-floor support if a workload changes, as orders vary on a day-to-day basis. Statistics are also gathered such as takt time, how many batches are completed in an hour, truck unloading time, and sequencing of events. Despite the clarity provided by the above metrics, the model revealed a problem due to the random distribution of work. Employees' workloads were uneven, with one being faster and one slower. By balancing the workload, employees began working at a similar pace and congestion decreased dramatically. By minimizing congestion using AnyLogic software, Cardinal Health was able to decrease the average shift length from 10.5 to 7.25 h and increase the amount of employee capacity. Cardinal Health saves over 3 million dollars annually using ABM with AnyLogic Simulation technology. "AnyLogic's agent libraries, flexible architecture, and integrated animation enables the continuing success of this project", declares Brian Heath, Director of Advanced Analytics at Cardinal Health; you can view his presentation and learn more about using ABM for real world application.

10.5 Key Points

A layout is the physical arrangement of objects in a space. Fundamental objectives of layout planning are related to cost minimization for internal transportation, lead time reduction or reasonable arrangement of departments in facilities. In addition, layout planning can be used in order to reduce the risks of good damages because of accidence in the warehouse, e.g., a fire.

In general, there are four basic types of layouts in manufacturing:

- fixed position layout
- process flow layout
- product flow layout
- cell-based layout.

These forms of layouts depend on the process flow design. In warehouses the layout is determined by the process flow, which includes the following stages:

- incoming and inspection area
- storage area
- put-away area
- pick-up area
- packing area
- shipment area.

Methods of layout planning can be divided into qualitative and quantitative. We considered in this chapter a qualitative method "REL-charts" and a quantitative method "quadratic assignment problem". REL-charts can be applied to cases where considerations of desirable/undesirable proximity of some areas are important. The quadratic assignment problem is an optimization method for optimal layout planning with the objective of minimizing total transportation costs.

Discussion

In our examples, production facilities were described (e.g., the creation of brake systems) or the layout of retail warehouses for distribution centers for spare parts and food retailing. Please discuss how the layout planning consideration might be transferred to layout problems in...

- offices in an insurance company
- departments at your local authorities
- structure of supermarkets or shopping malls
- organisation of functional areas at hospitals or clinics

What do you think are the relevant criteria that influence the decisions on these layouts?

Acknowledgments

Introductory Case-Study "OTLG Ludwigsfelde"
The authors thanks the OTLG GmbH & Co. KG for the permission to use the company materials in this textbook.

Layout Planning in Warehouses
The authors thank the logistics direction of REWE East for the permission to use the company data in this case-study.

Layout Examples in Production
The authors thank the *Knorr-Bremse Berlin Systeme für Schienenfahrzeuge GmbH* for the permission to use the company materials in this textbook.

Bibliography

Bicheno J (2004) The new lean toolbox. PICSIE Books, Buckingham
Brunner FJ (2011) Japanische Erfolgsrezepte. Hanser Verlag, München
Dolgui A, Proth J-M (2010) Supply chain engineering: useful methods and techniques. Springer, Berlin
Gogate AS, Pande SS (2008) Intelligent layout planning for rapid prototyping. Int J Prod Res 46(20):5607–5631
Günther H-O, Tempelmeier H (2012) Produktion und logistik, 9th edn. Springer, Heidelberg
Heizer J, Render B (2013) Operations management: sustainability and supply chain management, 11th edn. Pearson, Harlow
Ioannou G (2006) Time-phased creation of hybrid manufacturing systems. Int J Prod Econ 102(2): 183–198
Martin JW (2007) Lean six sigma for supply chain management – the 10-step solution process. McGraw Hill, New York
Nee AYC, Ong SK, Chryssolouris G, Mourtzis D (2012) Augmented reality applications in design and manufacturing. CIRP Ann Manuf Technol 61(2):657–679
Okulicz K (2004) Virtual reality-based approach to manufacturing process planning. Int J Prod Res 42(17):3493–3504
Saad SM, Lassila AM (2004) Layout design in fractal organizations. Int J Prod Res 42(17): 3529–3550
Schenk M, Wirth S, Müller E (2014) Fabrikplanung und Fabrikbetrieb. Methoden für die wandlungsfähige, vernetzte und ressourceneffiziente Fabrik, 2nd edn. Springer, Berlin
Schonberger RJ (2008) Best practices in lean six sigma process improvement – a deeper look. Wiley, Hoboken, NJ
Slack N, Chambers S, Johnston R (2010) Operations management, 6th edn. Pearson, Harlow

Demand Forecasting   11

The Learning Objectives for This Chapter Are to

- understand the role of demand forecasting in SCOM
- understand the forecasting process and methods in SCOM
- understand the role of expert methods in forecasting
- apply statistical methods for forecasting
- calculate the forecasts based on statistical methods
- understand and apply the measures for forecast quality assessments.

11.1 Introductory Case Study

Good forecasting is vital for any business planning. If the estimates are too high, a company over-produces goods that cannot be sold. On one hand this is unnecessary and moreover increases costs for resources such as raw materials, workforce or storage space. On the other hand, underproduction can result in shortages and lost business opportunities and a potential loss of customers who could not be served.

Good forecasting can become a competitive advantage. For example, Walt Disney Entertainment Parks put extremely high emphasis on predicting the next hours', days' and weeks' demand. While they have been almost managing to accurately predict the future, revenue has been increasing immensely. Moreover, forecasting can be useful for analysing areas for improvement.

Predictions about demand need to be made. However, forecasts are almost always wrong, as operations are rather complex. Demand sometimes changes

---

Find additional case-studies, Excel spreadsheet templates, and video streams in the *E-Supplement* to this book on www.global-supply-chain-management.de!

© Springer International Publishing Switzerland 2017
D. Ivanov et al., *Global Supply Chain and Operations Management*, Springer Texts in Business and Economics, DOI 10.1007/978-3-319-24217-0_11

without prior warning and usually the effects set in later, making it difficult for operations managers to react.

However, some demand swings can be taken into consideration, such as for example seasonal changes. These can include weather or particular holidays. For example, a city hotel, a supermarket, a metal producer and a knitwear shop are all differently dependent on these external factors. A city hotel has most customers during the holiday season, whereas a knitwear shop sells primarily in autumn and winter. The supermarket may face peak times, for example during lunch and after work hours. The factory producing metals is the most likely to be independent of seasonal swings and has a steady demand throughout the year. However, many businesses have discovered the correlation of weather and sales, which is why demand for meteorological forecasting services has rapidly increased.

Forecasts are generally expressed in terms that are also useful for capacity management, production and SC planning. The aim is not only to be as accurate as possible but also to know the difference between the plan and actual data. This range can help to improve forecasts in future and to estimate which forecasting techniques perform better. Moreover, forecasts are made for the close and long-term future. Generally, short-term forecasts tend to be more accurate.

There are various tools to create a demand forecast, such as:

- expert estimates
- time series analysis
- regression analysis.

An expert estimate is a qualitative analysis tool that is drawn from historic demand and expert opinions on future development. Sport Obermeyer, a sports clothing retailer, applied this method. Initially, the whole team was involved in a decision about the next forecast. However, when management noticed that some people would always dominate the decision process, then decisions were made independently and the results were compared and clustered. If most team members had forecast a similar result the product was categorized as easy to forecast. Otherwise, it was labelled "hard to forecast". For these products the sports retailer delayed forecasting in order to reduce the errors. In the case of Sport Obermeyer, using expert opinions worked extremely well with the new method.

Time series analysis, for instance exponential smoothing, takes sales data from the past to estimate the new demand. The restaurant chain "Red Lobster" is making use of that tool with demand forecasting software. Each evening the software creates a new forecast for the next day listing exactly which meals need to be prepared. Managers adjust these forecasts based solely on local specialties.

Regression analysis can be applied to estimate the dependence between two factors. For example, in a telecommunication company, monthly repair efforts can be analysed to estimate the numbers of service employees needed. There are various other options for predicting future demand such as simple probability, neutral networks and fuzzy logic, to name just a few.

11.1 Introductory Case Study

Demand forecasting in medical care has an extraordinary role. Unlike for production companies, an insufficient supply of resources does not mean an unhappy customer, but affects the condition of a patient's health. Even though hospitals are serving the public they also need to make a profit. Hence, the sector is facing the same dilemma in forecasting matching demand with supply while not providing the way for too many or too few resources; lost sales opportunities equal lost treatment opportunities. On the other hand the aim is to minimize excess capacities and to minimize cost.

Forecasts in hospitals can be useful for human resources such as nurses and doctors, customers (patients needing treatment), and operational goods such as beds and medicines. For staffing beds, queuing models can be applied. These methods help to analyse the capacity utilization of beds. This can be relevant for long-term planning of how many rooms and beds are needed. Those are then fixed costs, which it is difficult to reduce in future. Average methods are not an appropriate measurement here. If the mean of all flu patients is taken over the year, there would be empty beds in summer and not nearly enough beds in winter.

In medical care, emergency departments are facing the most extreme role. Patients arrive randomly at any time of the day. This means the workload is highly variable. The severity of the sickness also varies. To manage patient arrivals, hospitals apply systems of categorizing patients as seriously ill, non-urgent and routine. The latter are likely to be turned away from the emergency department and asked to arrange a doctor's appointment. For the first two categories a schedule is developed. Crowding in emergency departments endangers health-care provision. Hence, forecasting plays an important role; therefore models are being used to enable patients' needs to be met more efficiently. Researchers have spent much effort in finding the best forecasting methods in this field.

In a sample emergency department, researchers came to the conclusion that time series analysis can provide a good method of indicating future needs. Daily patient attendances can be computed. For estimates, the autoregressive integrated moving average (ARIMA) method can be used, including such variables as holidays, air pollution, temperature and humidity. The variables are taken to prove a correlation between those and emergency department attendances. The application of the ARIMA method can improve resources and especially staff planning.

Questions
What are the fields where (demand) forecasting is used?
Why is demand forecasting in medical care particularly challenging?
Why are means or averages not sensible measures for planning bed capacities?
Which analysis methods can be used to evaluate the crowding problem in emergency departments?

11.2 Forecasting Process and Methods

Forecasting future demand belongs to the major decisions in SCOM. Forecast sales data represent the input for further production, transportation, sourcing and inventory planning. Moreover, many strategic decisions such as facility location planning, revenue management and process design interact with demand forecasts (see Fig. 11.1).

Forecasts can be made for operative or strategic issues. Similar, different methods can be applied to forecast demand. In this section, we consider the process of forecasting, different time horizons and basic forecasting methods.

11.2.1 Forecasting Process and Time Horizons

The forecasting process begins with the definition of the objective. The second step is to determine the time horizon over which the forecasts should be performed. For example, for an airline, the objective can be to define how many airplanes should be purchased over the next 10 years. Next step is to select the method of forecasting. This depends on both the defined horizon and the available data. After data acquisition, forecasting is performed, typically using software.

The results should be controlled continuously since any SCOM system and its environment is highly dynamic and subject to many external and internal changes.

The forecasting process is presented in Fig. 11.2 using an example for forecasting the number of printed materials for a university lecture based on the prediction of student attendance.

A professor should define every week how many handouts should be printed for the next lecture. In this case the time horizon is a week. For such short-term issues, time series analysis is a preferred method. Based on the attendance list from the last lectures, exponential smoothing can be performed to predict demand.

Other time horizons may include anything from 3 months to 3 years. Examples of the decisions for this medium-range horizon can be sales and operations planning or budgeting. *Long-term forecasting* is typically referring to a period over 3 years, e.g., new product planning, facility location planning, and research and development (R&D). *Medium-range* forecasts are used to deal with more comprehensive

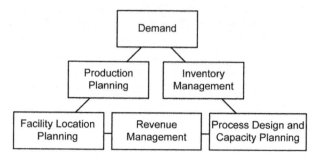

Fig. 11.1 Role of demand forecasting in SCOM

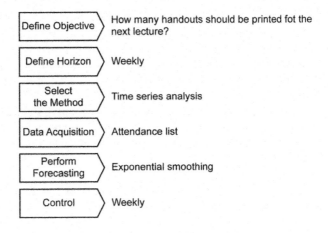

Fig. 11.2 Forecasting process

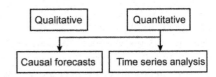

Fig. 11.3 Forecasting methods

issues and support management decisions regarding planning and products, plants and processes. *Short-term forecasts* tend to be more accurate than longer-term forecasts.

11.2.2 Forecasting Methods

The forecasting methods can be divided into qualitative and quantitative methods (see Fig. 11.3):

Qualitative methods are used when the situation is vague and little data exist. Typically, such situations have a long-term nature or decisions are to be taken about new technology or product. The forecasting for such cases involves intuition and experience. In many cases, the forecasting process relies on historical data such as demand numbers or turnovers. This works well as long as a company has reliable data which is available for the required forecasting. But how does it work when a company wants to launch a new technology? In this case they have to rely on expert views and customers' opinions.

This expert type of forecasting is normally based on professional knowledge and experience. A company uses this input from different experts to develop forecasting for the next period. The problem with the expert methods is that they are based on opinions, experiences and knowledge of human beings.

There are different methods for qualitative forecasting. One of the methods is *sales estimation*. For that method a company asks their sales expert about the latest turnover figures and aggregates the data for overall turnover, using the data to develop a forecast. The next qualitative method is the *customer survey*. It is a good tool to use when a company launches a new product when there are no historical data or expert experiences. A company can ask their customers directly what they are thinking of the new product and try to develop a forecasting for the product launch.

The third method is the basic idea of qualitative forecasting—the *expert view*. A company asks proven experts about new technologies or their experiences with related products in the past. These experts are normally working in different departments of the same company.

The best known qualitative forecasting method is the *Delphi Method*. It is an extension of the expert view and the feature is a structured multiple expert survey using specialists from different companies and institutions. The Delphi Method runs into two or more rounds. A moderator develops a questionnaire and all the experts reply anonymously. After the first round the moderator creates a new questionnaire based on the information he got. Answers to the first round are published to all other experts so everybody can rethink their view. Next, they fill out the new questionnaire and so on until it leads to a consensus.

Quantitative methods are used when historical data exist, e.g., existing products, existing technology or existing markets. These methods are based on statistics. Statistical methods can be classified into two different forecasting methods:

- causal forecast
- time series analysis.

In *causal forecasting*, the demand (y) for a product depends on a known factor (x) and because of this it can be forecast (see Fig. 11.4). For example: Demand for axis (y) depends on the number of citizens in a district (x). Linear trends can be found using the least squares technique that results in Eq. (11.1):

$$\hat{y} = a + bx \qquad (11.1)$$

where $\hat{y}$ is the computed value of the variable to be predicted (dependent variable); a is y-axis intercept; b is the slope of the regression line; and x is the independent variable.

Non-linear regression is more complicated but also more realistic. For a causal forecasting method, it is important to have reliable historical data for the known factor (the independent variable).

Fig. 11.4 Regression analysis

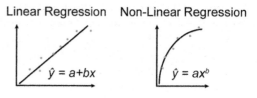

11.2 Forecasting Process and Methods

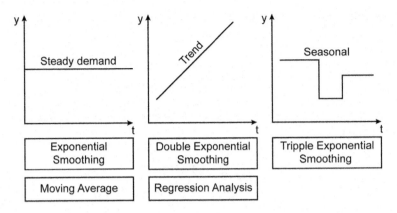

Fig. 11.5 Time series analysis

On the other hand, there is the *time series analysis*. It is based on historical sales data. Sets of evenly spaced numerical data can be obtained by observing response variables at regular time periods. This method actually forecasts on the basis of the past values and assumes that factors influencing past and present will continue to influence in future.

There are different methods to forecast demand depending on the temporal progress of demand (see Fig. 11.5):

If there is a constant demand for a product we can use the *Moving Average* or the *Simple Exponential Smoothing*. For products with a demand which is based on trends, we can use *Regression Analysis* or *Double Exponential Smoothing*. Products with seasonal demand can be forecast using *Triple Exponential Smoothing*.

11.2.3 Forecasting Quality

Different forecasting methods can provide different *forecast quality*. In order to estimate the quality of a forecast, some measures are used in practice, including

- mean absolute deviation (MAD)
- mean squared error (MSE)
- mean absolute percentage error (MAPE)

MAD measures the absolute deviation (ε) of forecast and actual data over T-periods according to formula (11.2):

$$\text{MAD} = \frac{1}{T} \sum_{t=1}^{T} |\varepsilon_t| \qquad (11.2)$$

MSE measures the quadratic deviation of forecast and actual data according to formula (11.3):

$$\text{MSE} = \frac{1}{T}\sum_{t=1}^{T} \varepsilon_t^2 \qquad (11.3)$$

MAPE measures the percentile deviation of forecast and actual data according to formula (11.4):

$$\text{MAPE} = \frac{1}{T}\sum_{t=1}^{T} \left|\frac{\varepsilon_t}{y_t}\right| \qquad (11.4)$$

The practical problem with the MAD measure is that it expresses the absolute values and is therefore quantity-dependent. This makes it difficult to apply MAD for comparison of forecasts for different products. MSE is frequently used because of its good theoretical properties but may be negatively affected by so-called outliers or freak values. MAPE is intuitively good and understandable and can be used for comparison of different forecasts where MAD/MSE values differ.

> ▶ **Practical Insight** In practice, statistically computed measures for forecast quality analysis needs to be checked carefully. For example, consider actual sales data for five periods: 10–10–11–10–11 and two forecasts: (a) 8–8–9–8–9 and (b) 8–12–9–12–9. From statistical point of view, both forecasts have the same MAD = 2. But from management point of view first forecast (a) has a bias since we always produce less than demand. So for managers it is more important to identify bias rather than strive for minimal forecast error.

11.3 Statistical Methods

In this section, we learn how to compute demand forecasts with the help of different statistical methods in more detail.

11.3.1 Linear Regression

Linear regression is normally used as a causal forecasting method. The procedure will be explained by taking as an example sales in a newly established small tea shop that depends on the number of customers, as shown in Table 11.1.

The first step is to calculate the regression function $\hat{y}(x) = \hat{a} + \hat{b}x$ with the parameter $\hat{a}$ and $\hat{b}$. It is important to find the $\hat{a}$ and $\hat{b}$ where the MSE has its minimum. To find the parameters we need to fill out the following table (Table 11.2).

11.3 Statistical Methods

Table 11.1 Initial data for linear regression

Week n	Customer x_n	Sales (in €) y_n
1	26	269
2	35	389
3	43	432
4	67	536
5	78	685
6	80	709

Table 11.2 Results for calculating parameters

Week n	Customer x_n	Sales y_n (in €)	x_n^2	$x_n \cdot y_n$
1	26	269	676	6994
2	35	389	1225	13,615
3	43	432	1849	18,576
4	67	536	4489	35,912
5	78	685	6084	53,430
6	81	709	6561	57,429
Σ	330	3020	20,884	185,956

In order to calculate the coefficient $\hat{b}$, formula (11.5) can be used:

$$\hat{b} = \frac{(6 \cdot 185,956) - (330 \cdot 3020)}{(6 \cdot 20,884) - (330)^2} = \frac{119,136}{16,404} \approx 7.263 \qquad (11.5)$$

The computed value 7.263 means that when there is one more customer per week, sales income is rising by approximately 7.26 €.

There are two options to calculate $\hat{a}$. The first option is the usage of Eq. (11.6):

$$\hat{a} = \frac{\sum_{n=1}^{N} x_n^2 \sum_{n=1}^{N} y_n - \sum_{n=1}^{N} x_n \sum_{n=1}^{N} (x_n \cdot y_n)}{N \sum_{n=1}^{N} x_n^2 - \left(\sum_{n=1}^{N} x_n\right)^2} \qquad (11.6)$$

The easier way is as follows (Eq. 11.7):

$$\hat{a} = \bar{y} - \hat{b}\bar{x} \qquad (11.7)$$

In the case of using formula (11.7) we have to calculate the average values:

$$\bar{y} = \frac{\sum_{n=1}^{N} y_n}{N} \quad \text{and} \quad \bar{x} = \frac{\sum_{n=1}^{N} x_n}{N}. \quad \text{For our example:}$$

$\hat{a} = \frac{3020}{6} - \left(7263 \cdot \frac{330}{6}\right) \approx 103.868$

The regression function now reads as follows: $\hat{y}(x) = 103.868 + 7.263x$

The next step is to calculate the MSE using the regression function (see Table 11.3).

Table 11.3 Results for calculating MSE

Week n	Customer x_n	Sales y_n (in €)	$y(x_n)$	ε_n	ε_n^2
1	26	269	292.706	23.706	561.974
2	35	389	358.073	−30.927	956.479
3	43	432	416.177	−15.823	250.367
4	67	536	590.489	54.489	2969.051
5	78	685	670.382	−14.618	213.686
6	81	709	692.171	−16.829	283.215
Σ	330	3020			5234.773

To calculate the forecast error ε_n we use formula (11.8):

$$\varepsilon_n = y(x_n) - y_n \tag{11.8}$$

To calculate the MSE we use formula (11.3):

$$\text{MSE} = \frac{5234.773}{6} = 872.462$$

11.3.2 Moving Average

The method of *moving average* is based on computing the average demand from the previous periods and using the values for forecasting. It is called "moving" because with every following period the average value is moving onwards.

Consider the following example and function to understand forecasting with the help of the moving average. Here, too, it is important to find the result with the lowest MSE. The demand for each next period is computed subject to formula (11.9):

$$\hat{y}_{t+1} = \frac{1}{T} \sum_{\tau=t-T+1}^{t} y_\tau \tag{11.9}$$

where $\hat{y}_{t+1}$ is the forecast for the next period, y_τ is the demand in period t and T is the number of periods. It is important to choose T that is not too large and not too small. Normally you calculate with different T-values to find the one with the lowest MSE.

Consider an example. Lebon Ltd wants to find its weekly average demand for Cupcakes. The following table (Table 11.4) illustrates the last weeks' demand.

Three different numbers of periods to be averaged are given: $T_1 = 2$; $T_2 = 3$; and $T_3 = 4$. The calculation results are presented in Table 11.5.

For example, to compute the forecast for the week #3: $31 \cdot = (26 + 35)/2 \rightarrow$ we add demand from the previous two periods and divide it through T_1.

11.3 Statistical Methods

Table 11.4 Initial data for moving average

Week t	1	2	3	4	5	6	7	8
Demand y_t	26	35	28	42	38	45	46	39

Table 11.5 Results calculating moving average with three different Ts

t	y_t	$\hat{y}(T_1 = 2)$	$\hat{y}(T_2 = 3)$	$\hat{y}(T_3 = 4)$
1	26	–	–	–
2	35	–	–	–
3	28	31*	–	–
4	42	32	30	–
5	38	35	35	33
6	45	40	36	36
7	46	42	42	39
8	39	46	43	43

* forecasted demand from this period onwards

Table 11.6 Results calculating MSE

t	y_t	$\hat{y}(T_1 = 2)$	ε_t	ε_t^2	$\hat{y}(T_2 = 3)$	ε_t	ε_t^2	$\hat{y}(T_3 = 4)$	ε_t	ε_t^2
1	26	–	–	–	–	–	–	–	–	–
2	35	–	–	–	–	–	–	–	–	–
3	28	31	–	–	–	–	–	–	–	–
4	42	32	–	–	30	–	–	–	–	–
5	38	35	−3	9	35	−3	9	33	−5	25
6	45	40	−5	25	36	−9	81	36	−9	81
7	46	42	−4	16	42	−4	16	39	−7	49
8	39	46	7	49	43	4	16	43	4	16
Σ				99			122			171

To check which T is the one with the smallest MSE we have to calculate the forecast error. It is important to start with a period where for all T-values the sales have been forecast in order to make the MSE values comparable. In this case it is week #5 (see Table 11.6).

Using the error calculation formula $\varepsilon_t = \hat{y}(T) - y_t$ and Eq. (11.3), we get:

$$\text{MSE}(T_1) = \frac{99}{4} = 24.75 \quad \text{MSE}(T_2) = \frac{122}{4} = 30.5 \quad \text{MSE}(T_3) = \frac{171}{4} = 42.75$$

As we can see the smallest T is the best one because there the MSE is at its minimum. For that reason the recommendation for forecasting the next periods will be using T = 2.

In some cases, a weighted moving average can be used. In this case, older data usually become less important and the weights are assigned to different periods based on experience and intuition.

11.3.3 Simple Exponential Smoothing

This method is close to that of the weighted moving average. The weightings decline exponentially and the most recent data are weighted higher. For sales forecasts, average demand/sales values of previous periods are exponentially weighted to forecast the next periods. The simple exponential average means working with a smoothing parameter α. The idea is to weight current demand higher and to assign lower weights to the previous demand.

In this method we use formula (11.10) to forecast the demand for the following periods:

$$\hat{y}_{t,t+1} = \alpha \cdot y_t + (1-\alpha) \cdot \hat{y}_{t-1,t} \qquad (11.10)$$

Where $\hat{y}_{t,t+1}$ is the forecast that we are making in the current period for the following period, y_t is the current demand and $\hat{y}_{t-1,t}$ is the forecast we made in the last period for the current period.

Consider the following example as an aid to understanding simple exponential smoothing. Demand for a product during the last six periods is provided (Table 11.7).

The smoothing parameters are $\alpha_1 = 0.3$ and $\alpha_2 = 0.5$. The idea is to choose the smoothing parameter which leads to a smaller MSE (see Table 11.8).

For example to compute the forecast sales for period #3: $54.5 = 0.3 \cdot 44 + (1-0.3) \cdot 59 \rightarrow$ we multiply the demand in week #2 by α and the forecast demand for week #2 by $(1-\alpha)$ to get the forecast for week #3. In this case, $MSE(\alpha_1) = \frac{338.75}{6} \approx 56.46$

Consider the calculations for Table 11.9:

Table 11.7 Initial data for single exponential smoothing

Week t	1	2	3	4	5	6
Demand y_t	59	44	61	58	49	52

Table 11.8 Results for single exponential smoothing with $\alpha_1 = 0.3$

t	y_t	$\hat{y}_{t,t+1}$	ε_t	ε_t^2
0		59	–	–
1	59	59	0	0
2	44	59	15	225
3	61	54.5*	−6.5	42.25
4	58	56.45	−1.55	2.40
5	49	56.92	7.92	62.65
6	52	54.54	2.54	6.45
Σ				338.75

* forecasted demand from this period onwards

11.3 Statistical Methods

Table 11.9 Results for single exponential smoothing with $\alpha_2 = 0.5$

t	y_t	$\hat{y}_{t,t+1}$	ε_t	ε_t^2
0		59	–	–
1	59	59	0	0
2	44	59	15	225
3	61	51.5	–9.5	90.25
4	58	56.3	–1.75	3.06
5	49	57.1	8.13	66.02
6	52	53.1	1.06	1.13
Σ				385.46

$MSE(\alpha_2) = 385.46/6 \approx 64.24$. As we can see, the second smoothing parameter leads to a higher MSE. For that reason it is advisable in this case to forecast demand for the following periods with the smoothing parameter of 0.3 instead of 0.5.

This method helps to forecast the call for products with a steady demand. But to forecast the sales for the products which have a trend-shaped or seasonal demand we need other methods.

11.3.4 Double Exponential Smoothing

Double exponential smoothing is used for situations where a trend already exists. This method works with two smoothing factors, α and β. The basic idea is that demand is normally over-rated when a trend is positive and under-rated in case of a negative trend. Consider the formula (11.11):

$$\hat{y}_{t,t+\tau} = a_t + b_t \cdot \tau \qquad (11.11)$$

Where $\hat{y}_{t,t+\tau}$ is the forecast for the following period performed in the current period, a_t is the smoothed forecast, b_t is the smoothed trend parameter (slope) and τ is the parameter which describes the number of periods for which we are making the forecast. We calculate a_t and b_t as follows from Eqs. (11.12) to (11.13):

$$a_t = \alpha \cdot y_t + (1 - \alpha) \cdot (a_{t-1} + b_{t-1}) \qquad (11.12)$$

$$b_t = \beta \cdot (a_t - a_{t-1}) + (1 - \beta) \cdot b_{t-1} \qquad (11.13)$$

Assume that we have the demand data of gluten-free bread in a small grocery shop for the last seven periods (Table 11.10).

To forecast the demand for 7 months in the following year we use the following parameters: $\alpha = 0.2$; $\beta = 0.35$; $\tau = 1$; $b_1 = 4$. The computational results are presented in Table 11.11:

By changing the smoothing factors we can obtain a more reliable forecast for the next periods where a trend exists.

Table 11.10 Initial data for double exponential smoothing

Months t	1	2	3	4	5	6	7
Demand y_t	249	257	269	285	298	302	312

Table 11.11 Results for double exponential smoothing

t	y_t	a_t	b_t	$\hat{y}_{t,t+1}$
1	249	249	4	
2	257	253.80	4.28	253
3	269	260.26	5.04	258.08
4	285	269.25	6.42	265.31
5	298	280.14	7.99	275.67
6	302	290.90	8.96	288.12
7	312	302.28	9.81	299.85

To handle forecasts for seasonal products we can use *triple exponential smoothing*. In this case, the third parameter, for seasonal fluctuations, is added to double exponential smoothing.

11.4 Key Points and Outlook

In this chapter, we learned methods and practical tools for demand forecasting. Let us summarize the key points of this chapter as follows. For SCOM, it is important to understand the role, process, and methods of demand forecasting, since forecasts are used for both tactical and strategic decisions. Production planning, inventory management, facility location and capacity planning rely on decisions that depend on demand forecasting.

The forecasting process consists of six steps: (1) define the objective; (2) determine the time horizon; (3) select the method of forecasting; (4) gather data; (5) perform the forecasting; (6) validate and control the results. The forecasting methods can be divided into qualitative and quantitative methods. Qualitative methods are used either for new product and technology or for long-term decisions where data from the past cannot be considered a reliable source. Qualitative methods use expert knowledge and experience and include such techniques as *sales estimation, customer survey, expert estimation*, and the *Delphi Method*.

We also learned several quantitative methods which are used when historical data exist and statistical tools can be applied. Regression analysis and time series analysis, including the moving average and exponential smoothing (simple, double, triple) belong to quantitative methods. We learned how to apply statistical methods for forecasting and to calculate the forecasts based on statistical methods.

For quantitative methods, it is important to understand the measures for forecasts' quality assessment which are based on error estimation. The most popular measures are MSE, MAD and MAPE.

Finally, it should be noted that a common problem with statistical methods are the reliability of historical data and future developments. If forecasting is only based on numeric data, it is not safe. Numeric data has often not considered external features such as ecological, economic or political factors. Assume that demand for ice cream has increased over the few last years by 10 % because of hot summers. The conclusion would be that the forecast for the following year would be high as well because the company assumes the weather will be hot again. If the company does not consider weather forecasts in its calculations or consider expert views, the forecast based only on historical data could be wrong. Another critical area is forecasting of product returns in online retail industry. For that reason it is common practice to combine expert and statistical methods to get safer forecasts. Such methods are known as ARIMA (autoregressive integrated moving average model) and ANOVA (analysis of variance).

Bibliography

Chase CW (2013) Demand-driven forecasting: a structured approach to forecasting, 2nd edn. Wiley, Hoboken

Chopra S, Meindl P (2012) Supply chain management. Strategy, planning and operation, 5th edn. Pearson, Harlow

Günther H-O (2005) Supply chain management and advanced planning systems: a tutorial. In: Günther H-O, Mattfeld DC, Suhl L (eds) Supply chain management und logistik. Physica-Verlag, Heidelberg, pp 3–40

Heizer J, Render B (2013) Operations management: sustainability and supply chain management, 11th edn. Pearson, Harlow

Render B, Stair RM, Hanna ME (2012) Quantitative analysis for management, 11th edn. Pearson, Harlow

Slack N, Chambers S, Johnston R (2010) Operations management, 6th edn. Pearson, Harlow

Stadtler H, Kilger C (2008) Supply chain management and advanced planning, 4th edn. Springer, Berlin

References for Sect. 11.1

Hoot NR et al (2008) Forecasting emergency department crowding: a direct event simulation. Ann Emerg Med 52(2):117–125

Sun Y, Heng BH, Seow YT, Seow E (2009) Forecasting daily attendances at an emergency department to aid resource planning. BMC Emerg Med 9:1

Thonemann U (2010) Operations management, 2nd edn. Pearson Studium, München

Production and Material Requirements Planning

12

Suresh Chandra has just received the demand forecast data for next year. He was new in the company and responsible for operations planning. His previous experiences in different companies provided him with valuable knowledge and tools for aggregate planning, master production scheduling, and material requirements planning. In the new position, his responsibility was to integrate all these activities within the operations planning.

The previous operations planning manager applied the following concept. First, sales and production plans were set up very early (typically in September of the previous year), and then agreements with customers and suppliers were signed. The problem with this system was that production and material procurement were not flexible enough to react to demand fluctuations. In addition, since the structure of the products was set up far in advance, the possibility of product individualization according to customer orders was missing.

Janna, who was a trainee in the SCOM department, should support Suresh in the redesign of the operations planning system. Janna and Suresh understood that matching demand and supply should take place as near as possible to the date when a customer order or demand is known. Janna made a suggestion: "We could make production planning on a weekly basis each Friday for the following week when customer orders and demands are known". Suresh saw two problems here. First, it would be difficult to plan material requirements since many purchased items had quite a long lead time. Second, frequent production set-ups were expensive and not always possible for technological reasons.

Then Janna proposed to analyse which data should be set up for a long period of time (so-called design variables) and which data could be adjusted during the planning process (so-called control variables). This idea was really good. Suresh

---

Find additional case-studies, Excel spreadsheet templates, and video streams in the *E-Supplement* to this book on www.global-supply-chain-management.de!

© Springer International Publishing Switzerland 2017
D. Ivanov et al., *Global Supply Chain and Operations Management*, Springer Texts in Business and Economics, DOI 10.1007/978-3-319-24217-0_12

and Janna invited marketing, sales, manufacturing, and procurement managers to a meeting and jointly analysed the as-is planning process.

They found out that rough demand data and production quantities for each month should really be known in advance. It was necessary to plan capacities and personnel, and to make basic agreements with customers and suppliers. But at the same time, such data were not required in detail for each product. It would be enough to aggregate products into some product families according to marketing and sales interests.

For manufacturing, it was important to know detailed data on production quantities at least 3–5 days before the beginning of the next month. This would be the basis for calculating master production schedules among all the production factories in the SC which were interconnected in the technological process. For procurement, such a timeline would also be okay for calculating material requirements and replenishing items from suppliers, taking into account lead times.

Then, daily production plans could be set up. Suresh asked if it could be demonstrated that it would be possible to update production plans twice a month on the basis of new demand information.

Janna also noticed that exact material specifications were not available for all products. This could create difficulties in procurement planning and result in missing items in production, and very expensive breaks in manufacturing. Indeed, each product was composed of 2000 parts on average. Even if one part was missing, delivery delay would occur. Suresh asked to rectify this problem and enter all the BOM (Bill-of-Materials) into the ERP system.

In this chapter, we learn basic methods of operations planning which will help Janna and Suresh to increase profits and reduce costs.

The Learning Objectives for This Chapter

- Understand different planning horizons
- Understand the role of aggregate planning
- Explain different options of matching demand and supply at aggregate level
- Understand rolling planning concept
- Explain the master production schedule concept
- Apply linear programming method to production planning
- Understand the principles of exploiting the bill-of-materials
- Compute dependent material requirements taking into account lead time

12.1 Introductory Case-Study SIBUR: Integrated Operations and Supply Chain Planning

The SIBUR Group is a gas processing and petrochemicals company that owns and operates Russia's largest gas processing business in terms of associated petroleum gas (APG) processing volumes. The group benefits from owning and operating Russia's largest and most extensive integrated infrastructure for the processing and

12.1 Introductory Case-Study SIBUR: Integrated Operations and Supply Chain Planning

transportation of APG and natural gas liquids (NGLs), located primarily in Western Siberia, which is the largest oil and gas producing region in Russia. SIBURS's business model is focused on integrated operations and the SC. The group has two operating segments: feedstock/energy and petrochemicals. The group's feedstock and energy segment comprises the gathering and processing of APG; transportation, fractionation and other processing of NGLs; and marketing and sales of energy products, such as natural gas, liquefied petroleum gases (LPG), naphtha, raw NGL, methyl tertiary butyl ether and other fuels and fuel additives.

APG is purchased from major Russian oil companies. NGLs are produced internally or purchased from major Russian oil and gas companies. The group sells these energy products in the Russian and international markets and uses some of them as feedstock for its petrochemicals segment, which processes them into more than 2000 different petrochemicals, including basic polymers, synthetic rubbers, plastics and products of organic synthesis, as well as intermediates and other chemicals. The group operates 27 production sites, has over 1500 big customers operating in the energy, automotive, construction, fast moving consumer goods (FMCG), chemical and other industries in approximately 60 countries and employs over 30,000 personnel (see Fig. 12.1).

The operations and SC planning department is composed of the department manager, planning manager, dispatch manager, and SC analysis manager. The planning process starts with demand forecasting. On the one hand, statistical methods such as time series analysis are applied. On the other hand, experts estimate numerous external factors at markets and suppliers. Demand forecast quality is crucial for planning quality, since small errors in demand forecast can lead to huge deviations in the planning and execution (see Fig. 12.2).

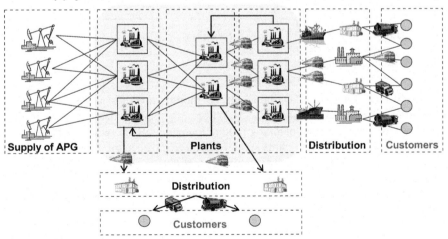

Fig. 12.1 SIBUR's SC structure

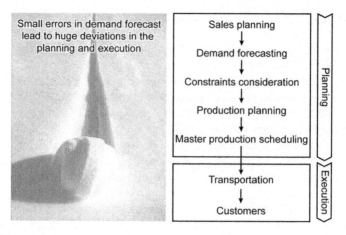

Fig. 12.2 Planning process

Different time horizons!

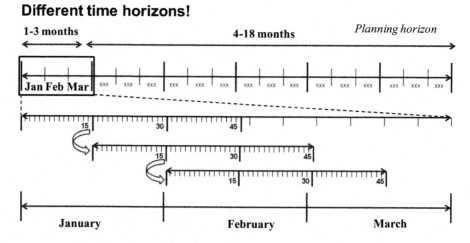

Fig. 12.3 Rolling planning

A mid-term forecast is available for 18 months, making it possible to start operations planning along the SC. Operations planning is based on the rolling planning procedure. Before planning production and material requirements, capacity, budget, and further constraints should be taken into account. After planning the master production scheduling (MPS) and transportation, products are delivered to customers.

Since demand forecasts, production and supply plans are updated frequently, a rolling planning procedure is implemented (see Fig. 12.3).

The rolling planning concept is based on the creation of a detailed MPS on a daily basis for 30–45 days for the whole SC. This MPS is updated every 15 days to take into account dynamics of real execution.

12.2 Planning Horizons/MRP-II

Planning decisions can be divided into

- Strategic,
- Tactical, and
- Operative

Strategic decisions are taken for a long period of time, typically for many years. *Tactical* decisions use information from strategic decisions and determining planning policies for some months. *Operative* decisions are taken in a weekly or daily manner for executing processes. Such a decomposition is needed since some data should be set up for a long period of time (so called design variables) and which data could be adjusted during the planning process (so called control variables). Some examples of different decisions at tactical and operative levels are presented in Fig. 12.4.

*Manufacturing resource planning—MRP-II—*means that, from a management point of view, the tools are being used for planning the activities of all functions of a manufacturing company. In the planning process, MRP II means the translation of business plans and demand forecasts, including customer orders, into production plans and purchasing plans using planned orders in a real-time multilevel scheduling environment (see Fig. 12.5).

MRP-II is a *hierarchical planning* approach. This means that decisions from the upper levels are used as input data for the lower levels (as opposed to *simultaneous planning* which is more complex).

Based on requirements and constraints from finance, marketing and manufacturing on one side and demand forecasts along with capacity decisions on the other side, aggregate planning is achieved. Results of aggregate planning are further used for master production scheduling (MPS), which is the base for material requirements planning (MRP), lot-sizing/procurement order quantity calculation, and finally for short-term scheduling and routing.

At each stage, *balancing* is mandatory to check that the results of the upper level may be implemented at the next level. Otherwise, incorrect calculations will be made throughout the planning levels. This could result in a situation where short-term daily schedules would have nothing in common with real demand; the wrong material could be purchased. In the following, we consider some important elements of the MRP-II concept.

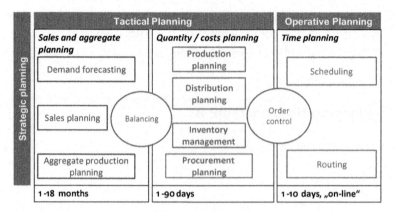

Fig. 12.4 Interrelations of strategic, tactical and operation planning decisions

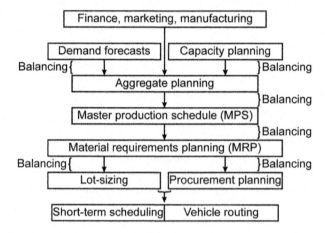

Fig. 12.5 MRP II process

12.3 Sales and Operations Planning

12.3.1 Role of Sales and Operations Planning

Production planning is usually done at an aggregate level, for both products and resources. *The objective of aggregate planning or so called sales and operations planning (S&OP) is to meet forecasted demand while minimizing cost over the planning period.* The concept of S&OP aimed at achieving a balance between demand and supply. Distinct but similar products are combined into aggregate product families that can be planned together so as to reduce planning complexity.

Consider some examples. Zara produces each year more than 12,000 different product designs. Barilla produces weekly more than 800 different pasta sorts. At

12.3 Sales and Operations Planning

BMW, more than 1000 different car variants are assembled daily. For such product variety, first planning decisions should be made at the aggregate level in order to manage complexity.

Similarly production resources, such as distinct machines or labor pools, are aggregated into an aggregate machine or labor resource. Care is required when specifying these aggregates to assure that the resulting aggregate plan can be reasonably disaggregated into feasible production schedules.

The quality of an aggregate plan has a significant impact on the profitability of a firm. A poor aggregate plan can result in lost sales and lost profits if the available inventory and capacity are unable to meet demand. A poor aggregate plan may also result in a large amount of excess inventory and capacity, thereby raising costs.

The aggregate planner's main objective is to identify the following operational parameters over the specified time horizon (Chopra and Meindl 2012; Heizer and Render 2013):

- Production rate: the number of units to be completed per unit time (such as per week or per month)
- Workforce: the number of workers/units of capacity needed for production
- Overtime: the amount of overtime production planned
- Machine capacity level: the number of units of machine capacity needed for production
- Subcontracting: the subcontracted capacity required over the planning horizon
- Backlog: demand not satisfied in the period in which it arises but carried over to future periods
- Inventory on hand: the planned inventory carried over the various periods in the planning horizon

An aggregate planner requires the following information:

- A logical overall unit for measuring sales and output
- A forecast of demand for an intermediate planning period in these aggregate terms
- A method for determining costs
- A model that combines forecasts and costs so that scheduling decisions can be made for the planning period
- Capacity planning results

Using this information, a company makes the following determinations through aggregate planning:

- Production quantity from regular time, overtime, and subcontracted time: used to determine number of workers and supplier purchase levels
- Inventory held: used to determine the warehouse space and working capital required
- Backlog/stockout quantity: used to determine customer service levels Workforce Hired/Laid Off: used to determine any labor issues to be encountered

- Machine capacity increase/decrease: used to determine if new production equipment should be purchased or idled

In order to match demand and supply at the aggregate level, companies can

- Use inventories to absorb changes in demand
- Accommodate changes by varying workforce size
- Use part-timers, overtime, or idle time to absorb changes
- Use subcontractors and maintain a stable workforce
- Change prices or other factors to influence demand

Application of these methods results in different options for aggregate planning.

12.3.2 Options for Aggregate Planning

In general, a company attempts to use its capacity and inventory to best meet demand. Therefore, the fundamental trade-offs available to a planner are among

- Capacity (regular time, overtime, subcontracted)
- Inventory
- Backlog/lost sales because of delay

There are essentially three distinct aggregate planning options for achieving balance between these costs. These options involve trade-offs among capital investment, workforce size, work hours, inventory, and backlogs/lost sales. Most options that a planner actually uses are a combination of these three and are referred to as tailored strategies. The three *options* are as follows.

- Capacity options
- Demand options
- Mixed options

Capacity options are based on the assumption that production capacity can be changed according to demand fluctuations. *First*, inventory levels can be changed in order to increase inventory in low demand periods to meet high demand in the future. The shortcoming of such policy is that it increases costs associated with storage, insurance, handling, obsolescence, and capital investment. In addition, shortages may mean lost sales due to long lead times and poor customer service.

Second, it is possible to change capacity by varying workforce size by hiring or layoffs. This allows to match the production rate to demand but creates training and separation costs for hiring and laying off workers. New workers may have lower productivity.

12.3 Sales and Operations Planning

Third, varying production rate through overtime is possible. This will allow constant workforce but overtime can be costly and may drive down productivity. In addition, overtime space is very limited; it may be difficult to meet large increases in demand. *Fourth*, subcontracting can be used as a temporary measure during periods of peak demand. Usually, it is a costly option with coordination problems regarding quality and delivery time.

Demand options are based on the assumption that it is possible to shift demand to slow periods or to use advertising or promotion to increase demand in low periods. Demand options include (1) longer lead time during high- demand periods and (2) mixing counterseasonal products and services. In other words, demand options intend to find a balance between supply and demand by influencing demand. An anecdotic example can be given here as an illustration. In a Russian restaurant on Brighton Beach, the cook cries to the waiter: "Pelmeni are ready!" The waiter responds: "Nobody has ordered pelmeni?!" The cook: "Then go and ask the quests, maybe somebody would like to order them!"

Mixed options combine elements from capacity and demand options. The common mixed options are as follows:

- Chase strategy and
- Level strategy

Chase strategy is based on using capacity as the lever. With the help of this strategy, we match output rates to demand forecast for each period. Typically, we can vary workforce levels or vary production rate. Such strategy is common in service organization.

Level strategy is based on using inventory as the lever. With the help of this strategy, a stable machine capacity and workforce are maintained with a constant output rate. While daily production is uniform, we use inventory as buffer. Stable production leads by tendency to better quality and productivity.

12.3.3 Methods for Aggregate Planning

Methods for aggregate planning can be based on empirical knowledge of the planers or on the mathematical models. Since a number of possible combinations of different methods is very high, a mathematical model would lead by tendency to a better results. But in many cases, the construction of such models is difficult since many "soft" factors should be taken into account. Basic quantitative method for S&OP is linear programming that allows allocate resources to demand in optimal way subject to capacity constraints. We will consider linear programming in the separate chapter. Here we reduce ourselves to consideration of empirical methods.

Task 12.1 Sales and Operation Planning

You have to prepare an aggregate plan for production of skateboards that will cover nine periods (Table 12.1):

Table 12.1 Demand forecast

Month	1	2	3	4	5	6	7	8	9	Total
Demand forecast	190	230	260	280	210	170	160	260	180	1940

You have 20 workers with a capacity (output) of 10 skateboards a month for each of them. The production cost is $6, the inventory holding cost is $5, and the backlog cost is $10 a unit. Overtime and subcontracting are not used. However, in this case the demand cannot be covered with the existing capacities. You have the possibility to employ two additional workers. In order to avoid the surplus production of 40 skateboards, you decide to hire the second worker for the first five months only. The cost of these two workers is $500.

We calculate an aggregate plan and its costs accordingly in Table 12.2 under the following assumptions:

- Inventory costs is calculated for average inventory on hand; average inventory on hand is calculated as 50 % from the sum of inventory at the beginning and end of each month;
- Our customer can wait: we can sell products in further periods to cover demand of the previous periods; but for each period we calculate backlog costs.

The total cost of this plan is $14,790. In order to make any judgments on its quality, you have to consider at least two other options.

Option 1) You can introduce flexible capacities to cover the discrepancies between output and demand in each month. This will cost you $4000 additionally.

(Comment: here you do not need the table calculation)
Answer: In this case, the demand and production volumes are equal, and neither backlogs nor inventory exist. However, the total cost is in this case $15,640. Therefore, this flexibility option costs more than the first option.

Option 2) You decide on subcontracting instead of hiring two workers. The supplier is able to deliver 50 units in the months 3, 5 und 7 at $7 a unit.

Answer: see Table 12.3
This option is also less efficient as compared with the first one. In order to make the subcontracting profitable, it should be used for the periods with the greatest backlogs (4)–(6).

12.3 Sales and Operations Planning

Table 12.2 Sales and operations plan

Month	1	2	3	4	5	6	7	8	9	Total
Demand forecast	190	230	260	280	210	170	160	260	180	1940
Production:										
Regular	220	220	220	220	220	210	210	210	210	1940
Overtime										
Subcontract										
Shortage/Overage	+30	−10	−40	−60	+10	+40	+50	−50	+30	0
Inventory:										
Beginning	0	30	20	0	0	0	0	20	0	
Ending	30	20	0	0	0	0	20	0	0	
Average	15	25	10	0	0	0	10	10	0	70
Backlog	0	0	20	80	70	30	0	30	0	230
Costs:										
Production	1320	1320	1320	1320	1320	1260	1260	1260	1260	11,640
Inventory	75	125	50	0	0	0	50	50	0	350
Backlog	0	0	200	800	700	300	0	300	0	2300
Total costs	1395	1445	1570	2120	2020	1560	1310	1610	1260	14,290

Table 12.3 Results of S&OP calculation

190	230	260	280	210	170	160	260	180	1940
200	200	200	200	200	200	200	200	200	1800
		50		50		50			150
10	-30	-10	-80	40	30	90	-60	20	10
0	10	0	0	0	0	0	50	0	
10	0	0	0	0	0	50	0	10	
5	5	0	0	0	0	25	25	5	65
0	20	30	110	70	40	0	10	0	280
1200	1200	1200	1200	1200	1200	1200	1200	1200	10800
0	0	350	0	350	0	350	0	0	1050
25	25	0	0	0	0	125	125	25	325
0	200	300	1100	700	400	0	100	0	2800
1225	1425	1850	2300	2250	1600	1675	1425	1225	14975

12.4 Sales and Production Planning with Linear Programming

12.4.1 Problem Description

In S&OP, overall production quantities and capacity have been defined. The next step is to decide on the product mix within these aggregate volumes. The *objective function* is to maximize the profit. The capacity is limited and demand is known that represents the *constraints*.

Consider an example. The demand in January for plastic windows of the types A and B is forecasted at 100 and 150 units respectively. The available capacity is 1000 time units. The price is $60 for windows of type A and $50 for windows of type B. For one unit of A and B, five and four capacity units are needed. For production of A and B, components #1 and #2 are required in proportion 40/60 and 70/30 respectively. These components are available in stock with 130 and 90 units respectively. The production of A and B implies material and manufacturing costs of $48 and $35 respectively for each unit.

Consider another example. A wholesaler deals with only two sorts of juice. Sort A is handled in barrels of 20 l. Sort B is handled in full boxes of 10 l per box. Since no chemical additives are used, refrigerated storage is needed. The capacity of this refrigerator is 10,000 units. Maximal storage time is 1 month. The producer of juice A is able to deliver 450 barrels a month at maximal. The producer of juice B is able to deliver 400 boxes a month at maximal. The profit for one sold barrel is $1 and for one sold box is $2.

12.4 Sales and Production Planning with Linear Programming

Both companies have to decide on quantities A and B in order to maximize their profit subject to demand and capacity constraints. Such problems can be represented as linear optimization problems with some decision variables and constraints. Our objective in the paragraph is to learn how to:

- represent such kinds of management problems in the form of an optimization model; and
- solve this model analytically and graphically.

Of course, in real life the number of decision variables (i.e., the number of products) is very high. To simplify the explanations, we will consider the cases with two variables (i.e., products A and B).

12.4.2 Method: Linear Programming

Linear programming (LP) is a widely used quantitative analysis tool to support the SCOM decisions on allocating available resources subject to demand in order to maximize the profit or minimize costs (e.g., in the transportation problem). The following is characteristic for LP models and describes its requirements and assumptions:

- objective function that describes the management goal (e.g., profit maximization);
- constraints that limits the degree to which we can pursue our objective;
- alternative ways for resource allocation should exist;
- both objective and constraints must be expressed as linear functions.

Let us formulate the LP models for the two cases described above. For the case with plastic windows, the objective is to maximize the profit. We can state the following general objective function [Eq. (12.1)]:

$$Z = \sum_{i=1}^{n} p_i \cdot x_i \rightarrow \text{or } Z = p_A \cdot x_A + p_B \cdot x_B \rightarrow \text{max!} \qquad (12.1)$$

where p_A and p_B and x_A and x_B are the profits and quantities of products A and B respectively.

Since the price for A is $60 and the variable costs are $48, $p_A = \$12$. Similarly, $p_B = \$15$. We can rewrite the objective function as follows [Eq. (12.2)]:

$$Z = 12x_A + 15x_B \rightarrow \text{max!} \qquad (12.2)$$

What is the maximal possible value of the objective function? Without having any constraints, the profit can be unlimited when we decide to produce an unlimited quantity of product B. However, we have limited demand and capacity and have therefore to consider a constraint system. The solution to this constraint system will allow us to find such quantities as x_A and x_B so that the Z-value will be the maximal possible profit under the considered constraints, prices and costs.

The constraint system is general form can be written as follows [Eqs. (12.3–12.5)]:

$$\text{Production capacity:} \sum_{i=1}^{n} c_i \cdot x_i \leq C_{total} \text{ or } C_A \cdot x_A + C_B \cdot x_B \leq C_{total} \quad (12.3)$$

$$\text{Demand}: x_A \leq D_A; x_B \leq D_B \quad (12.4)$$

$$\text{Non-negativity constraint}: x_A, x_B \geq 0 \quad (12.5)$$

where

C_A and C_B is the number of capacity units required for production of one unit of A and B respectively,

C_{total} is the overall available capacity, and

D_A and D_B is the demand for A and B respectively,

The constraint system for the case with plastic windows can be therefore written in the following way [Eqs. (12.6–12.9)]:

$$\text{Production capacity:} \; 5x_A + 4x_B \leq 1000 \quad (12.6)$$

$$\text{Demand:} \; x_A \leq 100; \; x_B \leq 150 \quad (12.7)$$

$$\text{Non-negativity constraint}: x_A, x_B \geq 0 \quad (12.8)$$

Additional constraints for components:

$$\text{Component 1}: 0.4x_A + 0.7x_B \leq 130; \quad \text{Component 2}: 0.6x_A + 0.3x_B \leq 90 \quad (12.9)$$

Similarly, we can formulate the LP model for the case with the juice wholesaler [Eqs. (12.10–12.14)]:

$$\text{Objective function:} \; Z = 1x_A + 2x_B \to \max! \quad (12.10)$$

$$\text{Storage capacity:} \; 20x_A + 10x_B \leq 10,000 \quad (12.11)$$

Supply:

$$x_A \leq 450 \quad (12.12)$$

$$x_B \leq 400 \quad (12.13)$$

$$\text{Non-negativity constraint:} \; x_A, x_B \geq 0 \quad (12.14)$$

12.4 Sales and Production Planning with Linear Programming

▶ **Practical Insights** For such LP models, different solution techniques exist. In real-life cases, special software, such as CPLEX, Lindo, AMPL, Matlab, GAMS, Gurobi, XPRESS, etc., are used. All these software apply solution algorithms based on the *simplex method* and modern advanced computational techniques. LP is really a working tool in practice.

12.4.3 Graphical Solution

In this paragraph, we will consider a graphical solution method for LP models. First, we must identify the set of feasible solutions. To do that, we plot the constraints on a graph. The variables x_A and x_B will be plotted as the horizontal and vertical axes respectively. Consider the solution to the case with plastic windows. To plot the line for Eq. (12.6) we need to define the points where the line $5x_A + 4x_B \leq 1000$ intersects the x_A and x_B axes. When $x_A = 0$, $x_B = 250$. When $x_B = 0$, $x_A = 200$. Similarly, we do this for the lines subject to Eq. (12.9), see Fig. 12.6.

It can be observed that the *feasible region* is formed by four lines: demand A, demand B, component #1 and component #2. According to the *corner-point solution* method, the optimal solution belongs to one of the corner points in the feasible regions. For example, take point (100;0). For this point the profit is $12 \cdot 100 + 15 \cdot 0 = \$1200$. We have to calculate the profit at different corner points. Having

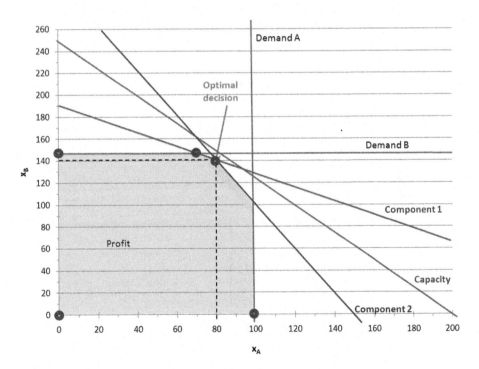

Fig. 12.6 Graphical solution to LP problem with the help of corner-point method

done that, we will get maximal profit at $x_A = 80$ and $x_B = 140$ units. The objective function is in this case $12 \cdot 80 + 15 \cdot 140 = \$3060$. We can also observe that only 960 of 1000 available capacity units will be used. The reason is the limited component quantities.

Consider the second case about the juice wholesaler. We plot the constraints in the same way as for the first case but solve this task with the help of another method, namely the *iso-profit line* method (see Figs. 12.7 and 12.8). We define the decision variables for products A and B as x_1 and x_2 respectively. The constraints (12.11)–(12.13) are marked as NB1–NB3 respectively.

Having defined the feasible region, the *iso-profit line* is now used to find the optimal solution. We start by letting the profit be equal to some arbitrary amount, that is, to select a relatively small value. In our example, letting the profit be $500, we get the iso-profit line G_{500} (see Fig. 12.8).

The farther we move the iso-profit line from the origin, the higher our profit will be. In our case the highest possible profit of $1100 will be achieved at $x_1 = 300$ and $x_2 = 400$.

> ▶ **Practical Insights** In SCOM, managers are typically interested not only in the optimal solution but also in the assessment of its robustness, since many risks and uncertainties can influence the input parameters, such as capacity, material supply, and demand. An analysis of how sensitive the optimal solution is regarding changes in demand and supply is called *sensitivity analysis*. Sensitivity analysis is a standard tool in LP solvers.

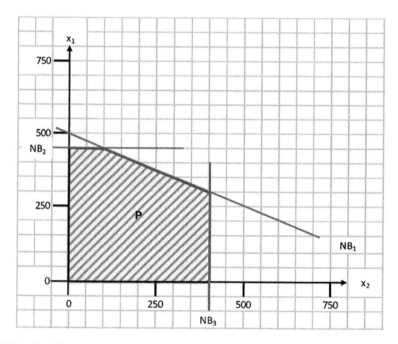

Fig. 12.7 Feasible region in the LP problem

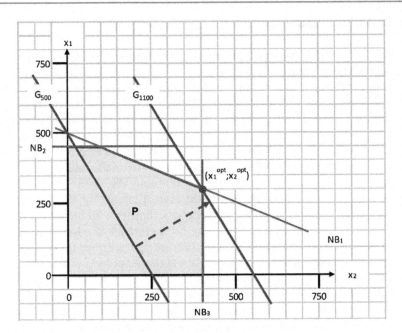

Fig. 12.8 Solution to the LP problem with the help of iso-profit line

12.5 Master Production Schedule and Rolling Planning

12.5.1 Master Production Schedule

Master production schedule (MPS) specifies what is to be made and when in accordance with the aggregate production plan. The MPS is the main result of the production planning process. If aggregate planning works with product families, MPS disaggregates them. MPS is established in terms of specific products. For example, aggregate planning determined to produce in August 2000 tables. MPS would determine that in first week 600 tables, in second week 400 tables, in third week 700 tables, and in fourth week 300 tables will be produced.

> ▶ **Practical Insights** In practice, the MPS is quite often fixed or "frozen" in the near term part of the plan. For example, in the automotive industry, so called *"pearl chain"* concept is used. The sequence of car production is fixed for seven days and remains unchanged throughout the whole production cycle. This allows increase efficiency of manufacturing, improve capacity balancing, and make planning process more convenient for managers.

12.5.2 Rolling Planning

Planning at the MPS level is typically done in a rolling or (adaptive) horizon fashion. *Rolling planning* is a continuous, event-driven, real-time (re)planning and control process. It uses not only simple open time slots (in contrast to incremental planning) but employs conflict-driven plan changes during the system execution (see Fig. 12.9). Rolling (or adaptive) planning is a method of planning in which a plan is modified periodically by a change in the system parameters or the characteristics of control influences on the basis of information feedback about a current system state, the past and the updated forecasts of the future.

In *adaptive planning*, the precision of planning decisions decreases while moving away from the decision point (see Figs. 12.9 and 12.10). As shown in Figs. 12.9 and 12.10, planning decisions become fuzzier with increasing distance from the decision-making point. This may be interpreted as a sequence of inter-inserted funnels. At certain intervals, the plans are updated, the "fuzzy" part of the plans becomes precise and a new funnel for the further process course appears.

Such an approach provides the required flexibility with regard to dynamics and uncertainty. Hence, adaptive planning implies problem resolution and redefinition through the learning process, rather than problem solving. This allows us to interpret planning and scheduling not as discrete operations but as a continuous

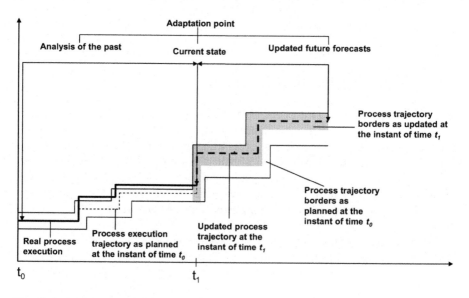

Fig. 12.9 Adaptive planning logic

12.6 Material Requirements Planning

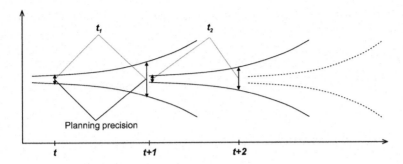

Fig. 12.10 Precision of planning decisions

adaptive process. The adaptive planning procedure can be interconnected with the adaptive procedure. This allows reaction in the real-time mode to necessities for replanning due to disruptions in SCs (unplanned regulations).

If there is not sufficiently full information about the system and operation dynamics, certain key operations and events must be determined, of which the uncertainty of states does not allow operation plans to be formed. As a result, a number of alternative operation dynamics scenarios can be elaborated. Further, with time, the uncertain (at the time of planning) operations' states become certain and possess certain characteristics (parameters).

12.6 Material Requirements Planning

Each of us buys sometime furniture which should be assembled at home. As assistance we get prospects which explain us:

- Which items are contained in the package and in what quantity
- How these items can be assembled
- Which items are necessary for sub-assembly
- In which sequence we should perform sub-assemblies and final assembly
- What time is needed for sub-assemblies and final assembly

You can observe from the assembly instructions that:

- We have got a list of materials needed and their interrelations
- We can determine quantity of items required for furniture assembly.

In terms of operations management, we would describe this case as follows:

- We have got a *bill-of-materials* (BOM)
- We have performed *material requirements planning* (MRP)

If the demand for one item is related to the demand for another item, we call it *dependant demand*. Given a quantity for the end item, the demand for all parts and components can be calculated. For any product for which a schedule can be established, dependent demand techniques should be used. The most common techniques in this area are BOM and MRP.

12.6.1 Bill-of-Materials

First, BOM represents a list of components, ingredients, and materials needed to make the product. Second, BOM provides a product structure (see Fig. 12.11). This structure can be re-written simpler if we depict number of items requires for one unit at the upper level (see Fig. 12.11). From the product structure, we can determine how many items are required at different levels of the BOM (Fig. 12.12) (see Table 12.4).

This is important to synchronize manufacturing and procurement since we can produce items at the upper level only after the items from the lower level are purchased or manufactured.

From the product structure, we can also determine total quantity of all items. If we perform this procedure, we *explode the BOM*. For the given structure, we can explode the BOM as shown in Table 12.5.

Consider as an example total requirements for material #2 (M2). Three pieces are needed for one component 12. In turn, three pieces of Component 12 are needed for one module #1, and one module #1 is needed for one end item. So the dependant demand on

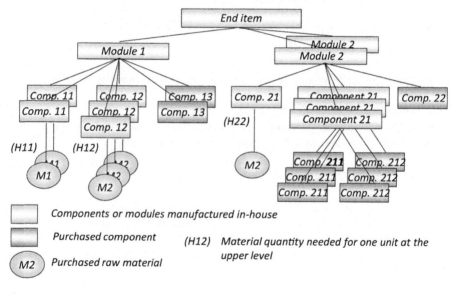

Fig. 12.11 Structure of an end product

12.6 Material Requirements Planning

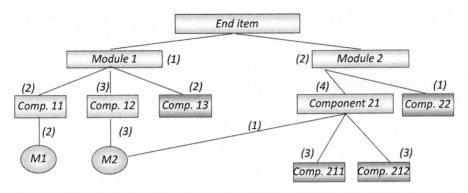

Fig. 12.12 Structure of an end product with item quantities

Table 12.4 Level BOM

Level				Item	Quantity
0				End item	1
	1			Module 1	1
		2		Component 11	2
			3	Material 1	2
		2		Component 12	3
			3	Material 2	3
		2		Component 13	2
	1			Module 2	2
		2		Component 21	4
			3	Component 211	3
			3	Component 212	3
			3	Material 2	1
		2		Component 22	1

Table 12.5 Explode the BOM

Item	Quantity
End item	1
Module 1	1
Module 2	2
Component 11	2
Component 12	3
Component 13	3
Component 21	8
Component 22	2
Component 211	24
Component 212	24
Material 1	4
Material 2	17

M2 is now $3 \cdot 3 \cdot 1 = 9$ pieces. In addition, one piece of M2 is needed for one component 21, and four components 21 are needed for one module #2. Two modules #2 are needed for one end item. So the dependant demand on M2 is now $9 + 1 \cdot 4 \cdot 2 = 17$ pieces.

Exploding the BOM is important for manufacturing and procurement to determine aggregate quantities for production and purchasing. This data is needed for production and procurement planning

> ▶ **Practical Insights** In practice, BOM calculation is a complex task. A Mercedes-Benz (SL) is composed of nearly 9100 items. Amounts of 600 kg steel and 25 kg colour are needed. An Airbus is composed at average of more than 4000 thousands items. Even if only one item is missing, delivery and production delays can happen. BOM and MRP calculations are automated in the ERP system. For really complex products, these procedures are integrated within CAD (computer-aided design) and PDM (product data management) systems. In addition, so called *module BOMs* are typical for complex products. This means that BOM is created separately for each module.

12.6.2 MRP Calculation

With the help of BOM, the product structure is defined. However, manufacturing and procurement of items happens not immediately. This requires a certain *lead time*. For production, lead time is the sum of the order, wait, move, setup, store, and run times. For purchased items, lead time is the time between the recognition of a need and the availability of the item for production. The lead time is taken into account to calculate MRP.

For MRP calculations, the following data are required:

- MPS
- BOM
- Inventory availability
- Purchase orders outstanding (scheduled receipts)
- Lead/manufacturing times for each item

On the basis of this data, the MRP system calculates orders for manufacturing and purchasing (see Fig. 12.13).

MRP calculation is based on the following algorithm:

1. From exploding the BOM, so called *gross requirements* on items are defined beginning with the upper level down to the lower levels.
2. Taking into account inventory availability and purchase orders outstanding (scheduled receipts), *net requirements* can be determined.
3. Net requirements = Gross requirement—(inventory availability + scheduled receipts)
4. Finally, net requirements are used to determine actual order release time subject to lead time. This step is often called "lead time offset" or "time phasing"

12.6 Material Requirements Planning

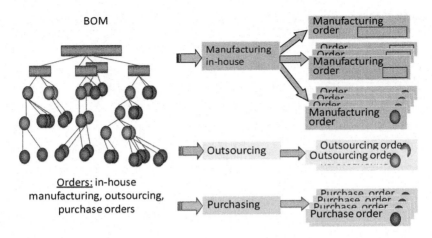

Fig. 12.13 Structure of MRP system

Consider an example.

Task 12.2 MRP Calculation
MPS for an end product is composed as follows (Table 12.6):

We are given the following BOM (Fig. 12.14):
We assume that no inventory is available and no scheduled receipts are planned. Lead time for all items is 1 month. In this case, *gross requirements equal net requirements* and the following represents results of MRP calculations (see Table 12.7).

We start with the net requirements for an end item. This data is taken from the MPS. Next step is to determine net requirements for the items at the first level. Since for all items, exactly one piece is needed for one end item, their net requirements are identical to those of the end item. Net requirements for the items at first level should be shifted according to 1 month of lead time. Similarly, net requirements for the items at the second level are determined subject to net requirements of the items at first level and lead-time shifting.

For example, 20 units of item D in period #2 means that we have to manufacture 20 units of item D in February in order to be able to assemble 10 units of end item E in April. By processing the BOM by level, items with multiple parents are typically only processed once, saving time and resources and reducing confusion. We transform Table 12.7 as follows (see Table 12.8).

The above transformation is based on aggregating the net requirements of the same items over different levels in each period. For example, in period #2, we aggregated net requirements for item #2 from the second level (30) and third level (80). Net requirement for item #2 in the second period is 110 pieces. This information is important for purchasing planning for February.

Table 12.6 MPS for an end product

April	May	June	July
10	10	20	50

Fig. 12.14 BOM

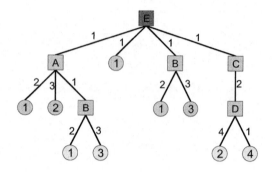

Table 12.7 MRP calculation

Level	Item	Months						
		1	2	3	4	5	6	7
0	E				10	10	20	50
1	A			10	10	20	50	
	B			10	10	20	50	
	C			10	10	20	50	
	1			10	10	20	50	
2	B		10	10	20	50		
	D		20	20	40	100		
	1		40	40	80	200		
	2		30	30	60	150		
	3		30	30	60	150		
3	1	20	20	40	100			
	2	80	80	160	400			
	3	30	30	60	150			
	4	20	20	40	100			

Table 12.8 MRP calculation

Item	Months						
	1	2	3	4	5	6	7
E				10	10	20	50
A			10	10	20	50	
B		10	20	30	70	50	
C			10	10	20	50	
D		20	20	40	100		
1	20	60	90	190	220	50	
2	80	110	190	460	150		
3	30	60	90	210	150		
4	20	20	40	100			

12.6 Material Requirements Planning

Table 12.9 Initial data

Period	8	9	10
Demand	125	90	110

Table 12.10 MRP calculation

Period	4	5	6	7	8	9	10
Demand					125	90	110
Additional demand					25	10	10
Gross requirement					150	100	120
On-hand inventory					35	0	0
Scheduled receipts					7	0	5
Net requirement					108	100	115
Planned order release				108	100	115	

Consider the calculations for plates (lead time = 2):

Period	4	5	6	7	8	9	10
Gross requirement				108	100	115	
On-hand inventory				25	0	0	
Scheduled receipts				0	0	0	
Net requirement				83	100	115	
Planned order release		83	100	115			

Consider the calculations for legs (lead time = 1):

Period	4	5	6	7	8	9	10
Gross requirement				432	400	460	
On-hand inventory				32	0	0	
Scheduled receipts				0	0	0	
Net requirement				400	400	460	
Planned order release			400	400	460		

Now we are going to include inventory and schedule receipts into the consideration. Assume the following problem statement.

Task 12.3 MRP Calculation

You are given the following MPS for table production (Table 12.9):

Lead time for the table production is one period. To produce one table we need four legs and one plate. For tables, you have got additional demand of 25 units in period #8, 10 units in periods #9 and #10 respectively. We have 35 tables, 25 plates and 32 legs as beginning inventory. The retailer announced that it will send back seven tables in period #8 and five tables in period #10. For plate production, we need two periods, and one period is needed for leg production.

First, we perform calculations for tables (lead time = 1) (see Table 12.10):

Managers frequently use so called closed-loop MRP systems. This allows production planners to move work between time periods to smooth the load or to at least bring it within capacity.

In practice, managers need to know how to group the "planned order releases". Indeed, we can order 400 legs for June as one large order, or split this order into four orders of 100 units in each order. Here the trade-off is how to balance *ordering fixed costs* and *inventory holding costs*. We will consider order quantity planning and *lot-sizing* decisions in Chap. 13.

12.7 Key Points

Planning decisions can be divided into strategic, tactical, and operative. MRP II means the translation of business plans and demand forecasts incl. customer orders into a production and purchasing plans. The objective of aggregate planning or so called sales and operations planning (S&OP) is to meet forecasted demand while minimizing cost over the planning period. The concept of S&OP aimed at achieving a balance between demand and supply.

In general, a company attempts to use its capacity and inventory to best meet demand. Therefore, the fundamental trade-offs available to a planner are among capacity, inventory, and backlog/lost sales because of delay. Three *options of S&OP* are capacity options, demand options, and mixed options. Mixed options combine elements from capacity and demand options. The common mixed options are as chase strategy and level strategy.

MPS specifies what is to be made and when in accordance with the aggregate production plan. Planning at the MPS level is typically done in a rolling or (adaptive) horizon fashion. If the demand for one item is related to the demand for another item, we call it dependant demand. The most common techniques in this area are BOM and MRP. BOM represents a list of components, ingredients, and materials needed to make product. Second, in the BOM, the product structure is defined. However, manufacturing and procurement of items happens not immediately. This requires certain *lead time*. Lead time is taken into account while calculating MRP. MRP system calculates orders for manufacturing and purchasing.

Bibliography

Chopra S, Meindl P (2012) Supply chain management. Strategy, planning and operation, 5th edn. Pearson, Harlow

Heizer J, Render B (2013) Operations management: sustainability and supply chain management, 11th edn. Pearson, Harlow

Hendricks KB, Singhal VR (2014) The effect of demand-supply mismatches on firm risk. Prod Oper Manag 23(12):2137–2151

Mangan J, Lalwani C, Butcher T (2008) Global logistics and supply chain management. Wiley, New York

Silver EA, Pyke DF, Peterson R (1998) Inventory management and production planning and scheduling, 3rd edn. Wiley, Hoboken

Thomé AMT, Sousa RS, do Carmo LFRRS (2014) The impact of sales and operations planning practices on manufacturing operational performance. Int J Prod Res 52(7):2108–2121

Wallace TF, Stahl RA (2006) Sales and operations planning. TF Wallace & Co., Cincinnati

Reference for Sect. 12.1

SIBUR (2013) www.sibur.com

Inventory Management 13

The Learning Objectives for This Chapter

- Understand the trade-off "service level vs. costs" in inventory management
- Understand the role of inventory in the supply chain
- Conduct ABC and XYZ analysis
- Explain and use the EOQ/EPQ models for independent inventory demand
- Compute a reorder point
- Calculate service levels and probabilistic inventory models
- Explain and use the dynamic lot-sizing models
- Understand and compute the effects of inventory aggregation
- Explain ATP/CTP concept

13.1 Introductory Case-Study: Amazon, Volkswagen and DELL

Trade-off "service level vs. costs" is one of the most important issues in inventory management. Its resolution strongly depends on the manufacturing, sourcing, distribution, and SC strategy. Consider three examples.

Amazon
Amazon.com, Inc. is the world's largest online retailer, founded in 1994. It started as an online bookstore but has diversified over the last 20 years selling DVDs, CDs, MP3, software, games, furniture, food, toys and more. The basic idea is that everybody with access to the internet can buy nearly worldwide a massive range of products at any time and get them delivered wherever they want. Amazon apps

---

Find additional case-studies, Excel spreadsheet templates, and video streams in the *E-Supplement* to this book on www.global-supply-chain-management.de!

make it possible to buy their products easily even with smartphones or tablets. Their inventory management for books is based on the number of sales for each book. Best-selling books are stocked in many regional warehouses to enable fast responsiveness for customers in any region. Books with a smaller number of sales are stocked in only a few regional warehouses to reduce inventory costs. The slowest moving books are not even held in stock but are obtained directly from the publisher or distributor. Through this strategy it is possible for Amazon to reduce inventory costs for slow-moving products and to have the best possible service level and reliability for their customers.

Volkswagen
Founded in Germany in 1937, Volkswagen implemented the JIT-based SC strategy in Germany. This means that components and items are delivered to the assembly line when they are needed. In this case only a small amount of safety stock is held for critical parts. This strategy helps to reduce inventory, transport, labour and administration costs. Often suppliers locate their plants close to the manufacturer to deliver the required components and items at the right moment and also to reduce their transport costs. This choice of location reduces the risk of delivery delays and supply shortages. Examples of these JIT components are the dashboard with all electronic devices or seats. JIT is normally used for A-, B-, X- and Y-items. For C-items Volkswagen uses a Kanban replenishment system to have them in stock at any time. These items normally have low inventory holding costs. Based on the JIT strategy and Kanban replenishment system Volkswagen is able to minimize inventory costs.

DELL
Founded in US in 1983, DELL runs a MTO production strategy. The assembly starts and materials are replenished only after a customer order. In such a business model, DELL is able to drastically reduce its inventory. For some components, DELL has 90 inventory turns a year which means that inventory is only 4 days on hand at average. Such inventory dynamics allows Dell to respond to a wide range of quantities demanded, meet short lead time, handle a large variety of products, build innovative products, and handle supply uncertainty.

13.2 Role, Functions and Types of Inventory

The *role of inventory management* is to strike a balance between inventory investment and customer service. Inventory is one of the most expensive assets of many companies representing as much as 50 % of total invested capital. In SCOM we must therefore balance inventory investment and customer service level.

Inventory has different *functions*, e.g.:

le the company and the SC from fluctuations in demand and hold a
oods that will provide a selection for customers

13.2 Role, Functions and Types of Inventory

- to increase SC flexibility by placing inventory at right places
- to hedge against facility disruptions in the case of natural catastrophes
- to decouple or separate various parts of the production process
- to take advantage of quantity discounts and hedge against inflation

Typically, inventory is classified in the following *types*:

- *Raw material* (items which are purchased but not processed)
- *Work-in-process (WIP)* (items which underwent some change but are not completed)
- *Maintenance/repair/operating (MRO)* (items which are necessary to keep machinery and processes productive)
- *Finished goods* (completed product awaiting shipment).

In taking decision in the scope of inventory management, the following two *basic questions* are put in the forefront of consideration:

- How much should I replenish?
- When should I replenish?

In calculating inventory amounts, the following *costs* are typically considered:

- Holding costs (variable)—the costs of holding inventory over time;
- Ordering costs (fixed)—the costs of placing an order and receiving goods
- Setup costs (fixed)—the costs to prepare a machine or process for manufacturing an order
- Stockout costs (variable)—the costs of lost customer order because of a product shortage, loss-of-goodwill costs.

Holding costs include operating costs, labour costs, material handling costs, etc. and vary considerably depending on the business, location, and interest rates. Generally this costs is greater than 15 % of the item price, some items have holding costs greater than 40 %. Holding costs depend on the order quantity.

Setup costs (in manufacturing) and ordering costs (in procurement) are fixed and do not depend on the order quantity. At present, this cost tends to be reduced due to e-business developments. At the same time, setup/ordering costs can be increased in the case of high variety of the assortment and market dynamics.

According to the inventory functions and types, inventory can be used to manage:

- Economy of scale—this is *cycle inventory*;
- Uncertainty—this is *safety inventory*.

Cycle inventory exists because producing or purchasing in large *lots* or *batches*. A lot or *batch size* is the quantity that a stage in the SC either produces or purchases at a time. SC can exploit economy of scale and order in large lots to reduce fixed costs. With the increase in lot size, however, also comes an increase in carrying costs. As an example of a cycle stock decision, consider an online book retailer. This retailer's sales average around 10 truckloads of books a month. The cycle inventory decisions the retailer must make are how much to order for replenishment and how often to place these orders. We will consider cycle inventory optimization in the "Deterministic models" section (for one period) and "Dynamic lot-sizing models" section for many periods.

Safety inventory is carried to satisfy demand subject to unpredictable demand fluctuations and reduce product shortages. Safety inventory can help the SC manager improve product availability in the presence of uncertainty. In the presence of safety inventory, costs of shortage or costs of overage can occur. Calculation of safety inventory is based on a pre-determined *service level*. Choosing safety inventory involves making a *trade-off* between the costs of having too much inventory and the costs of losing sales due. We will consider methods to support decisions on safety inventory in the "Stochastic models" section.

For many industries, some products are sold in high quantities in summer, and lower quantities in winter (e.g., mineral water). *Seasonal inventory* is built up to counter predictable variability in demand. Companies using seasonal inventory build up inventory in periods of low demand and store it for periods of high demand when they will not have the capacity to produce all that is demanded. Managers face key decisions in determining whether to build seasonal inventory, and if they do build it, in deciding how much to build. If a company can rapidly change the rate of its production system at very low cost, then it may not need seasonal inventory, because the production system can adjust to a period of high demand without incurring large costs. The basic trade-off SCOM managers face in determining how much seasonal inventory to build is the cost of carrying the additional seasonal inventory versus the cost of having a flexible production rate.

> ▶ **Practical Insights** It is clear intuitively that car tyres and pins will have different inventory management policies. However, in a distribution centre which runs over two million items, it can be quite a complicated task to find the right policy for each item. Many companies that ask for inventory optimization want to start immediately with software and mathematical models. But before starting any calculations, items should be properly analysed and classified. False organization of inventory management is in many cases the key point of problems in optimization.

13.3 Material Analysis

13.3.1 ABC Analysis

First step in the item classification is the *ABC analysis*. ABC analysis divides inventory into three classes based on annual dollar volume:

13.3 Material Analysis

Fig. 13.1 ABC analysis

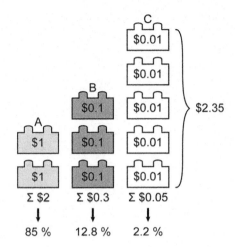

- Class A—high annual dollar volume
- Class B—medium annual dollar volume
- Class C—low annual dollar volume

ABC analysis is used to establish policies that focus on the few critical parts and not the many trivial ones. This method implements the Pareto Principle which states that "there are few critical and many trivial". Consider a simple example. Imagine that you have ten Lego blocks: two of them are red, three green, and five blue (see Fig. 13.1). To perform the ABC analysis, we measure the annual demand of each inventory item times the cost per unit. Assume that one red block costs $1, one green block costs $0.1, and one blue block costs $0.01.

You can easily calculate that total inventory costs is $2.35. Two red blocks take only 20 % of the total inventory amount, but they create 85 % of inventory costs. These are critical items in the A group. A-items have to be managed especially carefully. First, it has to be managed for the relationships with suppliers of A-items, i.e., supplier development. Second, tighter physical inventory control for A-items is needed. Third, we need more care in forecasting A-items.

Consider a numerical example for ABC analysis.

Task 13.1 ABC Analysis
Quarted Ltd is a company which sells table lamps.

In Tables 13.1 and 13.2, a numerical example is provided.

Table 13.1 Initial data for ABC analysis

Table lamp	Annual demand	Cost per unit	Annual expenditure
X1	100	0.5	50
X2	200	0.05	10
X3	50	1.65	82.5
Y1	40	10.75	430
Y2	200	0.11	22
Y3	200	0.19	38
Y4	50	2.4	120
T1	90	0.6	54
T2	10	13.6	136
T3	60	1.35	81

Table 13.2 Results of ABC analysis

Table lamp	Annual demand	Cost per unit	Annual expenditure	Cumulative expenditure	Percentage expenditure	Category
Y1	40	10.75	430	430	42.0 %	A
T2	10	13.6	136	566	55.3 %	A
Y4	50	2.4	120	686	67.0 %	A
X3	50	1.65	82,5	768.5	75.1 %	A
T3	60	1.35	81	849.5	83.0 %	B
T1	90	0.6	54	903.5	88.3 %	B
X1	100	0.5	50	953.5	93.2 %	B
Y3	200	0.19	38	991.5	96.9 %	C
Y2	200	0.11	22	1013.5	99.0 %	C
X2	200	0.05	10	1023.5	100.0 %	C

We are given annual demand and the costs. To determine which table lamps are in the A, B or C-category we need to calculate the annual expenditure:

$$\text{annual expenditure} = \text{annual demand} \cdot \text{costs per lamp} \qquad (13.1)$$

Next step is to arrange the different types of table lamps according to their annual expenditure. After calculating the cumulative expenditure we have to compute the percentage of the cumulative expenditure. Then we can classify the A, B and C items. Assuming that the classification is 80:15:5 we can label the different table lamps as follow (see Table 13.2):

We can observe that 150 table lamps generate around 80 % of inventory costs (A) whereas 600 table lamps generate only 5 % of inventory costs (C). This relationship can be presented in graphic form as shown in Fig. 13.2.

13.3 Material Analysis

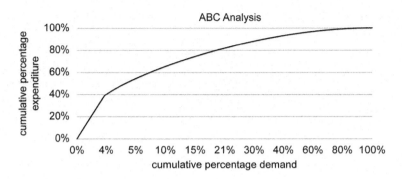

Fig. 13.2 ABC analysis in graphical form

From Fig. 13.2 it can be observed that 80 % of expenditure is created by only 20 % of demand.

13.3.2 XYZ Analysis

Monetary value of capital commitment is not the only criterion to classify materials. Other criteria can be physical volume of items, demand patterns, or delivery time. For example, regarding the physical volume of items, it is possible to classify unwieldy items in group X and small and handy items in groups Y and Z. The principle will be the same as for ABC analysis. Another option for XYZ analysis is to divide inventory into three classes based on different demand patterns:

- Class X: constant, non-changing demand
- Class Y: neither constant nor sporadic demand (fluctuating demand)
- Class Z: sporadic or strongly fluctuating demand

Changes in demand make it possible to determine the prediction accuracy of each inventory class. Information on XYZ analysis provides the opportunity to develop strategies concerning alternative stocking arrangements, reorder calculations, and intervals of inventory control. Consider Fig. 13.3 to understand the connection between ABC and XYZ analysis.

XYZ analysis can be used to enhance ABC analysis. A combined ABC/XYZ analysis helps to define the purchasing method for different inventory classes and helps to determine which parts must be in stock, when they should be ordered JIT and when it is only viable for them to be ordered on a forecast basis.

Fig. 13.3 ABC/XYZ analysis

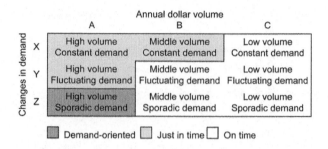

Table 13.3 Initial data for ABC/XYZ analysis

	Quantity	Cost per unit ($)	Annual expenditure	Volume per unit (in dm^3)	Total volume (in dm^3)
Blouses	120	200	24,000	1.00	120
Pantsuits	420	200	84,000	1.00	420
Jeans	50	200	10,000	2.00	100
Dresses and skirts	450	500	225,000	2.00	900
Costumes	280	1000	280,000	2.00	560
Fur coats	120	10,000	1,200,000	10.00	1200
Sport britches	10	80	800	2.00	20
T-Shirts	1200	80	96,000	0.50	600
Scarfs	100	50	5000	0.40	40
Underwear	500	75	37,500	0.02	10
Belts	600	95	57,000	0.05	30
Total	3850		2,019,300		4000

Task 13.2 ABC/XYZ Analysis

A Hollywood star is constantly complaining of the lack of space in her wardrobe that can be represented as Tables 13.3 and 13.4.

Perform a combined ABC/XYZ analysis to help the Hollywood star to gain at least 50 % of space and to reduce the expenditure by 70 %!

Solution. First, we sort the items according to their volume (see Table 13.5).
Second, we perform ABC analysis (Table 13.6).
Finally, we sort the items according to the XYZ classification in order to observe the potential for space reduction. Obviously, we will have to identify X-items and the percentage of never used X-items which are the primary candidates for leaving the wardrobe. In parallel, we will have to identify A-items since our second goal in this task is also to reduce the expenditure to 70 % (Table 13.7).

13.3 Material Analysis

Table 13.4 Initial data for ABC/XYZ analysis

	Quantity	Frequent use	Seldom use	No use	% of no use from quantity
Blouses	120	30	30	60	50.00 %
Pantsuits	420	100	120	200	47.62 %
Jeans	50	20		30	60.00 %
Dresses and skirts	450	10	20	420	93.33 %
Costumes	280	20	30	230	82.14 %
Fur coats	120	5	15	100	83.33 %
Sport britches	10	4	2	4	40.00 %
T-Shirts	1200	300	400	500	41.67 %
Scarfs	100	30	30	40	40.00 %
Underwear	500	200	100	200	40.00 %
Belts	600	200	200	200	33.33 %

Table 13.5 XYZ analysis

	Quantity	Volume per unit (in dm^3)	Total volume (in dm^3)	Percentage	Cumulative percentage
Fur coats	120	10	1200	30	30
Dresses and skirts	450	2	900	22.5	52.5
T-Shirts	1200	0.5	600	15	67.5
Costumes	280	2	560	14	81.5
Pantsuits	420	1	420	10.5	92
Blouses	120	1	120	3	95
Jeans	50	2	100	2.5	97.5
Scarfs	100	0.4	40	1	98.5
Belts	600	0.05	30	0.75	99.25
Sport britches	10	2	20	0.5	99.75
Underwear	500	0.02	10	0.25	1
Total	3850	20.97	4000	100.00 %	100 %

It can be observed that due to the high value, high volume, and high percentage of never used items, fur coats, dresses and skirts as well as costumes are key items to achieve both the objectives, i.e. value reduction of 70 % and space reduction of 50 %. The clearing of the wardrobe of never used fur coats, dresses and skirts as well as costumes will enable the Hollywood star both to reduce the value of the wardrobe items to 70 % and space to 50 %.

Table 13.6 ABC analysis

	Quantity	Cost per unit ($)	Annual Expenditure	Cumulative expenditure	Percentage expenditure	Category
Fur coats	120	10,000	1,200,000	1,200,000	59.4	A
Costumes	280	1000	280,000	1,480,000	73.3	A
Dresses and skirts	450	500	225,000	1,705,000	84.4	B
T-Shirts	1200	80	96,000	1,801,000	89.2	B
Pantsuits	420	200	84,000	1,885,000	93.4	B
Belts	600	95	57,000	1,942,000	96.2	C
Underwear	500	75	37,500	1,979,500	98.0	C
Blouses	120	200	24,000	2,003,500	99.2	C
Jeans	50	200	10,000	2,013,500	99.6	C
Scarfs	100	50	5000	2,018,500	99.7	C
Sport britches	10	80	800	2,019,300	100	C
Total	3850		2,019,300	2,019,300	100	

Table 13.7 Integrated ABC-XYZ analysis

	Quantity	% of never used items	Cumulative percentage (volume)	Space saving	ABC	Cost saving
Fur coats	120	50.00 %	30	25.00 %	A	1,000,000
Dresses and skirts	450	47.62 %	52.5	21.00 %	B	210,000
T-Shirts	1200	60.00 %	67.5	6.25 %	B	40,000
Costumes	280	93.33 %	81.5	11.50 %	A	230,000
Pantsuits	420	82.14 %	92	5.00 %	B	40,000
Blouses	120	83.33 %	95	1.50 %	C	12,000
Jeans	50	40.00 %	97.5	1.50 %	C	6000
Scarfs	100	41.67 %	98.5	0.40 %	C	2000
Belts	600	40.00 %	99.25	0.25 %	C	19,000
Sport britches	10	40.00 %	99.75	0.20 %	C	3200
Underwear	500	33.33 %	100	0.10 %	C	15,000
Total	3850		100 %	100 %		1,577,200

We thank Mr. Martin Pruy for preparing this task.

13.4 Deterministic Models

After having classified the items, the next step is to determine order quantities. In this section, we consider items with independent deterministic demand in the settings of the economy of scale, i.e., the *cycle inventory*. Why do we need to determine optimal order quantities? Theoretically, we could order each day exactly

13.4 Deterministic Models

the quantity that corresponds to the daily demand. However, in this case we would have each day ordering costs. We would also pay each day for transportation.

In most cases, it is reasonable to exploit *economy of scale* and order in large lots to reduce fixed ordering costs. We are going to learn how to determine when and how much to order. We will consider the following methods:

- Basic economic order quantity (EOQ)
- Economic production order quantity (EPQ)
- Quantity discount model
- Reorder point (ROP)

13.4.1 EOQ Model

Let us start with the *EOQ model*. It is simple and helps us to understand the relationship between ordering and holding costs. Consider the system that exhibits the following characteristics (see Fig. 13.4):

- Demand and lead-time are known and constant
- Receipt of inventory is instantaneous and complete
- Quantity discounts are not possible
- Only variable costs are setup and holding
- Stock-out can be avoided

We introduce the following notation:
q is the number of units per order
q^* is optimal number of units per order (EOQ)
b is annual demand in units for the inventory item
f is set-up or ordering cost for each order
c is holding or carrying cost per unit per year

Under the assumption of linear inventory consumption, cycle inventory and lot-sizes are related as follows in Eq. (13.2):

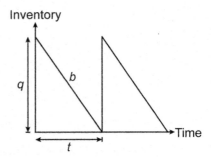

Fig. 13.4 Inventory consumption and replenishment pattern in EOQ model

$$\text{Cycle inventory} = \frac{q}{2}. \qquad (13.2)$$

This means that average inventory on hand is equal to 50 % of the order quantity.

$$\text{Then annual inventory holding costs is } c \cdot \frac{q}{2}. \qquad (13.3)$$

In order to calculate ordering costs we have to know the number of order per year. This number can be easily calculated as shown in Eq. (13.4):

$$\text{Number of orders per year} = \frac{b}{q} \qquad (13.4)$$

$$\text{Then, annual fixed ordering costs is} = f \cdot \frac{b}{q} \qquad (13.5)$$

Optimal order quantity is found when an annual ordering cost equals annual holding costs [see Eq. (13.6)]:

$$c \cdot \frac{q}{2} = f \cdot \frac{b}{q} \qquad (13.6)$$

In solving Eq. (13.6) for q*, we get the EOQ formula as follows [Eq. (13.7)]:

$$q^* = \sqrt{\frac{2b \cdot f}{c}} \qquad (13.7)$$

Consider graphical representation (see Fig. 13.5):

It can also be observed from the graph that the smallest total cost (the top curve) is the sum of the two curves below it. Minimal total costs are achieved at the

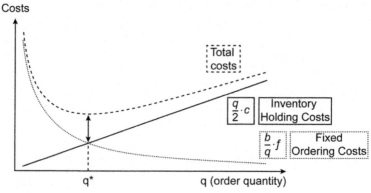

b: Demand   c: Holding costs per unit   f: Fixed costs

Fig. 13.5 Graphical representation of EOQ model

13.4 Deterministic Models

intersection point of the fixed and variable costs curves. This corresponds to the EOQ point q*. It can also been observed that total cost function is quite flat in the minimal region. This means that moderate EOQ changes will not influence a significant increase in total costs by tendency. This exemplifies useful *robustness property* of this method.

We can also determine expected number of orders per year [Eq. (13.8)] and expected time between orders [Eq. (13.9)]:

$$N = \frac{b}{q*} \qquad (13.8)$$

$$T = \frac{365}{N} \qquad (13.9)$$

Total annual cost is calculated as shown in Eq. (13.10):

$$TC = c \cdot \frac{q*}{2} + f \cdot \frac{b}{q*} \qquad (13.10)$$

Consider an example.

Task 13.3 EOQ
Demand for the Sakri2 LED TV at Amillos is 3200 units per quarter. Amillos charges fixed costs of $2500 per order. Annual holding costs per LED TV is $80. Calculate the number of LED TVs that the store manager should order per refill.

Solution
Annual demand: b = 3200 × 4 = 12,800 units; Ordering cost/order: f = $2500
Holding cost per unit per year: c = $80
Using the EOQ formula, the optimal order quantity is

$$q* = \sqrt{\frac{2 \cdot 12,800 \cdot 2500}{80}} = 895$$

To minimize total cost at Amillos, the store manager orders 895 LED TVs per refill. The cycle inventory is the average resulting inventory and is calculated as follows: cycle inventory = 895/2 ≈ 448 units
For an order size of q* = 895, the store manager evaluates:
Number of orders per year: N = 12,800/895 = 14.3
Expected time between orders: T = 365/14.3 = 25.5 days
Total cost: TC = 80 · 895/2 + 2500 · 12,800/895 = $71,554
Total cost for 1 year is $71,554 for 14.3 orders with 895 LED TVs in each order.

> ▶ **Practical Insights** The EOQ model was developed around the beginning of the twentieth century in the era of mass production and economy of scale. By that time, procurement processes were being

performed manually and were quite costly and time-consuming. Today, economy of flexibility and small lot-sizes exists in many industries and services. Transportation costs and SC coordination becomes more and more important. Procurement processes have been automated; many of them performed via the internet. A significant part of fixed ordering cost (telephone, fax, etc.) has been cut.

▶ **Practical Insights** In applying EOQ computation results and inventory control policies, practical reality needs to be considered. For example, in some cases suppliers fix the dates for new orders (e.g., each Friday) or allow the orders at fixed quantities (e.g., 50, 150 or 300 units) only.

Deliberate the following questions:

- Can we include transportation costs in the EOQ model?
- Is EOQ of each firm really an optimal solution for the whole SC?
- For which department is EOQ really "optimal"? (Just a hint: what happens with transportation costs, if EOQ decreases?)

Consider an example. EOQ is 40 units. This corresponds to 25 deliveries a year subject to annual demand of 1000 modules. Consider the following procedure for transportation costs determination: 400 € per delivery + 4 € per module. It is possible to transport up to 100 units at a time.

Costs Analysis for 100 Units
- Transportation costs = 10 deliveries · (400 + 4 · 100) = 8 € per unit
- Cycle inventory = (100/2) · 29 + (1000/100) · 23.2 = 1682 €
- Safety inventory = 1.65 · 4 · 10 = 66 items · 29 = 1914 €
- Total costs per module: 11.6 €

Costs Analysis for 40 Units
- Transportation costs = 25 deliveries · (400 + 4 · 40) = 14 € per unit
- Cycle inventory = (40/2) · 29 + (1000/40) · 23.2 = 1160 €
- Safety inventory = 1.65 · 4 · 10 = 66 units · 29 = 1914 €
- Total costs per module: 17.1 €

Conclusion: EOQ is not optimal in the integrated inventory–transportation setting. At the lot-size 100 units, total costs are reduced from 17.1 € to 11.6 € per unit. For annual demand of 1000 modules, the cost savings is 5500 €.

13.4.2 EOQ Model with Discounts

Inventory costs can also be calculated on the basis of the unit prices p (i.e., actual costs of the material purchased) as shown in Eq. (13.11):

13.4 Deterministic Models

$$\text{Costs}(q) = p_1(1-r_1)b + \frac{q}{2}p_1(1-r_1)I + \frac{b}{q}f \qquad (13.11)$$

In this case for calculating EOQ, Eq. (13.12) is used:

$$q^* = \sqrt{\frac{2 \cdot b \cdot f}{p \cdot I}}, \qquad (13.12)$$

where I is the *interest rate (capital commitment)* and p is the unit price.

As such, different prices can be included in the analysis. This allows us to apply the EOQ model for situations with quantity discounts. Reduced prices are often available when larger quantities are purchased. In this case, the *trade-off* is between reduced item cost and increased holding cost.

The *algorithm of calculating EOQ with discounts* involves the following steps:

- For each discount, calculate q*.
- If q* does not qualify for a discount, choose the smallest possible order size to get the discount.
- Compute the total cost for each q* or adjusted value from Step 2.
- Select the q* that gives the lowest total cost.

Task 13.4 EOQ with Discounts

Carlo Inc. operates a chocolate shop in New York. The chocolate is ordered from a supplier in Switzerland. Normally cost for one unit of chocolate is $5.00, but a quantity discount is provided by the manufacturer (see Table 13.8).

Carlo Inc.'s annual demand for chocolate is 10,000 units and the setup cost per order is $50. Interest rate is 20 %.

Solution:

$$\text{For discount } 0\%, q^* = \sqrt{\frac{2 \cdot 10,000 \cdot 50}{5 \cdot 0.2}} = 1000$$

$$\text{Costs}(1000) = 5 \cdot (1-0) \cdot 10,000$$
$$+ \frac{1000}{2} \cdot 5(1-0) \cdot 0.2 + \frac{10,000}{1000} \cdot 50 = \$51,000$$

Table 13.8 Initial data for EOQ calculation with discounts

Discount quantity in units	Discount in %	Discount price p
0–999	0	$5.00
1000–1999	4	$4.80
2000–10,000	10	$4.50

For discount 4%, $q^* = \sqrt{\dfrac{2 \cdot 10{,}000 \cdot 50}{4.8 \cdot 0.2}} = 1021$

$q^* = 1021$ units qualifies for the interval [1000–1999] units and therefore can be used for costs calculation:

$Costs(1021) = 5 \cdot (1 - 0.04) \cdot 10{,}000$
$+ \dfrac{1021}{2} \cdot 5(1 - 0.04) \cdot 0.2 + \dfrac{10{,}000}{1021} \cdot 50 = \$48{,}980$

For discount 10%, $q^* = \sqrt{\dfrac{2 \cdot 10{,}000 \cdot 50}{4.5 \cdot 0.2}} = 1054$

$q^* = 1054$ units does not qualify for the interval [2000–10,000] units and therefore the smallest possible order size to get the discount of 10 % should be used for costs calculations:

$Costs(2000) = 5 \cdot (1 - 0.1) \cdot 10{,}000$
$+ \dfrac{2000}{2} \cdot 5(1 - 0.1) \cdot 0.2 + \dfrac{10{,}000}{2000} \cdot 50 = \$46{,}150$

It can be observed that we have the lowest total cost with 2000 units of chocolate per order. We can also determine an expected number of orders per year $N = 10{,}000/2000 = 5$ and expected time between orders: $T = 365/5 = 73$.

13.4.3 EPQ Model

The EPQ model is fairly similar to the EOQ model but it is applied to manufacturing. This model is used when:

- inventory builds up over a period of time after an order is placed
- units are produced and sold simultaneously.

In the EPQ model, we realize the assumption that receipt of inventory is instantaneous and complete. Now we are allowing receipt of inventory *over a period of time* and introduce three new parameters:

- r is daily production rate
- d is daily demand
- t is the length of the production run in days

Setup costs remain unchanged; holding costs are now calculated subject to the relation of production and demand as follows [Eq. (13.13)]:

$$c \cdot \dfrac{q}{2}[1 - (d/r)] \tag{13.13}$$

13.4 Deterministic Models

For example, if we produce each day the quantity that corresponds exactly to the daily demand, we will not have any holding costs (the expression in brackets will always equal zero) but we will have very high set-up costs.

Then, the following EPQ formula (13.14) can be stated as follows:

$$q^* = \sqrt{\frac{2b \cdot f}{(1 - d/r) \cdot c}} \qquad (13.14)$$

Maximal inventory level in the system can be calculated as per Eq. (13.15):

$$I_{max} = q\left(1 - \frac{b}{r}\right) \qquad (13.15)$$

Note: in EPQ, we consider daily demand. If we are given annual demand it should be divided through number of working days.

Consider an example.

Task 13.5 EPQ

Natural Inc. produces high-quality food processors. It sells 18,000 processors per year and is able to produce 125 machines per day. Natural Inc. is working on 250 days per year. Annual holding cost per food processor is $18 and setup cost is $800. Calculate the economic production quantity for Natural Inc. and the maximal inventory level.

Solution

d = 18,000/250 = 72 units per day

$$q^* = \sqrt{\frac{2 \cdot 18,000 \cdot 800}{(1 - 72/125) \cdot 18}} = 1943 \quad I_{max} = 1943\left(1 - \frac{72}{125}\right) = 824$$

It can be observed that the optimal lot-size is 1943 units. At this quantity, minimal setup and holding costs can be achieved. Taking into account the actual consumption rate of 72 units a day and production rate of 125 units a day, maximal inventory level in the system will be 824 units.

13.4.4 Re-order Point

The EOQ model answers the "how much" question. The *re-order point* (ROP) tells "when" to order. ROP is introduced to take into account the so called *lead time*, i.e. the time between placement and receipt of an order (see Fig. 13.6).

With the assumption of constant demand and during lead time and lead time itself, ROP is calculated as in Eq. (13.16):

$$ROP = d \cdot L, \qquad (13.16)$$

where d is daily demand and L is lead time.

Fig. 13.6 Re-order point

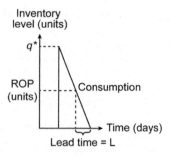

Note: In ROP, we consider daily demand. If we are given annual demand it should be divided through the number of working days in a year. Consider an example.

Task 13.6 Re-order Point
A company experiences an annual demand of 8500 cheese knives per year (250 working days). Lead time for an order is 5 working days. Calculate the ROP and explain its meaning.

Solution

1. Daily demand $= 8500/250 = 34$ units
2. ROP $= 34 \cdot 5 = 170$ units

After selling 170 cheese knives we have to place a new order.

13.5 Stochastic Models

We already know how to determine order quantities and ROPs for situations where demand and lead time are deterministic. However, in many practical cases, both demand and lead time are fluctuating. We do not know their determined values, but can only estimate them on the probability basis. For such cases, *stochastic (probabilistic)* models are needed.

13.5.1 Service Level and Safety Stock

Imagine that on one Saturday evening you are sitting at home and notice that you have only 16 nappies left for your baby. You are in a province city in Germany where all stores are closed on Sunday. You recall that normally you need eight nappies a day. Normally, you would need three nappies for the rest of Saturday, eight for Sunday, and three for the Monday morning until the stores open again. So

13.5 Stochastic Models

normally 16 nappies would be enough and you would not need to go out now to buy a new packet of nappies (the stores close in 1 h and it is rainy). But what will happen if the demand on nappies increases and deviates from the mean value? So here the trade-off in your decision is to balance the risk of being out of stock and the additional costs for driving the car to the store and spending your time.

Uncertainty in demand makes it necessary in SCOM to maintain a certain customer service level or *level of product availability* to avoid stock-outs. Level of product availability is the fraction of demand that is served on time from a product held in inventory. A high level of product availability provides a high level of *responsiveness* but increases cost because a much inventory is held but rarely used. In contrast, a low level of product availability lowers inventory holding cost but results in a higher fraction of customers who are not served on time. The basic trade-off when determining the level of product availability is between the cost of inventory to increase product availability and the loss from not serving customers on time.

For example, 0.05 probability of stock-out corresponds to a 95 % service level (see Fig. 13.7). In a situation of demand uncertainty, *safety inventory* is introduced. It can be observed from Fig. 13.6 that ROP is enlarged by the safety stock subject to a 95 % service level. In order to calculate service level, Eq. (13.17) is used:

$$ss = z \cdot \sigma_{dLT}, \qquad (13.17)$$

where ss is safety stock, σ_{dLT} is standard deviation of demand during lead-time and z is the number of standard deviations.

Demand deviation can be gleaned, e.g., from the analysis of demand forecasts and actual sales in the past. For example, $\sigma = 1.25 MAD$ is a typical value. Z-value can easily be determined (see Table 13.9).

For example, $z = 1.65$ for service level 95 %, $z = 2.33$ for service level 99 %, and $z = 1.28$ for service level 90 %. If standard deviation of demand during lead time is 10, then safety stocks equals $1.65 \cdot 10 = 16.5$; $2.33 \cdot 10 = 23.3$; $1.28 \cdot 10 = 12.8$.

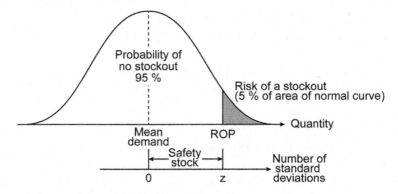

Fig. 13.7 Interrelation of demand distribution, ROP, service level and safety stock [adapted from Heizer and Render (2013)]

Table 13.9 Table of normal distribution

z	0.00	0.01	0.02	0.03	0.04	0.05	0.06	0.07	0.08	0.09
0.0	0.5000	0.5040	0.5080	0.5120	0.5160	0.5199	0.5239	0.5279	0.5319	0.5359
0.1	0.5398	0.5438	0.5478	0.5517	0.5557	0.5596	0.5636	0.5675	0.5714	0.5753
0.2	0.5793	0.5832	0.5871	0.5910	0.5948	0.5987	0.6026	0.6064	0.6103	0.6141
0.3	0.6179	0.6217	0.6255	0.6293	0.6331	0.6368	0.6406	0.6443	0.6480	0.6517
0.4	0.6554	0.6591	0.6628	0.6664	0.6700	0.6736	0.6772	0.6808	0.6844	0.6879
0.5	0.6915	0.6950	0.6985	0.7019	0.7054	0.7088	0.7123	0.7157	0.7190	0.7224
0.6	0.7257	0.7291	0.7324	0.7357	0.7389	0.7422	0.7454	0.7486	0.7517	0.7549
0.7	0.7580	0.7611	0.7642	0.7673	0.7704	0.7734	0.7764	0.7794	0.7823	0.7852
0.8	0.7881	0.7910	0.7939	0.7967	0.7995	0.8023	0.8051	0.8078	0.8106	0.8133
0.9	0.8159	0.8186	0.8212	0.8238	0.8264	0.8289	0.8315	0.8340	0.8365	0.8389
1.0	0.8413	0.8438	0.8461	0.8485	0.8508	0.8531	0.8554	0.8577	0.8599	0.8621
1.1	0.8643	0.8665	0.8686	0.8708	0.8729	0.8749	0.8770	0.8790	0.8810	0.8830
1.2	0.8849	0.8869	0.8888	0.8907	0.8925	0.8944	0.8962	0.8980	0.8997	0.9015
1.3	0.9032	0.9049	0.9066	0.9082	0.9099	0.9115	0.9031	0.9147	0.9162	0.9177
1.4	0.9192	0.9207	0.9222	0.9236	0.9251	0.9265	0.9279	0.9292	0.9306	0.9319
1.5	0.9332	0.9345	0.9357	0.9370	0.9382	0.9394	0.9406	0.9418	0.9429	0.9441
1.6	0.9452	0.9463	0.9474	0.9484	0.9495	0.9505	0.9515	0.9525	0.9535	0.9545
1.7	0.9554	0.9564	0.9573	0.9582	0.9591	0.9599	0.9608	0.9616	0.9625	0.9633
1.8	0.9641	0.9649	0.9656	0.9664	0.9671	0.9678	0.9686	0.9693	0.9699	0.9706
1.9	0.9713	0.9719	0.9726	0.9732	0.9738	0.9744	0.9750	0.9756	0.9761	0.9767
2.0	0.9772	0.9778	0.9783	0.9788	0.9793	0.9798	0.9803	0.9808	0.9812	0.9817
2.1	0.9821	0.9826	0.9830	0.9834	0.9838	0.9842	0.9846	0.9850	0.9854	0.9857
2.2	0.9861	0.9864	0.9868	0.9871	0.9875	0.9878	0.9881	0.9884	0.9887	0.9890
2.3	0.9893	0.9896	0.9898	0.9901	0.9904	0.9906	0.9909	0.9911	0.9913	0.9916
2.4	0.9918	0.9920	0.9922	0.9924	0.9927	0.9929	0.9931	0.9932	0.9934	0.9936
2.5	0.9938	0.9940	0.9941	0.9943	0.9945	0.9946	0.9948	0.9949	0.9951	0.9952
2.6	0.9953	0.9955	0.9956	0.9957	0.9958	0.9960	0.9961	0.9962	0.9963	0.9964
2.7	0.9965	0.9966	0.9967	0.9968	0.9969	0.9970	0.9971	0.9972	0.9973	0.9974
2.8	0.9974	0.9975	0.9976	0.9977	0.9977	0.9978	0.9979	0.9979	0.9980	0.9981
2.9	0.9981	0.9982	0.9982	0.9983	0.9984	0.9984	0.9985	0.9985	0.9986	0.9986

We can observe that the increase of service level from 90 % to 99 % results in doubling the inventory.

> ▶ **Practical Insights** The service level is determined subject to SC strategy (efficient vs responsive). The higher the service level, the higher the SC responsiveness, but also the higher inventory costs. If managers were to set up the service level to 100% this would mean that each customer order would be satisfied from the inventory without delay. However, 100 % service level would result in a huge inventory. This cost can scatter positive effects from high customer satisfaction. That is why service level is typically set up at less than 100 %.

Another important issue is that stock-outs can be objective and subjective. For example, the absence of a certain sort of milk in a supermarket does not automatically mean that milk is missing totally since other sorts are available. In retail, 3–8 % of stock-out is typical and results not only from false inventory planning but could also be for many other reasons, e.g., false shelf placement.

The inclusion of safety stock changes the calculation of ROP [see Eq. (13.18)]:

13.5 Stochastic Models

$$ROP = d \cdot L + ss \tag{13.18}$$

In order to calculate ROP, four situations are possible:

- demand is assumed to be normally distributed during the lead time,
- daily distribution of demand is given (i.e., demand is variable) and lead time is constant,
- daily demand is constant and lead time is variable,
- both demand and lead time are variable.

In order to calculate ROP if demand is assumed to be normally distributed during the lead time, formula (13.19) can be used:

$$ROP = d \cdot L + z \cdot \sigma_{dLT} \tag{13.19}$$

If daily distribution of demand is given (i.e., demand is variable) and lead time is constant, formula (13.20) can be used:

$$ROP = d \cdot L + z \cdot \sigma_d \cdot \sqrt{L} \tag{13.20}$$

If daily demand is constant and lead time is variable, formula (13.21) can be used:

$$ROP = d \cdot L + z \cdot \sigma_L \tag{13.21}$$

▶ **Practical Insights** Equation (13.21) nicely provides evidence of importance to reduce the lead time variability. We can observe that lead time variability reduction directly influences the safety stock level. This observation depicts the integration of supplier selection, contracting, and inventory management decisions.

Finally, if both demand and lead time are variable, formula (13.22) can be used:

$$ROP = d \cdot L + z\sqrt{L \cdot \sigma_d^2 + d^2 \cdot \sigma_L^2} \tag{13.22}$$

Consider an example.

Task 13.7. ROP with Safety Stock
Average demand for toothbrushes is 35 units per day. Standard deviation of normally distributed demand during lead time is ten toothbrushes per day. Lead time is 3 days. Service level is 95 %. Calculate ROP and safety stock.

Solution

$$\begin{aligned} ROP &= 35 \cdot 3 + 1.65 \cdot 10 = 122 \text{ units}; \text{ Safety stock is } 1.65 \cdot 10 \\ &= 16.5 \text{ units} \end{aligned}$$

Now we assume that we are given daily distribution of demand instead of standard deviation of normally distributed demand during lead time. Consider ten units as daily standard deviation of demand and calculate ROP:

Solution

$$ROP = 35 \cdot 3 + 1.65 \cdot 10 \cdot \sqrt{3} = 134 \text{ units}$$

Next consider a situation where demand is constant but lead-time may fluctuate with standard deviation of one day. Calculate ROP.

Solution

$$ROP = 35 \cdot 3 + 1.65 \cdot 35 \cdot 1 = 163$$

Finally we assume that both demand and lead-time are variable. Calculate ROP.

Solution

$$ROP = 35 \cdot 3 + 1.65 \sqrt{3 \cdot 10^2 + 35^2 \cdot 1^2} = 170$$

▶ **Practical Insights** Practical implementation of the statistical methods to inventory management is not easy. In many companies, decisions have been taken manually for many years on the basis of expert knowledge. In this case, it can be reasonable to allow re-writing of the calculated results in software manually to start working with new technology. As practice shows, in a short period of time, inventory managers will see the advantages of the new system and accept 95 % of automatically generated orders.

13.5.2 Single Period Systems ("Newsvendor Problem")

The newsvendor problem is a mathematical model for calculating the optimal inventory level for one single period. It is called the news-boy or newsvendor problem. A newspaper vendor who must decide every day how many daily newspapers he wants to stock for the next day is faced by uncertain demand and knowing that unsold copies will be almost worthless next day.

The newsvendor problem is characterized by the following conditions:

- fixed price for each unit,
- perishable product,
- uncertain demand,
- no additional delivery in period t,
- short purchase time.

13.5 Stochastic Models

Consider the following notation for single period model:
- c is purchase price
- r is retail price
- v is salvage price
- c_o is overage cost
- c_u is underage cost
- z is number of standard deviations
- σ is standard deviation of demand
- μ is expectation of demand
- S is order quantity
- S^* is optimal order quantity
- $Z(S^*)$ is expected cost for optimal order quantity
- $\prod(S^*)$ is expected profit for optimal order quantity

To calculate the *overage* and *underage cost* we can use the Eqs. (13.23) and (13.24):

$$c_o = c - v \quad (13.23)$$

$$c_u = r - c \quad (13.24)$$

Then we use the *critical ratio* (CR) to find z-value from the table of normal distribution [Eq. (13.25)]:

$$CR = \frac{c_u}{c_u + c_o}; F(CR) = z \quad (13.25)$$

For example, $CR = \frac{0.75}{0.75 + 0.25}; F(0.75) = 0.68 = z$

Next step is the calculation of S* according to Eq. (13.26):

$$S^* = \mu + z \cdot \sigma \quad (13.26)$$

In order to calculate the expected cost and profit for optimal order quantity, Eqs. (13.27) and (13.28) can be used:

$$Z(S^*) = (c_o + c_u) \cdot f_{01}(z) \cdot \sigma \quad (13.27)$$

$$\Pi(S^*) = c_u \cdot (\mu - Z(S^*)) \quad (13.28)$$

Consider an example:

Task 13.8 Newsvendor Problem

Coff&Co., a coffee shop, sells vegan chocolate croissants. They purchase the croissants from a small bakery shop at the end of the street. The bakery shop sells chocolate croissants to Coff&Co. for $0.70 each. Coff&Co. sells them for $2.40 to their customers. Unsold croissants can be returned to the bakery for $0.15 each. On the basis of the last months, Coff&Co. expects a normal distributed demand for chocolate croissants. Expectation of demand is 14 croissants per day and a standard deviation is four per day. Calculate the optimal order quantity, expected cost and profit for the chocolate croissants.

Solution

$$\text{Overage cost}: c_o = c - v = 0.70 - 0.15 = \$0.55$$
$$\text{Underage cost } c_u = 2.40 - 0.70 = \$1.70$$
$$CR = \frac{1.70}{1.70 + 0.55} = 0.75; F(0.7556) = 0.7 = z$$

$S^* = 14 + 0.7 \cdot 4 = 17$ units; therefore Coff&Co. should order 17 vegan chocolate croissants per day.

$Z(S^*) = (0.55 + 1.70) \cdot f_{01}(0.7) \cdot 4 = \$2.81/day$; so expected cost is \$2.81 per day.

$\Pi(S^*) = 1.70 \cdot (14 - 2.81) = \$20.99/day$; so expected profit is \$20.99 per day.

Note: $f_{01}(z)$ value can be taken from the full version of normal distribution table.

13.5.3 Safety Stock and Transportation Strategy: Case DailyMaersk

This case study focuses on the impact of a global transportation concept on inventory management on the example of the Daily Maersk. It illustrates how the sea-leg part of SCs relates to shippers' inventory management at destination countries. It shows that Daily Maersk can offer substantial benefits to shippers in terms of safety stock reduction.

Maersk Line is part of Denmark's largest corporation, the Copenhagen-based Maersk Group. Within the Maersk Group, Maersk Line makes up roughly half of the revenues, making it the group's largest segment. Maersk Line operates in the container shipping industry, offering liner services between seaports. It is the largest container line worldwide with a fleet of 576 vessels. Normally, customers can be split into either direct customers (producers) or forwarders (e.g. Kuehne&Nagel, DHL, DB Schenker) who book slots for the cargo on container vessels to the respective locations.

In 2011, Maersk announced the introduction of Daily Maersk, a first-of-its-kind concept offering daily departures from key ports in Asia to key ports in Europe, instead of departures only once a week. Maersk started by offering a daily departure instead of as formerly only weekly departures from Asian key ports Shanghai, Ningbo, Yantian (all Chinese) and Tanjung Pelepas (Malaysia) to Felixstowe (UK), Rotterdam (Netherlands) and Bremerhaven (Germany) (Fig. 13.8).

Consider an example. The sea journey from Yantian to Felixstowe takes on average 30 days; now one departure of a Maersk vessel is offered each day instead of only once a week. We assume constant demand of 10 units a day, 98 % service level, and normally distributed lead-time from Yantian to Felixstowe. The safety stock (ss) at destination (Felixstowe) can be then defined as

$$ss = z \cdot d \cdot \sigma_{LT}, \qquad (13.29)$$

where z is number of standard deviations, d is daily demand and σ_{LT} is standard deviation of lead time.

13.5 Stochastic Models

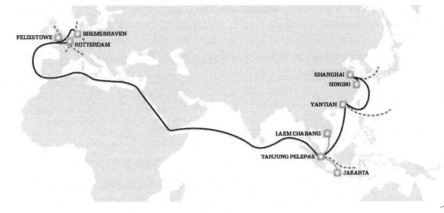

Fig. 13.8 Daily Maersk's transportation network

First, the analysis of lead-time has been performed for weekly departures. It showed that standard deviation of lead-time for weekly departure is 2 days. Subsequently, the analysis of lead-time has been performed for daily departures and showed standard deviation of lead-time for daily departure of 0.3 days.

Assuming a service level at 98 % and daily demand of 10 units, safety stocks can be calculated as follows:

$$\text{ss (weekly departure)} = 2.055 \cdot 10 \cdot 2.0 = 41.1 \text{ units}$$
$$\text{ss (daily departure)} = 2.055 \cdot 10 \cdot 0.3 = 6.2 \text{ units}$$

The calculation above shows that safety stock level falls significantly due to Daily Maersk concept with only 6.2 units required in stock versus 41.1 units in a weekly service. This translates into lower inventory costs for direct customers or intermediaries such as forwarders at destination points and offers a measurable benefit to Maersk Line's customers.

Discussion Questions

What impact does daily vessel departures have on inventory?

Daily vessel departures have two impacts: (1) lower average lead time (due to shorter average waiting time at port of origin); and (2) a lower standard deviation of lead time (as the increased sailing frequency leads to a high probability of catching a vessel within 24 h, even if a vessel is missed for one day).

Which other factors could be included in this analysis?

We restricted our analysis only to sailing lead-time and included no other elements of lead time (thus ignoring e.g., hinterland transportation).

Why is Maersk Line able to provide the daily service and what risks might be encountered?

As the largest player in the market, Maersk exploits the economy of scale, being among the few able to offer sufficient capacity for daily departures. To offer a daily instead of a weekly departure, Maersk Line must deploy more vessels instead of only one on respective routes, demanding much higher investment in containerships. Its environmental footprint can be assumed higher, as a larger number of vessels travels on the same route. Maersk faces the risk of not being able to fully utilize the increased capacity on Daily Maersk routes. This risk can be reduced by re-routing of other services.

13.6 Inventory Control Policies

Inventory control policy is a managerial procedure that helps to define how much and when to order. The review may happen periodically (e.g., at the end of a month) or continuously (i.e., tracking each item and updating inventory levels each time an item is removed from inventory). Four parameters are important in the setting up of inventory control policies:

- t is replenishment interval
- q is order quantity
- s is re-order point
- S is target inventory level.

Since order quantity and replenishment interval may be both fixed and variable, four basic inventory control policies can be classified (see Fig. 13.9).

If the period between two orders is always the same, we talk about *periodic review systems*. If the point of time of the next replenishment depends on the ROP, we talk about ROP method of stock control or *continuous review system*. The above-mentioned four parameters can be fixed or changed (adjusted) in dynamics regarding the changes in demand and supply. Therefore, *static* and *dynamic* views on inventory control policies can be considered.

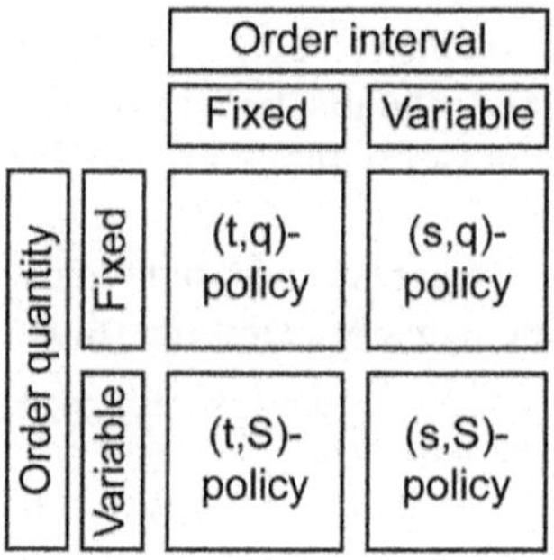

Fig. 13.9 Inventory control policies

		Order interval	
		Fixed	Variable
Order quantity	Fixed	(t,q)-policy	(s,q)-policy
	Variable	(t,S)-policy	(s,S)-policy

13.6.1 Fixed Parameters

In case where replenishment interval, order quantity, ROP, and target inventory level are fixed, the following policies can be classified.

Policy 1: t,q
- t: fixed time between two orders
- q: fixed order quantity

In (t,q) policy, a fixed amount (q) is ordered accordingly for a fixed period of time (t) (see Fig. 13.10).

(t,q) is a simple policy for handling the ordering process. This policy opens possibilities to further automatic control, which improves quality and saves resources, such as labour, energy or materials. However, (t,q)-policy is inflexible and used very seldom in the business. Should uncertainty or fluctuation in demand exist, this policy cannot be adjusted. In addition, shortage or overstocking make (t,q)-policy an unattractive tool for many companies. Thus, it is recommended to implement this policy under constant demand.

Policy 2: t,S
- T: fixed time between two orders
- Q: variable order quantity to stock up to the target level S

In the (t,S)-policy, the order quantity (q) is variable, q is placed at a fixed time (t). We need to order a certain amount of inventory to reach the desired quantity S subject to lead-time (lt). Order quantity is calculated as the target level S—stock on hand (see Fig. 13.11).

This policy avoids excessive inventory, which cannot be used for any other purpose and thus involves opportunity costs. The model is easy to use for control of

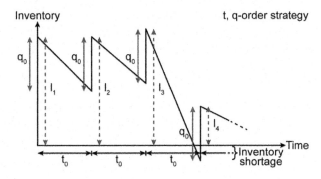

Fig. 13.10 (t,q)-inventory control policy

Fig. 13.11 (t,S)-inventory control policy

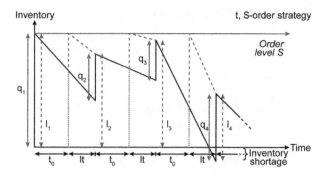

orders. However, the physical control of the inventory could be so expensive that the exact count is only performed for example once a month. In certain cases the (*t,S*)-policy can lead to relatively high capital commitment because of high average inventory. This policy also implies high ordering costs because we might not place a large order on the fixed day. At the same time, we might need to wait too long to fulfil our target inventory and thus shortage can occur. The (*t,S*)-policy is recommended for use in companies with a cycled replenishment.

Policy 3: s,q
- t: variable time between two orders
- q: fixed order quantity.

This model operates when order quantity (*q*) is fixed and interval (t) between orders can vary. In this case, the order point (*s*) is defined as ROP (see Fig. 13.12). Every order arrives to replenish inventory after a *lead time*. The lead time is assumed known and constant. The only uncertainty is associated with demand. In the following analysis one should be most concerned with the possibility of shortage during an order cycle, that is, when the inventory level falls below zero. This is also called the stock-out event. Every time we extract inventory, we compare what is left with *s*.

Note: for calculating the ROP, Eq. (13.20) should be slightly modified to take into account the replenishment interval [see Eq. (13.30)]:

$$ROP = d \cdot (T+L) + z \cdot \sigma \cdot \sqrt{(T+L)} \tag{13.30}$$

If the stock level is less than *s*, then we place an order at the rate of *q*. Similar to (*t, q*)-policy, in (*s,q*)-policy, *q* refers also to the optimal order quantity. The policy (*s,q*) results in shorter time between orders if there is inventory shortage. Because of its simple operation and full control over results this policy is broadly spread in

13.6 Inventory Control Policies

Fig. 13.12 (s,q)-inventory control policy

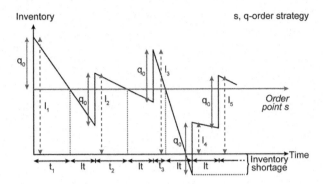

organizations. An advantage of the model is that it considers demand fluctuations. Disadvantages lie in regular inventory control.

Policy 4: s,S
- t: variable time between two orders
- q: variable order quantity between the order level S and ROP s.

This strategy is used to define the drop of order quantity s after every inventory usage. Should it be the case, a manager should re-fill inventory to raise the inventory position to the level S, which is desirable property (see Fig. 13.13).

Therefore, both order quantity and the time interval between orders is variable. This system can handle any level of demand and at any time include demand fluctuations in the planning. Target level is calculated as Eq. (13.31):

$$S = (ROP + q) - \text{min rate of usage} \cdot \text{lead time} \quad (13.31)$$

Order policy (s,S) avoids excessive level of inventory and ensures that the business has the right goods on hand to avoid stock-outs. However, this policy requires much effort and high control. It is used in industrial and commercial areas of business, given the fact that flexible order quantity is possible and target quantity can be predetermined.

Task 13.9 Inventory Control Policy

Consider the given data and determine parameters and annual holding costs for (s,S)-policy for 95 % and 98 % service level respectively:

- demand per day (d)
  100 units

Fig. 13.13 (s,S)-inventory control policy

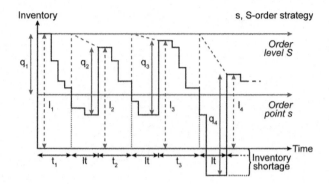

- standard daily deviation of demand (σ)
  20 units
- annual holding costs (h)
  $10 per unit
- fixed ordering costs (f)
  $100 per order
- order interval (T)
  4 weeks
- lead time (L)
  2 weeks

Solution

1. Find z-values for 95 % and 98 % service level; we get 1.65 and 2.05 respectively.
2.
$$ss = z \cdot \sigma \cdot \sqrt{(T+L)} = 1.65 \cdot 20 \cdot \sqrt{4+2} = 81 \text{ units.}$$
3.
$$ROP = 100 \cdot (4+2) + 81 = 681 \text{ units.}$$
4. $S = ROP + q$; $q^* = \sqrt{\frac{2 \cdot 36500 \cdot 100}{10}} = 855$ units; $S = 681 + 855 = 1536$ units.
5. The policy is (681;1536); Average inventory position is $(681 + 1536)/2 = 1108$.
6. Costs $= 1108 \cdot 10 = \$11{,}082$.
7. $ss = 2.05 \cdot 20 \cdot \sqrt{4+2} = 100$; $ROP = 100 \cdot (4+2) + 100 = 700$ units.
8. $S = ROP + q$; $q^* = \sqrt{\frac{2 \cdot 36500 \cdot 100}{10}} = 855$ units; $S = 700 + 855 = 1555$ units.
9. The policy is (700;1555); Average inventory position is $(700 + 1555)/2 = 1128$.
10. Costs $= 1128 \cdot 10 = \$11{,}282$.

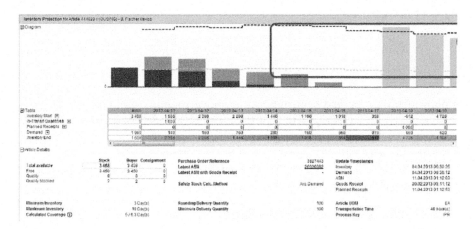

Fig. 13.14 Dynamic view of inventory control (based on SupplyOn VMI solution, used with permission)

13.6.2 Dynamic View

In case where replenishment interval, order quantity, ROP, and target inventory level are not fixed, but change in dynamics subject to changes in demand, the following changes to the above-mentioned policies need to be considered. We have to take into account demand, current and projected inventory, in-transit quantities as well as planned deliveries (see Fig. 13.14).

It can be observed from Fig. 13.14 that both target inventory level and re-order point change in dynamics subject to changes in demand. The calculation basis is the planned days of supply.

13.7 Dynamic Lot-Sizing Models

We already know how to manage inventory with both deterministic and stochastic demand. However, our previous discussion addressed one period problems. Now we will consider *multi-period* problems. Assume that you need tickets for the tram, say 20 tickets for a month. You can buy all of them right at the beginning of the month. In this case, you spend your time for buying tickets only once but you invest quite a lot of money at a time. Alternatively, you can buy tickets every day. Your capital commitment will be lower but you will spend more time.

In multi-period problems, the parameters (e.g., demand, lead time, costs) can vary in different periods. In addition, inventory from the previous periods can be used to cover demand in future. That is why the basic *trade-off in multi-period models* is how to balance inventory holding costs and ordering costs over time.

Dynamic lot-sizing models help us to decide in every period if we should order/ produce only for one period or if we should build lot-sizes over several periods together to minimize order and holding costs. These models can be divided into two

Table 13.10 Demand data

t	1	2	3	4	5	6
b_t	500	200	600	300	200	100

groups: optimization and heuristics. An example for optimization is the Wagner-Whitin model, which is a generalization of the EOQ model considering changes in demand over time. The second group contains the heuristics, e.g., Silver-Meal heuristic, the least unit cost heuristic and the part-period heuristic.

To explain the different dynamic lot-sizing models we use an example to show the different procedures and results.

Task 13.10 Dynamic Lot-Sizing Problem
Sheeran Ltd reveals the following periodic demand for a material they need for their production (Table 13.10):

Orders take place at the beginning of each period and the product is immediately available. Every order generates fixed cost f of \$100 and there are holding costs c per unit per period of \$0.5.

13.7.1 Least Unit Cost Heuristic

Least unit cost heuristic is based on average unit cost per period K_t^{unit}. For the calculation of the average costs for the first period we can use Eq. (13.32):

$$K_1^{unit} = \frac{f_1}{b_1} \tag{13.32}$$

In the second step, the task is to find out if it is more efficient to order the material for period #1 and period #2 jointly in the first period. To find out the average unit cost jointly for the first and second period we use Eq. (13.33):

$$K_{1,2}^{unit} = \frac{f_1 + b_2 \cdot c}{b_1 + b_2} \tag{13.33}$$

We continue with this extension until we reach the minimum of the average costs. This means that as soon as the cost increases we stop the calculation and start from the beginning with the next period onwards.

An example:

$$K_{1,1}^{unit} = \frac{100}{500} = 0.2 \quad K_{1,2}^{unit} = \frac{100 + 200 \cdot 0.5}{500 + 200} = 0.286$$

13.7 Dynamic Lot-Sizing Models

We can see the average cost per unit increases so we decide not to order the demand for period #1 and period #2 together. Instead of ordering them together we start the calculation with period #2 again and order in period #1 only the material for this single period:

$$K_{2,2}^{unit} = \frac{100}{200} = 0.5 \quad K_{2,3}^{unit} = \frac{100 + 600 \cdot 0.5}{200 + 600} = 0.5$$

Because the average unit cost remains at the same level we continue the calculation:

$$K_{2,4}^{unit} = \frac{100 + 600 \cdot 0.5 + 300 \cdot 2 \cdot 0.5}{200 + 600 + 300} = 0.636$$

Note: since the inventory for period #3 is hold over two periods, we multiply $(300 \cdot 0.5)$ by 2.

In the case we might want to order material in period #2 for periods #3, 4 and 5 jointly and start the calculation for period #4 again.

$$K_{4,4}^{unit} = \frac{100}{300} = 0.33 \quad K_{4,5}^{unit} = \frac{100 + 200 \cdot 0.5}{300 + 200} = 0.4$$

The average cost increases again so we decide to order only the material for period 4 and not for periods #4 and #5 together.

$$K_{5,5}^{unit} = \frac{100}{200} = 0.5 \quad K_{5,6}^{unit} = \frac{100 + 100 \cdot 0.5}{200 + 100} = 0.5$$

In the result, order quantities for each period are determined as follows:

$$q_1 = 500; \ q_2 = 800; \ q_3 = 0; \ q_4 = 300; \ q_5 = 300; \ q_6 = 0$$

In order to calculate the total cost we add up the fixed ordering costs for every order and the holding costs for every period in which we generate them:

$$K^{total} = 4 \cdot 100 + (600 \cdot 0.5) + (100 \cdot 0.5) = \$750$$

We order in four periods and in period #2 and #5 we order material for the next period as well. Total cost is $750.

13.7.2 Silver-Meal Heuristic

The Silver-Meal method uses the average cost per period instead of the average unit cost. As long as the cost is decreasing, the lot-size is extended similarly to the least unit cost heuristics.

For period #1 Eq. (13.34) can be used:

$$K_1^{period} = \frac{f_1}{1} \tag{13.34}$$

If we want to find out if it is less expensive to order the material for period #2 in period #1, we use Eq. (13.35):

$$K_{1,2}^{period} = \frac{f_1 + b_2 \cdot c}{2} \tag{13.35}$$

Consider an example:

$$K_{1,1}^{period} = \frac{100}{1} = 100 \quad K_{1,2}^{period} = \frac{100 + 200 \cdot 0.5}{2} = 100$$

Now we expand the first calculation with the material holding costs for period #2. Because they do not increase we continue with period #3.

$$K_{1,3}^{period} = \frac{100 + 200 \cdot 0.5 + 600 \cdot 2 \cdot 0.5}{3} = 267$$

As you can see the average period cost increases remarkably. For that reason we order only material for period #1 and #2 together and start our calculation again with period #3.

$$K_{3,3}^{period} = \frac{100}{1} = 100 \quad K_{3,4}^{period} = \frac{100 + 300 \cdot 0.5}{2} = 125$$

The cost increases again and that is why we order the material for period 3 only.

$$K_{4,4}^{period} = \frac{100}{1} = 100 \quad K_{4,5}^{period} = \frac{100 + 200 \cdot 0.5}{2} = 100$$

$$K_{4,6}^{period} = \frac{100 + 200 \cdot 0.5 + 100 \cdot 2 \cdot 0.5}{3} = 100$$

As we can see we can order the material for periods 4, 5 and 6 jointly, resulting in the following solution.

$$q_1 = 700 \quad q_2 = 0 \quad q_3 = 600 \quad q_4 = 600 \quad q_5 = 0 \quad q_6 = 0$$

$$K^{total} = 3 \cdot 100 + (200 \cdot 0.5) + (200 \cdot 0.5 + 100 \cdot 2 \cdot 0.5) = \$600$$

The total cost is lower with Silver-Meal heuristic than with the least unit cost heuristic. In this case the Silver-Meal order strategy is the preferable way because we can save $150.

▶ **Practical Insights** Silver-Meal heuristic is most preferable in cases with sporadically fluctuating demand.

13.7.3 Wagner-Whitin Model

The *Wagner-Whitin model* considers the deterministic demand that changes over several periods, for one product. This model helps us to find the optimal solution that will tend to be (but not necessarily!) better than Silver-Meal and offer the least unit cost heuristic solutions. The Wagner–Whitin method provides optimal results for the periods under consideration but not beyond them. The basic idea of the model is to minimize holding and order costs. Unlike with the heuristics, the Wagner–Whitin method does not stop when costs are increasing in one period because the optimization method compares different periods with each other.

For the first period we only have the fixed ordering cost as $K_1^{WW} = f_1$. In the second step, we want to find out the costs for ordering periods #1 and #2 jointly in the first period instead of ordering them separately.

Consider the basic Wagner–Whitin formula for costs calculation (13.36):

$$K_{t,t+1} = Min\left[Min(1 \leq t < j)\left[f + c \cdot \sum_{t=t+1}^{j} b_t \cdot n + K_{t-1}\right]; f + K_{j-1}\right] \quad (13.36)$$

According to formula (13.36), for each period t, all possible options to order for n-periods in this period until the j-period or to not order at all are considered. The option with minimal costs is selected.

The calculation for the first period is performed as $K_{1,2}^{WW} = f_1 + b_2 \cdot c$. Normally, this calculation is continued for all possible option. That is remarkable for the Wagner–Whitin method and differentiates it from the heuristics. It is safer to calculate one or two more costs rather than building the wrong lot-sizes. In case we want to calculate costs for the next period, we do not start only with the fixed ordering cost in this period. We have to add up the ordering cost from this period and the total cost from the previous ordering period.

Consider the following example to better understand the procedure of the Wagner–Whitin method (Table 13.11).

$K_{1,1}^{WW} = 100$;
$K_{1,2}^{WW} = 100 + 200 \cdot 0.5 = 200$; $K_{1,3}^{WW} = 100 + 200 \cdot 0.5 + 600 \cdot 2 \cdot 0.5 = 800$
$K_{2,2}^{WW} = K_{1,1}^{WW} + 100 = 200$; $K_{2,3}^{WW} = K_{1,1}^{WW} + 100 + 600 \cdot 0.5 = 500$

In this case the costs for ordering the materials for periods #1 and #2 jointly (strategy 1) is similar to ordering them separately (strategy 2). We can follow both ways and decide at the end which is the preferred strategy.

Table 13.11 Wagner-Whitin calculation

	Demand b_t					
	500	200	600	300	200	100
Period t	1	2	3	4	5	6
1	100	200	800			
2		200	500	800		
3			300	450	650	
4				400	500	600
5					500	**550**
6						600
K_t^{WW}	100	200	300	400	500	550

The bold value indicates minimal total costs

$$K_{2,2}^{WW} = K_{1,1}^{WW} + 100 + 600 \cdot 0.5 + 300 \cdot 2 \cdot 0.5 = 800$$

$$K_{3,3}^{WW} = K_{1,2}^{WW} + 100 = 300$$

In the case we decide to order in period 1 for the first and second periods jointly, the calculation we use for period #3 is the total cost of $K_{1,2}^{WW}$. If we decide to order for the first and second periods separately we use the total cost of $K_{2,2}^{WW}$ for the calculation of $K_{3,3}^{WW}$. We will continue with strategy 1.

$$K_{3,4}^{WW} = K_{1,2}^{WW} + 100 + 300 \cdot 0.5 = 450$$

$$K_{3,5}^{WW} = K_{1,2}^{WW} + 100 + 300 \cdot 0.5 + 200 \cdot 2 \cdot 0.5 = 4650$$

$$K_{4,4}^{WW} = K_{3,3}^{WW} + 100 = 400 \;;\; K_{4,5}^{WW} = K_{3,3}^{WW} + 100 + 200 \cdot 0.5 = 500$$

$$K_{4,5}^{WW} = K_{3,3}^{WW} + 100 + 200 \cdot 0.5 + 100 \cdot 2 \cdot 0.5 = 600$$

$$K_{5,5}^{WW} = K_{4,4}^{WW} + 100 = 500 \;;\; K_{5,6}^{WW} = K_{4,4}^{WW} + 100 + 100 \cdot 0.5 = 550$$

$$K_{6,6}^{WW} = K_{5,5}^{WW} + 100 = 600$$

The costs K_{min}^{WW} at the end of the table in the last period are the total costs. When trying different strategies we will realize that the total cost can never be below $550.

> **Practical Insights** The dynamic lot-sizing models considered are basically applied to make-to-stock (MTS) production strategy (see Chap. 6). In small series manufacturing and assemble-to-order (ATO) production strategies, other methods are typically used. These methods are based on bottleneck-based manufacturing control such as *EPEI* (Every Part Every Interval) lot-sizing, *heijunka* or DBR (*drum-buffer-rope*). Lot-size can also be constrained by limited storage capacity within the production processes. In addition, integration of

manufacturing lot-sizing and vehicle scheduling belong to practical trends, e.g., as so-called BIB (*batch-in-batch*) lot-size.

13.8 Aggregating Inventory

In a number of cases, *many markets* are replenished from the same warehouse. In this setting, interesting *trade-offs* between number of facilities, inventory and transportation costs may arise when comparing different options, e.g.:

- building warehouse in each market or
- centralizing inventory

Some important questions can be discussed regarding these options.

How does the replenishment interval affect the safety stock requirement at warehouses?

A larger replenishment interval results in higher safety stock requirements, because safety stock is often used at the end of replenishment intervals; if replenishment intervals are larger it is important that safety stock is available to be used.

How does the replenishment interval affect the level of inventory (and thus the size of the warehouse)?

A smaller replenishment interval means a lower level of inventory within the warehouse and thus a smaller warehouse is useful. On the other hand, a higher replenishment interval leads to a higher level of inventory and thus a bigger warehouse needs to be provided.

How does the replenishment interval affect other warehouse costs (such as labour cost)?

A shorter replenishment interval probably results in higher labour cost because of greater material handling.

Furthermore it is necessary to evaluate other factors that affect the decision, such as the market in which the firm produces. Perhaps in a smaller market the firm would focus on responsiveness rather than efficiency, and in a larger market the opposite. Also other SC drivers affect the decision. Since sustainability is becoming more important nowadays, firms also have to find a trade-off between transportation costs and responsiveness while considering *sustainability*.

Another specific case is a situation where two warehouses have to be merged in order to save warehousing fixed and operating costs. How to determine the right safety stock in the new larger warehouse? Here are two possible situations:

- Two warehouses served the same market previously
- Two warehouses served different markets previously.

In the case where two warehouses served the same market previously, safety stock should remain unchanged, according to the formula $ss = z \times \sigma_{dLT}$. Indeed, if deviation of demand for tomatoes in Berlin is 100,000 tons, it will not change just because we merge our warehouses. However, if two warehouses served different markets previously, the following holds true: $\sigma_{new} = \sqrt{\sigma_{new}^2}$ where $\sigma_{new}^2 = \sigma_1^2 + \sigma_2^2$.

Note: If average demand and demand deviation differ significantly from each other at two warehouses which previously served the same market, the formula for different markets has to be applied.

Task 13.10 Merging Warehouses

Mr. Tsching has two wholesale flower markets and his most important products during the Christmas period are Christmas stars. Mr. Tsching has to order Christmas stars for the next season from his supplier. His markets are located in Berlin and Cologne and provide Christmas stars for different regions in Germany, Switzerland and Austria. The warehouses serve different markets. Cologne serves west and south Germany and Switzerland, and Berlin serves north and east Germany and Austria. Based on sales data from the last year Mr. Tsching assumes demand to be evenly distributed. Demand for his market in Cologne is 12,000 Christmas stars with a standard deviation of 4600 stars. The market in Berlin has demand for14,300 Christmas stars with a standard deviation of 6200 stars. The purchase price for one Christmas star is 1.12 € and the retail price is 3.65 €. Christmas stars which are not sold can be sold on to the textile industry for 0.31 € per star. The textile industry can use the red pigments for dying. Mr Tsching thinks about merging his markets. Merging will involve extra transport costs of 22,500 € but a reduction in fixed costs of 20,000 €.

Calculate optimal order volume, expected cost and profit for every market and decide if a merging of Mr Tsching's markets is a profitable idea.

Solution

We refer to the newsvendor model considered in Sect. 13.5.2. First, the expected costs and profit for the non-merged case are considered as follows:

$$c_o = 1.12 - 0.31 = 0.81€ \quad c_u = 3.65 - 1.12 = 2.53€$$
$$CR = \frac{2.53}{2.53 + 0.81} \approx 0.76 F(0.76) = z = 0.71$$
$$f(0.71) = 0.31 S^*_{Berlin} = 14,300 + 0.71 \cdot 6200 = 18,702$$
$$S^*_{Cologne} = 12,000 + 0.71 \cdot 4600 = 15,266$$

Expected cost for Christmas season:

$$Z\left(S^*_{Berlin}\right) = (0.81 + 2.53) \cdot 0.31 \cdot 6200 = 6420€$$

$$Z\left(S^*_{Cologne}\right) = (0.81 + 2.53) \cdot 0.31 \cdot 4600 = 4763€$$

Expected profit for Christmas season:

$$\Pi\left(S^*_{Berlin}\right) = 2.53 \cdot 14,300 - 6420 = 29,759 €$$

$$\Pi\left(S^*_{Cologne}\right) = 2.53 \cdot 12,000 - 4763 = 25,597 €$$

$$\Pi(total) = 25,597 + 29,759 = 55,356 €$$

Merging the markets:

$$\mu_{new} = \mu_{Berlin} + \mu_{Cologne} = 14,300 + 12,000 = 26,300$$

$$\sigma_{new} = \sqrt{\sigma^2_{Berlin} + \sigma^2_{Cologne}} = \sqrt{6200^2 + 4600^2} = 7720$$

$$S^*_{new} = 26,300 + 0.71 \cdot 7720 = 31,781$$

Expected cost for the merged the market:

$$Z(S^*_{new}) = (0.81 + 2.53) \cdot 0.31 \cdot 7720 = 7993 €$$

Compare expected cost with total cost for two markets:

$$Z\left(S^*_{Berlin}\right) + Z\left(S^*_{Cologne}\right) - Z(S^*_{new}) = 6420 + 4763 - 7993 = 3190 €$$

Do not forget to add the costs of merging (22,500€ − 20,000€) when calculating the expected profit:

$$\Pi\left(S^*_{new}\right) = 2.53 \cdot 26,300 - (7993 + 2500) = 56.046 €$$

We opt for merging the warehouses because the expected profit of 56,046 € is higher than in initial situation (55,356 €).

13.9 ATP/CTP

John was browsing the internet to find new furniture for his flat. After having entered the desired parameters he has an overview of beds. The overview contained offers from four suppliers. The prices were quite similar but lead times differed significantly. Two suppliers indicated 3 weeks of lead time, one supplier indicated 2–3 days; the last one indicated 8–10 days since it does not have the item in stock but will be able to produce it and deliver within a week. John selected the offer of the third supplier, since the prices were almost equal and lead time became the competitive advantage. His friend Alex selected the offer of the fourth supplier since the price was a bit lower than that of the third supplier, but lead time was shorter than for suppliers 1 and 2.

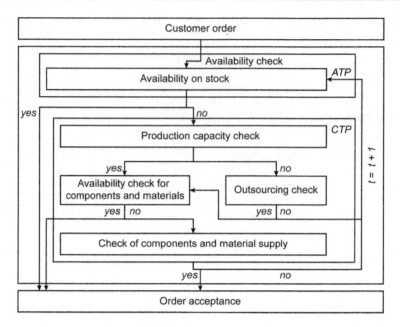

Fig. 13.15 ATP/CTP process [based on Teich (2003)]

Indication of a lead time of "3 weeks" is a signal that the supplier works with standard lead times. This means that it does not take into account actual inventory or production capacity load. If there is inventory or slack in production capacity, delivery time can be significantly shorter than 3 weeks. Otherwise, it may be longer.

Suppliers 3 and 4 apply so-called ATP/CTP (available-to-promise/capable-to-promise) systems. This means that they have introduced IT [e.g., SAP APO (advanced planning and optimization)] which has the ability to check actual inventory and production capacity along the SC and to define an exact lead time and delivery date (see Fig. 13.15).

At the order fulfilment stage, customer orders are matched with quantities available on stock and from scheduled receipts. In addition, customer requests for delivery of a product with regard to quantity, time and location have to be answered.

The investigation into whether a delivery can actually be made is called ATP. The standard method of ATP is to search for available stocks, which can be promised for delivery.

CTP can be applied when conventional ATP checks fail, i.e., the requested product is not in stock at respective locations and not available from scheduled receipts. CTP refers to the planning and scheduling run with regard to work-in-progress (WIP) during an ATP check. CTP checks whether it is possible to modify existing scheduled production orders with regard to time and order size or whether to create a new production order, taking production capacities and component availability into account.

Such concepts are used by many online retail companies such as Amazon. Manufacturing companies apply such systems to manage complexity which frequently involves thousands of orders per day which may be placed for hundreds of thousands of items. Investment in IT for ATP/CTP can be high but will be paid for through the achievement of competitive advantages.

13.10 Key Points and Outlook

In this chapter, we learned about methods and practical tools for inventory management. Let us summarize the key points of this chapter as follows.

The role of inventory management is to strike a balance between inventory investment and customer service. Inventory is one of the most expensive assets of many companies representing as much as 50 % of total invested capital. Operations and SC managers must balance inventory investment against levels of customer service. Inventory has different functions and types. Trade-off of "service level vs costs" is one of the most important issues in inventory management. Inventory creates costs but at the same time it can be used to increase SC flexibility. The most important costs in inventory optimization are holding, ordering and stock-out costs.

In taking decisions on the scope of inventory management, the following two basic questions are put in the forefront for consideration:

- How much should I replenish?
- When should I replenish?

According to the inventory functions and types, inventory can be used to manage:

- economy of scale—this is cycle inventory;
- uncertainty—this is safety inventory.

Basic methods for item classification are the ABC and XYZ analysis. ABC analysis divides inventory into three classes A-B-C based on annual dollar volume. ABC analysis is used to establish policies that focus on the few critical parts and not the many trivial ones. XYZ analysis is used to classify items according their demand dynamics.

For cycle inventory, the basic methods are as follows:

- basic EOQ and EPQ
- quantity discount model
- reorder point (ROP).

The EOQ method helps us to understand the relationship between ordering and holding costs. EOQ finds the optimal order quantity for deterministic demand in one period mode. The EOQ model answers the "how much" question.

In the quantity discount model, inventory costs can also be calculated on the basis of different unit prices. The EPQ model is fairly similar to the EOQ model but is applied to production. This model is used when:

- inventory builds up over a period of time after an order is placed
- units are produced and sold simultaneously.

The reorder point (ROP) tells "when" to order. ROP is introduced to take into account the so-called lead time, i.e. the time between order placement and receipt.

However, in many practical cases, both demand and lead time can be fluctuating. We do not know their actual values, but can only estimate them on a probability basis. For such cases, stochastic (probabilistic) models are needed. Uncertainty of demand makes it necessary to maintain certain customer service levels to avoid stock-outs. In the presence of demand uncertainty, safety inventory is introduced.

The essential difference between multi-period problems and single-period problems is that all the relevant parameters (e.g., demand, lead time, costs) can vary in different periods. In addition, inventory from previous periods can be used to cover demand in following periods. That is why the basic trade-off in multi-period models is how to balance inventory holding costs and ordering cost over time. Basic methods for multi-period problems are the Wagner–Whitin method (optimization) as well as Silver–Meal and unit cost methods (both methods are heuristics).

In many practical cases, EOQ and ROP cannot be applied because of business policies. For example, many companies in electronics retail industry have to place their orders on Fridays on the basis of demand forecasts since this is required by OEMs. In other cases, deliveries may be possible only on certain dates (e.g., on Monday). In these cases, inventory control policies are applied.

In many cases, interesting trade-offs between number of facilities, inventory and transportation costs may arise when comparing different options. That is why integrated inventory–transportation models are considered. In order to take into account actual inventory on stock production capacities, the ATP/CTP concept is used. It allows right delivery dates to be determined.

Many additional problems and methods of inventory management exist in practice, e.g. multi-echelon inventory management in the SC. Multi-echelon inventory management is a way to cut costs and increase customer service levels.

Single-echelon inventory management has some major problems. The SC carries excess inventory in the form of redundant safety stock. End customer service failures occur even when adequate inventory exists in the network. Customer-facing locations experience undesirable stock-outs, even while service between echelons is more than acceptable. External suppliers deliver unreliable performance when they have received unsatisfactory demand forecasts. Shortsighted internal allocation decisions are made for products with limited availability.

The objective of multi-echelon inventory management is to deliver the desired end customer service levels at minimum network inventory, with the inventory divided among the various echelons. However, multi-echelon techniques are more complex. The complexity of managing inventory increases significantly. All locations should be under the internal control of a single enterprise. Instead of simply replenishing the warehouse that sits between supplier and end customer, as in the single-echelon situation, we also need to contend with the problems of replenishing the multi-stage inventory system.

Additional problems and methods of inventory management which could also be considered for practical issues are as follows:

- different kinds of service level (alpha, beta, and gamma)
- dynamic safety stock calculations
- inventory-lot-size problems
- inventory-routing problems, especially in the context of vendor-managed inventory (VMI)
- production–inventory–transportation problems
- stochastic economic lot-sizing and scheduling problems with constraints on budget, capacity, etc.

These and a wide range of other problems of inventory management in the supplychain are truly fascinating and deserve much attention.

Bibliography

Axsater S (2010) Inventory control, 2nd edn. Springer, New York
Bowersox DJ, Closs DJ, Copper MB (2013) Supply chain logistics management, 5th edn. McGraw-Hill, Boston
Chopra S, Meindl P (2012) Supply chain management. Strategy, planning and operation, 5th edn. Pearson, Harlow
Christopher M (2011) Logistics and supply chain management. Creating value-adding networks, 4th edn. FT Press, New Jersey
Drexl A, Kimms A (1997) Lot sizing and scheduling – survey and extensions. Eur J Oper Res 99(2):221–235
Günther H-O (2005) Supply chain management and advanced planning systems: a tutorial. In: Günther H-O, Mattfeld DC, Suhl L (eds) Supply chain management und logistik. Physica-Verlag, Heidelberg, pp 3–40
Heizer J, Render B (2013) Operations management: sustainability and supply chain management, 11th edn. Pearson, Harlow
Hwang H-C (2010) Economic lot-sizing for integrated production and transportation. Oper Res 58(2):428–444
Render B, Stair RM, Hanna ME (2012) Quantitative analysis for management, 11th edn. Pearson, Harlow
Sainanthuni B, Parikh PJ, Zhang X, Kong N (2014) The warehouse-inventory-transportation problem for supply chains. Eur J Oper Res 237(2):690–700
Stadtler H, Kilger C (2008) Supply chain management and advanced planning, 4th edn. Springer, Berlin
Stadtler H (1996) Mixed integer programming model formulations for dynamic multi-item multi-level capacitated lot-sizing. Eur J Oper Res 94(3):561–581
Teich T (2003) Extended value chain management. GUC Verlag, Chemnitz (in German)
Tempelmeier H (2005) Bestandsmanagement in supply chains. 3. Aufl.

Thonemann U (2010) Operations management: konzepte, methoden und anwendungen, 2nd edn. Pearson, München

Wagner HM, Whitin TM (1958) Dynamic version of the economic lot-size model. Manage Sci 5(1):89–96

Waters D (2008) Supply chain management: an introduction to logistics, 2nd edn. Palgrave Macmillan, Basingstoke

Waters D (2013) Inventory control and management, 2nd edn. Wiley, Chichester

Wolsey LA (2006) Lot-sizing with production and delivery time windows. Math Program 107(3): 471–489

Zipkin PH (2000) Foundations of inventory management. McGraw-Hill, Boston

Zipkin PH (1991) Computing optimal lot sizes in the economic lot scheduling problem. Oper Res 39(1):56–63

Reference for Sect. 13.5

http://www.maerskline.com.

Routing and Scheduling 14

Routing and scheduling belong to operative decisions which are required for running the *daily operations*. The prerequisites are as follows. Typically, we are given known capacities that cannot be extended at short hand so that resource scarceness cannot be prevented in some situations. Furthermore, detailed information about the demand to be fulfilled is available.

The central challenge of operative decision making is now to match the demand with the available capacities on a daily basis. Here, two basic decision tasks have to be solved (isolated or in parallel): (1) demand has to be assigned to resources and (2) schedules have to be set up. A *schedule* describes the sequence in which the assigned tasks are executed and at which starting points individual operations are initiated. The major difficulty is to ensure that the available capacities are not exceeded and that the resources are deployed at highest efficiency.

In Sect. 14.1 we introduce a typical case for operative decision making. Section 14.2 introduces *mathematical graphs* as a tool for the representation of decision situations in a network structure. Additionally, the first insights into the algorithmic processing of graph-data as the basic ingredient for decision making in network structures are provided. The consideration of complex restrictions during the deployment of a resource is discussed in Sect. 14.3 by means of the so-called *traveling salesman problem* (TSP) in which the sequencing of operations to build a schedule for a resource is in the focus of decision making. The integrated consideration of *assignment and scheduling/sequencing* decision problems under limited resource availability is addressed in Sect. 14.4 in the context of the *capacitated vehicle routing problem* (CVRP). In Sect. 14.5 a short introduction into the scheduling of the production machines is given. Finally, Sect. 14.6 summarizes the key aspects of this chapter.

Find additional case-studies, Excel spreadsheet templates, and video streams in the *E-Supplement* to this book on www.global-supply-chain-management.de!

The Learning Objectives for This Chapter

- Learn about typical operative process planning tasks from transportation as well as production.
- Understand the representation of networks in mathematical graphs.
- Define the decision models in mathematical graphs.
- Select adequate algorithms for solving optimization models defined on graphs.
- Understand basic ingredients of heuristic algorithms for solving complex routing and scheduling models with several constraints.
- Understand basic objectives and trade-offs in routing and scheduling.
- Compute optimal and sub-optimal (heuristic) production schedules.

14.1 Introductory Case Study RED SEA BUS TRAVEL

The leading actor in this chapter is Christina. She has just completed her study programme. Equipped with a recently acquired bachelor degree certifying her successful studies in leisure and tourism management, she wants to achieve some job experience abroad. So she applies for several jobs in the well-known Hurghada Red Sea area in Egypt. After several interviews, she finally gets a job at RED SEA BUS TRAVEL (RSBT). This company offers transport services in the Hurghada region. International travel agencies book RSBT service operations in order to ensure that their tourists are moved to their preferred holiday region.

At her first working day, Christina is assigned to the planning and dispatching office of RSBT in downtown Hurghada. After several complicated years of business due to a lack of tourists, RSBT has detected an increasing number of bookings from travel agencies but also from individual customers. These bookings can be classified into the following four categories:

- Limousine Services (LS)
- Sightseeing Tours (SST)
- Airport Arrival Transfer (AAT)
- Airport Departure Transfer (ADT)

RSBT receives all bookings at short hand, e.g. on the day before the transport service is executed. Service (transport) processes have to be set up in order to cover customer demand. RSBT operates a fleet of (mini)buses of different sizes and also has qualified drivers. Assignment of bookings to buses has to be decided, and for each bus the daily schedule has to be determined.

Christina's task is now to analyse the four products LS, SST, AAT and ADT and to make suggestions how the day-to-day deployment of the available buses (which are the available resources) must be carried out in order to use these resources in the most efficient manner while all booking requests are fulfilled. Having accompanied several transport services during her first week at RSBT, Christina has identified the core planning challenges in the four business sectors:

LS: What is the *shortest (quickest) path* through the local street network to travel from the limousine service headquarters to the airport? How can this path be identified?

SST: In which *sequence* should all the nice places be visited so that visitors have enough time to enjoy their leisure time in the hotel?

AAT: What is the minimal travel *distance* to bring all inbound passengers associated with an inbound flight to their hotels? What is the minimal number of required buses?

ADT: Which bus should *pick up* which guests from which hotel in order to take them to the airport on time if customers do not accept a pickup more than 5 h earlier than their scheduled flight departure?

Christina is now looking for suitable planning models for the four types of transportation service situations. Her intention is to make the determination of the processes traceable but, at the same time, she wants to ensure that efficiency of the deployment resources is as high as possible.

14.2 Shortest Paths in a Network

This section addresses the optimization of travel paths in a network structure. In particular, we are looking for shortest (or quickest) connections between a given start location and a given destination location. These two locations are both part of a network but there is no direct connection available between them. Instead, it is necessary to determine a sequence of concatenated direct connections between intermediately passed connections/points that finally connects the start with the terminus location.

14.2.1 Outline of the Shortest Path Problem (SPP) in a Network

Christina first turns towards the LS business. In the first step, she is asking the booking department for data about the usual as well as about the most frequently booked relations for limousine transport. Her survey results in the observation that six locations contribute to the daily LS operations (see Table 14.1).

The fare for an LS booking is calculated based on the travel distance between the booked pickup location and the booked delivery location. From discussions with the RSBT customer care manager Christina has learned that there are several complaints from customers who think that they have to pay too much, since drivers do not follow the shortest travel route.

Christina wants to find out if these complaints are justified and she decides to have conversation with some drivers. After her interviews, she was convinced that the complaints were not justified. All of the complaints are as a result of a misunderstanding: the infrastructure in the area is quite different from the typical European street network. Since all hotels have been built around the populated

Table 14.1 Locations for LS

Notation	Locations
A	Reefside—The Fisherman's Village
B	The Palace Hotel
C	Downtown 5star
D	Mermaid's Inn
E	Red Sea Diver's Base
F	Hurghada International Airport

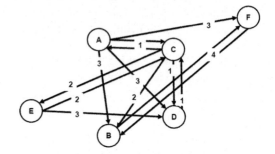

Fig. 14.1 Street network connecting the Airport (F) with the most important hotels (A–E) in the Hurghada area

downtown area there are only streets that connect the biggest hotels. That means going from a pickup point to a delivery point often requires a visit to several hotel places. The street network is significantly less dense than in a typical European city and "felt detours" are needed when travelling in the area.

In order to provide more transparency for customers and in order to instruct the limousine drivers, Christina decides to create a list for each pair of pickup and delivery point combinations. She wants to add the shortest route to each pair (to inform the drivers) and the corresponding travel distance (to inform the customers).

In the first attempt to compile the desired list, Christina collects data from the street map. She marks the six locations A to F (Fig. 14.1). Furthermore, she looks for streets connecting these locations. Whenever she finds out that there is a street connecting a hotel with the airport or the airport with a hotel or a hotel with another hotel, she connects the origin location with the terminal location by an arc. That is, an arc represents an existing street connecting these two points and the arc direction indicates the direction of travel (Fig. 14.1). Finally, she appends the length (given in km) of such a street (section) between two points. From the compiled simplified map, she learns, for example, that there is a street that goes from A (Reefside—The Fisherman's Village) to D (Mermaid's Inn) but this street cannot be used to go from D to A. The length of the street section from A to D is 3 km. But what is the distance of a trip from E to F? Christina is looking for a comfortable method to determine the least travel distance (i.e., to solve the shortest path problem [SPP]) between a pair of pickup and delivery locations not directly connected by an arc.

14.2.2 Mathematical Graphs

A mathematical *graph* is a tool to describe network structures. A *network* consists of some points as well as connections between these points. In a mathematical graph these points are represented by *nodes* and all nodes are collected in a *node set* which is often labelled N. If there is a connection between two points then there is also a connection (i.e., an *arc*) between the two corresponding nodes, say i and j, taken from the node set N ($i, j \in N$). If it is only necessary to be aware that these two nodes are connected, then this connection is expressed by putting the two connected nodes into a set $\{i; j\}$. This set is called an *edge*. In most situations it is necessary to save information about the type of connection between the nodes i and j. For example, if i as well as j are cities served by an airline, it is necessary to know if an offered flight goes from i to j and/or from j to i. It is therefore necessary to distinguish a connection from i to j and a connection from j to i. In such a situation the connection is established by the ordered pair (i; j) which indicates that there is a connection originating from i and going to j. If there is also a connection from j to i then a second ordered pair (j; i) is used to represent this additional connection. An ordered pair (i; j) connecting two nodes is called an *arc*. All required arcs and/or edges are saved in another set, called the arc (or edge) set typically labelled E. Information associated with a node or an arc (edge) can be stored by mappings f and g, so that f(i) respectively g(i; j) or g($\{i; j\}$) is the stored information. The quadruple (N; E; f; g) is called a *weighted mathematical graph*.

14.2.3 The SPP as Graph-Based Optimization Model

Christina wants to represent the LS problem setting in a mathematical graph. She starts with setting up a graph-based optimization model for the network structure shown in Fig. 14.1. Therefore, it is necessary to represent the given information as a mathematical graph G = (Ω; Θ; d) with evaluated arcs. The node set Ω consists of the six nodes $\Omega = \{A; B; C; D; E; F\}$. The arc set Θ comprises exactly those arcs connecting the nodes as shown in Fig. 14.1, so that $\Theta := \{(A; B), (A; C), (A; D), (A; F), (B; F), (C; A), (C; B), (C; D), (C; E), (D; C), (E; C), (E; D), (F; B)\}$. We incorporate the real-valued mapping d to assign the travel distance d(i; j) to each arc (i; j) $\in \Theta$.

In order to prepare the analysis of the derived graph, we introduce several definitions. These definitions help us to discuss the specific properties of a graph-based decision model.

Let (i; j) as well as (k; l) be two arcs in a given graph G. We call arc (k; l) a "successor of arc (i; j)" if and only if the two nodes j and k coincide, i.e. if and only if j = k. In such a situation, we also say that arc (k; l) follows arc (i; j) if and only if (k; l) is a successor of (i; j) in the given graph G. In our example arc (F; B) is a successor of arc (A; F), which means that arc (F; B) follows arc (A; F).

We are now prepared to introduce the term "*path*" into a network G. Let s and t be nodes from the node set Ω of G. In our example, s might be node A and t could be node E. Let $(i_0; i_1)$, $(i_1; i_2)$, ..., $(i_{k-1}; i_k)$ be a finite sequence of following arcs with the properties $i_0 = s$ and $i_k = t$. We call the arc sequence $(i_0; i_1)$, $(i_1; i_2)$, ..., $(i_{k-1}; i_k)$ a path in G from s to t. For short, we call this arc sequence an s-t-path in G.

$$L((i_0; i_1), (i_1; i_2), \ldots, (i_{k-1}; i_k)) := d(s, i_1) + d(i_1; i_2) + \ldots + d(i_{k-1}; t) \quad (14.1)$$

The length of a given s-t-path $(i_0; i_1)$, $(i_1; i_2)$, ..., $(i_{k-1}; i_k)$ in G is defined by Eq. (14.1). In a case where all nodes contained in path $(i_0; i_1)$, $(i_1; i_2)$, ..., $(i_{k-1}; i_k)$ are pairwise different, we call the s-t-path a "simple path".

The property "pairwise different" refers to a situation in which each two nodes of a given subset of the node set Ω are not the same. A simple path in the graph shown in Fig. 14.1 is, for example, the path (A; D), (D; C), (C; E). In contrast, the path (A; D), (D; A), (A; F) is not a simple path since node A is visited more than once.

Using the aforementioned definitions, we are now prepared to describe Christina's task to determine the shortest path between a pair of nodes in the given network structure formally. Let s be the pickup point of an LS booking and let t be the planned drop-off point of this LS booking. Christina is looking then for a simple s-t-path $(s; i_1)$, $(i_1; i_2)$, ..., $(i_{k-1}; t)$ in G with minimal length $L((s; i_1), (i_1; i_2), \ldots, (i_{k-1}; t))$.

14.2.4 Dijkstra's Algorithm for the Identification of a Shortest s-t-Path

There is a very efficient and quick algorithm available to identify the shortest s-t-path in a given graph G. The only requirement for the applicability of this algorithm is that all arcs (i; j) of G have a non-negative length d(i; j). Applied to determine a shortest s-t-path in G this algorithm does a little more than needed; it calculates the shortest paths from *s* to each other node in G. The basic idea of this algorithm has been contributed by E.W. Dijkstra (1959). For this reason, the algorithm is often called the "Dijkstra-Algorithm".

Dijkstra's algorithm works as follows. Let $|\Omega|$ be the number of nodes in the given graph G, in which we are going to identify the shortest s-t-path.

Algorithm Start At the beginning, each node is assigned a so-called temporary label value l(v). This value equals the shortest path length known so far (not the path itself!) from start node *s* to node *v*, i.e. it carries the length of the shortest s-v-path found so far. Since, at the beginning, no s-v-path is known, we set l(v) equal to infinity ($l(v) := \infty$), for all $v \in \Omega$, $v \neq s$ but we set $l(s) = 0$.

Algorithm Iteration Dijkstra's algorithm iterates the following steps $|\Omega|$ times.

(1) Each iteration starts with the selection of a node k with a temporary label value l(k). If there is such a node we select node k with a minimal temporary label value among all temporarily labelled nodes. If there is no temporarily labelled node left then the algorithm terminates.

14.2 Shortest Paths in a Network

(2) The label value l(k) of the selected node k is declared to be "permanent" and it will not be changed any more in later iterations.

(3) For all remaining nodes $w \in \Omega \setminus \{k\}$ with a label value l(w) which is not permanently labelled so far, we check the following: if the arc (k; w) is contained in G and if l(k) + d(k;w) < l(w) then we update l(w) by l(w):=l(k) + d(k; w). We have found a shorter s-w-path in G. If there is no such arc (k; w) or if l(k) + d(k; w) ≥ l (w) then we do not change l(w) and check the next node w ≠ k.

The following definitions help to ease the execution of the Dijkstra algorithm for even larger networks. Let v be a node from the node set Ω of graph G. In step (ii) of the iteration of Dijkstra's algorithm, we need to analyse all those nodes in Ω that are directly connected with v by an arc that originates from v. The termination node of such an arc is called a "successor of v". Let SUCC(v) be the set that contains all temporarily labelled successors of v, i.e. SUCC(v):={$k \in \Omega | (v; k) \in \Theta$ and k is temporarily labelled}.

Let (i; j) be an arc taken from the arc set Θ of graph G. We define i as a "predecessor" of j in G. For short, we write pred(j) := {i} if (i; j) $\in \Theta$. In the Dijkstra algorithm we use the predecessor convention to recursively store the shortest s-t-path, e.g. the sequence of visited nodes in the shortest s-t-path. Starting from the terminal node t, we store pred(t) and for the node pred(t) we store pred (pred(t)) and so on (right-to-left path determination).

Let Ω^T be the subset of the node set Ω that contains all nodes that are currently labelled temporarily and let Ω^P be the subset of Ω formed by the nodes that are already labelled permanently.

Dijkstra algorithm	
(a)	set $\Omega^T:=V$ and $\Omega^P:= \emptyset$
(b)	set l(v):= ∞ and pred(v):= $\emptyset$ for all $v \in \Omega \setminus \{s\}$, l(s):=0 and pred(s):= $\emptyset$, l(s) = 0
(c)	proceed with steps (d)–(g) if $\Omega^T \neq \emptyset$, otherwise go to (h)
(d)	select a node $k \in \Omega^T$ so that l(k) is minimal over Ω^T.
(e)	declare the label l(k) as permanent and update $\Omega^T:= \Omega^T \setminus \{k\}$ and $\Omega^P:= \Omega^P \cup \{k\}$
(f)	for all $w \in$ SUCC(k) that fulfil l(k) + d(k; w) < l(w) update l(w):=l(k) + d(k; w) and pred (w):={k}
(g)	goto (c)
(h)	stop the algorithm

Such an algorithm description is quite close to a computer programming code. It is written in pseudocode. Pseudocode descriptions are often used in order to make the "real" implementation (coding) with a programming language like BASIC, Java or C++ easier.

The Dijkstra algorithm starts with the initialization of the two node sets Ω^T as well as Ω^P (the symbol $\emptyset$ represents an empty set) in the steps (a) and (b). The steps (c)–(g) are repeated as long as there is still a node with a temporary label available. In each repetition, exactly one node is moved from the set of temporarily labelled nodes into the set of permanent nodes (d), (e) and the temporary labels are updated if a shorter s-w-path to a node w is found (f).

Table 14.2 Structured table-based presentation of the iterations of the Dijkstra algorithm

Iteration	Node recently selected and labelled as permanent	Recent label values					
		A	B	C	D	E	F
0 (Start)	–	∞	∞	∞	∞	0(–)	∞
1	E	∞	∞	2(E)	3(E)	0*(–)	∞
2	C	3(C)	4(C)	2*(E)	3(E)	0*(–)	∞
3	A	3*(C)	4(C)	2*(E)	3(E)	0*(–)	6(A)
4	D	3*(C)	4(C)	2*(E)	3*(E)	0*(–)	6(A)
5	B	3*(C)	4*(C)	2*(E)	3*(E)	0*(–)	6(A)
6	F	3*(C)	4*(C)	2*(E)	3*(E)	0*(–)	6*(A)

Christina has read about the Dijkstra algorithm and the shortest path problem. She applies it now to the problem situation shown in Fig. 14.1. She starts with the identification of the shortest path between point E and point F.

In order to ease the repetitive applications of steps in the Dijkstra algorithm it seems to be appropriate and helpful to represent the working data and intermediate results in a table as shown in Table 14.2. The recent label values are contained in the columns headed by the nodes. The recent pred(X)-value of node X is given in brackets right to the recent label value. In a case where the label value has been declared to be permanent it is marked by *. Each row represents one iteration of the Dijkstra algorithm.

Iteration 0 (Start): $\Omega^P = \emptyset$ and $\Omega^T = \{A; B; C; D; E; F\}$. The label value l(E) of the starting node E is set to 0. All remaining nodes are temporarily labelled by ∞.

Iteration 1: $\Omega^P = \emptyset$ and $\Omega^T = \{A; B; C; D; E; F\}$. Node E is labelled with the minimal temporary label value 0. For this reason, E is moved from Ω^T to Ω^P ("permanently labelled"). SUCC(E) = {C; D}. Since l(E) + d(E; C) = 0 + 2 < ∞, we update l(C):=2 and set pred(C):={E}. Since l(E) + d(E;D) = 0 + 3 < ∞, we update l(D):= 3 and set pred(D):={E}.

Iteration 2: $\Omega^P = \{E\}$ and $\Omega^T = \{A; B; C; D; F\}$. Node C is labelled with the smallest temporary label value. For this reason C is moved from Ω^T to Ω^P ("permanently labelled"). SUCC(C) = {A; B; D}. Since l(C) + d(C; A) = 2 + 1 < ∞, we update l(A):=3 and update pred(A):={C}. Since l(C) + d(C; B) = 2 + 2 < ∞, we update l(B):=4 and update pred(B):={C}. Since l(C) + d(C; D) = 2 + 1 $\geq$ 3, we do not update l(D) und pred(D).

Iteration 3: $\Omega^P = \{C; E\}$ und $\Omega^T = \{A; B; D; F\}$. Both nodes A and D are labelled with the same minimal temporary label value 3. Node A is selected since it comes first in a lexicographic order. For this reason we move A from Ω^T to Ω^P and update SUCC(A):={B; F}. Since l(A) + d(A; B) = 3 + 3 $\geq$ 4, we preserve l(B) and pred(B). Since l(A) + d(A; F) = 3 + 3 < ∞, we update l(F):=6 as well as pred(F):= {A}.

Iteration 4: $\Omega^P = \{A; C; E\}$ and $\Omega^T = \{B; D; F\}$. Node D has the minimal temporary label value 3. Therefore, we move D from Ω^T to Ω^P and update SUCC (D):= $\emptyset$. No temporary label value must be checked for being updated.

Iteration 5: $\Omega^P = \{A; C; D; E\}$ and $\Omega^T = \{B; F\}$. Node B is labelled with the smallest temporary label value, which is 4. Thus, we move B from Ω^T to Ω^P and we set SUCC(B) = {F}. Since $l(B) + d(B; F) = 4 + 4 \geq 4$, we preserve l(F) and we neither update prec{B}.

Iteration 6: $\Omega^P = \{A; B; C; D; E\}$ and $\Omega^T = \{F\}$. Node F is labelled with the minimal temporary label value 6. We therefore move F from Ω^T to Ω^P and set SUCC(B):= $\emptyset$. No further checks are necessary.

Iteration 7: $\Omega^P = \{A; B; C; D; E; F\}$ and $\Omega^T = \emptyset$. There is no further node available that has been labelled temporarily. The Dijkstra algorithm terminates here.

The found permanent label value l(F) of the designated goal node gives the length of the shortest E-F-path in graph G. The path is determined by a recursive backtrack-analysis of the final pred-values. We have found that pred(F):=A, pred(A):=C, pred(C):=E. The shortest E-F-path in G is ((E; C), (C; A), (A; F)).

There is a chance of the existence of more than one E-F-path with the same minimal distance. The Dijkstra algorithm can find only one shortest E-F-path. Christina can use the Dijkstra algorithm to determine the shortest distances between each pair of nodes in the network in the Hurghada area.

14.3 Round Trip Planning/Travelling Salesman Problem

Now that Christina has successfully solved the planning challenge for the LS operations, she turns towards the next open challenge. In the SST department of RSBT it is necessary to determine round trips of buses that contain exactly one visit for each location contained in a given list of sightseeing objects.

Christina examines the SST situation and she finds out that there are some similarities with the shortest path identification problem which she solved as explained in Sect. 14.2. First, the SST challenge also lives in a network structure. Second, for a given list of points of interests, a connecting path in the given network structure is required. Third, also in the SST situation, a path with minimal length is searched. However, Christina discovers an important difference between the LS and SST situations. In the LS challenge only the starting as well as the terminating node of the requested s-t-path is given. There are no requests to visit other nodes. In contrast, the necessity to visit all locations contained in the aforementioned list of points of interests is postulated. For this reason, Christina concludes that the Dijkstra algorithm is not a sufficient tool to solve the SST challenge since this algorithm does not provide the opportunity to manage the constraint that each node contained in the network is visited exactly once.

In this section we accompany Christina while she learns how optimization problems on network structures can be solved if restrictions on the solution must be considered. In Sect. 14.3.1, the underlying basic decision problem of the SST situation is introduced and explained in detail. In Sect. 14.3.2, a mathematical optimization model for a restricted network optimization problem is introduced. Techniques to determine feasible solutions for these models are presented in Sect. 14.3.3.

14.3.1 Travelling Salesman Problem

Christina wants to know if her SST challenge has already been solved by anybody else. She remembers a lecture she visited during her studies. It was named "Operations Research Methods for Management Decision Problems". She sends an email to one of her study friends and asks him to send her a copy of the presentations delivered in this lecture. Several days later she receives these printouts and starts scanning the documents.

After some minutes she discovers the picture of a network (Fig. 14.2) that attracts her attention. The slide that contains this graphic is headed by the words "Travelling Salesman Problem".

Christina starts reading the remarks given by the instructor. She reads that the *Traveling Salesman Problem (TSP)* represents the basic decision task of many vehicle deployment problems. It is quite similar to the shortest path problem since also in the TSP it is necessary to fulfil a transportation task in a network structure with minimal resource utilization.

However, the TSP is distinct from the shortest path problem since all nodes in the network have to be visited but no node is allowed to be visited more than once (which means that each available node must be visited *exactly once*). There is also a distinct node, called the starting node, or the depot from which the travelling salesman starts his journey and to which he returns after all other nodes have been visited exactly once. The salesman wants to keep its total sum of travel distances between the visited nodes as small as possible.

Christina summarizes these findings and transfers her finding to the SST challenges. She is convinced that the TSP represents exactly the SST problem setting: there is a set of nodes given and these nodes (in the SST case: the given

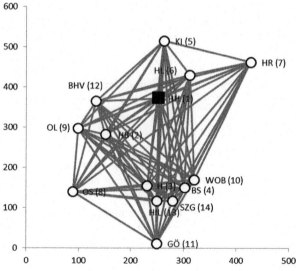

Fig. 14.2 Problem setting of the travelling salesman problem (TSP)

14.3 Round Trip Planning/Travelling Salesman Problem

points of interests) must all be visited by a vehicle but the length of the travel path must be minimal.

Christina continues to read the instructor's notes. Without going into details she understands that the TSP can be modelled as a *linear program* (cf. Chap. 12) but that it is impossible to apply the standard approach for linear programs, which is the Simplex algorithm, to solve this model. For this reason her instructor proposes to apply other decision support methods which are called heuristics. Now, Christina's attention is awakened and she decides to study in detail the information given in the course material about the TSP, its modelling and the heuristic model solving techniques.

First, Christina wants to understand the case that motivates Fig. 14.2. The outline of the case study is as follow. A sales representative lives in Hamburg (city numbered 1 according to Table 14.3). Each week, she has to visit the remaining 13 cities in Northern Germany which are given in Table 14.3 (cities 2–14). She wants to visit all these cities with one trip (if necessary, she will have an overnight stay in one of the cities) in order to show up at the retail outlet stores of her company. According to her contract with this company, she has to pay for the fuel costs on her own. In order to keep the fuel expenses as low as possible the sales representative is searching for a least-distance round trip that starts in Hamburg, terminates in Hamburg and visits all remaining 13 cities exactly once.

Christina continues to learn more about the case. The sales representative (which is in the role of the travelling saleswoman) can travel directly from each given city and each given other city as indicated by the graph in Fig. 14.2. Such a graph in which each node has a connection to each other node is called a complete graph. At first look, such a network structure seems to make the determination of a round trip easier than the determination of a round trip in a general graph like the one given in Fig. 14.1: Detours on the way from one node to another node are not necessary.

Table 14.3 Coordinates of major cities in Northern Germany

Name of location (abbreviation)	i	Coordinates x_i	y_i
Hamburg (HH)	1	253	372
Bremen (HB)	2	151	282
Hannover (H)	3	231	155
Braunschweig (BS)	4	302	150
Kiel (KI)	5	262	515
Lübeck (HL)	6	311	425
Rostock (HR)	7	427	462
Osnabrück (OS)	8	89	140
Oldenburg (OL)	9	99	297
Wolfsburg (WOB)	10	320	170
Göttingen (GÖ)	11	249	12
Bremhaven (BHV)	12	133	365
Hildesheim (HIL)	13	249	117
Salzgitter (SZG)	14	279	117

Fig. 14.3 Infeasible TSP solution with too short cycles

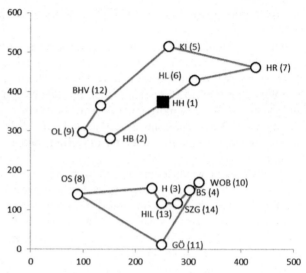

▶ **Practical Insights** A high number of nodes and arcs in the network let the determination of the shortest path become a management problem of high *complexity*. The following calculation emphasizes this statement. How many round trips are available that visit each node exactly once? For the first customer node, the sales representative can select from 13 so far unvisited nodes. For the second customer node to be visited, she can still select from 12 remaining customer locations and so on. In the given example, this leads to $13 \cdot 12 \cdot \ldots \cdot 2 \cdot 1 = 13! = 6.227.020.800$ possible trips that visits each node exactly once. Such a path that contains a node exactly once and that is closed (start and end node coincide) is called a Hamiltonian path. Now assume that the identification and the calculation of the length of each individual Hamiltonian path lasts 1 s. The compilation of a list of all evaluated Hamiltonian paths would last around 1200 days. For this reason, this so-called complete enumeration is not an appropriate approach with which to identify a shortest Hamiltonian path due to practical problems.

Christina is happy. She knows now that the SST challenges match the TSP challenges. Therefore, she is sure that she can solve her SST task after she has learned how the TSP is solved. She continues to inspect the lectures notes about the TSP and finds out that, again, a model-based approach is proposed to identify a solution for the given decision task. First, a model for the TSP is needed and, second, an algorithm for identifying a solution of the model is required.

14.3.2 A Mixed-Integer Linear Program for TSP-Modelling

All N = 14 locations to be visited are numbered by 1, 2, ..., N in order to ease the further problem description (cf. Table 14.3). These locations form the node set. An arc (i; j) connects two nodes and indicates that it is possible to travel from i to j. The node set in the TSP is equal to $\{1, ..., N\} \times \{1, ..., N\} \setminus \{(1; 1), ..., (N; N)\}$. Therefore, the graph in the TSP is complete.

The basic idea for modelling the TSP is that each arc (i; j) contained in the aforementioned node set is either contained in the Hamiltonian path (the round trip through all N nodes) or not. In the first mentioned case node j is visited immediately after node i but in the latter case node j is not visited immediately after i has been left. The TSP decision problem reduces to the question of which arcs form the requested Hamiltonian path and which arcs are ignored. In order to represent these binary decisions the family of binary decision variables x_{ij} (i ∈ $\{1, ..., N\}$, i ∈ $\{1, ..., N\}$) is introduced. Each decision variable x_{ij} is either 0 or 1 and x_{ij} represents the decision whether arc (i; j) is contained in the Hamiltonian path or not. We declare x_{ij} to be 1 if and only if arc (i; j) is included in the Hamiltonian path. It equals 0 if this is not true.

Let d(i; j) be the distance between node i and node j if the arc (i; j) is used.

$$Z(x_{11}, x_{12}, \ldots, x_{NN}) = \sum_{i=1}^{N} \sum_{j=1}^{N} d(i;j) \cdot x_{ij} \to \min \quad (14.2)$$

Equation (14.2) determines the sum of travel distances of all arcs that are selected to be included in the Hamiltonian path. This value $Z(x_{11}, \ldots, x_{NN})$ must be minimized.

$$\sum_{j=1}^{N} x_{ij} = 1 \quad \forall i \in \{1, \ldots, N\} \quad (14.3)$$

$$\sum_{j=1}^{N} x_{ji} = 1 \quad \forall i \in \{1, \ldots, N\} \quad (14.4)$$

In order to ensure that the selected arcs form a Hamiltonian path through the node set $\{1, ..., N\}$ it is necessary to restrict the selection of the arcs. First, each node must be left once (14.3) and the salesman has to go to each node exactly once (14.4).

It is not sufficient (but it is necessary) that the two restrictions (14.3) as well as (14.4) are fulfilled in order to ensure that a Hamiltonian path through N = $\{1, ..., N\}$ is determined. Figure 14.3 shows a selection of arcs that fulfills (14.3) and (14.4) but a Hamiltonian Path is not achieved. Instead, two so-called short-cycles are generated. One of these two short cycles does not contain the start node 1. Therefore, it is necessary to add other constraints in order to ensure that a Hamiltonian path is generated.

$$u_i - u_j + Nx_{ij} \leq N - 1 \quad \forall i,j \in \{2,\ldots,N\} \tag{14.5}$$

The article of Desrochers and Laporte (1991) proposes the constraint family (14.5) as short-cycle elimination constraints. They demonstrate that, by means of these constraints and with the incorporation of the real-valued u_i-decision variables, short cycles that do not contain the start node 1 can be prevented.

$$x_{ij} \in \{0;1\} \quad \forall i,j \in \{1,\ldots,N\} \text{ and } u_i \text{ real-valued for all } i \in \{1,\ldots,N\} \tag{14.6}$$

Jointly, Eqs. (14.5) and (14.6) ensure that only round trips that contain the designated starting point 1 are allowed.

The TSP is now represented by the linear program (14.2)–(14.6). Since some of the decision variables included in this model are limited to integer (binary) values while other decision variables are real-valued this model falls into the class of a mixed-integer linear program (MILP). A linear program containing only integer-valued decision values falls into the class of integer linear programs (ILP) according to Grünert and Irnich (2005).

Having studied the derivation of the mathematical model and having learned that the model consists of a linear objective function as well as a collection of linear constraints, Christina re-implements the reported problem instance in an Excel spreadsheet model and tries to solve this model with the Excel Solver add-in. Quite rapidly, the solver returns a feasible solution. Christina studies the returned decision variable values. She is worried by the proposed values, e.g. she finds the proposal to set an x-decision variable to the value 0.25. She asks herself how she can interpret this value. After a while, she finds out the reason for this unexpected proposal: she forgot to declare the x-decision variables to be binary. She corrects this shortcoming and restarts the solver. Unexpectedly, the solver is unable to return a feasible solution. The calculation lasts more than 20 min so that she decides to interrupt it, being disappointed that there is no straightforward way to solve the TSP.

From her previous experience Christina has learned that the Simplex algorithm fails to return a feasible solution since this algorithm is unable to ensure that integer values are returned. An explicit limitation of the decision variable domains to binary or integer values significantly prolongs the model solving times. Christina supposes that in the latter mentioned situation another algorithm is called. Her interest is aroused. She wants to know if there are other algorithmic approaches to solve mathematical optimization models. She returns to the textbook and continues to read the instructor's ideas about solving a TSP-like problem.

14.3.3 Heuristic Search for High Quality Round Trips

An algorithmic approach to solve a decision model by exploiting a rational strategy of planning without mathematical proof that the proposed (return) feasible model solution cannot be dominated by another feasible solution is called a *heuristic* or a non-optimizing algorithm. In contrast, an algorithm for which the returned solution proposal is proven to be minimal (maximal) is called an *exact* or optimization algorithm or approach. The Simplex algorithm is an example of an exact algorithm. Heuristics are incorporated into model solvers in case no exact algorithm is available or if the processing times provided by an exact algorithm are expected to be prohibitively long. Since the *processing time* for solving relatively small instances of a TSP is in general quite long it seems to be reasonable to think about a heuristic approach for the TSP.

This paragraph introduces heuristics for the management of TSP-like planning tasks. Two types of algorithms are distinguished. First, we discuss the construction of a first feasible solution for the TSP, i.e. we explain the construction of a first Hamiltonian path in the given network. Second, we discuss approaches for the improvement of the Hamiltonian path, i.e. we want to reduce the travel length associated with the Hamiltonian path. Therefore, we need to analyse the already existing Hamiltonian path in order to find out which modifications are promising for a reduction in the length of the Hamiltonian path. The most promising modifications are tentatively implemented and, if leading to a travel distance reduction, finally implemented.

Algorithms for the Construction of an Initial Feasible Model Solution
Joereßen and Sebastian (1998) describe a quite intuitive approach for the construction of a Hamiltonian path. The central idea is to consecutively insert the nodes after the last visited node until all nodes are contained in the path. A Hamiltonian path is created. This approach is also known as a *"nearest neighborhood heuristic"*.

It starts with an empty path. For a first step, the starting node (in our example node 1) is inserted. Next, the node with the shortest distance from the starting node is inserted just after the starting node. This path extension is iterated until no further node is remaining. This path construction procedure follows the rational strategy to keep the additional travel distance associated with serving the next customer after the previously inserted customer as low as possible. Therefore, the applied rational strategy can be characterized as *"greedy"*. Consequently, this construction heuristic is named "greedy construction procedure". A major shortcoming of the greedy construction procedure is its myopic insertion strategy. After all nodes have been inserted into the node sequence it is necessary to return to the start node. The travel distance for the return to the depot is not considered in the calculation of the additional travel distance to serve the next customer. Consequently, the greedy strategy cannot be proven to return the shortest possible Hamiltonian path. However, it returns a first Hamiltonian path.

Task 14.1 TSP Solution with Greedy Heuristic
Consider a transportation company that has to deliver products from Hamburg to 13 cities in Germany according to the TSP. The data refer to Table 14.3 and the distances are reflected in Fig. 14.4.

	j													
		1	2	3	4	5	6	7	8	9	10	11	12	13	14
i	1		136	218	227	143	79	196	284	171	213	360	120	255	256
	2	136		150	201	258	215	330	155	54	203	287	85	192	209
	3	218	150		71	361	282	364	143	194	90	144	232	42	61
	4	227	201	71		367	275	336	213	251	27	148	273	62	40
	5	143	258	361	367		102	173	413	272	350	503	198	398	398
	6	79	215	282	275	102		122	361	248	255	418	188	314	310
	7	196	330	364	336	173	122		467	367	311	484	310	388	375
	8	284	155	143	213	413	361	467		157	233	205	229	162	191
	9	171	54	194	251	272	248	367	157		255	322	76	234	255
	10	213	203	90	27	350	255	311	233	255		173	270	89	67
	11	360	287	144	148	503	418	484	205	322	173		372	105	109
	12	120	85	232	273	198	188	310	229	76	270	372		274	288
	13	255	192	42	62	398	314	388	162	234	89	105	274		30
	14	256	209	61	40	398	310	375	191	255	67	109	288	30	

Fig. 14.4 Distance matrix for the TSP instance defined by the nodes in Table 14.3 (values for d(i; j) in kilometers)

Obviously, the length d(i, j) of the arcs are very important for the decision about the inclusion of the next node. Typically, these values are composed in the distance matrix as shown for the example from Table 14.3 in Fig. 14.4. The entry in the i-th row in column j corresponds to the length of the arc (i; j). Headers are not considered in this numbering.

Greedy construction procedure	
(a)	initialize: L = 0, start = 1, k = 1;
(b)	Repeat steps (c)–(i) until all columns are blocked
(c)	DEST:=min{d(START, q)l column q is not blocked}
(d)	L:=L + d(START, DEST);
(e)	block row of START as well as column associated with START;
(f)	stop[k]:=START;
(g)	START:=DEST;
(h)	k = k + 1;
(i)	goto (b);
(j)	stop[k] := 1;
(k)	L:=L + d(START, 1);
(l)	End;

14.3 Round Trip Planning/Travelling Salesman Problem

This pseudocode represents the greedy construction procedure that consists of an initialization phase (a), iteration loops (b)–(i) as well as a termination phase (j)–(l). During the initialization phase, the travel distance is set to 0 and the first node in the path is set to the starting node start :=1 (home of the salesman). The iteration counter k is initialized.

Exactly one node is appended to the already existing partial path in each iteration. Each iteration starts with the check whether there are still unblocked columns. Such an unblocked column represents a node that has not yet been appended. Among all unblocked column (available nodes) a node DEST with the least distance d(START, DEST) from the last appended node START is chosen (c). Afterwards, the so far travelled path length L is increased by L(START; DEST) (d). Next, the row as well as the column associated with DEST is blocked (e). The recently selected node DEST is appended to the already existing partial path (f) and DEST will be set to the latest inserted node (g). The iteration counter is increased by 1 (h) and the procedure jumps back to the beginning of the loop (i). In the case of no further unblocked column being available, the path will be closed, i.e. the arc from the last appended node to the starting node is selected (j) and the travel distance is updated (k). Further details can be found in the examples in E-Supplement.

In the example, we have framed the cells representing the arcs (1; 6), (2; 3), (3; 13), (4; 10), (5; 7), (6; 5), (7; 12), (8; 1), (9; 2), (10; 11), (11; 8), (12; 9), (13; 14) as well as (14; 4). These arcs lead to the Hamiltonian path 1, 6, 5, 7, 12, 9, 2, 3, 13, 14, 4, 10, 11, 8, 1. The length is 1746 km. This path can be found in Fig. 14.5.

Figure 14.5 visualizes the proposal generated by the greedy construction procedure. Obviously, the generated Hamiltonian path is not optimal, i.e. it is possible to reduce the travel length. Within the route segment $1 \rightarrow 6 \rightarrow 5 \rightarrow 7 \rightarrow 12$ as well as in the route segment $9 \rightarrow 2 \rightarrow 3 \rightarrow 13 \rightarrow 14 \rightarrow 4 \rightarrow 10 \rightarrow 11 \rightarrow 8 \rightarrow 1$ a modification of the visiting order leads to a shorter Hamiltonian path. This is not a surprising observation since the primary goal of the greedy construction procedure is the generation of a feasible (but not necessarily a least-distance) Hamiltonian path. The idea of inserting one customer after another, even with least marginal costs, does not result in a least-distance Hamiltonian path.

The phenomenon observed here refers to a general shortcoming of heuristic search for solutions if several constraints have to be considered while trying to optimize the objective function. It is either trying to fulfil the optimization property or it is trying to achieve feasibility of the generated solution proposals. At first glance, it seems that the greedy construction procedure fails for the TSP but it is worth getting a first feasible Hamiltonian path, since it is possible to improve the objective function using so-called improvement heuristics that modify the initial feasible solution. These improvement heuristics focus on the minimization of the objective function value but also keep the feasibility of the modified solution.

Fig. 14.5 Visualization of the greedy construction procedure proposal

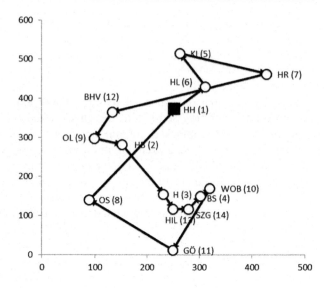

Improvement Heuristics for the Travel Distance Reduction

We design and apply improvement heuristics in order to update an already existing feasible decision problem solution. During the update it is necessary to preserve the feasibility but the objective function value should be brought closer to the (unknown) optimization goal. For a given Hamiltonian path in the TSP an improvement heuristic tries to find another Hamiltonian path with reduced travel distance by modification of the visiting sequence as proposed by the construction heuristic. Detours should be eliminated. The 2-opt-improvement heuristic presented here is based on ideas discussed by Croes (1958). In its most simple realization the 2-opt heuristic tries to reduce the length of a given Hamiltonian path by swapping two adjacent nodes in the path. Therefore, the swap is applied tentatively. Then, it is checked to see whether length reduction is achieved. In this case, the tentative swap is confirmed. Otherwise, the swap is cancelled (Fig. 14.6).

We now apply the 2-opt-improvement logic to reduce the travel distance by swapping adjacent nodes in the available Hamiltonian path proposed by the greedy construction heuristic. We start with the partial path 1; 6; 5; 7 and try to swap nodes 6; 5, i.e. we tentatively replace 1; 6; 5; 7 with 1; 5; 6; 7 (cf. Fig. 14.6).

Iteration 1: The sub-path 1; 6; 5; 7 has a length of 354 km. Swapping 6 and 5 will lead to the sub-path 1; 5; 6; 7 with a length of 367 km. This swap is therefore not beneficial and it is not confirmed.

Iteration 2: The sub-path 6; 5; 7; 12 has a length of 605 km. Swapping 5 and 7 will lead to the sub-path 6; 7; 5; 12 of length 493 km. Since the executed swap

14.3 Round Trip Planning/Travelling Salesman Problem

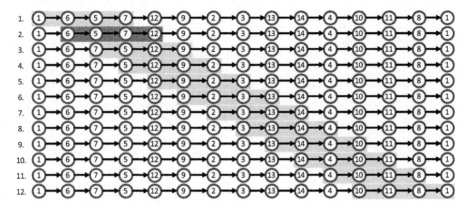

Fig. 14.6 Processing of 2-opt-improvement-algorithm

leads to a length reduction it is confirmed and the sub-path 6; 5; 7; 12 is replaced by the sub-path 6; 7; 5; 12.

Iteration 3: The sub-path 7; 5; 12; 9 has a length of 447 km. Swapping nodes 12 and 5 leads to the sub-path 7; 12; 5; 9 of length 780 km. This swap is therefore not beneficial and it is not confirmed.

Iteration 4: The sub-path 5; 12; 9; 2 has a length of 328 km. Swapping nodes 12 and 9 leads to sub-path 5; 9; 12; 2 with length 433. This swap is not confirmed.

Iteration 5: The sub-path 12; 9; 2; 3 has a length of 280 km. Swapping nodes 2 and 9 leads to sub-path 12; 2; 9; 3 with length 333 km. This swap is not confirmed.

Iteration 6: The sub-path 9; 2; 3; 13 has a length of 264 km. Swapping nodes 2 and 3 leads to sub-path 9; 3; 2; 13 with length 536 km. This swap is not confirmed.

Iteration 7: The sub-path 2; 3; 13; 14 has a length of 222 km. Swapping the nodes 3 and 13 leads to sub-path 2; 13; 3; 14 with length 295. This swap is not confirmed.

Iteration 8: The sub-path 3; 13; 14; 4 has a length of 112 km. Swapping nodes 13 and 14 leads to sub-path 3; 14; 13; 4 with a length of 153 km. This swap is not confirmed.

Iteration 9: The sub-path 13; 14; 4; 10 has a length of 97 km. Swapping nodes 14 and 4 leads to sub-path 13; 4; 14; 10 with a length of 169 km. This swap is not confirmed.

Iteration 10: The sub-path 14; 4; 10; 11 has a length of 240 km. Swapping nodes 4 and 10 leads to sub-path 14; 10; 4; 11 with a length of 242 km. This swap is not confirmed.

Iteration 11: The sub-path 4; 10; 11; 8 has a length of 405 km. Swapping nodes 10 and 11 leads to sub-path 4; 11; 10; 8 with a length of 554 km. This swap is not confirmed.

Iteration 12: The sub-path 10; 11; 8; 1 has a length of 662 km. Swapping nodes 11 and 8 leads to sub-path 10; 8; 11; 1 with a length of 798 km. This swap is not confirmed (Fig. 14.7).

The existing Hamiltonian path is now completely processed. A length reduction of 112 km has been achieved. The improved Hamiltonian path is shown in

Fig. 14.7 Hamiltonian path after first application of the 2-opt-improvement heuristic

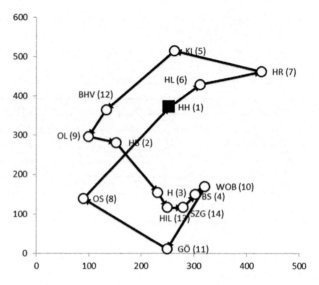

Fig. 14.8 Solution of inversion of the sub-path from 3 to 8

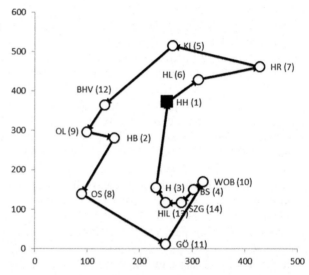

Fig. 14.7. Despite significant improvement, we see immediately that further improvements are needed. However, the required improvement cannot be achieved by interchanging adjacent nodes, so that a 2-opt improvement procedure call is useless. In the situation reported here it is beneficial to invert the sub-path 3; 13; 14; 4; 10; 11; 8, i.e. to replace this sub-path by 8; 11; 10; 4; 14; 13; 3 (see Fig. 14.8). However, the identification of a sub-path whose inversion is beneficial is a challenging task in itself.

In general a restart of the 2-op procedure to the already improved solution can be useful in order to identify further length-saving swapping. In our example swapping

Fig. 14.9 Map of hotels in the example

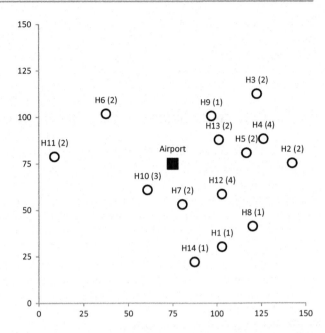

of nodes 6 and 7 is now possible (but was not possible in the first application of the 2-opt procedure). Sometimes nodes are moved from a position at the beginning of a Hamiltonian path to a later position or vice versa.

14.4 Vehicle Routing

Having solved the first two operative vehicle deployment tasks (LS and SST) successfully, Christina turns to the next large business area, which is the local transfer of inbound tourists. RSBT provides this service to international travel agencies. These agencies sell all-inclusive travel packages to customers. Such a package includes

- a return flight ticket from the selected origin airport to Hurghada international airport (HRG)
- accommodation in the selected hotel in the Hurghada region including breakfast or half board or full board or all-inclusive food & beverage
- transfer on day of arrival with a pickup at the airport and a drop-off at the selected hotel
- transfer on the day of departure from the hotel to the airport.

Christina finds out that RSBT generates a significant amount of income from the transfer services but the profits are quite small. She discusses this observation with the responsible division manager. The manager mentions that the transfer of incoming passengers (AAT) is easier to plan than the transfer of outbound passengers (ADT) since in the ADT setup pickup times at the hotels have to be considered. In the AAT setup, such time windows do not play any role.

14.4.1 Case Study ORION: Vehicle Routing at UPS

ORION (**O**n-**R**oad **I**ntegrated **O**ptimization and **N**avigation) is a routing optimization system that suggests an optimized route to get from point A to point Z and all potential stops in between while also considering specified delivery windows. It aims to determine routes by a heuristic that uses predominantly right-hand-turns in order to increase efficiency by maximizing both time savings and safety (therefore saving on repairs, etc.). ORION uses a database of 250 million addresses, customized map data and takes into account different variables such as distances, delivery times, different types of customers, and package types. ORION constantly re-evaluates alternative routing options, up to the last moment before a driver leaves the depot and thereby provides optimal routing instructions to UPS drivers – in a planned second phase of the ORION project, UPS plans to enable live recalculations even during delivery.

What has been the business value of ORION?
Through the deployment of ORION, UPS had optimized 10,000 routes by the end of 2013 and aims to optimize all 55,000 routes being served in the US by 2017. The optimization of routes had effects on three dimensions: efficiency, sustainability and service level. The results stated refer to the pilot year 2013.

By optimizing routes, UPS managed to reduce the total distance travelled by trucks by 20 million miles and to deliver 350,000 additional packages. Estimations indicate that a reduction of one mile per day per driver for 1 year results in savings amounting to $50 million.

These efficiency gains in turn positively affect the use of resources, as a reduction in miles travelled causes a diminution of CO_2 emissions (14,000 metric tons) and leads to gasoline savings (5.7 million litres of fuel). At the same time UPS also increased its service "My Choice", a service that allows consumers to actively choose delivery preferences, reroute shipments and adjust delivery locations and dates as needed, could be further optimized.

What are the disadvantages of ORION?
The costs connected with the development of soft- and hardware as well as the setup of vehicle routing solutions such as ORION can be extremely high. UPS dedicates 700 employees to the operation and maintenance of ORION, even though there are no official comments regarding the costs directly attributable to ORION.

14.4 Vehicle Routing

UPS' overall annual budget of $1 billion on technology suggests that the investment on innovation and improvement of technology is material. Also, the lead time needed for the set-up can often be considerable. In UPS' case, the ORION algorithm was initially developed in a laboratory and tested at various UPS sites from 2003 to 2009. In order to gather the huge amount of data necessary to develop the ORION system, UPS installed GPS tracking equipment and vehicle sensors on UPS delivery trucks in 2008. The company prototyped ORION at eight sites between 2010 and 2011, before deploying the system to six beta sites in 2012.

Furthermore, the *complexity* of vehicle routing problems in the real world is often very high requiring special experts for the implementation of VRP solutions. The complexity can easily be understood when thinking of the number of possibilities for determining only one route: an average UPS driver has about 125 customers to reach a day. The number of options for scheduling a route for 125 different locations is 125! which is a number with 210 digits which by far exceeds the number of nanoseconds the earth has existed. Another hint for the complexity of the problem is the fact that after 6 years of research, UPS was able to determine an algorithm that takes 90 pages to describe and 1000 pages of code to implement.

Finally, at this stage, ORION is not able to consider *dynamic data* such as weather, traffic jams, or accidents which might slow down a driver's route, and is therefore only providing an optimal solution at the moment a vehicle leaves the depot and not later, as changes might occur.

14.4.2 Decision Situation Outline

Christina and the manager commonly decide that for the reason of the time, they have to separate the AAT from the ADT operations planning. Furthermore, they decide to analyse the AAT set-up first. Since Christina is not familiar with the AAT business she asks for an example in order to get an insight into the preparation and execution of some AAT services. The manager selects a certain day from the last month. On that day, there was one evening flight that carried overall 29 passengers to HRG. Different travel agencies have booked the corresponding AAT service at RSBT.

Overall, 14 hotels have to be served. The number of passengers q_i to be brought to a hotel H_i varies between 1 and 4 as shown in Table 14.4. The hotels are distributed around the airport (Fig. 14.9).

Next, Christina wants to know how the passengers are transported to the hotels. She learns that four minibuses are available to fulfil the AAT services. Each minibus offers ten passenger seats. All minibuses start their operations from a large parking lot at the airport. From there, a minibus moves to the exit of HRG's arrival hall where the passengers to be served enter the minibus. Next, a minibus goes to the requested hotel(s) where passengers are dropped off. Within a service trip, a minibus regularly visits one or more hotels before it returns empty to the parking lot at HRG.

Table 14.4 Hotels to be served in the AAT example

Hotel (code)	Hotel number i	Coordinates		Number of passengers
		x	y	q_i
Marina *** (H1)	1	103	30	1
Blue Lagoon (H2)	2	143	75	2
Three Palms (H3)	3	123	113	2
Golf Resort (H4)	4	126	88	4
Delphin (H5)	5	117	81	2
Pyramid (H6)	6	38	102	2
Inn at the Beach (H7)	7	81	53	2
Sharky Corner (H8)	8	120	41	1
Diver's Paradise (H9)	9	97	101	1
Red Sea Exclusive (H10)	10	60.75	60.75	3
Water Palace (H11)	11	8.75	78.75	2
Grand Hotel Landside (H12)	12	103	58.5	4
Desert Castle (H13)	13	101.25	87.75	2
Wonder World (H14)	14	87.5	22	1

*** It is a three star rated hotel

The AAT manager tells Christina that he has the feeling that the performance of the AAT operations is quite low. In particular, he thinks that the distances travelled (and therefore trip durations) are quite high. As a consequence the number of deployed vehicles seems to be quite high. Overall, AAT operations seem to produce unnecessary travel costs (fuel costs resulting from detours) as well as personal costs (for the drivers). In order to demonstrate this, the AAT manager produces Table 14.5 showing the trips executed by the four vehicles. Four vehicles are deployed and the total distance travelled is 232.42 km + 285.77 km + 204.08 km + 150.81 km = 873.07 km.

14.4.3 Current Approach for the Route Compilation

Having seen only the vehicle trips already executed, Christina feels uncomfortable in giving a statement about the suitability of the proposed trips. She looks for hints that support the evaluation of the proposed service processes (the vehicle trips). In a first attempt to estimate the quality of the proposed trips she visualizes the proposed solution (the trips) in the map provided in Fig. 14.9. Therefore, she connects the hotels by lines in the sequence proposed by the visiting sequences shown in Table 14.5. As the result, she gets the route map shown in Fig. 14.10.

14.4 Vehicle Routing

Table 14.5 Vehicle trips in the AAT example

Location	X	y	Occupied seats at departure	Route of
Airport	300	300	9	Vehicle 1
H1	412	121	8	Trip length: 232.42
H2	570	301	6	
H3	490	450	4	
H4	505	353	0	
Airport	300	300		
Airport	300	300	8	Vehicle 2
H5	467	323	6	Trip length: 285.77
H6	150	407	4	
H7	322	212	2	
H8	481	165	1	
H9	388	402	0	
Airport	300	300		
Airport	300	300	9	Vehicle 3
H10	243	243	6	Trip length: 204.08
H11	35	315	4	
H12	412	234	0	
Airport	300	300		
Airport	300	300	3	Vehicle 4
H13	405	351	1	Trip length: 150.81
H14	350	88	0	
Airport	300	300		

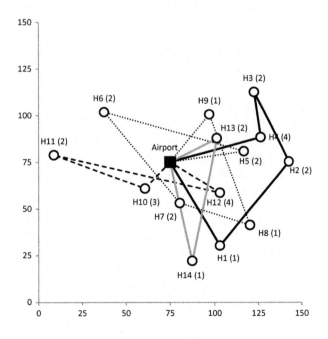

Fig. 14.10 Vehicle trips in the AAT-example

Vehicle 1 follows the continuous line but vehicle 2 travels along the dotted line. In addition, vehicle 3 operates along the dashed line, while the fourth vehicle follows the grey line. Christina thinks about generating trips in the AAT business and she tries to uncover similarities and differences compared to the two previous investigations. Here is what she finds out:

1. Since several vehicles are available it is necessary to distribute all nodes representing locations to be visited among the available vehicles. No node is allowed to be left uncovered.
2. In order to save travelled distances each node must be served by one visit, i.e. by exactly one vehicle.
3. Since the vehicle capacity is limited there is a constraint that must be considered: the maximal payload capacity is not allowed to be exceeded.
4. For each vehicle, a TSP has to be solved (a Hamiltonian path through the common starting point and the locations assigned to this vehicle).

According to the first two properties of AAT's current situation it is necessary to decide about the assignment of customer locations to the vehicles, i.e. the set of customer nodes is clustered into pairwise disjoint sets which are called tours. Each tour is extended by the central position (the depot) from where all vehicles are located before the trip execution starts and to which all vehicles return after they have served all assigned customers (all deliveries have been executed).

The third property implies that the clustering is a decision that is constrained, e.g. some clustering decisions are not allowed (they are infeasible). The fourth observation demonstrates that there is also a sequencing problem (a TSP) which must be solved.

Christina leans back and summarizes her findings. The current AAT situation is a constrained combined clustering and sequencing problem. In order to find out if such a decision situation has been discussed before, she starts an Internet search and learns that the current AAT decision was a problem that had been quite well and intensively studied, called the *capacitated vehicle routing problem* (CVRP).

14.4.4 Capacitated Vehicle Routing Problem

Solving a CVRP is the process of finding the optimal transportation routes for a given fleet of vehicles under capacity constraints. There are different variations of the CVRP in regard to the specific constraints that an organization faces. In Fig. 14.11, the most important CVRP determinants are summarized.

Consider the most important CVRP determinants. First, *objectives* may relate to time, distance, costs or sustainability. Second, the consideration of *customers* may be subject to different numbers of customers, demand patterns and time windows. Third, the *drivers* can be classified regarding different working periods and regulations for working conditions and time.

Fourth, the *fleet* can be considered in different ways depending on the size of vehicles (homogenous or heterogeneous), capacity utilization rules (e.g., LTL: less than truck load or FTL: full truck load) and depot of references (e.g., the requirement on returning to the start depot). Fifth, representation of the *road network* may be different

14.4 Vehicle Routing

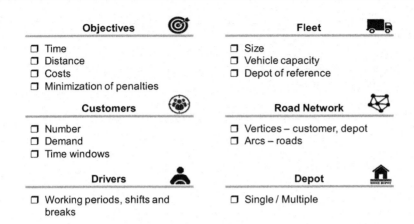

Fig. 14.11 CVRP characteristics

for different CVRP cases. Finally, the *depots* can be considered as single or multiple. The solution methods used for the CVRP consider *heuristic* and *exact* approaches.

> ▶ **Practical Insights** CVRP solutions in practice are typically based on heuristic methods since the complexity of CVRP is even higher than in TSP. In addition, up-to-date information technology allows using real-time data about traffic jams, weather conditions, etc. This makes it possible to implement *dynamic* or *adaptive* vehicle routing models in combination with sophisticated software to increase flexibility and customer service level.

Having learned that the AAT challenge can be represented as CVRP, Christina wants to know how the vehicle trips (routes) are derived from the requests submitted by the travel agencies. She discusses this issue with the AAT manager. First, she hears that all requests are submitted from the travel agencies to AAT three days prior to the due day, which is the execution day. Second, she is told that the consecutively arriving requests are processed in the order of their arrival ("first come/first serve"). Hotel H1 belongs to the first request received, H2 to the second, and so on. The request received first is assigned to the first vehicle, i.e. vehicle 1 visits H1. The second request received is appended to this route after the first request, i.e. H2 is visited by vehicle 1 immediately after H1 has been visited. The next requests are processed similarly as long as the residual capacity (number of free seats) of the vehicle currently under consideration is large enough to serve the next request, i.e. as long as adding the next request would not result in exceeding the capacity of the vehicle. The route of this vehicle is then closed, i.e. the return of the vehicle to the central depot (parking lot) is added and the route of this vehicle is not changed any further. A new vehicle route is opened and the drop-off location for the request that has caused excess capacity is inserted as the first customer location in the route of the second vehicle. Altogether, a greedy strategy similar to the strategy introduced for the TSP is applied to the CVRP. Two differences must be mentioned.

1. The next request is not determined by the smallest distance increase but by the arrival time of the request.
2. A capacity limit assigned to each vehicle is observed. In a case where the addition of the next request would lead to a capacity excess, a new vehicle route would be started.

The pseudocode description for the applied construction procedure for the CVRP is as follows.

Construction Procedure for the CVRP	
(a)	initialize: START=0; DEST=1; k=1; v=1; cap_used(v)=0; L(v)=0; PATH[v,k]=START;
(b)	Repeat steps (c)-(p) until DEST > CUSTOMERS
(c)	if cap_used(v)+q(DEST) ≤ CAP(v) then goto (j)
(d)	PATH[v;k+1] := 0;
(e)	L:=L+d(START,0);
(f)	v:=v+1;
(g)	L(v):=0;
(h)	cap_used(v):=0;
(i)	k=0; START:=0;
(j)	L(v):=L(v)+d(START,DEST);
(k)	cap_used(v) := cap_used(v)+q(DEST);
(l)	k:=k+1;
(m)	PATH[v;k]:=DEST;
(n)	START:=DEST;
(o)	DEST:=DEST+1
(p)	goto (b);
(q)	return PATH;
(r)	End;

All vehicles start at the depot node 0 and have the remaining payload capacity CAP[v]. The vehicle currently under consideration is represented by v. The assigned payload of vehicle v is labelled by cap_used(v), and L(v) carries the length of the route of vehicle v. PATH[v;k] contains the node that is the k-th customer location in the route of vehicle v. START gives the last visited node and DEST contains the node associated with the request at position DEST in the sequence of requests.

The CVRP construction procedure starts with the initialization of the used variables (a). In each iteration, the steps (b)–(p) are processed. Iteration starts with the check of whether there are still unassigned customer locations (b). After that the assignment of the next request to vehicle v is tested to see if it will lead to an excess in capacity of this vehicle (c). If this is not the case then the trip length is updated (j), the used capacity is increased (k), the vehicle customer location is appended to the existing partial route (m) and the next customer to be considered is selected (n)–(o). If the capacity test fails, i.e. if the next customer cannot be

14.4 Vehicle Routing

assigned to the current vehicle then the depot is appended as last visited location to the route (d) and the return distance is added (e). Afterwards, the route of the next vehicle is initialized (f)–(i).

Christina asks for the ratio behind the planning logic represented by the CVRP construction procedure. She learns that this planning procedure is very simple and can be applied very quickly. In studying this information Christina is sure that she can improve the route plan, because the proposed CVRP construction procedure does not consider any information about the geographic location of the hotels to be visited. This results in unnecessary detours. For example, she refers to the dashed and to the dotted vehicle routes in Fig. 14.10. Here, the two vehicles are "zig-zagging" through the area; travelling back and forth between different regions causes detours.

14.4.5 The Sweep Algorithm

Task 14.2. Solving the CVRP by the Sweep Algorithm
Consider the locations with transformed coordinates (Table 14.6).

In order to overcome shortcomings associated with the CVRP construction procedure Christina thinks about opportunities to identify and exploit similar locations of different hotels. One characteristic of a customer location (hotel) is its direction in relation to the central reference point which is the airport parking lot at point (75; 75). Another characteristic of a hotel location is the distance between the airport parking lot and the hotel. If and only if both values, direction as well as distance

Table 14.6 Locations with transformed coordinates

Location	No. i	(x; y)-coordinates		q_i	Polar coordinates		Angle
		x	y		r_i	$\deg_i$	α_i
Airport	0	75	75	0	0	0	0
H6	6	37.50	101.75	2	46.06	0.95	54.51
H11	11	8.75	78.75	2	66.36	1.51	86.78
H10	10	60.75	60.75	3	20.15	2.36	135.01
H14	14	87.50	22.00	1	54.45	3.37	193.27
H7	7	80.50	53.00	2	22.68	3.39	194.04
H1	1	103.00	30.25	1	52.79	3.70	212.04
H8	8	120.25	41.25	1	56.45	4.07	233.29
H12	12	103.00	58.50	4	32.50	4.18	239.50
H2	2	142.50	75.25	2	67.50	4.72	270.21
H5	5	116.25	80.75	2	42.14	4.85	277.84
H4	4	126.25	88.25	4	52.94	4.96	284.50
H13	13	101.25	87.75	2	29.18	5.16	295.91
H3	3	122.50	112.50	2	60.52	5.38	308.30
H9	9	97.00	100.50	1	33.68	5.57	319.22

from the airport of different hotels, are similar then both hotels are situated close together. However, if the direction components are similar then it is perhaps beneficial to assign both customers to the same vehicle since detours are unlikely and the vehicle is already heading for the same direction for both customers (hotels) (Fig. 14.12).

The analysis of the x-y-coordinates that describe the hotel locations does not help Christina to find similarities between the hotel sites. For this reason, she thinks about transforming the x-y-coordinates into polar-coordinates. Therefore, she defines the grey vertical reference line as shown in Fig. 14.12 and determines the direction of a hotel, e.g. H6, by drawing a line from the airport's coordinates to H6. Each hotel, i.e. H6 is now defined by the distance r_i between the airport and the hotel ("radius") plus the direction as defined by the angle α_i between the vertical reference line and the direction line to the hotel side. In column 7 of Table 14.6 this angle is given by deg_i of the grey arc (the length of the circumference of a complete circle $= 6.282$). If deg_i is multiplied by $360°/6.282$ then we get the angle α_i.

Christina now sorts the requests according to increasing α_i-values. She gets the request sequence shown in columns 1 and 2 in Table 14.6. She saves this sequence in the list SEQ, so that SEQ[1] = H6, SEQ[2] = H11, SEQ[3] = H10, SEQ[4] = H14, SEQ[5] = H7, SEQ[6] = H1, SEQ[7] = H8, SEQ[8] = H12, SEQ[9] = H2, SEQ[10] = H5, SEQ[11] = H4, SEQ[12] = H13, SEQ[13] = H3, SEQ[14] = H9.

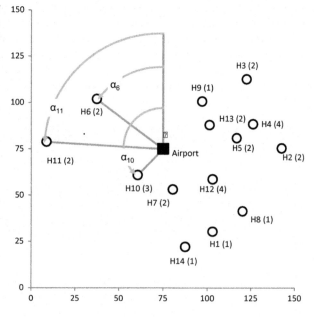

Fig. 14.12 Determination of polar-coordinates of locations in relation to the *vertical grey line*

14.4 Vehicle Routing

	Sweep-procedure for the CVRP
(a)	initialize: START = 0; REQ = 1; DEST = SEQ[REQ]; k = 1; v = 1; cap_used(v) = 0; L(v) = 0; PATH[v,k] = START;
(b)	Repeat steps (c)–(q) until DEST > CUSTOMERS
(c)	if cap_used(v) + q(DEST) $\leq$ CAP(v) then goto (j)
(d)	PATH[v;k+1] := 0;
(e)	L:=L + d(START,0);
(f)	v:=v + 1;
(g)	L(v):=0;
(h)	cap_used(v):=0;
(i)	k = 0; START:=0;
(j)	L(v):=L(v) + d(START,DEST);
(k)	cap_used(v) := cap_used(v) + q(DEST);
(l)	k:=k + 1;
(m)	PATH[v;k]:=SEQ[REQ];
(n)	START:= SEQ[REQ];
(o)	REQ:=REQ + 1;
(p)	DEST:=SEQ[REQ];
(q)	goto (b);
(r)	return PATH;
(s)	End;

The aforementioned pseudocode depicts the modified construction procedure that now incorporates the determined sequence of requests ordered by increasing angle α_i. This procedure appends requests in the sequence SEQ to a vehicle as long as this vehicle has enough capacity. In a case where vehicle capacity is not sufficient to also serve the next request according to the SEQ-order, it continues with the next vehicle. If we fix the lower corner of the vertical grey line at the depot at (75; 75) and if we move the other corner counterclockwise around the depot then the grey line "sweeps" consecutively over all locations in the sequence SEQ. For this reason, the procedure represented in the pseudocode is called the "sweep algorithm for the capacitated vehicle routing problem" (Gillett and Miller 1974).

Christina applies the sweep algorithm to the AAT example and gets the route collection printed in Table 14.7. She adds up the travel distances of the three generated routes and finds out that they add up thus: 239.45 km + 209.02 km + 172.42 km = 620.90. Compared to the travel distance sum achieved from the application of the construction procedure shown in Fig. 14.12, which was 873.07 km, Christina calculates a travel distance saving of $\approx$ 29 % as a consequence of the variation of the sequence in which the request locations are appended to the existing routes. She learns that a careful analysis of the locations to be inserted next at the end of a tentative route significantly contributes to the saving of travel distances. The resulting vehicle routes are plotted in Fig. 14.13.

The number of vehicles required is also reduced if the sweep procedure is applied. However, Christina concludes that this is an achievement that has not been addressed by the sweep procedure. Her analysis of the sweep procedure

Table 14.7 Vehicle trips in the AAT example proposed by the sweep-algorithm

Location	x	Y	Occupied seats at departure	Route of
Airport	75.00	75.00	10	Vehicle 1
H6	37.50	101.75	8	Trip length: 239.45
H11	8.75	78.75	6	
H10	60.75	60.75	3	
H14	87.50	22.00	2	
H7	80.50	53.00	0	
Airport	75.00	75.00		
Airport	75.00	75.00	10	Vehicle 2
H1	103.00	30.25	9	Trip length: 209.02
H8	120.25	41.25	8	
H12	103.00	58.50	4	
H2	142.50	75.25	2	
H5	116.75	80.75	0	
Airport	75.00	75.00		
Airport	75.00	75.00	9	Vehicle 3
H4	126.25	88.25	5	Trip length: 172.42
H13	101.25	87.75	3	
H3	122.50	112.50	1	
H9	97.00	100.50	0	
Airport	75.00	75.00		

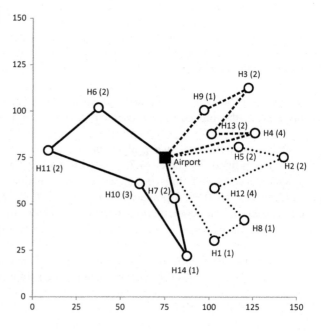

Fig. 14.13 Routes proposed by the sweep algorithm

reveals that the reduction is not addressed here. However, Christina concludes that a reduction in the number of vehicles used has the potential to contribute to the reduction of the total sum of travelled distances. Her statement is mainly inspired by the following observation. If there are two vehicles following two routes, then each vehicle must travel to the first customer in its route and each vehicle has to travel back from its latest visited customer location to the depot. We have two outbound route segments from the depot with length d1 (to node p) and d2 (to node q) and the inbound travel distances from the nodes s and t to the depot of length d3 and d4. If both routes are integrated, then we can save one outbound segment (say of the second vehicle) and one inbound segment which summarize to d2 + d4. If this sum is larger than the distance of the additional route segment from s to p of length d(s, p), i.e. if d2 + d4 − d(s, p) > 0 then the combination of the two trips realizes travel distance reductions. Clarke and Wright (1964) have proposed a so-called saving algorithm that starts with pendulum routes between the depot and a single customer location and continues to combine two routes to save travel distances. Further details on ADT scenario can be found in the example in E-Supplement.

14.5 Machine Scheduling

Christina wants to thank her study colleague (his name is Mark) for providing all the information about the TSP that enables her to understand the algorithmic ideas to improve the operations at RSBT. She calls him one evening and they talk for a long time about their current professional involvement. Mark mentions that he is working on scheduling problems but in the manufacturing business where he is responsible for setting up machine schedules. Christina is interested and invites him to talk about his experiences.

14.5.1 The Problem of Scheduling a Machine

Mark explains the general setup of a simple one-machine scheduling challenge in a manufacturing environment (Fig. 14.14).

There is a machine that is able to process one manufacturing task at a time. A manufacturing task is part of a customer *order*. All received orders are collected in the order or job backlog. At a specific time, all jobs are prepared for fulfilment. Fulfilling a job means using the machine to execute the manufacturing tasks requested by the customer that are associated with a job.

All jobs from the job backlog are ordered and jobs from the backlog are consecutively processed by the machine in the order determined by the job sequence $o_1, o_2, \ldots, o_N$. The executed tasks create the assets $A_1, A_2, \ldots, A_N$ requested by the customers. The basic decision problem associated with the outlined machine scheduling scenario is to determine the job *processing sequence* that determines the *schedule of the machine*.

Fig. 14.14 Machine scheduling problem

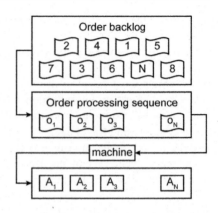

Christina wants to know how a manufacturing request can be evaluated in order to find an appropriate job processing sequence. Mark explains that each individual job is associated with different attributes. According to these attributes jobs can be compared and prioritized. Thonemann (2010) proposes the following three attributes to compare jobs in a job backlog. First, the *due date* d_i of job i is used. The due date determines the latest allowed completion time associated with a job. Second, each job has a specific *processing or flow time* p_i which is the time needed to process job i on the machine. Third, the *release time* t_i of job i is used to characterize a job. The release time is the time at which the job is completely specified so that its processing can be started.

Christina interrupts Mark and tells him that she would have been faced with a similar situation if she had handled the TSP. She had experienced the problem of finding good sequences as a very challenging task due to the strong increase in possible permutations of operations. Furthermore, she wants to know from Mark about the planning objectives in machine scheduling. Mark continues and states that there are several commonly used *performance indicators*:

The *completion time* of a job i determines the time when the job is completely fulfilled, i.e. it is the time when the job "leaves" the machine. The completion time is typically denoted by c_i.

The *flow (lead-time) time* f_i of a job i is the difference between the completion time c_i and the release time r_i of a job i. It can be interpreted as the time span necessary to respond to a customer job release.

Lateness or *tardiness* TD_i of job i measures the amount of time in excess of the due date associated with a job'

Work-in-process inventory and *capacity utilization*.

Lead time is composed of processing time, set-up time, waiting time, lying time and transportation time (Fig. 14.15).

Set-up time is needed to prepare the machine for processing the next job. *Lying time* is needed because of some technological restrictions (e.g., drying).

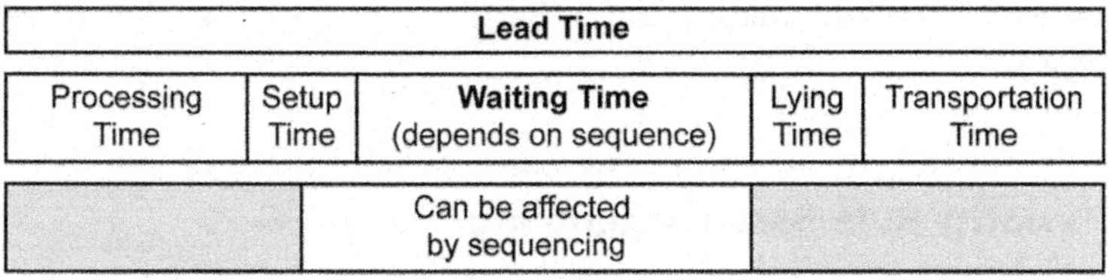

14.5 Machine Scheduling

Lead Time				
Processing Time	Setup Time	Waiting Time (depends on sequence)	Lying Time	Transportation Time
		Can be affected by sequencing		

Fig. 14.15 Lead time

Transportation time reflects the physical movement of jobs through the machines. *Waiting time* exists because a job cannot be processed at the next machine since this machine is occupied on another job. Even the waiting time and partially the set-up time can be affected by sequencing.

Completion times, flow times and tardiness are performance indicators for quantifying the scheduling decisions from the perspective of an individual request. In order to evaluate the quality of a complete job processing sequence additional performance indicators are used.

The *makespan* MS(S) associated with a job processing sequence S is defined as the length of the period that starts with the release of the first job and that ends with the completion of the last job in the sequence S.

The *average completion time* ACT(S) associated with sequence S is the average value of the completion times of the processed jobs if the jobs are processed in the sequence S by the machine.

The *maximal completion time* MCT(S) is the maximal value observed among all completion times after the application of the job processing sequence S.

Mark concludes his short introduction to machine scheduling with the remark that all the performance indicators can be used as primary planning goals. This creates *trade-offs* or goal conflicts since some of the goals are in contradictory relation to each other.

A typical trade-off in production scheduling is lead time and capacity utilization. Just imagine that you are in a supermarket on a Tuesday morning. Probably, you will be the only person there at this time. So you will not have to wait anywhere and will exit the supermarket in a short time. The time of your shopping will be short. But what about the supermarket? If you are the only customer, their capacity utilization is very low. The same effect can be encountered in manufacturing and service systems in regard to customer order lead time and resource capacity utilization.

This typical *trade-off in scheduling* is called *the scheduling dilemma*. According to the scheduling dilemma, we cannot achieve a reduction in lead time and an increase in capacity utilization at the same time. Mark gives an example. Students at Berlin School of Economics and Law arrive at the subway station Berliner Strasse, which is about 10 min walk from university. They can also use bus 104 to get to the school from the subway station. Assume that the buses run every 10 min and every minute one student comes to the bus stop. In this case, the waiting times and the lead times will be quite long, but the bus will take ten students and have good capacity utilization. Should the buses run every minute, the lead times would be very short (no waiting time), but the capacity utilization of each bus would be low.

14.5.2 Priority Rule-Based Scheduling

After she has learned that the schedule generation is also based on the sequencing of operations, as is the visit sequencing in the TSP, Christina wants to know how appropriate job processing sequences are determined. She asks Mark whether he also uses "greedy" strategies to add operation by operation to a partial sequence. Mark confirms her speculation but he tells Christina that there are some sort of *priority* or *dispatching rules* whose applications make the sequencing straightforward.

Mark explains that a priority rule is a "rule of thumb" to sort a set of jobs according to increasing or decreasing values of the release times r_i, the flow times f_i or the due dates d_i. The application of such a "simple" rule seems to be promising since the evaluation value of an individual job is not affected by the earlier or the subsequently processed job. This is a major difference from the sequencing in the TSP when the travel distances between consecutively visited nodes impacts the overall objective which is the total sum of travelled distances. Priority rules can be applied both for *job shop* and *flow shop* (cf. Chap. 9).

Task 14.3 Scheduling by Priority Rules

In order to demonstrate the effects of determining a job processing sequence using a priority rule, Mark introduces an example with eight jobs. The attributes of the jobs from the job backlog are summarized in Table 14.8.

The most intuitive approach for the determination of the job processing sequence is to process the jobs in the sequence of their arrival or release time. Those jobs

Table 14.8 Job backlog

Job i	1	2	3	4	5	6	7	8
Release time r_i	1	2	3	5	6	7	8	1
Duration p_i	4	2	3	7	2	8	3	4
Due date d_i	14	29	16	23	24	18	31	14

Table 14.9 Job processing sequence and machine schedule generated by FCFS

Job i	Release time r_i	Duration p_i	Due date d_i	Start time	Finish time	Tardiness	Flow time	Delayed?
1	1	4	14	8	12	0	11	0
2	2	2	29	12	14	0	12	0
3	3	3	16	14	17	1	14	1
4	4	7	28	17	24	0	20	0
5	5	7	23	24	31	8	26	1
6	6	2	24	31	33	9	27	1
7	7	8	18	33	41	23	34	1
8	8	3	31	41	44	13	36	1

14.5 Machine Scheduling

Table 14.10 Job processing sequence and machine schedule generated by SPT

Job i	Release time r_i	Duration p_i	Due date d_i	Start time	Finish time	Tardiness	Flow time	Delayed?
2	2	2	29	8	10	0	8	0
6	6	2	24	10	12	0	6	0
3	3	3	16	12	15	0	12	0
8	8	3	31	15	18	0	10	0
1	1	4	14	18	22	8	21	1
4	4	7	28	22	29	1	25	1
5	5	7	23	29	36	13	31	1
7	7	8	18	36	44	26	37	1

arriving first will be processed first. This sequencing rule is called *First Come/First Serve (FCFS)*. It does not apply to any "intelligent" sorting but it is a fair approach.

Table 14.9 shows the machine schedule resulting from the FCFS-processing job. The makespan is $44 - 1 = 43$ time units. The average completion time equals 27 time units but the maximal completion time is 44 time units. Five jobs are completed with delays. The average tardiness is 6.75 time units and the maximal tardiness is 23 time units. On average, the flow time is 22.5 time units.

The application of FCFS does not consider processing times or due dates while determining the sequence of processing. In order to enable a quick delivery of jobs it is useful to try to minimize the completion times of jobs. Here, it is beneficial to process those jobs first that can be processed rapidly in order to make the machine available for the next job as quickly as possible. According to the *Shortest-Processing-Time rule (SPT-rule)* the jobs are sorted by increasing processing time. The job with the shortest processing time in the job backlog is processed first.

The SPT-generated job processing sequence is listed in column 1 of Table 14.10. Again, the makespan is 43 time units but the average completion time is reduced from 27 time units to 23.25 time units. The maximal completion time remains 44 time units. Four jobs are still delayed with a slightly reduced tardiness of 6 time units. However, the maximal tardiness is prolonged to 26 time units but the average flow time is reduced to 18.75 time units.

Neither the application of the SPT rule nor the application of FCFS is able to control the maximal tardiness since none of these two rules considers the due date information associated with the jobs. In order to minimize the maximal tardiness the *Earliest Due Date rule (EDD-rule)* is proposed. According to the EDD-rule the most urgent job is processed first, followed by the job with the second highest urgency.

The makespan remains 43 time units (since there is no slack time in the schedules) as shown in Table 14.11. The average completion time is 29.5 time units and the maximal completion time equals 44 time units. An average flow time of 25 time units is observed. The application of the EDD-rule leads to a significant

Table 14.11 Job processing sequence and machine schedule generated by EDD

Job i	Release time r_i	Duration p_i	Due date d_i	Start time	Finish time	Tardiness	Flow time	Delayed?
1	1	4	14	8	12	0	11	0
3	3	3	16	12	15	0	12	0
7	7	8	18	15	23	5	16	1
5	5	7	23	23	30	7	25	1
6	6	2	24	30	32	8	26	1
4	4	7	28	32	39	11	35	1
2	2	2	29	39	41	12	39	1
8	8	3	31	41	44	13	36	1

reduction in maximal tardiness from 23 (FCFS) respectively 26 (EDD) down to 13 time units. Unfortunately, the number of delayed requests is increased (6 jobs). The same development is observed for the average tardiness, which is increased by up to 7 time units compared to 6 time units (SPT) and 6.75 time units (FCFS).

> ▶ **Practical Insights** The application of a priority rule enables the minimization of a single performance indicator value. There is no priority rule known that minimizes all three performance indicators (1) number of delayed requests (2) average completion time and (3) maximal delay. However, priority rules are easy to apply. That is why these simple heuristics are widely used in practice. In sophisticated scheduling software, so-called *meta-heuristics* such as *genetic algorithms* and *ant colony optimization* (ACO) are used. They provide solutions of very high quality.

14.5.3 Scheduling Algorithm of Moore

Moore (1968) published a paper about a one-machine scheduling algorithm that minimizes the number of delayed jobs. The basic idea is to extend the EDD rule by identifying those jobs that block the machine. Those jobs are then moved to the end of the sequence hoping that now one or even more jobs can be started earlier so that the number of delayed jobs can be reduced. Mark is going to explain to Christina how the Moore algorithm works by means of the example previously introduced.

First, the job backlog is scheduled according to the EDD rule. If there are no delayed jobs then the schedule construction is finished. Otherwise, the first delayed job according to the EDD-induced schedule is marked; here job 7 is the first delayed job (Table 14.12).

The basic idea of the Moore algorithm is to find out the reason of this delay. Moore supposes that the marked or a previously processed job is responsible for the delay. There, Moore suggests moving the labelled job 7 or one of the previously scheduled jobs (job 1 or job 3) to the end of the sequence so that all subsequent jobs can be started earlier. In order to identify the most appropriate job to be moved to the end, Moore proposes to compare the processing times p_i of the marked job and

14.5 Machine Scheduling

Table 14.12 Moore-algorithm (start): job processing sequence and machine schedule generated by EDD and marked first delayed job 7

Job i	Release time r_i	Duration p_i	Due date d_i	Start time	Finish time	Tardiness	Flow time	Delayed?
1	1	4	14	8	12	0	11	0
3	3	3	16	12	15	0	12	0
7	7	8	18	15	23	5	16	1
5	5	7	23	23	30	7	25	1
6	6	2	24	30	32	8	26	1
4	4	7	28	32	39	11	35	1
2	2	2	29	39	41	12	39	1
8	8	3	31	41	44	13	36	1

Table 14.13 Moore-Algorithm (2nd iteration): Job processing sequence and machine schedule generated by EDD and marked first delayed job 4

Job i	Release time r_i	Duration p_i	Due date d_i	Start time	Finish time	Tardiness	Flow time	Delayed?
1	1	4	14	8	12	0	11	0
3	3	3	16	12	15	0	12	0
5	5	7	23	15	22	0	17	0
6	6	2	24	22	24	0	18	0
4	4	7	28	24	31	3	27	1
2	2	2	29	31	33	4	31	1
8	8	3	31	33	36	5	28	1
7*	7	8	18	36	44	26	37	1

of the earlier scheduled jobs and to select the job among the aforementioned jobs with the longest processing time in order to achieve a maximal left shift of the job starting times. In the example (Table 14.12), job 7 exhibits the longest processing time $p_7 = 8$ so that it is moved to the end of the sequence. This job is marked by * in Table 14.13.

In the next iteration, the first delayed job (job 4) is marked. This job and job 5 have the same maximal processing time of 7 time units among all requests started after the marked job. Job 5 is selected (since it appears first in the intermediate sequence) and job 5 is moved to the end of the sequence (Table 14.14).

Table 14.14 contains the final scheduling sequence (1; 3; 6; 4; 2; 8; 7; 5). None of the so far unmoved jobs is delayed so that the algorithm terminates. The minimal number of delayed jobs is two.

14.5.4 Scheduling Two Machines in a Flow Shop

Christina detects similarities between the machine scheduling problem outlined by Mark and the TSP. There are the jobs which correspond to the requests in the TSP and there are resources: in the TSP there is a vehicle but in Mark's setup there is a

Table 14.14 Moore-Algorithm (3rd iteration): Final job processing sequence and machine schedule with minimal number of delayed requests

Job i	Release time r_i	Duration p_i	Due date d_i	Start time	Finish time	Tardiness	Flow time	Delayed?
1	1	4	14	8	12	0	11	0
3	3	3	16	12	15	0	12	0
6	6	2	24	15	17	0	11	0
4	4	7	28	17	24	0	20	0
2	2	2	29	24	26	0	24	0
8	8	3	31	26	29	0	21	0
7*	7	8	18	29	37	19	30	1
5*	5	7	23	37	44	21	39	1

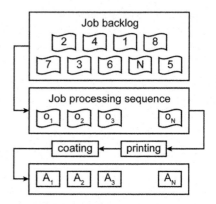

Fig. 14.16 Two machine scheduling situation

manufacturing machine. Christina wonders if there is a machine scheduling setup with two or even more machines that corresponds to the CVRP (Fig. 14.16).

She asks Mark about this question. Mark affirms but tells Christina that there are several multi-machine setups. Christina wants to know what the schedule generation is like in such a multi-machine scenario. Mark starts with the description of the system setup (Fig. 14.16). Each job requires two production steps. In a first step, the work piece is painted and in the second step, the painted piece is protected by a coating. Of course, it is necessary that painting precedes coating for all jobs. Each job i is characterized by the two processing times p_i^{paint} for the painting procedure as well as p_i^{coat} for the coating procedure (Table 14.15).

Mark explains that there is a famous approach to this setting for minimizing the completion time of the complete job backlog. This algorithm was originally proposed by Johnson (1954) and is hence called the *Johnson's algorithm*. This algorithm follows the principle to keep the *idle times* of the second machine as short as possible. This is achieved by starting those jobs first on the first machine with the shortest p_i^{paint}-values. These jobs are quickly processed by the first machine and then forwarded to the second machine in order to avoid idle times on the last

14.5 Machine Scheduling

Table 14.15 Job backlog for the two-machine set-up

Job i	1	2	3	4	5	6	7	8
Release time	3	4	5	6	7	8	9	10
Paint duration p_i^{paint}	4	2	3	7	2	8	3	4
Coating duration p_i^{coat}	7	6	1	5	4	3	4	2

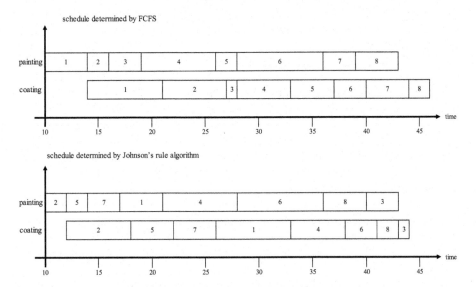

Fig. 14.17 Two machine schedules generated by FCFS and Johnson's algorithm

mentioned machine. The starting sequences of the jobs on the two machines should be kept unchanged. Therefore, it is sufficient to define the job processing sequence only for the first machine. The determined sequence then also applies for the second machine.

The Johnson's algorithm starts with splitting up the job backlog into two subsets J_1 and J_2. All jobs i whose processing times p_i^{paint} are shorter than their processing times p_i^{coat} are put into J_1. The remaining jobs are collected in the set J_2. In the example setting, the first set is $J_1:=\{1; 2; 5; 7\}$ and the second set is $J_2:=\{3; 4; 6; 8\}$.

In the second step, both sets are ordered. The set J_1 is sorted by increasing processing times p_i^{paint} and the set J_2 is sorted by decreasing processing times p_i^{coat}. In the example, we have the sequence $S_1:=(2; 5; 7; 1)$ as well as the sequence $S_2:=(4; 6; 8; 3)$.

In the third step, sequence S_1 is combined with sequence S_2 by appending S_2 to S_1. In the example, we get the complete job backlog sequence $S:=(S_1, S_2)=(2; 5; 7; 1; 4; 6; 8; 3)$.

Mark outlines the generated schedule in a *Gantt-chart* (i.e., a special form of schedule representation) and compares it with the schedule that results from starting the jobs in the order in which they have been released (Fig. 14.17). It can be observed that makespan has been reduced with the help of Johnson's algorithm.

14.5.5 Further Challenges in Machine Scheduling

In reality, there is a variety of other more complicated machine scheduling situations (Kovalyov et al. 2007; Dolgui et al. 2010; Berrichi and Yalaoui 2013). Li and Chen (2010) investigate a one-machine set-up in which the exact processing times of the jobs in the backlog are unknown but estimated by a distribution function. Albers (1997) analyses a set-up in which the job backlog is not available. Instead, no arriving job is scheduled before it arrives or without considering a job arriving subsequently.

If two or more machines must be scheduled in order to fulfil a set of jobs, two general set-ups are distinguished. The case outlined by Mark falls into the category of *flow production* (Dolgui and Proth 2010; Pinedo 2010): all jobs are processed in the same sequence on all available machines. In the *job shop* setup (Mattfeld 1996; Werner 2013) each job maintains an individual machine processing sequence. In many industries, flexible flow and job shops with alternative parallel machines are used (Kyparisis and Koulamas 2006; Ivanov and Sokolov 2012). In the process industry, continuous flows represent an additional challenge (Shah 2004; Bożek and Wysocki 2015; Ivanov et al. 2015).

Next, SC coordination belongs to future trends in scheduling research and practice. In this area, *integration of scheduling and routing* problems is studied (Agnetis et al. 2006; Chen 2010). In addition, integration of *inventory-routing* decisions as well as supplier selection and scheduling is a promising research area (Sawik 2013).

Finally, *uncertainty* is challenging the scheduling and routing decisions. In this setting, the issues of schedule *stability and robustness* along with the development of rescheduling policies become more and more important (Kolisch and Hess 2000; Vieira et al. 2003; Artigues et al. 2005; Aytug et al. 2005; van de Vonder et al. 2007; Hazir et al. 2010; Gomes et al. 2013; Sotskov et al. 2013; Harjunkoski et al. 2014; Liu and Ro 2014).

14.6 Key Points

In this chapter, you have been introduced to typical operative process planning tasks from transportation as well as production. In particular, you are now familiar with the shortest path problem, the travelling salesman problem, the CVRP, with a single machine scheduling problem and a simple two-machine flow-shop problem.

You have learned the basics about the formulation of decision models on mathematical graphs and you are familiar now with the concept of modelling operative decision tasks as graph-based optimization models. Decision variables are used to represent atomic decision tasks and constraints must be considered in order to compile a feasible solution of a complex decision problem from the atomic decisions.

14.6 Key Points

You are aware now that a careful selection of adequate algorithms for solving optimization models defined on graphs is important. For some decision problems, such models like the one presented for the shortest path problem, there are exact algorithms. As an example you have been introduced to the Dijkstra algorithm.

Christina leans back and recapitulates on what she has learned. First, a network-based optimization model for TSP was introduced. This model falls into the category of a mixed-integer linear problem since some decision variables must be integer or even binary. Within such a model it is possible to add constraints to control the decision variable value determination.

Compared to the shortest path problem in a network, which does not have any constraints about nodes to be visited, the complexity of the TSP is significantly increased. Therefore, it is reasonable to refrain from using exact algorithms for the identification of the best possible Hamiltonian path (with the least travel distance). Instead heuristics are proposed to approximate an optimal Hamiltonian path. There are different types of heuristics. Construction heuristics are used to set up an initial feasible solution for a constraint optimization model. Improvement heuristics (e.g. a 2-opt improvement procedure) are used to improve the objective function value of the best found feasible solution, i.e. to replace an existing feasible solution with another feasible solution having an improved objective function value). Christina is happy since she can use the proposed techniques to model and to solve RSBT's SST challenge.

Section 14.4 introduced the decision problem class of combined assignment and sequencing problems from operation fleet management. The basic decision task is described in the CVRP. We started the discussion of the CVRP with the outline of a typical planning situation. By means of this example we discussed the sophisticated decision challenges of a simultaneously conducted partition of the set of request locations, and the sequencing of the locations in order to determine vehicle routes. We have seen that failures in the assignment of requests to vehicles typically result in detours and an increase in the number of required vehicles. Both issues contribute to the additional costs for fulfilling customer requests.

In order to contribute to the striving to keep the fulfilment costs as low as possible we proposed to analyse customer locations, i.e. the locations that require a visit. For this reason, we proposed to sort all locations by means of their angle relative to a reference line. We then proposed the sweep algorithm which exploits the information about vicinity of different locations. The sweep algorithm tries to compile closely situated locations into one route in order to keep the sum of travelled distances low. We are now prepared to manage all decision situations that are in the form of the AAT challenge.

Finally, we have learned how to design simple heuristics for complex routing and scheduling models. But you are also aware that the computation of (sub)-optimal model solutions is often very complicated. Nevertheless, you understand the importance of formulating an appropriate decision model as the interface between applications and computers. The formulation is the most important ingredient for the setup of computerized decision support systems.

Toth and Vigo (2002) discuss model formulations for the CVRP. These models are used to apply special solver tools like CPLEX or LINGO in order to derive proven optimal solutions to the CVRP. However, depending on the actual data of a CVRP scenario and depending on the number of available vehicles and requests to be served, the processing times are often prohibitive so that for practical real-world problem settings heuristics are applied preferentially (Gendreau et al. 2002).

For other decision models, it is necessary to incorporate heuristics like the greedy heuristic or the sweep heuristic. There are also priority rules that can be applied to sequence tasks in machine scheduling. You can distinguish between construction and improvement procedures as basic ingredients of heuristic algorithms for solving complex models with several constraints. Fleet routing and machine scheduling belong to the most exciting tasks in SCOM!

Bibliography

Agnetis A, Hall NG, Pacciarelli D (2006) Supply chain scheduling: sequence coordination. Discrete Appl Math 154(15):2044–2063

Albers S (1997) Better bounds for online scheduling. SIAM J Comput 29(2):459–473

Andersson A, Hoff A, Christiansen M, Hasle G, Løkketangen A (2010) Industrial aspects and literature survey: combined inventory management and routing. Comput Oper Res 37:1515–1536

Artigues C, Billaut J-C, Esswein C (2005) Maximization of solution flexibility for robust shop scheduling. Eur J Oper Res 165(2):314–328

Aytug H, Lawley MA, McKay K, Mohan S, Uzsoy R (2005) Executing production schedules in the face of uncertainties: a review and some future directions. Eur J Oper Res 161(1):86–100

Berrichi A, Yalaoui F (2013) Efficient bi-objective ant colony approach to minimize total tardiness and system unavailability for a parallel machine scheduling problem. Int J Adv Manuf Tech 68 (9-12):2295–2310

Blazewicz J, Ecker K, Pesch E, Schmidt G, Weglarz J (2001) Scheduling computer and manufacturing processes, 2nd edn. Springer, Berlin

Bożek A, Wysocki M (2015) Flexible job shop with continuous material flow. Int J Prod Res 53 (4):1273–1290

Chen Z-L (2010) Integrated production and outbound distribution scheduling: review and extensions. Oper Res 58(1):130–148

Clarke G, Wright JW (1964) Scheduling of vehicles from a central depot to a number of delivery points. Oper Res 12(4):568–581

Croes G (1958) A method for solving traveling-salesman problems. Oper Res 6(6):791–812

Desrochers M, Laporte G (1991) Improvements and extensions to the Miller-Tucker-Zemlin subtour elimination constraints. Oper Res Lett 10:27–36

Dijkstra EW (1959) A note on two problems in connexion with graphs. Numer Math 1:269–271

Doerner KF, Gronalt M, Hartl RF, Kiechle G, Reimann M (2008) Exact and heuristic algorithms for the vehicle routing problem with multiple, interdependent time windows. Comput Oper Res 35:3034–3048

Dolgui A, Eremeev AV, Kovalyov MY, Kuznetsov PM (2010) Multi-product lot-sizing and scheduling on unrelated parallel machines. IIE Trans 42(7):514–524

Dolgui A, Proth J-M (2010) Supply chain engineering: useful methods and techniques. Springer, Berlin

Gendreau M, Laporte G, Potvin J-Y (2002) Metaheuristics for the capacitated VRP. In: Toth P, Vigo D (eds) The vehicle routing problem. Society for Industrial and Applied Mathematics, Philadelphia, pp 129–154

Gillett BE, Miller LR (1974) A heuristic algorithm for the vehicle-dispatch problem. Oper Res 22 (2):340–349

Gomes MC, Barbosa-Póvoa AP, Novais AQ (2013) Reactive scheduling in a make-to-order flexible job shop with re-entrant process and assembly a mathematical programming approach. Int J Prod Res 51(17):5120–5141

Grünert T, Irnich S (2005) Optimierung im transport - band I: grundlagen. Shaker, Aachen

Harjunkoski I, Maravelias CT, Bongers P, Castro PM, Engell S, Grossmann IE, Hooker J, Méndez C, Sand G, Wassick J (2014) Scope for industrial applications of production scheduling models and solution methods. Comput Chem Eng 62:161–193

Hazir O, Haouari M, Erel E (2010) Robust scheduling and robustness measures for the discrete time/cost trade-off problem. Eur J Oper Res 207(2):633–643

Ivanov D, Sokolov B, Dolgui A, Werner F, Ivanova M (2016) A dynamic model and an algorithm for short-term supply chain scheduling in the smart factory Industry 4.0. Int J Prod Res 54(2):386–402

Ivanov D, Sokolov B (2012) Dynamic supply chain scheduling. J Sched 15(2):201–216

Joereßen A, Sebastian H-J (1998) Problemlösung mit Modellen und Algorithmen. Teubner, Stuttgart, Leipzig

Johnson SM (1954) Optimal two- and three-stage production schedules with setup times included. Nav Res Logist Q 1(1):61–68

Kolisch R, Hess K (2000) Efficient methods for scheduling make-to-order assemblies under resource, assembly area and part availability constraints. Int J Prod Res 38(1):207–228

Kovalyov MY, Ng CT, Cheng TCE (2007) Fixed interval scheduling: models, applications, computational complexity and algorithms. Eur J Oper Res 178:331–342

Kyparisis GJ, Koulamas CP (2006) Flexible flow shop scheduling with uniform parallel machines. Eur J Oper Res 168:985–997

Li Y, Chen R (2010) Stochastic single machine scheduling to minimize the weighted number of tardy jobs. In: Cao B-Y, Wang E, Guo S-Z, Chen S-L (eds) Fuzzy information and engineering 2010. Springer, Berlin, Heidelberg, pp 363–368

Liu Z, Ro YK (2014) Rescheduling for machine disruption to minimize makespan and maximum lateness. J Sched 17(4):339–352

Maccarthy BL, Liu J (1993) Addressing the gap in scheduling research: a review of optimization and heuristic methods in production scheduling. Int J Prod Res 31(1):59–79

Mattfeld DC (1996) Evolutionary search and the job shop. Physica-Verlag, Heidelberg

Moore JM (1968) An n job, one machine sequencing algorithm for minimizing the number of late jobs. Manage Sci 15(1):102–109

Pinedo ML (2010) Theory, algorithms, and systems, 4th edn. Springer, New York

Ritzinger U, Puchinger J, Hartl RF (2016) A survey on dynamic and stochastic vehicle routing problems. Int J Prod Res 54(1):215–231

Sawik T (2013) Integrated selection of suppliers and scheduling of customer orders in the presence of supply chain disruption risks. Int J Prod Res 51(23-24):7006–7022

Shah N (2004) Process industry supply chains: advances and challenges. Comput Aided Chem Eng 18:123–138

Solomon MM (1987) Algorithms for the vehicle routing and scheduling problems with time window constraints. Oper Res 5(2):254–265

Sotskov YN, Lai T-C, Werner F (2013) Measures of problem uncertainty for scheduling with interval processing times. OR Spectrum 35(3):659–689

Thonemann U (2010) Operations management: konzepte, methoden und anwendungen, 2nd edn. Pearson, München

Toth P, Vigo D (2002) Models, relaxations and exact approaches for the capacitated vehicle routing problem. Discrete Appl Math 123(1–3):487–512

Van de Vonder S, Demeulemeester E, Herroelen W (2007) A classification of predictive-reactive project scheduling procedures. J Sched 10(3):195–207

Vieira GE, Herrmann JW, Lin E (2003) Rescheduling manufacturing systems: a framework of strategies, policies, and methods. J Sched 6(1):35–58

Werner F (2013) A survey of genetic algorithms for shop scheduling problems. In: Siarry P (ed) Heuristics: theory and applications. Nova Science, New York, pp 161–222

References for Sect. 14.4.1

Konrad A (2013) Meet ORION, software that will save ups millions by improving drivers' routes. http://www.forbes.com/sites/alexkonrad/2013/11/01/meet-orion-software-that-will-save-ups-millions-by-improving-drivers-routes/, accessed 19 Jan 2015

Noyes K (2014) *The shortest distance between two points? At UPS, it's complicated.* Fortune Online, July 25, 2014, 10:58. http://fortune.com/2014/07/25/the-shortest-distance-between-two-points-at-ups-its-complicated/, accessed 2 Dec 2014, 12:03

Shontell A (2011) *Why UPS Is So Efficient: "Our Trucks Never Turn Left"*. Business Insider, March 24, 2011, 16:28. http://www.businessinsider.com/ups-efficiency-secret-our-trucks-never-turn-left-2011-3, accessed 28 Nov 2014, 19:33

Wohlsen M (2013) *The Astronomical Math behind UPS' New Tool to Deliver Packages Faster.* Wired Magazine Online, December 13, 2013, 6:30). http://www.wired.com/2013/06/ups-astronomical-math/, accessed: 9 Dec 2014, 13:05

Erratum to: Global Supply Chain and Operations Management

Dmitry Ivanov, Alexander Tsipoulanidis, and Jörn Schönberger

© Springer International Publishing Switzerland 2017
D. Ivanov et al., *Global Supply Chain and Operations Management*,
Springer Texts in Business and Economics,
DOI 10.1007/978-3-319-24217-0

DOI 10.1007/978-3-319-24217-0_15

In the Front matter page X, the last paragraph stated "This book is accompanied by a free Web site www.supply-chainmanagement.de".

This website link has been updated to www.global-supply-chain-management.de.

The updated online version of the original book can be found at
http://dx.doi.org/10.1007/978-3-319-24217-0

Appendix Case-Study "Re-designing the Material Flow in a Global Manufacturing Network"

With the help of this case-study, materials of many chapters in this book can be applied to practical decision-making. In particular, knowledge on sourcing and production strategies, inventory management, transportation planning, linear and mixed-integer linear programming can be summarized.

Problem Description

In many cases, outsourcing or global sourcing is applied to cost reductions in material flows. At the same time, it can be possible to achieve similar effects by redesigning the material flow within the existing manufacturing network. Especially in industries with deep manufacturing penetration, such as plant engineering, there are many options to extend existing internal customer–supplier relations. In this situation, make-or-buy analysis should be performed for different modules and components at each location. The basis for the comparison of the make and buy efficiency is the total cost, comprised of production, logistics and follow-up costs. In addition, risks should be considered.

Consider an enterprise that produces systems for energy transmission and has two locations: factory A is located in Europe and factory B is located in China. Both factories have deep manufacturing penetration; in other words they are able to produce almost all the components and modules needed for the final product assembly. Both factories can assemble the same final products from the same components, known as shared components (see Fig. 1).

The final assembly always takes place in the country where the customer builds its energy system. It should be analysed to see whether the production of the shared components can be distributed within the network so that total network costs are minimized.

For analysis, a module has been selected that is needed for 54 % of all the energy system types. This makes the analysis representative and the results scalable. The module is produced according to ATO strategy and built into the final product at both factories. The module is composed of 13 components sourced from seven suppliers. At the first stage, four options for process design have been formulated (see Fig. 2).

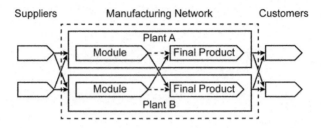

Fig. 1 Manufacturing network

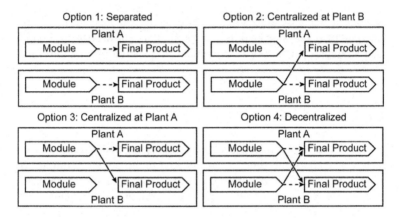

Fig. 2 Options for process design

At present, option 1 is used.

Questions

1. Formulate a mathematical model for the problem considered above! Select a standard model from Operations Research!

2. The model has now to be filled out with data. Describe your approach to get the necessary data!

Assumptions
- Material costs at location A is 212 €, labour costs is 40.50 € and overhead costs is 20.78 € for one module. Transportation costs for one module is 14 €.
- Material costs at location B is 143 €, labour costs is 20.0 € and overhead costs is 14 € for one module. Transportation costs for one module is 14 €.
- Consider inventory costs as composed of cycle and safety inventory costs. Select for calculation appropriate models of inventory management. Use transit price for the calculation.
- The following is true for location A: interest is 10 %, fixed costs is 23.2 €, service level is 95 %, standard deviation of lead time is 10 days and there are 250 working days in a year!

Appendix Case-Study "Re-designing the Material Flow in a..."

Table 1 Costs analysis for global sourcing

Costs	GER-GER	GER-CH	CH-GER	CH-CH
Material costs				
Labor costs				
Overhead costs				
Production costs				
Profit (5 %)				
Transfer price				
Customs duty (1.7 %)				
Transit price				
Transport costs				
Inventory costs				
Total landed costs				
Implementation costs				
Coordination costs				
Total costs				

- The following is true for location B: interest is 10 %, fixed costs is 13.2 €, service level is 95 %, standard deviation of lead time is 10 days and there are 250 working days in a year!
- Consider complexity issues if setting up coordination costs!
- Capacity at each location is 1200 units. Demand for one period is 1000 units at location A and 100 units and location B.

The cost analysis includes so called Total Landed Costs and follow-up costs (Table 1):

3. Solve the model with the help of Excel Solver! Explain the results and link them to one of the four options! Do we have any costs savings if we change from the Option 1? What is your recommendation?

Costs c_{ij}	Location A (i = 1)	Location B (i = 2)	Capacity a_i
Location A (j = 1)			
Location B (j = 2)			
Demand b_j			

The objective function can be written as follows:
subject to restrictions:
As the basis for comparison, the *as-is* situation can be taken which is described as follows:

Quantity x_{ij}	Location A (i = 1)	Location B (i = 2)	Sum
Location A (j = 1)			
Location B (j = 2)			
Sum			

$Z(x) =$
The optimization model provides the following result:

Quantity x_{ij}	Location A (i = 1)	Location B (i = 2)	Sum
Location A (j = 1)			
Location B (j = 2)			
Sum			

$Z(x) = €$
The network costs is now €. The cost savings is €.

4. Analyse advantages and limitations of each option considering the following criteria:

- Coordination efforts
- Reaction speed
- Supplier management
- Scale effects
- Material and labour costs
- Transportation costs and lead-times
- Manufacturing complexity
- Quality
- On-time delivery
- Inventory
- Single sourcing risks

With the help of scoring analysis, the following results can be indicated (see Table 2):

5. Consider a third location in India which can be used as a hub in the network. The capacity is 1200 units, and there is no demand in India at present. Sourcing costs from India to Germany is 198 € and from India to China −181 €.

- calculate optimal solution!
- what qualitative factors would you consider?
- perform sensitivity analysis and explain its results!

Optimal solution is:

Quantity x_{ij}	Location A (i = 1)	Location B (i = 2)	Location C (j = 3)	Sum
Location A (j = 1)				
Location B (j = 2)				
Location C (j = 3)				
Sum				

$Z(x) = €$

6. Consider five markets (China, Germany, Russia, Egypt, and India) and three factories in China, Germany, and India. The capacity in China can be increased at 3000 € (Table 3).

Appendix Case-Study "Re-designing the Material Flow in a..."

Table 2 Scoring analysis

Criterion	Option 1	Option 2	Option 3	Option 4
Coordination efforts				
Reaction speed				
Supplier management				
Scale effects				
Material and labour costs				
Transportation costs and leadtimes				
Manufacturing complexity				
Quality				
On-time delivery				
Inventory				
Single sourcing risks				
Total				

Table 3 Represents initial data

Supply region	Demand region production and transportation cost per X units					Fixed costs	Low capacity	Fixed costs	High capacity
	GER	CH	IND	EGT	RUS				
GER	273	303	303	295	292	0	1.200	0	1.200
CH	200	177	182	190	195	0	1.200	3.000	1.600
IND	198	181	170	188	193	0	1.200	0	1.200
Demand	1.000	100	150	50	100				

Formulate and solve a mathematical model for the problem considered above! Select a standard model from Operations Research!

Additional Task

Consider another module for which production capacity of 1000 units in Germany and 600 units in China is available. The corresponding costs are given as follows:

Costs c_{ij}	Location A (i = 1)	Location B (i = 2)	Capacity a_i
Location A (j = 1)	12.276	13.990	1000
Location B (j = 2)	9.518	8.167	600
Demand b_j	1000	100	1100/1600

Formulate the mathematical model!
Calculate costs for Option 1!
$Z(x) =$
Calculate optimal solution and costs savings!

Quantity x_{ij}	Location A (i = 1)	Location B (i = 2)	Sum
Location A (j = 1)			
Location B (j = 2)			
Sum			

$Z(x) =$

This results in savings of € or % of costs reduction.

Additional Discussion Questions

1. Global sourcing is reasonable for items with high volumes, low demand fluctuations and low transportation costs as compared with the item value. Which methods of operations management could help you identify such items? Think up a numerical example for each method to describe your approach!
2. In the case study we considered deterministic demands. Which methods would you use to forecast demand if statistical information is (is not) available?
3. The plant in China was engineered with an excessive capacity. What could be the reasons for that? Which methods could be used to support this decision?
4. We considered one period analysis. Which methods could you use to lot-size optimization for multi-period problems?
5. Which trade-offs can you see between inventory and transportation costs? Is the *economic order quantity* (EOQ) optimal for integrated inventory and transportation costs? If yes, why? If not, which methods could be used to minimize total costs? Think up a simple numerical example to explain your approach!

Index

A
ABC analysis, 348
Action research, 63
Adaptive planning, 334
Added value, 3
Additive manufacturing, 54
Advanced planning systems (APS), 46, 48–50
Aggregate planning, 322, 324
Agile supply chain, 76–78
Andon system, 267, 269
Ant colony optimization, 426
Arc, 393
Architecture of Information Systems (ARIS), 43
Assemble-to-order, 121, 132
Assembly line, 257–262
Automated shipping notification (ASN), 46
Available-to-promise (ATP), 384

B
Backlog, 323
Batch shop, 257
Batch size, 347
Bill-of-materials, 335
Bottleneck analysis, 244–245
Branch-&-Bound, 155–160
Break-even analysis, 246–248
Bullwhip effect, 79
Business analytics, 52–54
Business case, 249
Business intelligence, 52–54
Business process, 41
Business process management, 41–44
Business process modeling, 43–44
Business process re-engineering, 44
Business-to-consumer, 30
Buyback contracts, 87

C
Capacitated plant location model (CPLM), 160
Capacitated vehicle routing problem (CVRP), 389, 414
Capacitated warehouse location problem (WLP), 160–166
Capacity, 240
Capable-to-promise (CTP), 384
Capital commitment, 359
Case-study research, 63
Causal forecasting, 306
Cell-based layout, 288–290
Center-of-gravity model, 167, 170
Chase strategy, 325
Cloud computing, 46
Cluster storage, 291
Collaboration, 39, 134
Collaborative networks, 53
Collaborative planning forecasting and replenishment (CPFR), 18, 85–86
Completion time, 422
Computer integrated manufacturing, 45, 272
Consolidation of shipments, 194–196
Constraint, 325
Continuous flow, 262
Continuous improvement, 266
Continuous review system, 370
Control, 3, 50
Corner-point solution method, 331
Critical ratio (CR), 367
Cross-docking, 224
Cyber-physical systems, 54, 272
Cycle inventory, 347, 354, 356
Cycle time, 235

D
Decision, 54, 55
Decision tree, 248–249

Decision variable, 147
Dedicated storage, 291
Delphi method, 306
Demand planning, 131
Dependant demand, 336, 338
Design capacity, 241
Dijkstra algorithm, 394
Disaster management, 25–29
Disaster recovery, 21
Disruption management, 20
Distribute-to-order, 133
Distribution centre, 29
Distribution management, 19–20
Distribution network design, 224
Double exponential smoothing, 313–314
Drum-buffer-rope, 245, 380
Dual sourcing, 107
Due date, 422
Dynamic lot-sizing, 375–381Dynamics, 55
Dynamic vehicle routing problem (VRP), 415

E
Earliest due date rule (EDD-rule), 425
E-business, 52–54
E-commerce, 46
Economic order quantity (EOQ) model,
    355, 356
Economic production quantity (EPQ) model,
    360Economy of scale, 4
Effective capacity, 241
Effectiveness, 42
Efficiency, 42, 260
Efficiency strategy, 74
Electronic data interchange (EDI), 38, 46, 83
Emergency operation, 27
Engineer-to-order, 132
Enterprise management, 5
Enterprise resource planning (ERP), 38, 45,
    47–48
E-operations, 30–34
E-procurement, 38–39
Ergonomic workplace, 287
Event-process chains, 44
Every part every interval (EPEI) lot-size, 380
Exact algorithm, 403
Excel solver, 151
Expected monetary value, 248

F
Facility location, 141–186
Factor-ranking analysis, 175–184
Factor-rating method, 175–180
Factory planning, 233–235

Feasible region, 331
Feasible solution, 148
First come/first serve (FCFS), 425
First-in-first-out (FIFO), 291
Flexibility, 139
Flow shop, 424
Flow time, 425
Forecasting, 304
Forecasting process, 304
Forecast quality, 307
Full truck load (FTL), 196

G
Gantt-chart, 429
Genetic algorithms, 426
Global optimization, 168
Global sourcing, 108
Graph, 389
Gross requirement, 338

H
Health, Safety and Environment (HSE), 236
Heijunka, 380
Heuristic, 61, 402
Hierarchical planning, 321
Holding costs, 347
Hub-and-spoke network, 225
Humanitarian logistics, 25–29

I
Idle time, 258, 428
Industry 4.0, 45, 54, 270
Information, 6
Information technology, 45
Innovation strategy, 74
Integrated supply chain, 15–17
Integration definition for function modeling
    (IDEF), 44
Interest rate, 359
Intermodal transportation, 230
Internet of things, 54, 272
Inventory, 82
    control, 370
    management, 346
    on hand, 323
Iso-profit line, 332
IT project, 46

J
Jidoka, 98, 269
Job shop, 256, 424

Johnson's algorithm, 428
Just-in-time (JIT), 4, 98, 110, 268

K
Kaizen, 98, 266–267, 269
Kanban, 263, 269

L
Last-in-first-out (LIFO), 291
Layout planning, 279–299
Lead time, 338, 422
Lean production, 4, 98, 263–271
Lean supply chain, 75
Least unit cost heuristic, 376–377
Less than truck load (LTL), 414
Level strategy, 325
Linear programming, 211, 329Linear
   regression, 306, 308–310
Little's Law, 242–244
Local sourcing, 108
Logistics management, 18–19
Logistics network, 29
LTL. *See* Less than truck load (LTL)

M
Machine-to-machine (M2M), 273
Make or Buy, 102
Makespan, 423
Make-to-order, 132
Make-to-stock, 132
Management information systems, 45–54
Manufacturing execution systems (MES), 45
Manufacturing resource planning
   (MRP II), 321
Many-to-many network, 193
Mass production, 4
Master production schedule, 321, 333
Material requirements planning, 335–342
Mathematical graph, 393
M-commerce, 30, 34
Mean absolute deviation, 307
Mean absolute percentage error, 307
Mean squared error, 307
Meta-heuristics, 426
Miehle algorithm, 171
Milk-runs, 197–199
Mixed integer linear programming (MILP),
   148, 402
Model, 58
   information, 43, 65

Model-based decision approach, 154
Modelling, 58
MODI method, 211
Modular factory, 236
Modularization, 126
Moving average, 310–311
Muda, 263
Multi-objective decision making, 56
Multiple objectives, 42
Multiple sourcing, 106

N
Nearest neighborhood heuristic, 403
Net requirement, 338
Network, 393
Newsvendor problem, 366–368
Node, 393

O
Objective function, 147, 325
One-piece single flow, 285
Operational risks, 91
Operations, 1–14
   management, 3
   planning, 317
   research, 61
   strategies, 74
Optimality, 56
Optimization, 61
Order
   fulfillment, 42
   management, 101
   penetration point, 130
   pick-up, 291
Ordering costs, 347 .
Outsourcing, 15, 104
Overtime, 323

P
Pacing, 258
Pareto-optimal, 56
Path, 393
Pearl chain, 333
Performance, 4, 55
Periodic review systems, 370
Pick by Light, 291
Pick by Voice, 291
Pick-up list, 291
Planning, 3
Postponement, 126, 196–197
Priority rules, 424–426

Problem, 54
Process, 41
    flow layout, 282–284
    optimization, 43
Processing time, 422
Procurement, 100
Product data management, 38
Product flow layout, 284–287
Production floor, 281Production footprint, 235
Production rate, 260, 323
Production strategies, 132
Product-process matrix, 262–263
Pull process, 130, 265
Purchasing, 100
Push/pull, 130, 265
Put-away, 291

Q
Quadratic assignment problem, 295–297
Quality strategy, 74
Quantity flexibility contracts, 87
Queuing theory, 250

R
Radio frequency identification (RFID), 46
Random storage, 291
Rapid plant assessment, 243
Raw material, 374
Real-time control, 50
Real-time (re)planning, 334
Recurrent risks, 91
Re-engineering, 41–43
Regression analysis, 306
Relationship (REL)-charts, 293–295
Release time, 422
Reorder point, 361
Replenishment interval, 370, 371, 375
Resilience, 87
Responsiveness, 363
Responsiveness strategy, 74
Retail warehouse, 293
Revenue-sharing contracts, 87
Ripple-effect, 92
Risk, 20
    management, 21, 57
    objective, 57
    perceived, 57
    pooling, 126
Rolling planning, 321, 333–335

S
Safety inventory, 348
Safety stock, 363
Sales and operation planning, 325–328
Salvage price, 367
SC Event Management (SCEM), 46, 50–51
Schedule, 421
Scheduled receipts, 338
Scheduling, 421–423Scheduling dilemma, 423
Seasonal inventory, 348
Sensitivity analysis, 116, 333
Sequencing, 424
Service level, 348
Service operations, 3
Services, 21–29
Setup costs, 347
Setup time, 422
Shortest path, 391–397
Shortest-processing-time (SPT-rule), 425
Silver-meal heuristic, 377–379
Simple exponential smoothing, 312–313
Simplex method, 331
Simulation, 61, 254–256, 27–298
Simultaneous planning, 321
Single exponential smoothing, 312
Single period system, 366–368
Single sourcing, 106
Six Sigma, 267–268
Smart factory, 272
Society, 6
Software as a service (SaaS), 38
Sort, systemize, sweep, standardize and sustain (5S), 290
Sourcing, 22, 101
Sourcing process, 101
Sourcing strategy, 15, 106
Spend analysis, 112
Spreadsheet approach, 149–155
Standard deviation of demand, 363
Steiner–Weber model, 170
Stochastic inventory management, 362
Stockout costs, 347
Storage, 291
Strategic fit, 74
Structure dynamics, 55
Subcontracting, 323
Supplier analysis, 112–114
Supplier base, 31–32, 101
Supplier collaboration portal, 116
Supplier development, 116
Supplier integration, 116–117

Supplier relationship management, 111–117
Supplier selection, 114–116
Supply chain, 5
    coordination, 79–87
    design, 144
    management, 5, 6
    resilience, 92
    segmentation, 109
    strategy, 74
Supply chain operations reference (SCOR), 43
Supply contract, 86
Sustainability, 20, 42, 87
Sweep algorithm, 417–421
System, 54

T
Takt time, 235, 245, 260
Tardiness, 422
Target inventory level, 370, 371, 375
Target planning, 236
Task time, 258
Theory of constraints, 245
3D printing, 21
Throughput time, 262
Time series analysis, 307
TOPSIS, 56
Total cost of ownership, 46
Total productive maintenance, 284
Total quality management (TQM), 4
Toyota production system, 265–266
Trace and tracking, 19
Trade-off, 42, 56, 348, 359
Transformation process, 3
Transportation, 19
    costs, 195
    matrix, 212
    modes, 228–231
    network design, 206–208
    problem, 210
Transport network, 192
Transshipment, 199–206
Transshipment problem, 204
Travelling salesman problem (TSP), 398–400
Triple exponential smoothing, 307

U
Uncertainty, 57
    factors, 57
Unified modelling language (UML), 44
U-shape, 287
Utility value analysis, 180

V
Value, 264
Value added, 73
Value stream mapping, 264
Vehicle routing, 409–421
Vendor-managed inventory (VMI), 18, 40, 82–85
Virtual enterprises, 53
Virtual store, 34
Visibility, 39

W
Wagner–Whitin, 379
Waiting time, 423
Warehouse location problem (WLP), 146–149
Warehouse management systems (WMS), 45
Warehouse process, 290
7+1 Waste, 267
Weighted moving average, 311
Workforce, 323
Work-in-process, 347

X
XYZ analysis, 351–354

Y
Yamazumi chart, 261

Z
Zero defects, 290

Printed by Printforce, the Netherlands